The Shape of Qumran Theology

The Didsbury Lectures published by Paternoster

1979 F.F. Bruce
Men and Movements in the Primitive Church
(*now part of Paternoster's 'Biblical Classics Library' Series*)

1980 I.H. Marshall
Last Supper and Lord's Supper
(*now part of Paternoster's 'Biblical and Theological Classics Library' Series*)

1981 J. Atkinson
Martin Luther: Prophet to the Church Catholic*

1982 T.F. Torrance
The Meditation of Christ*
(*re-published by T & T Clark with an additional chapter*)

1983 C.K. Barrett
Church, Ministry and Sacraments

1984 A. Deasley
The Shape of Qumran Theology
(forthcoming 2000)

1985 D. Guthrie
The Relevance of John's Apocalypse*

1986 A. Skevington-Wood
Revelation and Reason†

1987 A.F. Walls
The Making of the Nineteenth-Century Missionary*

1988 M.D. Hooker
Not Ashamed of the Gospel

1989 R.E. Clements
Wisdom in Theology

1990 C.E. Gunton
Christ and Creation

1991 J.D.G. Dunn
Christian Liberty

1992 P. Bassett
A Redefinition of Heresy

1993 D.J.A. Clines
The Bible Today†

1994 J.B. Torrance
Worship, Community and the Triune God of Grace

1995 R.T. France
Women in the Church's Ministry

1996 R. Bauckham
God Crucified: Monotheism and Christology in the New Testament

1997 H.G.M. Williamson
Variations on a Theme: King, Messiah and Servant in the Book of Isaiah

1998 D. Bebbington
Holiness in Nineteenth-Century England

1999 L.W. Hurtado
At the Origins of Christian Worship

2000 C. Pinnock
The Most Moved Mover
(forthcoming)

* no longer available
† not published

The Shape of Qumran Theology

Alex R.G. Deasley

First published in 2000 by Paternoster Press

06 05 04 03 02 01 00 7 6 5 4 3 2 1

Paternoster Press is an imprint of Paternoster Publishing,
P.O. Box 300, Carlisle, Cumbria, CA3 0QS, UK
Website – www.paternoster-publishing.com

British Library Cataloguing in Publication Data
A catalogue record for this book is available from the British Library

ISBN 0 85364 786 0

Cover Design by Campsie
Typeset by WestKey Ltd, Falmouth, Cornwall
Printed in the UK by Biddles Ltd, Guildford, Surrey

To

Richard and Pam,
Shauna and Robert,
Jeremy and Jan

with love

Contents

Preface

This book had its origin in an invitation to deliver the Didsbury Lectures for 1984 at the Nazarene Theological College, Manchester, and my first thanks are due to the then Principal, Dr. Hugh Rae, and his staff, for both the generosity of their invitation and the warmth of their welcome. The delay in the publication of the lectures has arisen from a variety of reasons, publishing and personal, which need not be recited here. The evident expansion of the lectures was part of the original intention though it could not be foreseen then that the Qumran texts in their entirety would become suddenly and dramatically accessible before the book was completed. In that respect, the delay has been advantageous, and while the book is a lineal descendant of the lectures, its scope, methods and conclusions have been considerably changed or refined in the light of the full corpus of texts now available.

Its increased scale notwithstanding, the book's purpose has not changed. Just as the lectures were directed to undergraduate students, so the book is intended for a similar audience, including the general reader who may desire an introduction to Qumran thought as a whole. Recent debate has required the treatment of aspects underlying this, hence the attention given to history and archaeology in the opening chapter. Hopefully, this will also provide useful background for the understanding of the later chapters.

In the writing of a book over so many years, I have inevitably incurred many debts. The first and greatest of these is to the late Professor F.F. Bruce, for many years Rylands Professor of Biblical Criticism and Exegesis in the University of Manchester. Not only did he direct my doctoral research (which was concerned with Qumran thought), but he also read and annotated the lectures, and encouraged me to expand them for publication. I also owe thanks to the libraries which have permitted me to use their resources. Not least among these is the William Broadhurst Library of the Nazarene Theological Seminary, Kansas City, Missouri, whose Director of Library Services, Dr. William C. Miller, went well beyond the bounds of duty to secure for me materials which I needed. I was also given access to the impressive Fred Young Qumran Collection in the library of the Central Baptist Theological Seminary, Kansas City, Kansas, for which I am deeply grateful. Finally, I wish to acknowledge with gratitude the use of the resources of the Cambridge University Library during a sabbatical leave in 1997 – a congenial duty for a Cambridge graduate.

A succession of typists has been involved in varying degrees in the four drafts through which the work has passed, and to all of them I am grateful. My greatest debt is to my wife who was not only involved at various stages throughout the process, but who typed the final draft in its entirety.

At a time when study of the entire corpus of the Qumran texts is proceeding with unwearying intensity, no work on Qumran thought as a whole can claim to be more than an interim contribution. But as an attempt to provide an overview where the overall shape can easily be lost in details, it may serve as a contribution to the understanding of one of the most dramatic archaeological finds of modern times.

Alex R.G. Deasley

Abbreviations

Included here are journals, series and works of reference. Short titles or abbreviations of editions of the texts and monographs referred to with some frequency are noted in the footnotes at their first occurrence.

ABD	*Anchor Bible Dictionary*
BA	*Biblical Archaeologist*
BAR	*Biblical Archaeology Review*
BASOR	*Bulletin of the American Schools of Oriental Research*
BBB	*Bonner Biblische Beitrage*
BBR	*Bulletin for Biblical Research*
BIB	*Biblica*
BJRL	*Bulletin of the John Rylands Library*
CBNT	*Coniectanea Biblica New Testament*
DSD	*Dead Sea Discoveries*
EQ	*Evangelical Quarterly*
HTR	*Harvard Theological Review*
HUCA	*Hebrew Theological Review*
IEJ	*Israel Exploration Journal*
INJ	*Israel Numismatics Journal*
IOS	*Israel Oriental Studies*
JBL	*Journal of Biblical Literature*
JJS	*Journal of Jewish Studies*
JQR	*Jewish Quarterly Review*
JSOT	*Journal for the Study of the Old Testament*
JSPseud.	*Journal for the Study of the Pseudepigrapha*
PEQ	*Palestine Exploration Quarterly*

QC	*Qumran Chronicle*
RB	*Revue Biblique*
RQ	*Revue de Qumran*
SUNT	*Studien zur Umwelt des Neuen Testaments*
TB	*Tyndale Bulletin*
TDOT	*Theological Dictionary of the Old Testament*
WUNT	*Wissenschaftliche Untersuchungen zum Neuen Testament*

Introduction

The Purpose, Problems and Method of the Study

Purpose

The intent of these pages is to explore the leading themes of Qumran theology and, on this basis, attempt a characterization of its overall shape. The underlying question comprehends a number of others: What is 'the given' with which Qumran thinking begins? What then is its point of departure? What are the factors which propel it from one step to the next? If or when it is viewed as a whole does the accent fall on subscription to a particular set of ideas; or conformity to defined practices; or the cherishing of a specific expectation; or some measure of all three?

Such an undertaking is essentially an attempt to reconstruct the mind of the Qumran sectaries in terms of *their* concerns and categories. It is fatally easy to reconstruct Qumran thought in terms of categories drawn from Western theology: the doctrines of God, of sin, of salvation and so on. But this can easily distort the picture not only by the imposition of alien categories, but also by forcing on the Qumran material a pattern, a tidiness and a rigidity which may be foreign to it. What is needed as far as it is obtainable, is an account of their understanding, outlook and mood in the categories, terms and emphases which they would have used. This is what will be attempted here.

Problems

Merely to state the purpose of this study is to prod into life a legion of slumbering (and not-so-slumbering) problems. Most fundamental of all is the question, pressed relentlessly by Professor Norman Golb,[1] as to whether there ever was any coherent Qumran community located at Qumran or anywhere else which would or could have produced what he sees as the widely diverse literature found in the Qumran caves.[2] Only slightly less challenging, even when the existence of a definable community at Qumran is conceded, is the question of whether all of the manuscripts found in the caves may be taken to be representative of the community's mind and in what measure. Few libraries today would be so regarded, and it cannot be taken for granted in the case of Qumran. Some means must be sought for resolving the question.

Beyond that problem lies the further difficulty that, even if all the manuscripts from the caves were used and accepted by the sect in some degree, yet they themselves show marks of literary growth. This poses the issue as to whether it is possible to speak at all of an entity called 'Qumran thought', rather than 'a history of Qumran thought'. For suchlike reasons J.H. Charlesworth has written: 'There is no "Qumran Theology" ... If the presupposition that there was only one system of thought at Qumran was ever valid, it is now no longer warranted. There were different ideas of the human ... and different explanations of God's responsibility for sin and evil, and apparently different messianic ideas ... Numerous theologies were found at Qumran'.[3] At the same time he goes on to affirm that 'obviously, the theologies at Qumran ... were united by certain overriding convictions and affirmations'.[4] It is not necessary to accept all of Charlesworth's specific conclusions to agree with his general principle that Qumran theology is held together 'by certain overriding convictions and affirmations'. It is in these that the shape of the theology is likely to be discovered. It is certainly with these that an inquiry such as this must begin. How much further it is possible to go only the investigation can make clear.

Method

Given the problems indicated, it is now incumbent to ask whether a method can be devised which holds out any hope of reconstructing Qumran thought in its coherent wholeness (always assuming that it has any). No small part of the difficulty arises from differing views of how the measure of divergence is to be evaluated. Is the appropriate procedure to approach the individual scrolls positively, admitting to the Qumran corpus those which show virtually any sizeable degree of affinity; or is it sounder to approach the individual scrolls negatively, and include only those which cannot be kept out? This question, with all of its evident loopholes, plays a large, if little discussed, part in the approach to this issue. Devorah Dimant has described it well:

> The sect's literary corpus attests to an overall unity of thought, terminology and style. Yet it also manifests a variety of manners of exposition, and of nuances in detail and formulation. This situation led to two different evaluations. One saw the sectarian literary corpus as reflecting a unified system of thought. Consequently, the aim of the analysis was a synthesis of the thought expressed in the various writings. More recently, scholars tend to detect various layers and stages of development in the sectarian literature, and the analysis aims at disentangling them.[5]

It may be worthwhile to review some attempts that have been made to resolve this problem.

In a recent treatment of Qumran anthropology, H. Lichtenberger bases his decision chiefly upon historical and palaeographical grounds.[6] Accepting that, despite some differences, the Qumran sectarians are to be identified with the Essenes;[7] and accepting further the conclusion of H. Stegemann that the Teacher of Righteousness was an ex-High Priest who assumed the leadership of the Qumran Community;[8] he concludes that the only documents which can be used with certainty as sources of Qumran thought are those which post-date 153–2 BC at which time, according to Stegemann, the Teacher of Righteousness broke with the Temple.[9] That is to say, the only texts admissible are those which reflect the work of the Teacher of Righteousness. This general picture Lichtenberger finds supported by the palaeographical evidence, which shows, according to him, that the texts are to be set in Roman times.[10] Accordingly, the only texts which he uses in reconstructing the anthropology of the sect are the leading documents (*Hauptschriften*) which stand with certainty within the Qumran community. For Lichtenberger, this means chiefly the *Damascus Document* (CD), the *Habakkuk Commentary* (IQpHab), the *Commentary on Psalm 37* (4Q171), the *Rule of the Community* (IQS), and its two appendices: the *Rule of the Congregation* (IQSa), and the *Benedictions* (IQSb); and those of the *Thanksgiving Hymns* (IQH) which derive from the Teacher of Righteousness.[11] While he is prepared to make use of other documents, e.g. the *Rule of the War* (IQM), for comparative purposes,[12] he depends primarily on those indicated. He is even more cautious in appealing to texts of the Apocrypha and Pseudepigrapha found at Qumran.[13]

The advantage of such a method is clear: it confines attention to that channel where the characteristic features are at their clearest. In so doing it may err by being too narrow; but perhaps that is better than the opposite error of being too broad. However, there are certain weaknesses in this type of approach which should not be overlooked. First, its point of departure is a particular reconstruction of the history of the sect, namely, that of H. Stegemann, and while such reconstructions may be helpful – not least for understanding the theology of the sect[14] – there is a tentativeness about them which makes it hazardous to place too much weight on them alone. Again, while there can be no doubting that the Teacher of Righteousness was vastly influential in shaping the sect's thought, the attributing of particular works or parts of works to him can be at best only a probability. Finally, on Stegemann's dating the sect continued for at least 150 years after the death of the Teacher of Righteousness and it is too large an assumption that in that time nothing happened to the sect's theology, or that anything that did happen to it must be discounted. There is at least as much to be said for reconstructing the thought of the sect from materials it valued during its later and mature years as from those which, on greater or lesser evidence, may be thought to represent its mind during its earlier history.

An alternative approach, using broader criteria, is that of Mathias Delcor.[15] Accepting the Essene character of the sect, which he takes to be the prevailing view,[16] Delcor proposes four criteria for distinguishing documents representative of the mind of the sect from those which are not:

(1) They must possess the doctrinal, institutional and legislative characteristics we know of the Essenes from ancient sources.
(2) They must show affinities of vocabulary, style and content with other non-biblical texts from the caves.
(3) Works which have not been transmitted by the Church or Synagogue are most likely to reflect the thought of the sect. Here he refers specifically to documents from Cave 1: the *Rule of the Community*, the *Habakkuk Commentary*, the *Rule of the War*, the *Thanksgiving Hymns* and the *Genesis Apocryphon*. To these he adds the *Damascus Document* of which fragments were found in Caves 5 and 6; and the *Prayer of Nabonidus*.
(4) Works which have been transmitted by the Christian Church which were also found at Qumran must be examined minutely alongside other Qumran writings to see if they are Essene in origin or influence. Here he has in mind the texts normally classed among the Pseudepigrapha such as *Enoch*, the *Book of Jubilees* and the *Testaments of the Twelve Patriarchs*, notably those of Levi and Naphtali.

Their presence at Qumran in either Hebrew or Aramaic rather than Ethiopic or Greek creates special problems which call for careful handling.

These criteria are generally sound even if they are not foolproof. Thus the first of them depends on the admission that the Qumran sectaries were Essenes, a conclusion which Delcor describes – albeit uneasily – as constituting a consensus.[17] However, it cannot be overlooked that there are differences between the accounts of the Essenes in the ancient classical sources and the picture which emerges from the Qumran texts, and at the very least it must be shown that these are not of such a magnitude as to overthrow the possibility of an Essene origin for the Qumran sect. While there was undoubtedly *some* relationship between the Essenes and the Qumran sect it is going too far to equate the two and much too far to make the accounts of the Essenes by Josephus, Philo and Pliny – themselves not wholly consistent – the measuring rod by which the Qumran documents are to be judged. The second and fourth criteria are essentially forms of what has come to be known in New Testament studies as the criterion of coherence[18] by which material showing kinship with that which on other grounds has come to be regarded as distinct may be viewed as emanating from the same source. The third criterion – again to echo the language of the New Testament studies – is basically the criterion of dissimilarity:[19] anything surviving only at Qumran may be concluded to represent the mind of that community since it has not been preserved by the Church or the Synagogue. This criterion is of greater value in establishing a *minimal* picture of Qumran thought than a *maximal* since its underlying assumption is that the Qumran sectaries had little or nothing in common with other religious groups. This is very improbable for a Jewish sect in the first century before the Christian era; indeed, the probability is rather that the men of Qumran had much more in common with *all* other Jews (even the Wicked Priest and Co.) than they had with any non-Jews; and while this does not disfranchise the criterion, it restricts its usefulness. The criterion is useful however, in enabling us to isolate those features which distinguish Qumran from other strands of Jewish thought and life.

More recently Devorah Dimant herself, in a ground-breaking article,[20] has analysed the collection from the caves at Qumran in an attempt to trace its contours and determine its character. She finds that the texts can be classified into three groups:

(1) biblical manuscripts (with a margin of uncertainty for the status at Qumran of texts like Ben Sira and Jubilees);
(2) documents employing terminology connected to the Qumran Community (= CT) by which she means terminology linked with a peculiar set of ideas, such as organization, community history, theological outlook and biblical exegesis;
(3) works which do not contain clusters of community terms and ideas (= NCT).[21]

The conclusions which Dimant derives from the foregoing analysis are as follows. First, the contents of most caves are essentially similar and interlinked, suggesting that all housed parts of the same collection. Second, the groups of texts noted are of roughly equal proportions. Of the 190 non-biblical works only nine were known before Qumran, all save one in the third group (NCT) and all handed down by Christians. No works in group two (CT) were transmitted by other channels. The absence of Jewish Greek works and pro-Hasmonean works (including I Maccabees and Judith) shows that the collection was intentional. Third, groups two (CT) and three (NCT) show both striking similarities and marked differences in terms of literary genre. The similarities are most evident in genres shaped by the Bible: liturgical, psalmodic and wisdom compositions. The halakhic texts present problems in that some contain Qumran terminology (e.g. the *Damascus Rule*, 4Q *Tohorot*), while others do not, even though the halakhah is identical with that of the community. Dimant speculates that such texts may be the product of circles close to the community, but not identical with it.[22]

The historical conclusions which Dimant draws from all of this are three. First, is the uniform character of the entire collection. The picture from all caves is roughly the same. Second, the presence of multiple copies of a number of works in Cave 4 shows its character as a library. Third, the Qumran library is that of a particular school, close to but not identical with the community: perhaps the parent group from which the Qumran community branched off. If so, the texts in group three (NCT) may hold the key for uncovering the origins and nature of the Qumran community.[23]

Dimant's analysis is exceedingly valuable in several respects. To begin with, her research shows the fundamental (even if not total) homogeneity of the Qumran texts. So large a measure of cohesion among a collection of texts numbering approximately 800 can hardly be accidental. Second, nonetheless, the existence of a group of manuscripts lacking the terminology peculiar to the community as indicated by texts which exhibit both distinctive ideas and terminology raises the question of the exact nature of the relationship. Her suggestion of a related circle, perhaps even the parent group from which the Qumran community branched off, could well be of the right order. It could have within it an explanation of why the sect might value, preserve and even make use of texts which shared much of their mentality, even if the form and expression differed.

An approach which suggests itself as an alternative to those described may be set out as follows.

(1) A text or texts from Qumran itself must be sought which, on the basis of content, date and use within the community, shows the greatest likelihood of speaking representatively for the sect at a mature stage of its history. The points of importance here are that the starting place must be evidence from Qumran itself, rather than from outside the sect – even reports about the sect; and that the

evidence must hold the probability of being able to speak normatively of the mind of the sect, whatever allowance may have to be made for anterior or later development. This may be called the criterion of distinctiveness.
(2) Other documents must be evaluated in relation to this by means of the criterion of coherence. It is important to recognize that, as applied to a phenomenon such as Qumran, two kinds of coherence must be distinguished. On the one hand there is what may be called *general coherence*, in which there is broad agreement with the overarching conceptions and frame of thought. On the other hand there is *particular or precise coherence* in which there is exact coincidence in terms of institutions, functionaries, specific beliefs, literary style, and language.
(3) Knowledge of the sect from sources external to the scrolls can function as a guide and control. Of greatest value here is the evidence of the archaeology of the Qumran ruins which makes possible in some measure the reconstruction of the history of the sect and its practices. This can offer confirmation that the contents of a given scroll are consistent with what is known of the history of the site and the practices carried out there. Similarly, references to the sect in other ancient writers can furnish guidance, though these sources have to be evaluated carefully. This third test may be called the criterion of external attestation.

None of these criteria in itself nor all of them together are to be applied woodenly. Each calls for a certain degree of flexibility within itself; while together they require an exploratory rather than a rigid approach which permits a measure of interaction. Nevertheless they provide a procedure in terms of which one may pursue a study such as this, without which it could become either overly narrow or overly broad in its result, and in both cases misrepresenting of the Qumran mind. As we have seen, Devorah Dimant leans towards the criterion of particular coherence, distinguishing texts exhibiting distinctive language and ideas (CT) from those exhibiting distinctive ideas only.[24] However, it is possible to press this distinction too far. Carol A. Newsom, whose work Dimant acknowledges,[25] has probed the question as to what is meant by labelling a text sectarian.[26] *Use* of a text is in some sense a mark of appropriation even if, in itself, it would not mark a text as sectarian. Again, distinctiveness of content, vocabulary and style cannot be demanded in all cases, especially where literary genre (psalms and prayers) might mute such features. Newsom concludes, 'The question of determining what is sectarian or non-sectarian literature from the Qumran library cannot be a matter merely of dividing the manuscripts into two separate piles with appropriate labels. The questions of content or rhetoric, of authorship and use must be posed for the document in question.' This means that for some the answer is not a simple yes or no.[27] The effect of this is not to say that it is impossible to reach a conclusion about any of the texts. It is rather to warn against a litmus-test approach, and preserve a measure of openness which facilitates a broader understanding of the Qumran mind.

Notes

1. For Professor Golb's fullest statement of his case see Norman Golb, *Who Wrote the Dead Sea Scrolls? The Search for the Secret of Qumran* (New York: Scribner, 1995).
2. The specifics of Golb's case will be addressed later.
3. Charlesworth, J.H., in the Introduction to the expanded edition of Ringgren, Helmer, *The Faith of Qumran* (New York: Crossroad, 1995), xviiif.
4. Op. cit, xix.
5. Dimant, Devorah, 'Qumran Sectarian Literature' in Michael E. Stone, (ed.), *Jewish Writings of the Second Temple Period*, (The Literature of the Jewish People in the Period of the Second Temple and the Talmud; 2; Compendia Rerum Iudicairum ad Novum Testamentum; section 2; hereafter *Jewish Writings of the Second Temple Period)*, (Assen–Philadelphia: CRINT, 1984), 532.
6. Lichtenberger, Hermann, *Studien zum Menschenbild in Texten der Qumrangemeinde* (Studien zur Umwelt des Neuen Testaments, Band 15, Göttingen, 1980), 13–19.
7. Ibid, 13f.

8. Ibid, 15f. For Stegemann's view see *Die Entstehung der Qumrangemeinde* (Bonn, 1971), 198–252.
9. Ibid, 15.
10. Ibid, 18f.
11. Ibid, 17.
12. Lichtenberger regards the *War Scroll* as pre-dating (at least in part) the Teacher of Righteousness, and therefore as being unusable in the reconstruction of Qumran anthropology. Ibid, 17, 26f.
13. Ibid, 14f.
14. The problems attendant upon the history of the sect will be examined in Chapter 2.
15. Delcor, M., 'Qumran et Découvertes au Désert de Juda' de H. Cazelles et Andre Feuillet (eds.), *Dictionnaire de la Bible, Supplément* (Paris, 1979), Tome Neuvième, cols. 832–3.
16. Art. cit, cols. 829–32. The issue will be considered below in the discussion of the history of the sect.
17. 'Après les hésitations du début des recherches qumrâniennes, un certain consensus s'est opéré dan le monde savant pour admettre l'origine essénienne des manuscrits' (art. cit. col. 829). A later sentence strikes a more cautious note, 'L'opinion qui prévaût actuellement soutient que la communauté de Qumrân est plus ou moins en relation avec les Esséniens' (col. 831).
18. Cf. Perrin, Norman, *Rediscovering the Teaching of Jesus*, (New York, 1967), 43–5.
19. Cf. Perrin, op. cit, 39–43.
20. Dimant, Devorah, 'The Qumran Manuscripts: Content and Significance' in D. Dimant and L.H. Schiffman (eds.), *Time to Prepare the Way in the Wilderness* (Leiden: Brill, 1995), 23–58.
21. Art. cit, 27–9.
22. Art. cit, 30–4.
23. Art. cit, 35f.
24. Cf. 'The distinctiveness of such clusters in the context of this peculiar corpus lies precisely in the close connection between terms and ideas.' (Art. cit, 28).
25. Art. cit, 28.
26. Newsom, Carol A., 'Sectually Explicit Literature From Qumran', in William Henry Propp, Baruch Halpern and David Noel Freedman (eds.), *The Hebrew Bible and Its Interpreters* (Winona Lake, Ind: Eisenbrauns, 1990), 167–85, especially 172–9.
27. Art. cit, 185.

Chapter One

In Search of the Sect

Qumran theology is a meaningful expression only if it can be shown that there was a Qumran community capable of producing it. The two realities, while distinguishable, rapidly become one. However, just as the existence of a coherent body of thought distinguishable as Qumran theology, has been questioned, so has the existence of a Qumran community. Our first task, therefore, is to inquire after and evaluate the available evidence which may sustain the conclusion that such a group, with ideas sufficiently distinctive as to validate with reasonable probability its identity, did in fact exist. This is not to stipulate ahead of time the character or quantity of evidence needed to support such a conclusion. It is simply to state that the theology and existence of the community may be mutually supportive, and to pursue the investigation on that premise.

On the assumption then, that the community at Qumran, if it can be shown to have existed, will shed light on Qumran theology, just as the theology will shed light on the community, we may ask by what procedure the search for the sect may best be prosecuted. Clearly, there is only one place to begin: with the scrolls in the caves. The question to be asked here is whether these give any indications not merely of being the work of a functioning group or community but, even more, of being prepared for use by and in such a community. If this can be shown convincingly, the next step will be to inquire whether there is any connection between the scrolls in the caves and the ruins of Khirbet Qumran to which they are adjacent. A third step will then be to ask what may be known of the history of such a sect from the scrolls and the ruins, as well as from any other sources where information may be had. From these three avenues of approach, it may then be possible to begin piecing together the thoughts of such a community as may have existed where the scrolls were found.

The Primary Clues: the Organizational Handbooks

It is undoubtedly a daunting task to seek to determine the key works in a collection of manuscripts numbering roughly 800.[1] Indeed, such an attempt could legitimately be criticized for its implicit assumption that the scrolls discovered in the eleven Qumran caves constitute a 'collection' at all in the sense of being the product of a homogeneous mindset.[2] For the point being made at present, however, all that is needed is the demonstration that one or more scrolls give evidence of the intent to serve the purposes of a definable religious community. If this can be shown, it would seem hard to resist the conclusion that they were the property of some religious community somewhere.

In any case, the proportions of the task are less formidable than appear at first sight, when due account is taken of the way in which the scrolls resolve themselves into fairly clear categories and groupings. For example, texts of the Hebrew Bible account form roughly 30 per cent of the 800 surviving manuscripts.[3] Again, the remaining 70 per cent of the manuscripts (which number approximately 545), reduce to about 190 documents, when account is taken of multiple copies or fragments.[4] At this point, it would be premature to contend that all of these reflect the same mindset, just as it would be equally premature to maintain that they do not. The conclusion for the moment is that the quest for texts which presuppose the organization and functioning of a community is by no means like looking for the proverbial needle in a haystack.

The Rule of the Community and its Relatives (IQS, IQSa, IQSb)

Approached from this angle, several documents present themselves as likely witnesses to and evidence of a functioning community. First among these are the *Rule of the Community* (IQS) and documents related to it by virtue of being parts of the same scroll (IQSa, and IQSb), as well as what have the appearance of being alternative versions of the Community Rule from Cave 4 (4QS^{a-j}) and Cave 5 (5Q11).

The copies of the Rule of the Community

The *Rule of the Community* from Cave 1 (IQS) is by far the fullest copy of the document we have and, for that reason, may be taken as the baseline, though some copies from Cave 4 may represent older recensions. For many reasons the *Community Rule* suggests itself as the place to start. However the first part of IQS I 1 be restored,[5] 4QS^{a} makes it plain that the middle hiatus reads *sēpher serek hayāhad*[6] 'book of the rule of the community'. The fact that this title was also found on the outside of IQS[7] is best understood as indicating that the work constituted some kind of community handbook. That the *Community Rule* underwent development during the sect's history is suggested not only by literary analysis;[8] it is made virtually certain by the character of the fragments from Cave 4. Thus one copy (4QS^{d}) not only begins with IQS V, but the disposal of the text suggests that this was the beginning of the document.[9] Again, the language of 4QS^{d}I 1 differs from that of the parallel matter in IQS V 1, describing itself as 'Midrash for the Instructor concerning the men of the law', where IQS V 1 reads, 'This is the rule for the men of the community'.[10] Still another linguistic difference is that, in 4QS^{d} I 2 the men of the law are required to 'acquiesce to the authority of the many', whereas in the *Community Rule* this requirement is defined as 'to the authority of the sons of Zadok, the priests who safeguard the covenant, and to the authority of the multitude of the men of the Community, those who persevere steadfastly in the covenant' (IQS V 2–3).[11] Pointing to a similar conclusion are certain features of 4QS[e]. This text contains IQS VII 10 – X 4 in its first four columns, but without IQS VIII 15 – XI 11. Whereas IQS VIII 1–14 is a discussion of the Community's purposes and principles, IQS VIII 15 – IX 2 embodies specific regulations for appropriate behaviour. The latter however, has no parallel in 4QSe.

These phenomena seem to be best accounted for on the theory that the documents in question reflect adaptations for different situations in the Community's life. Thus, G. Vermes says of the features of 4QS[d] and 4QS[b] noted above, 'The most likely hypothesis is that IQS in its final form is a composite document and that the congregation tradition of 4QS[d] and [b] corresponds to one of its components, probably the earlier one, and the sons of Zadok tradition to another.'[12] Similarly, the differences between 4QS[e] and the *Community Rule* are probably to be explained on the hypothesis that they are witnesses to adaptations of the *Rule* for differing functions or even stages of the life of the Community.[13] Taken together, the various forms of the *Rule* constitute sound evidence of the existence of a functioning religious organization.

Is it possible to characterize more precisely the nature of the Community and its working? Confining ourselves strictly to the surface phenomena of the various recensions of the *Community Rule*, several features emerge which help to give definition to the Community. IQS I 1 – III 12 appears to be a liturgy for an annual observance of covenant renewal which, however, is also spoken of as the door of entry into the covenant community (II 18–19; cf. I 16–17).[14] This tells us not only of the mechanics of community membership, but also of its character: the Community evidently regarded itself as standing in a special relationship to God; as parties to and keepers of a special covenant with God (I 16–18a).

Second, the Community had its own hierarchical structure modelled after that depicted in biblical tradition: priests, levites and the people (I 19–22), collectively referred to as the Many (VI 8–9). In addition there were officials entrusted with specific responsibilities within the community: the Instructor (*pāqîd*) 'who is at the head of the Many' (VI 14) and was responsible for examining candidates for membership (VI 13c–15); the Examiner (*mebaqqēr*), who presided at sessions of the council (VI 11–13); and a third functionary whose task seems to have lain in the realm of instruction, as is suggested by his name, *maskîl* (from the verb *sākal* which, in the Hiphil means 'to understand, have insight'). The descriptions of the maskil in IQS III 13–15, IX 12–19 and of his personal conduct in IQS IX 21–26 suggest that expertise in the distinctive doctrine and practice of the sect and the ability to impart it to others were his primary qualifications.[15]

This last item points to a further feature which, while not a matter of organization, is the *raison d'être* of the existence as well as of the form of the community organization, namely, its distinctive teaching. The description of the function of the Maskil in IQS III 13–15 stands as the introduction to the lengthy account (ending at IV 26) of the inner interpretation of human nature and human history in terms of the Two Spirits of Light and Darkness at work in humanity and the world, and of the ultimate triumph of the Spirit of Light in the visitation at the end-time and the inauguration of the new creation.

A fourth feature of the *Community Rule* is the code of conduct in V 1–VII 27. Following a general preamble (V 1–7), the code deals successively with avoidance of association with the 'men of sin' (V 7–20a); the testing of the spirits of those who have entered the covenant (V 20b–25a); regulations regarding communal life, including religious observances (V 25b – VI 7a); regulations for the conduct of official meetings of the Community (VI 8b–23); regulations for the trial of offences and the penalties for the same (VI 24–VII 27). As noted above one of the copies of the Rule from Cave 4 begins at the same point as IQS V, showing that for some purposes or at some stages in the history of the community, the *Rule* began here. The same may be the case with 4QS^{e}.[16] IQS VIII 1 – IX 25 seem designed to serve much the same purposes as columns V–VI except that they are less full, and are written more from the perspective of the aims and spirit of the Community, as well as from a more distinctly historical rather than a legislative vantage point.

These four features lie very much on the surface of the *Community Rule*, and constitute strong *prima facie* evidence that in this document we are encountering a distinct, defined and self-conscious religious community. The existence of so many copies – twelve if not thirteen – in the Qumran caves indicates, in the words of Geza Vermes, that 'the *Community Rule* figures fairly high on the list of the most popular documents, biblical and non-biblical, and is definitely the most copiously attested sectarian writing among the Qumran finds.'[17]

The Rule of the Congregation (IQSa) and the Rule of Benedictions (IQSb)

Attached to the scroll of the *Rule of the Community* (IQS) were two other documents distinct from it and yet evidently related. That the connection was more than physical is shown conclusively by the title which was sewed to the first column of the *Community Rule* and turned so as to be visible when the manuscript was rolled normally. As restored by the editor this reads: (*sere*) *k hayãḥad ûmin*:[18] 'rule of the community and excerpts from … ,' suggesting that the *Community Rule* was followed by something else which nonetheless was to be regarded as part of the first. In the words of Lawrence H. Schiffman, '*The Rule Scroll* is now seen as a three-part document including: (1) the *Manual of Discipline* (IQS), (2) the *Rule of the Congregation* (IQSa) and (3) the *Rule of Benedictions* (IQSb) … they were joined into the *Rule Scroll* by a scribe who recognized their conceptual unity.'[19]

A reading of the first lines of the *Rule of the Congregation* may seem at first sight to place a question mark against such a conclusion. To begin with, in the very first line, 'And this is the rule of the congregation of Israel in the final days' the word translated 'congregation' (Heb. *'ēdah*) is not the word translated 'community' (Heb. *yaḥad*) in the *Community Rule*. This impression is confirmed by the character of the congregation presupposed in the *Rule*, which consists of women and children, youths of different ages, adults and old men: a quite different picture from that conveyed by the *Community Rule*. But perhaps the distinction between the two can be overstated. On the one hand 'all the people' are present at least representatively in the *Community Rule*;[20] on the other side the *Rule of the Congregation* is for the congregation of Israel 'in the final days'.[21] The rule goes on to lay down regulations for the armies of the congregation (I 6) apparently in the eschatological war as well as for the behaviour appropriate at the meal following the arrival of the Messiah (II 11–21). The point need not be pursued further here. Suffice it to say that the evidence points to the existence of a religious group with two distinguishable aspects: community and congregation, which overlap without being co-extensive with each other.

If the *Rule of Benedictions* was placed intentionally as part of the *Rule Scroll*, as has been concluded above, then presumably it is to be understood in the context of the documents which stand before it.[22] This would mean that, just as the *Rule of the Congregation* contains the regulations for the assembling of the sect at the end of the days, the *Rule of Benedictions* will contain the blessings to be pronounced at that high moment when the victory of the children of light over the children of darkness is formally celebrated.[23] The text makes clear that they are to be pronounced by the Maskil (I 1, III 22) over various groups and individuals who will figure prominently in the new order. Schiffman points out that the *Rule of Benedictions* (as its name might imply) contains no curses such as are found in the liturgy for covenant renewal in the *Community Rule* (IQS II 4b–17), presumably because the wicked had been extirpated and there was no one to curse.[24]

The *Rule Scroll* thus bears witness to the existence of a structured community with defined procedures, regulations and religious liturgies. Moreover, even a *prima facie* survey of its organization has pointed to significant ideological concerns: with eschatology, covenant, purity. Taken together, all of these items constitute a significant starting-point from which to pursue the quest of a sect which in some way and degree was associated with the scrolls found in the Qumran caves.

The Damascus Document (CD)

Another text which invites examination as a possible witness to a community as its setting is that variously known as the *Damascus Rule or Document* or the *Covenant of Damascus* (CD). As is well known, the *Damascus Document* was discovered half a century before the Qumran scrolls in 1896 by Solomon Schechter, in the *genizah* or storeroom of the synagogue in Old Cairo.[25] However, numbers of fragments of it were found in Caves 4, 5 and 6 at Qumran, showing clearly that it was known there.[26] The Cairo manuscript consists of two groups of fragments: one of eight leaves written on both sides numbered by Schechter pages I–XVI and labelled Text A; and a second leaf also written on both sides giving two further pages which Schechter numbered pages XIX–XX and labelled Text B.[27] Pages XIX–XX are parallel to pages VII–VIII, though with enough differences to lead Schechter to conclude that Text B is another recension of the same text:[28] a conclusion that has been confirmed by later scholars.[29] Whether the fragments from Qumran caves buttress the multiple-recensions theory is disputed.[30]

Two matters concerning the *Damascus Document* have become clear with the discovery of the fragments from Cave 4.[31] First, the *Damascus Document* is much longer than had been thought, by some 363 lines.[32] Second, the bulk of this additional material is legal, being concerned with cultic purity, laws of diseases, laws of marriage and suchlike. This has a striking effect on the overall aspect of the document, which is now seen to consist two-thirds of halakhic material. Expressed otherwise, in the words of Baumgarten and Davies: 'The Admonition, which repeatedly calls for adherence to the proper interpretation of the Law, is thus to be viewed as essentially an introduction to a corpus of Torah interpretation and sectarian rulings.'[33]

What indications does the *Damascus Document* give, then, of being the witness to and manifesto of a functioning religious community? One feature that attests itself powerfully is a lively consciousness of its own history. This is not to say that that history is spelled out clearly, or that it is possible for us to reconstruct it; it is presupposed rather than told. But enough is said to indicate a corporate mindset that has been powerfully shaped by community experience, and is maintained by the recollection of it. There is the remembrance of confused beginnings, brought to an end by the arrival of a Teacher to be their guide (I 9–11). There is mention of a departure from Judah, evidently to live elsewhere (IV 2–4): in some contexts the destination is identified as Damascus (VI 4–5) which is also named as the setting of the new covenant (VI 19). There is the recollection, not untinged with bitterness of some who entered the new covenant but later withdrew (XIX 15–17, 33–5). This may have been connected in some way with the death of the Teacher (XX 13–15). Whatever the precise significance of these expressions, be they events or titles, a communal historical memory appears to be at work here.

A second feature which points to the *Damascus Rule* as being in some sense a community work – created by and for a community – is the evidence of ordered procedures to direct the operation of the group. Designations are used which appear to denote functionaries. Thus, serious infractions of the law are to be reported to the Examiner or Inspector (CD IX 17–22) (Heb. *mebaqqēr*): the same figure who presides at sessions of the council in IQS VI 11–13. This officer also has instructional and pastoral functions (CD XIII 5–10) together with the duties of admissions officer (CD XIII 11–13) which in the *Community Rule* are the responsibility of the *pāqîd* (IQS VI 14). The *maskîl* also appears in the *Damascus Document* (XII 21, XIII 22), apparently as the custodian of the Law. Such responsible officials presuppose in turn defined operational and legal procedures which safeguard the observance of the laws. The importance of this is made clear in the *Damascus Document* both in statements of principle as well as in specific legislation. More than once entry into the covenant is said to be 'in order to act according to the exact interpretation (Heb. *pērûsh*) of the law' (IV 8, VI 14, 18, 20, XIII 6, XIV 17). And, as was noted above, two-thirds of the *Damascus Document* consists of such interpretations together with prescribed procedures which enshrine them. These extend from regulations concerning the handling of lost property when the owner is unknown (IX 13–16) to the kind of water and amount of water which cleanse impurities (X 10–13) to raising a hand to move a stubborn animal, or wearing perfume, or restricting the movements of a wet-nurse on the sabbath (XI 6–11), to avoiding fornication by marrying more than once (IV 15–21).

A third factor which infuses and pervades the *Damascus Document* is a sense of religious purpose and vocation. Not only does the document evince a lively consciousness of the history of those for whom it speaks; it is equally instinct with an acute awareness of their own role in history. Both factors treated above contribute to this while others raise it to sharper definition. What is at stake for those behind the *Damascus Document* is nothing other than fidelity to the demands of God's covenant made with them after Israel had gone astray (III 12–16). This covenant is new, yet in essence is a return to the covenant with Moses (XV 7–10). In a word, it is Israel's second chance, but also her final chance. For the age of wickedness is about to be brought to an end (XIX 10–11). The task of the members of the community is therefore to keep the law perfectly, living in perfect holiness. Thus they will escape the destruction that will come upon Israel (VII 4–6).

All of these features find cohesion around the idea of covenant.[34] Indeed, there is such repeated mention throughout the document of 'those who enter or entered the covenant' (VI 11, 19; VIII 1, 21; IX 2f; XIII 14; XV 5; XIX 13f, 16, 33; XX 25) that it is unsurprising that the *Damascus*

Document should have come to be spoken of as 'the *Covenant of Damascus*'.[35] Before the text of the Cave 4 fragments became available J.T. Milik had indicated that 'our oldest manuscript of the *Damascus Document* places the ceremony of the renewal of the Covenant in the third month of the year':[36] a claim now validated by the text of 4QD[b] fragment 18 column V lines 16–18 which read that 'the sons of Levi and the men of the camps will meet in the third month and will curse whoever tends to the right or to the left of the law.'[37] It had already been conjectured on the basis of CD II 2, 'And now, listen to me all you who are entering the covenant,' that 'the *Damascus Document* in its final form was intended for use at the annual ceremony of the renewal of the covenant.'[38] 4QD[a] confirms this by showing that the *Damascus Document* concluded with a liturgy of thanksgiving.

On the basis of the evidence reviewed (which is merely a selection) the *Damascus Document* like the *Rule of the Community*, seems most naturally to be understood as some kind of community handbook. Its precise form is open to debate as is its literary history. But, in the words of M.A. Knibb, 'More important for our present purposes is the fact that the community for which the Laws were intended does seem to have had some kind of clearly defined structure.'[39] It has, indeed, been questioned whether the evidence cited can be used convincingly in support of such a conclusion. P.R. Davies has argued that the existence of a community is not necessarily 'a precondition for the origin of these documents,' making much of differences between IQS and the Cave 4 copies, and raising the question as to whether IQS is a community rule at all. 'At best it is a rather muddled archive, a receptacle of bits and pieces from different times and authors.'[40] For this reason Davies advocates 'a programmatic caution and even skepticism' as the proper methodology for interpretation. Caution no doubt is always in order, but it should attend programmatic skepticism as much as it should attend uncritical acceptance. The piecemeal aspect of the *Community Rule* may indicate no more than that, in some communities (not least in ancient times) the official handbook might well consist of a collection of pieces on various aspects of community life, linked together loosely to serve a common purpose.[41] That both the *Community Rule* and the *Damascus Document* should be mere exercises in creative pious hope and imagination down to the point of the production of multiple copies over a period approximating a century and a half[42] appears rather a tortuous explanation of data for which a less laboured solution seems ready at hand.

A more difficult question is whether the community in the *Damascus Document* is identical with that in the *Community Rule*. The differences are real, even if they have been exaggerated. The *Damascus Document* and the *Community Rule* seem clearly to legislate for different settings: the former for members living in 'camps' (CD VII 6b, XIX 2b, XII 22f, XIV 3), congregated into towns (CD X 21, XI 5, XII 19),[43] earning their living by agriculture alongside or in proximity to Gentiles (CD XII 6[b]–11); while the latter seems to presuppose a closed community, even if its isolation was not total (IQS V 14–20). The *Damascus Document* assumes marriage and family life (CD VII 6–7, XIX 2–3), whereas the *Community Rule* makes no mention of these and the community life presupposed would seem to make little allowance for them.

As to relations with the Jerusalem Temple, the *Community Rule* apparently regards the sect's religious praxis as an acceptable substitute for the Temple cult (IQS IX 3–5).[44] In harmony with this is the statement in CD VI 11f that 'all those who have been brought into the covenant shall not enter the temple to kindle his altar in vain;' and while there is no specific positive statement affirming that the sectarian observances are a substitute for the Temple cult, it is significant that the immediately following lines (CD VI 14–VII 6) are a description of the sectarian law which is enjoined upon the members. Complicating the picture however, are the laws from the legislative part of the document which give directions both for the sending of offerings to the Temple as well as for the offering of sacrifices in person (CD XI 17b–21a).

Some scholars have concluded that the problem is insoluble.[45] It certainly is not capable of easy or definitive solution, but the data would appear to indicate at least the direction in which a solution is to be sought. To begin with, if there are areas in which the two documents are at odds, there are also areas in which they coincide so strikingly that it is hard to suppose that their agreement is fortuitous. Thus, both use the same terms in a technical or quasi-technical sense to denote features of their organization. The body responsible for transacting the official business of the sect is known as 'the Many' (IQS VI 7, 8, 9 etc.; CD XIII 7; XIV 7). It is presided over by an official who bears the title of 'the Examiner' (*mebaqqēr* IQS VI 12, 20; CD XIV 10–12). However, the relationship between the Examiner and the Many differs in each document. In the *Damascus Document* he not only presides over the Many; he instructs them 'in the deeds of God, and shall teach them his mighty marvels, and recount to them the eternal events with their solutions' (XIII 7–8). In the *Community Rule* on the other hand, he appears to be no more than *primus inter pares*. Further, whereas in the *Damascus Document* candidates are admitted to the sect on the word of the Examiner alone (CD XIII 11–13), in the *Community Rule* a second stage is posited which requires examination by the Many as a body (IQS VI 13–20). Moreover, additional privileges attach to this second stage of membership according to the *Community Rule*: specifically, the incorporation of the member's possessions into the holdings of the sect, and his right to partake of the solid food of the common meal. Sharing the common drink requires an additional year of probation. The most probable explanation is that while the two communities were parts of the same movement, they functioned at different levels and it is this that is reflected in the diverse procedures.[46]

This would seem to be confirmed by the nomenclature used to refer to the two communities. It is striking that the term *yaḥad* is not used in the *Damascus Document* to refer to the community,[47] whereas in the *Community Rule* it is regularly used for that purpose. In the *Damascus Document* on the other hand the community is spoken of as 'the Congregation' (Heb. *'ēdah* as in VII 20; X 4, 5, 8 etc.) which occurs only twice in the *Community Rule*, and only one of these instances refers to the community itself (IQS V 20).[48] Both terms come together in the *Rule of the Congregation* in which all (sectarian) Israel constitutes the Congregation (IQSa I 1) but, now that the new era has arrived, is able without distinction to partake of the common meal hitherto restricted to the community of Qumran (IQSa II 21).[49]

It is not claimed that the divergent settings of the *Community Rule* and the *Damascus Document* account for all the differences between them, (not to mention those within them, like the variant attitudes to the Temple in CD). There are strong grounds for holding that the changing of regulations with the passage of time has also played a part: both the erasures and amendments to IQS VII–VIII are almost certainly to be accounted for in this way as are also the differences between the penal codes of the two documents.[50] The point of moment is that two of the manuscripts from the Qumran caves, whose importance is confirmed by the presence of multiple copies, bear witness to the existence of a community of distinctive shape and ideology. Is it possible to discover more about it?

The Dates of the Documents

There is one other piece of information the *Community Rule* and the *Damascus Document* can give us in our search for the sect: they can tell us something of its date. This information stands in a somewhat different category from that considered thus far, chiefly because it is conveyed unintentionally, by the form of the handwriting of the scrolls. The fundamental studies in this regard are those of N. Avigad[51] and F.M. Cross[52]. The method involved the establishment of a typological sequence on the basis of exemplars capable of independent dating. From the early work of Avigad and Cross to that based on the Bar Kokhba documents and the earliest indications from Masada[53] the conclusions of the experts have been unvarying that the sectarian manuscripts fall into two categories, Hasmonean or Herodian. The former, dating from 150–30 BC include the *Rule of the Community* which is dated slightly later than the great Isaiah scroll from Cave I, itself dated in the second half of the second century;[54] and the oldest copy of the *Damascus Document* from Cave 4 (4QD[a]) which, according to Baumgarten, Milik dates from 75–50 BC.[55] The second or Herodian group, dating from 30 BC to AD 70, includes most of the texts from Cave 1, specifically the *Pesharim*, the *Thanksgiving Hymns*, the *Rule of the War* and the *Genesis Apocryphon*.[56]

More recent advances in palaeography have taken two forms. First, the publication of vastly increased comparative material has both filled in gaps in the typological sequence as well as offering added evidence to existing data.[57] On the basis of this F.M. Cross sees no need for major changes in his typology.[58] Second, carbon 14 dating techniques have been refined so that they not only do not require such large amounts of material for testing as was previously the case, but they also yield more precise results.[59] Palaeographers believe that, in regard to Qumran texts, palaeography can date a manuscript to within twenty-five or fifty years of when it was written. In 1990 eight of the Qumran texts (together with six others from nearby sites) were subjected to the refined form of testing. Two facts emerged. In only one case was there a serious discrepancy – of 253 years (for no known reason). Second, in all cases, the palaeographical dates tended to be more conservative than the carbon 14 dates.[60]

The carbon 14 testing has not been without its critics. Indeed, the supposition of the objectivity of palaeography had itself been assailed by P.R. Davies before the recent carbon 14 tests were envisaged,[61] while the evaluation of the 1990 tests has been heavily criticized by Norman Golb.[62] It is probable that some factors either on the side of palaeography or the side of carbon 14 testing or both require re-adjustment.[63] James VanderKam expresses judiciously what may reasonably be concluded at this point, 'While these data do not prove that the paleographical dates are exact, they do show, as nearly as accelerator mass spectrometry (= carbon 14) testing can, that they are accurate and even that they tend to be conservative. Thus, although we may not know the exact date of a manuscript, we can be sure that paleographers have placed them in the correct periods. Such information proves that the scrolls came from the last centuries BC and the first century AD.'[64]

From the evidence surveyed thus far it is not concluding too much to say that some heavily-attested scrolls found in the Qumran caves point indubitably to the existence of a defined religious sect which functioned within the three centuries from 200 BC – AD 100. It remains to be investigated whether the nature, purpose and thought of this sect can be brought into sharper definition.

The Evidence of the Site

From relevant evidence from the caves we may now turn to the evidence of the site. Just as the question regarding the former was whether they contained any documentary evidence suggestive of a community, so the question regarding the latter is whether the character of the ruins is consistent with such a conclusion. It is worth repeating that, when the location of Cave 1, following its discovery by the Bedouin,[65] was established by Lankester Harding and de Vaux,[66] neither suspected any link between the ruins and the caves. Indeed, during their initial excavation of Cave 1 in the spring of 1949, a surface examination of the Qumran ruins was made, and two graves in the cemetery were excavated, but both archaeologists concluded that the ruins were the remains of a Roman military post from the end of the first century AD.

The excavation of Cave 1 led to steadily increasing pressure for a thorough examination of the site. Further soundings were taken in 1951, followed by four more campaigns from 1953 to 1956, and a final campaign at 'Ein Feshkha in 1958.[67] By the time the excavation of the site was completed, ten more caves had been discovered in the general vicinity of the ruins, including the celebrated Cave 4.[68] De Vaux's work necessarily constitutes the starting-point of all interpretation of the site. A number of specific issues enter directly into the larger question of whether the ruins are those of a religious community.

The Character of the Qumran Buildings

The first issue is whether any inferences regarding their function can be deduced from the character of the Qumran ruins. De Vaux's description is presented – appropriately enough for his purpose – in the context of a stratigraphic analysis which simultaneously traces the evolving history of the buildings in four stages which he labels Period Ia, Period Ib, Period II and Period III.[69] For our purposes it is not necessary (at least at this point) to trace the evolution of the structure. Indeed, de Vaux speaks of Period Ib as that 'when the buildings at Khirbet Qumran acquired what was virtually their definitive form.'[70] More important are its distinguishing features which de Vaux considered to be five.

First was the massive, two-storey tower which stood to the east of the main entrance on the north side and formed the north-west corner of the main buildings. The tower was accessible only from within. Second, was a group of rooms to the south-west of the tower, two of which were notable: the smaller in having a bench running along the walls, the latter in its unusual length. De Vaux thought both could have been assembly rooms.

The third distinguishing feature of the ruins to de Vaux, indeed, 'the most striking feature',[71] was the water system. Of note were the number and size of the cisterns, the system of channels which conveyed water to them from one side of the complex to the other, and the aqueduct which conducted the water from the Wadi Qumran at a point above the ruins into the building complex.

Fourthly is the assembly hall. 'This is a room 22 m long and 4.5 m broad, and orientated east and west ... This is the largest room in the whole of the ruins and it is clear that it was a meeting-place.'[72] However, it was more than simply a council-chamber. It also served as a formal dining-hall: a conclusion de Vaux inferred from the slope of the floor from west to south-east and the presence of conduits allowing for admission and emission of water and therefore ease of cleaning; as well as from the discovery of attached rooms containing more than a thousand eating vessels. The presence in open spaces throughout the complex of animal-bones half-buried in pots and sherds led de Vaux to conclude that at least some of the meals served in the assembly hall were of a sacred character.

Finally, de Vaux noted as significant the presence of workshops in various parts of the complex. Particularly notable are remains from all periods of potter's workshops: basins, circular cavities for wheels, and kilns. Indeed, the pottery workshop was the source of most of the pottery found on the site. This explains both its monotony and its uniqueness as compared with pottery from other sites of the same era.[73]

Putting all of this together, de Vaux concludes that the plan of the building as a whole is 'remarkable chiefly for its qualities of unification and organization. Khirbet Qumran is not a village or a group of houses; it is the establishment of a community. We must be still more precise: this establishment was not designed as a community residence but rather for the carrying on of certain communal activities. The number of rooms which could have served as dwellings is restricted as compared with the sites designed for group activities to be pursued.'[74] In short, the Qumran ruins are the remains of a religious settlement.

Discussion of this question, which had never really ceased, has achieved a new visibility of late as the full report of de Vaux's excavations, never published in his lifetime, has been undergoing preparation for publication,[75] and as alternative hypotheses have been advanced to account for the data.

Against de Vaux's conclusion that the buildings were a religious community centre, it has been suggested that they were a military fortress, a private villa, a hostelry or a selection of several of the above. These different options cannot be considered in any kind of detail; an attempt will be made at least to place them in some kind of perspective. In any case the ultimately determining factor is the ability of any view to account for the distinctive features of the Qumran ruins.

The claim that the ruins are those of a military fort or even fortress has been pressed most strongly by Norman Golb. In addition to amassing selective quotations from de Vaux and F.M. Cross implying that the site was fortified and was finally overthrown by military assault as the presence of Roman arrowheads indicates, Golb is careful to draw attention to the 'massive two-storey tower' and the 'remnants of a fortified surrounding wall'. On the basis of such evidence he concludes, 'What the Romans had to contend with at Qumran was clearly an armed camp in a heavily fortified location.'[76] More recently Golb has elaborated his position, with particular reference to Qumran as a link in the chain of defence fortresses designed to safeguard trade across the Dead Sea and protect Jerusalem and Judaea from military invasions from Nabataea.[77]

However, it is questionable whether this case is as impressive as it appears to be. There is no question that the Qumran buildings served military purposes – may indeed, have been constructed to that end to begin with – at different times in their history.[78] But it does not follow that a site with fortifications was therefore built as a military fortress. On the contrary, there is evidence that private homes built at the turn of the eras in rural settings had fortified features not unlike those at Qumran.[79] Moreover, it has been questioned whether the Qumran site fits into 'the defense system of encircling fortifications'[80] erected for the defense of Judaea.[81] Thus, the *prima facie* evidence can hardly be said to support the view that the Qumran buildings in the form in which they were finally destroyed were built for specifically military purposes.

Another interpretation of the Qumran ruins advanced recently is that they are those of a private villa. Interestingly, the view is advocated by Robert Donceel and Pauline Donceel-Vôute who have been entrusted with the task of publishing de Vaux's notebooks recording his excavations and interpretation of the site.[82] The Donceels' hypothesis rests chiefly upon two features: first, the character of the pottery and glassware found in the ruins, and second, its stratification. As to the former, they find that, while no detailed publication of the nearest sites – the Hasmonean and Herodian palaces at Jericho – is available, 'the common pottery shapes are far from being as isolated and particular to Qumran, its caves and its neighbourhood as it seemed in Father de Vaux's time.'[83] Regarding glassware several samples showed typological similarities especially in shape and ornamentation, with imports from Italy.[84] Lathe-turned stoneware, including urns, match those from patrician homes in Jerusalem;[85] while of particular note are coloured stone slabs, carefully cut for use in floors as in wealthy homes and palaces. The presence of these, as well as of the sophisticated glass and stoneware is astounding considering what has been said about the 'monastic simplicity' of the site.[86] As to stratification, fragments of stoneware (as well as of lamps believed to have appeared about 70 AD) have been found not only in different areas but different archaeological contexts, and found to join perfectly.[87]

A very different reading of the pottery found at Qumran has been carried out independently by Dr Jodi Magness.[88] Working either with published material or material personally examined, Dr Magness concludes that 'most of the material found at Qumran was produced locally.'[89] Noting that various types found at contemporary sites in Judaea are rare or unattested at Qumran – notably imports – Magness concludes that this must have been a deliberate policy on the part of the Qumran settlers.[90] Even more suggestive to Magness is the absence of locally-produced fine table ware of the first centuries BC and AD, as well as of wheel-made lamps with rims shaped to form spouts which were very common in Hasmonean times.[91] Her general conclusion is that 'fine wares are almost totally absent from the corpus at Qumran. In fact, one of the striking features of this pottery is its plainness ... [this] lends an air of austerity to the corpus which contrasts sharply with contemporary assemblages from Jericho, Jerusalem and Herodion.'[92]

Perhaps even more pressing a question for the villa-hypothesis is whether the ruins correspond in design with what is known of contemporary Judaean villas. Dr Jodi Magness addressed this question directly,[93] examining buildings of the Hasmonean, Herodian and Roman types, both palaces and mansions. In particular, she compares the site known as 'Hilkiah's palace', a Herodian-period rural villa west of Hebron. Her conclusion speaks for itself:

> In terms of layout and design, the settlement at Qumran has none of the features characteristic of the Hasmonean and Herodian palaces: the hall with two columns *in antis*, the colonnaded tri-clininium, the peristyle courtyard with garden, the bath-houses and the large swimming pools and landscaped gardens. It does have courtyards, without peristyles, around which rooms were grouped. There was a second storey of rooms in at least part of the settlement ... The most compelling argument against the identification of Qumran as a villa lies in the almost complete absence of interior decoration.[94]

Yet another identification proposed of late for the site is that of an inn or hostelry.[95] Rejecting other suggestions, Crown and Cansdale see Qumran as a significant point on the trade-route between Judaea and Arabia, with merchants and their wares being trans-shipped across the Dead Sea from Qumran to ports on the eastern shore. On this view the site is interpreted in commercial terms. The buildings with their splendid dining-room equipped with ample pottery and even fine glassware, would have served for the entertaining of travellers, to whose presence the large number of coins may bear witness. The water-system ensured adequate water supplies even during successive dry seasons. Besides spices from Arabia, salt mined or extracted from Sodom would be shipped through Qumran over the Salt Road[96] to Jerusalem which could be used by pack animals. Indeed, given a higher sea level, Qumran could well have been a port.[97] As for the scrolls, their presence in the adjacent caves was co-incidental: caves in the area were frequently used for this purpose, so that 'the depositing of scrolls in the caves around Qumran simply followed an old tradition.'[98]

While this case has a certain surface plausibility, it is doubtful whether it can bear close scrutiny either in its particulars or as a whole. Thus Qumran might have been a port, serving as a transit point for spices and salt to be shipped to Jerusalem via the Salt Road, but there is no hard evidence for any of these specifics. The fact that they – and others – may be spun together into a coherent whole does nothing to strengthen the tenuousness of the individual items. Individual possibilities do not become probabilities, let alone certainties, simply by being linked together.

Aside from these difficulties, there are two fundamental problems which the hostelry hypothesis faces. First, despite the claim of Crown and Cansdale to the contrary, the evidence does not sustain the view that Qumran is 'strategically sited ... an important node in this trade network.'[99] Either as the departure-point for goods being transported to Jerusalem or the transit point for merchants travelling to Arabia, Qumran is out of the way. In terms of what is known of both commerce and military strategy at the turn of the eras, the Qumran site commends itself by its isolation.[100] Second, it is hard to see the Qumran buildings as serving very readily the functions which the hostelry hypothesis requires of them. Indeed, one of the notable things in the exposition of Crown and Cansdale is the way in which one function after another is bundled into the definition: 'port, transit centre, entrepôt and perhaps an industrial site for manufacturing salt in drying pans, with a garrison troop community and the commercial outpost for Jerusalem and Jericho,' and a customs post besides.[101] The theory is imaginative and of heuristic value but it is hardly compelling.

A more plausible suggestion than the hostelry hypothesis has recently been advanced by Edward M. Cook in a popular but careful article which proposes that Qumran was a ritual purification centre.[102] Following a review of earlier proposals and their inability to satisfy all of the data of the site, Cook argues that the purpose of the settlement is to be found in these passages of the Temple Scroll which enjoin the creation of 'three places to the east of the city' as temporary residences for the purification of those who had become ritually defiled (*11Q Temp.* 46:16–18). This explains the elaborate water-system. Not only so but the Temple Scroll forbids the burial of the dead within cities (*11Q Temp.* 48:11–14), as well as the bringing into the city of the sanctuary the skins of animals slaughtered outside of it (*11Q Temp.* 47:7–11). These injunctions explain both the cemeteries at Qumran, as well as the collection of scrolls there. Cook concludes, 'Qumran, then, should be understood as an outpost or annex for the Jerusalem branch of sectarians. We must imagine the buildings as housing a small permanent staff as well as providing for a constant stream of incoming unclean members and outgoing clean ones. The bodies in the cemetery and the scrolls in the caves are all associated with the Jerusalem branch. The idea that Khirbet Qumran was the principal location of the group … should be discarded … Qumran was used primarily by the Jerusalem chapter of the Essenes.'[103]

Whether Cook's proposal offers a comprehensive solution to all of the data of the Qumran site – as he claims – need not be determined here. The strength of his suggestion is that it finds in the texts themselves the explanation of some of the main features of the site, including some of the most problematic. Its weakness is that the *Rule of the Community* does not read like the handbook of a community of transients. In any case, Cook's hypothesis does offer an alternative reading of the Qumran site, and that reading envisages its function as being religious.

The wide spectrum of views proposed: from religious community centre to trade and customs facility has not surprisingly led to the proposal that perhaps a spectrum of functions is to be envisaged – but not all simultaneously. Such a position has been propounded by J-B. Humbert.[104] Humbert's view however, is not just a piecemeal approach intent on solving individual difficulties. It is rather a comprehensive reinterpretation of the data prompted by what he perceives to be weaknesses in de Vaux's account. Within the framework of Humbert's understanding difficulties not readily resolved within de Vaux's scheme are held to be more readily soluble.

Humbert's starting-point is that de Vaux assumed *a priori* that Qumran was a community centre, and proceeded to interpret the data on that premise.[105] However, the data are more varied than de Vaux conceded, and include evidence of finer glass and pottery, columns and capitals which suggest a building of a different character.[106] Moreover, de Vaux's stratigraphy exhibits a rigidity which cannot be sustained by the evidence.[107] Humbert therefore proposes a new chronology (and accompanying stratigraphy) beginning with the construction of a resort-cum-hunting-lodge in Hasmonean times about 100 BC.[108] To this belong the remains of architectural and other refinement. This came to an end violently at a time which cannot be determined with precision: military attack in 57 BC, or earthquake and fire in 31 BC offer two possibilities. Sometime towards the end of the first century BC the site was occupied by the Essenes who were centred in the oases around the Dead Sea.[109] However, the Essenes did not occupy the site residentially (save for a small number: ten to fifteen[110]); rather, it became the religious centre – 'substitute Temple' – whither they resorted to keep the feasts and festivals and probably to offer sacrifices.[111] It is from this premise that Humbert reads the subsequent history of the site, envisaging a time when the cult site was established to the north (Period IIa), and later transferred to the south requiring the extension of the water system. Period IIb saw both expansion (of the hall of offerings – de Vaux's assembly-room) as well as the contraction (the abandonment of the same)[112] of the southern extensions.

Humbert's re-reading of the evidence of the Qumran

site is stimulating and suggestive. Its strength lies in its comprehensiveness. Not least impressive is its ability to offer promising solutions to questions that have vexed Qumran studies from their beginning: the harmonization of the evidence of the site with that of the ancient historians, notably Philo, Pliny and Josephus; the question of a gap in the occupation of the site during the latter half of the first century BC, and what occasioned it; the possibility of accounting for *both* the austere *and* the more elegant features of the remains within a single hypothesis; and, perhaps not least, the suggestion of a plausible role for the buildings as a religious community centre which does not require extensive living quarters for which at best tenuous possibilities have been proposed.

At the same time Humbert's interpretation has not gone unassailed. Dr Jodi Magness has criticized his proposals on archaeological grounds, declaring that they 'raise more problems than they solve'.[113] Thus, as to Humbert's alleged Hasmonean villa: she holds (and Humbert concedes) that much of his reconstruction is hypothetical; while she maintains that de Vaux's assembly-hall, which Humbert reads as an offering hall, is supported by comparative evidence from Hilkiah's palace.[114] Again, the ceramic evidence is clearly at odds with the dating of the buildings required by Humbert's scheme. This is especially the case with the 1000 vessels found in the storeroom (loci 86, 89) adjacent to the assembly hall (locus 77) which de Vaux judged were used for dining, but Humbert regards as vessels for offerings. But no comparative evidence is offered in support. Moreover, on Humbert's chronology these vessels belong to the pre-community stage. 'How then could these vessels have been used for cultic purposes by the Essenes at a time when the site supposedly functioned as a non-sectarian agricultural settlement?'[115]

Humbert's proposals have been questioned on other grounds than archaeological. L.H. Schiffman writes:

> While we have no problem with the notion that the original construction of the Qumran site may have been for purposes

> other than as a sectarian center we still cannot accept this view. First, it makes the assumption that the sect is to be identified with the Essenes, an issue which we regard as still unresolved. Second, the presence of so many ritual baths in the Hasmonean period ruins means that a religious group must have made use of this facility already in the Hasmonean period. Finally, we reject categorically the claim that sacrifices were performed at Qumran, and we cannot accept the analysis of the archaeological evidence as a basis for this claim.[116]

Is it possible to draw secure conclusions from such contested archaeological data? It seems clear that the comparative evidence will not sustain the conclusion that the ruins are those of a villa – either throughout their history or at any point in it. On the other hand the comparative evidence sustains the conclusion that the buildings had a defensive aspect, though not to the extent to require that their sole purpose was military. The trading-post theory depends on too many unproved assumptions to carry conviction. To this extent it is possible to say what the buildings were not. How far is it possible to infer from their form what they were?

Humbert's characterization of the buildings as 'an exploding settlement'[117] is not inapt. De Vaux himself had maintained that the beginnings of the occupation in Period Ia were modest whereas Period Ib saw an enlargement into 'an impressive complex of buildings.'[118] But Humbert is surely correct in seeing an adventitious (though certainly not purposeless) character to these additions. In a word, the complex suggests adaptation rather than design from the ground up.[119] If it be asked what purpose this expansion was intended to serve the answer appears to be twofold. First, the complex was intended for use by a sizeable number of people. This is suggested particularly by the largest room in the ruins (72½ × 15 feet) of which de Vaux says 'It is clear that it was a meeting-place'.[120] In short, the buildings were used by some kind of community. Second, if it be asked what was the nature of the community, the least that can be said is that it had a religious aspect. The numerous deposits of animal bones of sheep, goats and cattle, found carefully buried throughout the ruins at all levels suggest not only their use at religious meals but also careful disposal following the meals.[121]

Related data are not inconsistent with this understanding: for example, the large amount of pottery found in the ruins adjacent to the assembly-hall; and the water-channel for cleaning the building. The evidence as a whole seems to be most readily satisfied by the hypothesis that the Qumran complex was the meeting-place of some kind of religious community. The more exact definition of the nature of the community and its use of the buildings depends upon fuller evidence than that surveyed thus far.

The Relation of the Buildings and the Caves

The second critical issue to be faced in constructing the footings of a specifically Qumran theology is whether it can be shown, not merely that some of the scrolls from the caves legislate for a community and the ruins are those of a religious community, but whether there is evidence linking the two. It has been argued that there is not, by no one more strenuously than Professor Norman Golb.[122] It may be observed to begin with that it would be no small coincidence if a community handbook were discovered in a cave adjacent to community ruins and yet the two should be totally unconnected (though, of course, Dr Golb maintains that the ruins are those of a military fort).

However, recently discovered ostraca at the site: one apparently a list of supplies needed by the community[123], another, recording the gift of a horse and slave to the community[124] – the latter particularly, which uses the same word for community (*yaḥad*) as does the *Rule* of that name, make a link between cave and ruins virtually irresistible.

The discovery from the ruins of additional inkwells since de Vaux's excavations has strengthened the hypothesis, put forward by him almost from the start, that writing constituted a significant activity within the community.[125] If early versions of the scriptorium theory were overblown, they were early seen to be so.[126] It now appears that as many as five inkwells may have been found in the ruins: a discovery of considerable significance, since inkwells are relatively rare finds.[127] Stephen Goranson comments, 'the number of inkwells from a site like this is extraordinary. None has been found, for example, at Sepphoris, a major Galilean site, extensively excavated, where the Mishnah was completed.'[128]

The foregoing evidence must be taken in conjunction with the fact pointed out from the start by de Vaux – that the pottery found in the caves is of the same type as that found in the ruins.[129] After almost fifty years, marked by much debate and re-evaluation, Jodi Magness reaches essentially the same conclusions. The pottery at Qumran is monotonous, limited and repetitive: bowls, plates, cooking pots, jars, oil lamps. The same is true of that of the caves, except that it is even more limited. The scroll jars, though perhaps also used for other purposes, were probably made to hold scrolls: they occur elsewhere only rarely. Magness concludes that the pottery was made at the site.[130]

Such evidence seems most naturally to indicate that the caves and the ruins are to be taken together, each interpreted in the light of the other. If this is sound then one more footing has been found to serve as an underpinning for Qumran theology.

The Scale and Functioning of the Community

The evidence surveyed thus far both of the organizational texts and of the site, has disclosed an apparently double dimension to the sect. On the one hand the community (*yaḥad*) appears to stand in distinction from the congregation (*'ēdah*), the latter consisting of families living in the towns and villages, whereas the former exists in relative (though not total) isolation, and no hint of family life appears. Again, the assembly hall (locus 77), for all its generous proportions, is unlikely to have been able to accommodate more than a few score of individuals,[131] particularly if, as the presence of eating ware in an adjoining room suggests,[132] it served as the setting for ritual meals. On the other hand, the scale of the stock of pottery: more than one thousand items, including 708 bowls carefully stacked together, and constituting pottery necessary for eating purposes,[133] seems wildly out of proportion with the size of the hall.

This bifurcation of evidence comes to particular visibility in two respects which bear in turn, upon the functioning of the community. The first is that of living quarters. Aside from communal activities, where did the residents live and sleep? That they lived in the caves may be ruled out; for while artefacts have been found in most of the caves, they are objects which suggest hiding rather than habitation.[134] In any case, it is questionable whether there were enough caves within reasonable travelling distance of the Khirbeh to shelter a population of any size.[135]

De Vaux suggested that residents may have lived in huts or tents, identifying forked wooden posts as the supports for such shelters.[136] This suggestion has recently been revived by the explorations of a team of archaeologists led by Hanan Eshel and Magen Broshi in January 1996. So far, only unofficial reports have appeared[137] but these claim that outside newly discovered caves in the marl terrace, lines of stones have been found which may mark the location of tents. Such evidence can be fully weighed only when it has been published.

It is worth noting that the latest available evaluation of the evidence for living quarters is sceptical of the hypothesis of huts and tents. J. Patrich urges that the huts and tents theory be rejected, maintaining that the five-pole structure hypothesized by de Vaux was at best a temporary refuge. Patrich holds that living quarters should be sought inside the walls of the Khirbeh, probably on an upper storey. It is in view of this that he puts the likely population of the community at 50–70.[138]

The other phenomena which inject a measure of tension into reconstructing the functioning of the community are the cemeteries. Two conclusions about them may be set down forthwith. First, they give every sign of being linked to the ruins and therefore to the community. This is shown not only because pottery sherds found in the graves match the pottery of the buildings[139]; it is shown because of the unique mode of burial. For at a time when Jewish burial customs had changed from single burial in single graves to secondary burial (using ossuaries) in family tombs,[140] not only did the earlier style persist at Qumran, but the mode of burial was distinctive. Corpses were buried north to south, with the head at the south but propped by a stone so as to face east.[141] Moreover, the graves show a unique design, each corpse being positioned on a shelf cleared to the east of the bottom of the main shaft. Hachlili, commenting on the burial site as a whole (which contains approximately 1100 graves) concludes, 'It is too huge and different in form and customs to have served a regular Jewish community. To the contrary, the Qumran cemetery reflects a distinctive out of the ordinary community, who purposely used different customs.'[142]

The second notable fact about the Qumran burial site is that some of the tombs excavated were found to contain skeletons of women and children. In these cases however, the graves were located, not in the main cemetery which lies due east of the ruins and whose graves were arranged in ordered rows, but in the outward fringes of the main cemetery, as well as in two secondary cemeteries: one to the north of the main site, containing twelve graves, and the other, south of wadi Qumran, containing thirty graves. Of the fifty-two graves excavated, skeletons of women were found in seven and of children in five.[143] Certainly in three, possibly in five instances, there is evidence of burial in wooden coffins, though like the graves of the women and children these also were located on outer fringes of the main cemetery where the arrangement of the graves was irregular.[144]

Now the point of relevance of these data for this study is neither why the skeletons in the main cemetery are buried in the same, distinctive position,[145] nor even why they outnumber so completely the skeletons of women and children[146] (assuming that the sample of graves excavated is representative). The real point of moment is what the data say regarding the scale and functioning of the community. The least that can be said would appear to be that, while the presence of families was by no means unknown, and certainly not forbidden, the settlement served overwhelmingly as a gathering place for men dedicated to the cause which was nurtured there.

How much further it is possible to refine this statement remains to be seen. Additional related data certainly need to be fed into it. To begin with there is evidence, as de Vaux himself came to concede, that 'particularly during the second Iron Age and the Roman period the west bank of the Dead Sea was more thickly populated than we have been accustomed to imagine.'[147] Not only so, but there is evidence to suggest that there was probably significant Qumran influence in that region.[148] De Vaux's researches as far south as 'Ain Feshkha, including the building to the north of the spring at Feshkha and the related enclosures to its north and south are fully reported by him.[149] His conclusions were that the main period of occupation of the building was 'contemporaneous with Period II of Khirbet Qumran' as is shown by the pottery and confirmed by the coins;[150] and, that, while there is less evidence for Period I 'the fact remains that the coins which can be ascribed with certainty to Alexander Jannaeus and Antigonus Mattathias, as well as the entire ceramic material, do establish that Period I of Feshkha corresponds to Period Ib of Khirbet Qumran.'[151] 'All these signs point to the fact that the two were organically connected. They were inhabited by the same community, and it is this that explains their common history.'[152]

However, the evidence of a more widespread Qumran presence on the west bank of the Dead Sea goes beyond this – which, after all, merely demonstrates that the Feshkha settlement was an arm of that at Wadi Qumran: in de Vaux's words, 'an agricultural and industrial establishment used to benefit the community of Qumran.'[153] Fifteen miles south of Qumran a ruin was identified near 'En el-Ghuweir during construction of a new road. The site was excavated by P. Bar-Adon[154] who uncovered remains of a long, large building 43 × 19.5 m, comprising a large hall with a large kitchen and two rooms to the east.[155] Much of the pottery, including storage jars, jugs, cooking pots, bowls, lamps, 'was typical of the period 200 BCE – 68 CE, some of it resembling that found at Feshkha in strata I-II of Qumran'.[156] 800 m north of the building a cemetery was discovered. Of the twenty tombs investigated all but two were constructed to the same design as those in the Qumran cemetery; they were aligned north to south, with the head of the corpses to the south; and thirteen of them contained male skeletons, six female, and one that of a child.[157] While the pottery finds yielded a range from Qumran periods Ib to II, the coins dated from 37 BCE – 44 CE. Bar-Adon's conclusion is direct. 'One can assert that the inhabitants of 'En el-Ghuweir and Qumran belonged to the same desert sect. On the basis of the small dimensions of the cemetery at 'En el-Ghuweir, it seems to me that the center of this sect was at Qumran. 'En el-Ghuweir was a secondary settlement – perhaps one of a string of settlements spread out over the Judaean desert and along the shores of the Dead Sea, many of which have not yet been discovered.'[158] From the absence of any evidence of living-quarters, Bar-Adon draws the further conclusion that the building served as a public meeting-place for the sect.

Yet another cemetery discovered by Bar-Adon in the 1960s but not thoroughly excavated by him is located at Ḥiam El-Sagha, north of Murabba'at, and has been explored recently by Israeli archaeologists.[159] Of the twenty graves identified all but one are orientated north-north-east/south-south-west; in the two graves opened, the heads pointed south and faced east, one a mature male, the other a female child. No buildings were discovered in the vicinity of the cemetery, though Eshel and Greenhut noted two formations east of the cemetery which might have served that purpose.[160]

De Vaux was not unaware of much of this data, devoting an appendix to it.[161] He addresses chiefly the 'En el-Ghuweir evidence. While admitting that a connection between it and Qumran was a possibility, he nevertheless denied that it was likely, chiefly because of the absence of pottery forms most characteristic of Qumran during Period Ib; because the coins do not cover the span covered by coins from Qumran; and because no documents of the kind found at Qumran have been found at 'En el-Ghuweir.[162] It is questionable whether such data are needed to prove a connection or at least render it probable. The most telling evidence is the distinctive burial mode. This is particularly forceful not only because of its massive presence at Qumran, but because it stands in flat opposition to prevailing burial practices in Judaism at that time.

Now the evidence reviewed[163] may reasonably be said to support the conclusion that there was a Qumran presence on the western shore of the Dead Sea in addition to Qumran itself. But the comparative evidence also says something about the functioning of the community at Qumran. For not only does it show the vastly greater scale of the Qumran settlement; it also points to functions pursued there, such as the round-the-clock study of the law, for which resources could scarcely have existed at any of the other sites. At the same time, it also implies that the Qumran version of Judaism could also be practised and maintained without these other dimensions being pursued by each local group, though certainly they would have to be carried out somewhere. In short it becomes plausible to see Qumran as the active headquarters of the movement: a centre of study, worship and training. Is this not what the Community Rule presupposes? And if so, would not its population be likely to have a relatively small stable core, with a larger mobile dimension reaching its greatest scale at festivals such as the renewal of the covenant?

The history of occupation

A fourth contribution made by the site to the quest for the sect is the history of its occupation of the buildings. As was noted above, de Vaux's interpretation of the character of the buildings went hand in hand with his interpretation of their history. The most secure date obtainable is that of the destruction of the community in AD 68. The Jewish anti-Roman revolutionaries of AD 66–70 expressed their rebellion by minting their own coins. Of these 94 have been found at Qumran, 83 dating to the second year (68–9). Since it is known that the Roman armies led by Vespasian captured Jericho, eight miles north of Qumran in the summer of 68; and since Roman coins were found in the next layer of the Qumran ruins, de Vaux infers that the Qumran settlement was overthrown by the Romans in AD 68. The period of Roman occupation of the site, which apparently ended with the conquest of Masada in AD 74, he labels Period III.

When then did Period II begin? Here again the coin record offers guidance. Apart from ten coins from the reign of Herod the Great[164] there is a break in the record from Antigonus Mattathias (40–37 BC) until 4 BC when the record resumes with coins of Herod Archelaus (4 BC– 6 AD). The break in the coin record corresponds with a period when the buildings were devastated by fire. De Vaux dates the beginning of this to the massive earthquake of 31 BC attested by Josephus[165] and its end to the reconstruction of the buildings in 4 BC when the coin record resumes. This means therefore that Period II lasted from 4 BC to AD 68, while the preceding period – Period I – ended in 31 BC.

The first period de Vaux sees as falling into two distinct stages, the turning-point coming at about 130 BC with a marked increase in building activity to include a two-storey tower, an assembly hall, a refectory, workshops and a greatly enlarged water system. The coins in this layer led him to conclude that Period Ib as he called it coincided with the Hasmonean period, roughly from the time of John Hyrcanus (134–104 BC) to the beginning of the reign of Herod in 37 BC. Period Ia, beginning about 150 BC, was on a much smaller scale, when much older buildings were restored, and came to an end during the reign of Hyrcanus I.

It is safe to say that the case presented by de Vaux, which he argued with lucidity, cogency and judiciousness, became the benchmark for the interpretation of the Qumran site. This does not mean that it was universally accepted; it means rather that alternative views had to justify themselves over against de Vaux's. The fullest counter-reading to de Vaux's of the strictly archaeological evidence is that of E.M. Laperrousaz, himself a member of one of the original teams of excavators.[166] Laperrousaz' dissent focused on two aspects of the history of occupation of the site: a question of which more would be heard. First, he questioned whether the beginning of Period Ia could be dated before 100 BC, holding that the coin record cannot sustain this.[167] Second, he dissented from de Vaux's view that Period Ib ended in 31 BC,[168] placing it rather between 67 and 63 BC. This was followed by a literal exile to Damascus[169], with Period IIa beginning during the reign of Herod the Great and ending probably with the overthrow of Archelaus in AD 6.[170] The beginning of the Period IIb cannot be dated precisely, but its end came in 67–68.

As to the dating of the beginning of the Qumran settlement (Period Ia), de Vaux had conceded the difficulty of determining this. The modesty of the buildings, the fact that use was made of remains from the Israelite period, the virtual identity of the pottery in Periods Ia and Ib, and the absence of coins associated with it,[171] in contrast with the much fuller record for Period Ib including eleven Seleucid coins, one of John Hyrcanus I (135–104 BC) and one hundred and forty-three coins of Alexander Jannaeus (103–76 BC)[172], led de Vaux to conclude that the buildings of Period Ib could have been constructed at the earliest under John Hyrcanus. From this it followed that Period Ia must be earlier, 'but we cannot push it back very far because the modest nature of the buildings and the scarcity of archaeological material attest the fact that this first installation was of short duration.'[173]

In a recent re-evaluation of Qumran archaeology Magen Broshi has maintained that the archaeological evidence cannot demonstrate whether the site was settled in the middle or at the end of the second century BC, referring particularly to the numismatic evidence.[174] However, more recent excavations on Mount Gerizim have uncovered as many as two dozen coins of Hyrcanus I from various sites showing that the beginning of Hasmonean coinage belongs to the period 129–112/111 BC.[175] On the basis of this evidence F.M. Cross concludes that, 'this confirms anew De Vaux's chronology of the Qumran community center, placing its origin in the time of Jonathan or Simon.'[176]

The second demurrer of Laperrousaz was in respect to de Vaux's claim that Period Ib ended with the earthquake of 31 BC. Laperrousaz' proposed re-reading noted above, has not won many supporters, but enough hesitation has been expressed regarding related aspects of de Vaux's view (especially of a gap in occupation of the site between the earthquake and reoccupation in the time of Archelaus) to prevent the emergence of any kind of consensus.[177]

A re-reading of the evidence advanced recently by Jodi Magness appears to satisfy the typological data and avoid the objections raised against earlier proposals.[178] The heart of Magness' argument is that the hoard of 561 silver coins, the latest of which dates to 9/8 BC, and which de Vaux associated with the beginning of Period II, could equally be associated with Period Ib. Indeed, de Vaux's description suggests this: 'These three pots [containing coins] were buried *beneath* the level of Period II and *above* that of Period Ib.'[179] Assigning the hoard to the end of Period Ib permits a quite different reconstruction. It implies that the earthquake of 31 BC, which undoubtedly damaged the buildings did not bring occupation to an end. Repairs were effected and occupation continued unbroken until 9/8 BC, when fire, indicated by a layer of ash, and precipitated not by the earthquake but by a violent attack, brought occupation to an end – but only for a short period, until about 4 BC.[180] Period II then followed, as de Vaux suggested, beginning early in the reign of Archelaus, and lasting until the overthrow of AD 68.[181]

Conclusion

The purpose of this chapter has been to explore the question, pressed with increasing force and frequency of late, as to whether the evidence sustains the conclusion that a sect of any kind ever existed at Qumran. The approach adopted here has been to address that question on the basis of the surface evidence of the documents, and the typological evidence of the documents and the site, notably palaeography and archaeology. Of course, there is no evidence which does not require interpretation. But there is some evidence which requires less interpretation than others, and the evidence treated in this chapter is of that character. Clearly it has certain limitations. For example, while exhibiting data that point to the *existence* of the sect, it can say much less about the *nature* of the sect: a distinct circumscription of the meaning of the term *'sect'*. But what might be a disadvantage in other circumstances is an advantage in the present inquiry, for it is precisely the 'thatness' rather than the 'whatness' of the sect which requires to be demonstrated.

It is concluded here that the evidence set forth indicates that at least some of the documents of the Qumran caves and the evidence of the Qumran site are most readily accounted for on the hypothesis that both belong together and point to the existence of a religious community. In a word, there was an entity there which has to be accounted for. It had a discernible organization; it functioned in a distinct setting; it had a traceable history; and it apparently had distinct ideas which manifested themselves at least in some measure in distinct practices. With this we come to the threshold of our main interest: the theology of the sect.

Notes

1. Estimates have varied and will continue to do so. Scholars involved in the early stages of Qumran research implied a total of the order of 600. Cf.Trever, John C., *The Untold Story*

of Qumran (Grand Rapids, Eerdmans, 97–100), who refers to his own article 'Le Travail d'édition des Fragments Manuscrits de Qumran', in *RB* LX111, 1965, 49–67, ET (slightly updated) in *BA* 19, 1956, 75–96. More recently, a number of the order of 800 has been given. See the concluding observation of Geza Vermes to the Scroll Catalogue in the latest edition of his translation of the texts, in which he puts the total at 813. (*The Dead Sea Scrolls in English*, Revised and Extended Fourth Edition, Harmondsworth: Penguin Books, 1995, lvi). Dimant, Devorah, writes, 'The figure 800 represents, therefore, the manuscripts which are accounted for and which can at present be checked either through publication or with the help of photographs and inventory lists', art., 'The Qumran Manuscripts: Contents and Significance', in Dimant, Devorah and Schiffman, Lawrence H. (eds.), *Time to Prepare the Way in the Wilderness* (Leiden: E.J. Brill, 1995), (hereafter 'Qumran Manuscripts'), 30.

2. Cf. Yaacov Shavit, 'The Qumran Library in the Light of the Attitude Towards Books and Libraries in the Second Temple Period', in Wise, Michael O., Golb, Norman, Collins, John J. and Pardee, Dennis G. (eds.), Methods of Investigation of the Dead Sea Scrolls and the Khirbet Qumran Site, Present Realities and Future Prospects, in *Annals of the New York Academy of Sciences*, Volume 722, (New York: The New York Academy of Sciences, 1994) (hereafter 'Methods of Investigation'), 299–315. Shavit points to the scarcity of evidence suggesting the existence of libraries anywhere in Judaism, and warns against over-exactness in trying to deduce the Qumran sect from the Qumran texts.
3. See Dimant, 'The Qumran Manuscripts', 58.
4. Dimant, 'The Qumran Manuscripts', 32.
5. For a discussion see J. Carmignac, 'Conjecture sur la première ligne de la Règle de la Communauté,' *RQ* 2, 1959, 85–7.
6. So J.T. Milik, in a review of the Hebrew edition of Y. Yadin, '*The Scroll of the War of the Sons of Light Against the Sons of Darkness*', (Jerusalem, 1955), in *RB* 64, 1957, 586; repeated in a review of P. Wernberg- Møller, *The Manual of Discipline*, (Leiden: Brill, 1957), in *RB* 67, 1960, 410.
7. Barthélemy, D. and Milik, J.T., *Discoveries in the Judean Desert I, Qumran Cave I*, (hereafter DJD I), (Oxford, 1955), 107.
8. Murphy-O'Connor, J., 'La genèse littéraire de la Règle de la

Communauté', *RB*, 76, 1969, 528–49; Pouilly, J., *La Règle de la Communauté de Qumran, Son Évolution Littéraire*, Paris, (1976). For an evaluative account see Gagnon, R.J., 'How Did the Rule of the Community Obtain Its Final Shape?' in Charlesworth, James H. (ed.), *Qumran Questions*, (Sheffield, 1995), 67–85.

9. Vermes, Geza, writes, 'It would seem, moreover, that this constitutes the actual beginning of the manuscript, as it is preceded by a blank margin noticeably wider than that dividing the columns.' Art, 'Qumran Forum Miscellanea I,' *JJS*, 43, 1992, 301. A similar judgment is expressed by Garcia Martinez, Florentino, *The Dead Sea Scrolls Translated*, Leiden, (1994; hereafter *DSST*), 491. Cf. Hempel, Charlotte, 'Comments on the Translation of 4QSd I, 1,' *JJS*, 44, 1993, 127–8.
10. Translations of the scrolls are from DSST, unless indicated otherwise.
11. $4QS^b$ agrees with $4QS^d$ against IQS in this latter regard.
12. Vermes, G., 'Preliminary Remarks on Unpublished Fragments of the Community Rule from Qumran Cave 4,' *JJS*, 4, 1991, 255.
13. Cf. Metso, Sarriana, 'The Primary Results of the Reconstruction of $4QS^e$', *JJS*, 44, 1993, 303–8. She concludes, 'The manuscript of $4QS^e$ has preserved a more original text of the Community Rule than IQS' (307).
14. Parts of IQS I–III are preserved in $4QS^c$.
15. The exact relationship between these officials is less certain. For a useful note see Leaney, A.R.C., *The Rule of Qumran and Its Meaning*, London, (1966), 229f.
16. Cf. Metso, Sarrianna, (as in n.13), 307.
17. Art. cit, *JJS*, 4, 1991, 250f. The large numbers of copies, coupled with their differences, has been held to tell against the theory of a single community at Qumran. But this will depend on whether the Qumran Community is understood to constitute the sect without remainder. See below.
18. *DJD*, I, 107 with Plate XXII, photograph 28.
19. Schiffman, Lawrence H., *The Eschatological Community of the Dead Sea Scrolls, A Study of the Rule of the Congregation*, SBL Monograph Series Number 38, (Atlanta, Georgia: Scholars Press, 1989), 8.
20. E.g. in IQS II 20–22 those who enter the covenant consist of 'the priests ... the levites ... and all the children of Israel'. Again, in a session of the Many 'the priests will sit down

first, the elders next and the remainder of all the people will sit down in order of rank' (VI 8–9).

21. Schiffman aptly characterizes the *Rule of the Congregation* as 'an eschatological mirror image of *Rule of the Community.*' *Reclaiming the Dead Sea Scrolls*, (Philadelphia: The Jewish Publication Society, 1994), 133. (Hereafter *Reclaiming*).
22. Cf. Schiffman (in a discussion of the schema on which the text is to be reconstructed, 'There can be no question that an adequate schema would take into account the nature of the scroll as a whole in which the *Rule of Benedictions* appears as the last part.' (*Eschatological Community*, 73). Commending the reconstruction of J. Licht which takes the basis for analysis to be the eschatological community outlined in IQS[a], he continues, 'He expects to find in our text a series of benedictions for the very same officials mentioned in the *Rule of the Congregation*' (loc. cit.). J.H. Charlesworth adopts a similar stance (Charlesworth, J.H., *The Dead Sea Scrolls, Hebrew, Aramaic, and Greek Texts with English Translations Volume I, Rule of the Community and Related Documents* (hereafter Charlesworth, *DSS* Vol. I), (Louisville: Westminster John Knox Press, 1994), 119.
23. This is without prejudice to the suggestion of several scholars that the ritual meal of IQS[a] II 11–21 may have been observed proleptically in the community, and the Benedictions likewise. Cf. Vermes, G., *The Dead Sea Scrolls in English* (hereafter Vermes, *DSS*), (Harmondsworth, Fourth edition, 1995), 268; Rost, L., *Judaism Outside the Hebrew Canon*, Nashville, (1976), 169; Schiffman, L., *Sectarian Law in the DSS*, *Brown Judaic Studies*, 33, (Chico, 1983), 6. Schiffman has written more recently, 'The community described in the *Manual* (i.e. IQS) is an attempt to create messianic conditions, even before the coming of the *eschaton*, and to realize the sectarians' dreams of the future in the present … This banquet was of such great importance that the sectarians regularly ate communal meals in the present age in expectation of it' (*Eschatological Community*, 9). Milik, with less probability, regards the Benedictions as a purely literary exercise (*DJD*, I, 120).
24. Cf. 'Only the sect and its followers would survive the great battles described in the *Scroll of the War of the Sons of Light against the Sons of Darkness* and the resulting destruction of the wicked. Therefore, only the blessing formula would

have to be recited. The benedictions are intended to replace the blessing and curse recited as part of the mustering and covenant renewal.' (*Eschatological Community*, 75).

25. For details see Fitzmyer, J.A., 'Prolegomenon' in *Documents of Jewish Sectaries, Volume I: Fragments of a Zadokite Work*, edited and translated with introduction and notes by Schechter, S., (New York, 1970). A fuller account of the Genizah, its discovery and its contents is given by Kahle, Paul E., *The Cairo Genizah* 2nd ed., Oxford 1959), 3–13. Schechter's own account is contained in his *Studies in Judaism*, (Second Series, London, 1908), Vol. II, 5f.
26. The five fragments from Cave 6 were published by Baillet, M., in M. Baillet, J.T. Milik et R. de Vaux (eds.), *DJD III Les 'Petites Grottes' de Qumran*, (Oxford, 1962) 128–31; and the single fragment from Cave 5 by Milik, J.T., in the same volume (181). To that listing may now be added Charlesworth, J.H., *et al.* (eds.), *DSS, Vol. 2, Damascus Document, War Scroll and Related Documents*, (Louisville: Westminster John Knox Press, 1993), 59–79.
27. Why Schechter passed over the numbers XVII–XVIII has never been satisfactorily explained, though it has been a fruitful source of confusion. He has been followed by most editors, including (most recently) Qimron, Elisha, in Broshi, Magen (ed.), *The Damascus Document Reconsidered*, (Jerusalem: The Israel Exploration Society, 1992).
28. *Documents of Jewish Sectaries*, Volume I, (New York, 1970), p x.
29. Cf. Carmignac, J., 'Comparison entre les MSS, "A" et "B" du Document de Damas', *RQ*, 2, (1959–60), 53–67. Baumgarten, J.M., however, thinks the differences could be traced to copyists and leaves the matter open (*PDSS*, 2, 6).
30. Fitzmyer, J.A., while conceding that they agree substantially with Text A of the Cairo Genizah, maintains that they show divergences which 'reveal that the text itself was copied in different recensions and undoubtedly reflect differing stages of the community's existence' (*Documents of Jewish Sectaries*, I 17). Baumgarten, J.M., on the other hand, gives a negative (albeit tentative) answer, holding that the differences are minor, and that the Qumran fragments can be joined to the Genizah texts at appropriate points to yield a continuous text (*PDSS* 2, 59).
31. In addition to the fact, first noted by Milik, J.T., that columns

XIX–XX should follow columns I–VIII; columns XV–XVI columns XIX–XX; and columns IX–XIV columns XV–XVI. See Milik, J.T., *Ten Years of Discovery in the Wilderness of Judaea*, (London 1959), 151.

32. For the statistics (expressed somewhat differently) see Baumgarten, J.M., and Davies, Michael T, in Charlesworth, *DSS*, 2, 59.
33. Charlesworth, *DSS*, 2, 61.
34. The word *berîth* 'covenant' occurs no fewer than 42 times in the Damascus Document. Column XI is the only column in which it does not appear.
35. So Davies, P.R., *The Damascus Covenant: An Interpretation of the 'Damascus Document'*, (Sheffield, 1983). Davies was by no means the first to adopt this usage.
36. *Ten Years of Discovery*, 117.
37. The numbering of the text as 4QD[b] (4Q267) follows Garcia Martinez, *DSST*, 48. Reed, *Catalogue*, lists it as 4QD[a] (*olim* 4QD[b]) with number 4Q266. The same numbering is found in Eisenman, Robert and Wise, Michael, *The Dead Sea Scrolls Uncovered*, Rockport, Mass: (1992) (hereafter Eisenman-Wise, *DSSU*), 212, who provide a transliteration and translation of the section of the text from which the quotation comes (218–19) as well as photographs of the same (Plates 19 and 20). A transcription of the whole of 4QD[b] may be found in Wacholder, Ben Zion and Abegg, Martin G., *A Preliminary Edition of the Unpublished Dead Sea Scrolls, the Hebrew and Aramaic Texts from Cave Four, Fascicle One*, Washington, DC: Biblical Archaeological Society, (1991) (hereafter Wacholder-Abegg, *Preliminary Edition*), 3–22. Wacholder-Abegg list the text as 4QD[b], noting that others list it as 4QD[a]. To avoid confusion the symbols and numbering used in Garcia Martinez 'List of Manuscripts from Qumran' (*DSST* 467–513) will be used in this book.
38. See Knibb, Michael A., *The Qumran Community, Cambridge Commentaries on Writings of the Jewish and Christian World 200 BC to AD 200*, (Cambridge University Press, 1987), 26. Cf. 14.
39. Knibb, M.A., 'The Place of the Damascus Document' in *Methods of Investigation*, 152.
40. Davies, P.R., 'Redaction and Sectarianism in the Qumran Scrolls', in Martinez, F.G., Hilhorst, A., and Labuschague, C.J., (eds.) *The Scriptures and the Scrolls*, (Leiden: Brill, 1992),

152–63. (The sentence quoted is from 158). The differences between IQS and the Cave 4 copies which he has in mind include the absence from 4QS[d] of 'sons of Zadok' and '*yaḥad*' (IQS V 1–4).

41. The Cave 4 fragments of both IQS and CD are perhaps to be accounted for partly as updated versions; and partly as shortened versions for use for instructional purposes (e.g. Vermes suggests that 'IQS appears to have served as a handbook of instruction for the Master or Guardian of the community' (see Vermes, *The Dead Sea Scrolls: Qumran in Perspective*, Cleveland: Collins, 1978, 46). Roop, E.F., argues cogently on form critical grounds that, in its present form 'IQS was intended to be a manual or handbook for the Instructor ... IQS was not intended to be the constitution of the community, nor was it the juridical reference book, nor was it for use in liturgy ... IQS was a teacher's manual authorized by the Rabbim and intended to provide material from which the Instructor could draw in his didactic work and material which might serve to remind him of the kind of behavior the Rabbim expected from him.' (*A Form-Critical Study of the Society Rule (IQS) at Qumran*, Ann Arbor, University of Microfilms, 1984, 334f.) Lichtenberger, H., makes the further suggestion that the Cave 4 fragments may indicate the use of the *Rule* or parts of it as a 'Vademecum'. *Studien zum Menschenbild in Texten der Qumran-gemeinde* (Studien zur Umwelt des Neuen Testaments Band 15. Göttingen, Vandenhoeck und Ruprecht, 1980), 36. For an application of such possibilities to the Qumran penal code see Baumgarten, Joseph F., 'The Cave 4 Versions of the Qumran Penal Code', *JJS*, 43, 1992, 268–76.
42. The palaeographical evidence is presupposed here. It will be discussed more specifically below.
43. Dupont-Sommer suggested that CD XII 19a is the title of a section containing laws for towns (cf. XII 22b for camps), but of which the laws were eliminated by a copyist. A. Dupont-Sommer, *The Essene Writings from Qumran* (ed. G. Vermes, Gloucester, Mass: Peter Smith, 1973), 155, n.6 (hereafter Dupont-Sommer, *Essene Writings*).
44. The uncertainty arises from the division of words in the original as well as their translation as to whether the sectarian praxis is more effective than the Temple cult (i.e. the statement is comparative); or whether the Temple cult is ineffectual altogether (i.e. the statement is absolute). For a

discussion see Wernberg-Møller, P., *The Manual of Discipline*, translated and annotated with an introduction, in *Studies on the Texts of the Desert of Judaea*, ed, van der Ploeg, J., Volume I, (Leiden, 1957), 133 n.9, who concludes that the statement is absolute.

45. Cf. Fitzmyer, J. A., who says of the *Damascus Document*, 'This is a subsidiary rule book, but it is not known just how it is to be related to the Manual of Discipline of Cave 1', *Responses to 101 Questions on the Dead Sea Scrolls*, (New York/Mahwah: Paulist Press, 1992), 30.
46. Following a brief review of the data Schiffmann, L. E., concludes that it is best explained on the assumption that *Rule of the Community*, 'legislates specifically for the sectarian center at Qumran, and the *Zadokite Fragments* for groups scattered in camps throughout the Land of Israel ... Members could be inducted to full membership, including the right to touch pure solid and liquid food, only under the rigorous standards maintained, as far as we know, at Qumran alone.' *Reclaiming the Dead Sea Scrolls*, 101.
47. The sole exception is XX 32 which *DSST* renders 'the men of the Unique One', presumably in keeping with the use of the adjective on XX 1, 14. *PDSS* renders 'the men of the Community'. Cross, F.M., infers that 'the term *yaḥad* seems to be used only of the old community, the "Community" of the founder', *The Ancient Library of Qumran*, (3rd edition, Minneapolis: Fortress Press, 1995), 71, (hereafter Cross, *ALQ*^{3}). Either way the meaning is the same.
48. For a finely nuanced treatment of the nomenclature see Cross, *ALQ*^{3}, 70–1.
49. That a close connection exists between the community of the *Community Rule* and the congregation of the *Damascus Document* would seem to receive further support from the Cave 4 text 4QSD (4Q265), a preliminary study of which has appeared in Baumgarten, Joseph F., 'The Cave 4 Versions of the Qumran Penal Code', *JJS*, 43, 1992, 268–76. The offences discussed in 4QSD include some treated in IQS (disobeying seniors, deceiving colleagues, sleeping in assemblies, raucous laughter) but, whereas in IQS these incurred a single penalty, in 4QSD and the CD texts from Cave 4, they incurred a multiple penalty (exclusion from communal purities, reduction of rations and banning from community deliberations). Baumgarten concludes, 'These *mishpatim*

display affinities with the whole range of Qumran *serakhim* and halakic sources. It no longer seems appropriate to associate the *Damascus Document* exclusively with one uniform type of social organization', (273).

50. Baumgarten finds this to be particularly the case with the increased severity of the penalties in IQS as compared with CD and the Cave 4 Damascus fragments. Art. cit, 268.
51. Avigad, N., 'The Palaeography of the Dead Sea Scrolls and Related Documents', *Scripta Hierosolymitana* IV, (1958), 56–87.
52. Cross, F.M., 'The Development of the Jewish Scripts' in Wright, George E. (ed.), *The Bible and the Ancient Near East*, (Garden City, New York: Doubleday, 1961), 133–202.
53. For the Murabba'at finds see Milik, J.T., *Les grottes de Murabba'at, DJD*, II, Oxford, 1961, 70f. For an early account of the scrolls found at Masada see Yadin, Y., 'The Excavation of Masada, 1963/4, Preliminary Report', *IEJ*, 15, 1965, 103–9.
54. Avigad, art. cit, 69.
55. Baumgarten, Joseph M., 'The Cave 4 Versions of the Qumran Penal Code', *JJS*, 43, 1992, 269.
56. Some of the biblical fragments have been assigned to the pre-Hasmonean period, i.e. 225–150 BC, to which Cross gave the label 'Archaic'. See Cross, F.M., 'The Oldest Manuscripts from Qumran', *JBL* 74, 1955, 147–72, reprinted in Cross, F.M., and Talmon, S., *Qumran and the History of the Biblical Text*, (Harvard, 1975), esp. 167–9.
57. For a brief but well-documented survey, see Cross, F.M., *ALQ*^{3}, 171–4.
58. Cross writes, 'Archaic manuscripts of the first half of the second century need to be shifted up little if any and I believe that the dates of manuscripts in Jewish character which I have dated to the Hasmonean and Herodian periods need no adjustment.' *ALQ*^{3}, 173.
59. An account of an early attempt at carbon 14 dating of Qumran material may be found in *DJD*, I, 18–38. The test yielded a date between 167 BC and AD 237. (p. 27)
60. For an account of the process and the results see G. Bonani, M. Broshi, I. Carmi, S. Ivy, J. Strugnell and W. Wölfli, 'Radiocarbon Dating of the Dead Sea Scrolls,' *Atiqot II*, 1991, 27–32, 'Radio Carbon Dating of Fourteen Dead Sea Scrolls', *Radiocarbon*, 34, 1992, 843–9.
61. Davies, Philip R., *Behind the Essenes, History and Ideology in*

the Dead Sea Scrolls, (Atlanta, Georgia: Scholars Press, 1987), 136–7.

62. Golb, Norman, *Who Wrote the Dead Sea Scrolls? The Search for the Secret of Qumran*, (New York: Scribner, 1995), 251–6.
63. See 'Report and Discussion Concerning Radiocarbon Dating of Fourteen Dead Sea Scrolls' in Wise, Michael O., *et al. Methods of Investigation*, 441–53. The report of the radiocarbon tests itself, admitting that there is no simple explanation of the discrepancy in the case of the Testament of Qahat, concedes that the possibility of contamination in that case cannot be ruled out, since subsamples from the same material, subjected to ultrasonic cleaning alone, yielded dates significantly older (c. 350 years) than those cleaned both ultrasonically and chemically. The report accepts that more sophisticated chemical procedures may be necessary, and concludes, 'For the time being, this problem must remain unsolved'. G. Bonani, M. Broshi, I. Carmi, S. Ivy, J. Strugnell and W. Wölfi, 'Radiocarbon Dating of the Dead Sea Scrolls,' *Atiqot*, XX, July, 1991, 27–32. (The conclusions summarized above are from pp. 30–32).
64. Vander Kam, James C., *'The Dead Sea Scrolls Today'*, (Grand Rapids: Eerdmans, 1994), 19.
65. A vivid account, based on tape-recorded conversations with the Bedouin involved, and cross-checked again and again, is Trever, John C., *The Dead Sea Scrolls, a Personal Account*, (Revised edition, Upland Commercial Printers, 1988), Ch. 12, together with Appendix I.
66. A brief account by Harding may be found in *DJD*, I, 5–7.
67. De Vaux, R., *Archaeology and the Dead Sea Scrolls*, (London: Oxford University Press, 1973), vii–viii.
68. During this same period other caves containing significant material were discovered, but these were at a considerable distance from Qumran and bore no relation to it. For a brief documented account of subsequent explorations and their significance for Qumran see Cross, *ALQ*[3] 'Supplement to Chapter 1: Discovery of an Ancient Library and Related Discoveries' (1960–1993), 47–53.
69. See de Vaux, *Archaeology and the Dead Sea Scrolls*, Chapter 1.
70. Op. cit, 5.
71. Op. cit, 8. Cf. De Vaux's later comment, 'This highly developed and carefully constructed water system is the most striking characteristic of Khirbet Qumran. It reflects the

needs of a group which was relatively numerous, which had chosen to live in the desert, and for which, accordingly, the problem of how to ensure a supply of water was vital.' Op. cit, 10.

72. Op. cit, 11.
73. Op. cit, 17.
74. Op. cit, 10.
75. For a revealing account of the scale of the task see Donceel, Robert, 'Reprise des Travaux de Publication des Fouilles au Khirbet Qumran', *RB*, 99, 3, 1992, 557–73. To date, the first of five projected volumes has appeared, Humbert, Jean-Baptiste, et Chambon, Alain, *Fouilles de Khirbet Qumran et de Ain Feshkha I: Album de photographes* (Göttingen: Vandenhoeck und Ruprecht, 1995). In this connection Schiffman, L.H., makes the pertinent observation that 'until full publication of the excavation records and the records' reinvestigation by other scholars, the details of whatever we say here must to some extent remain tentative'. *Reclaiming*, 38.
76. Golb, Norman, 'The Problem of Origin and Identification of the Dead Sea Scrolls', *Proceedings of the American Philosophical Society*, 124, 1, 1980, 14 n.18. Golb largely repeats this case in 'Khirbet Qumran and the Manuscript Finds of the Judaean Wilderness', in *Methods of Investigation*, 51–4.
77. Golb, Norman, *Who Wrote the Dead Sea Scrolls?* 37–41.
78. Golb traces this history in *Who Wrote the Dead Sea Scrolls?* 13f.
79. See Magness, Jodi, 'A Villa at Khirbet Qumran?', *RQ*, 16, 3, 1994, 397–419. In particular, Magness quotes Hilkiah's Palace in Idumaea, observing, 'The villa sat within a fortified enclosure with a square tower on its western side. The tower is constructed of large stones, and its walls slope out towards the base.' (408). She adds later, 'The square towers at Qumran and Hilkiah's palace are also similar.' (411).
80. Golb, *Who Wrote the Dead Sea Scrolls?* 40.
81. See Tsafrir, Y., 'The Desert Fortresses of Judaea in the Second Temple Period', in Levine, L. I., (ed.) *The Jerusalem Cathedra 2*, (Jerusalem, 1982), 136.
82. Donceel, Robert, and Donceel-Voûte, Pauline, 'The Archaeology of Khirbet Qumran', in *Methods of Investigation*, 1–32.
83. Op. cit, 10.
84. Op. cit, 7.
85. Op. cit, 11.

86. Op. cit, 12.
87. Op. cit, 7, 13.
88. Magness, Jodi, 'The Community at Qumran in Light of Its Pottery', in *Methods of Investigation*, 39–48.
89. Op. cit, 40.
90. Op. cit, 42.
91. Op. cit, 42, 44.
92. Op. cit, 45–6.
93. 'A Villa at Khirbet Qumran?' *RQ*, 16, 3, 1994, 397–419.
94. Art. cit, 409–10, 412. Magness includes significant observations on the extensive water-system at Qumran, inasmuch as these were also found in Judaean palaces and mansions of the period, including Hilkiah's palace. However, whereas elsewhere there are elaborate bath-houses and swimming facilities, this is not the case at Qumran. 'The existence of an elaborate water-system at Qumran is significant because it indicates that the inhabitants possessed the technology necessary for construction the kinds of swimming pools and baths found in contemporary villas' (411). Her final conclusion is, 'De Vaux's interpretation of the site as a sectarian settlement still makes the most sense.' (419).
95. Crown, Alan D., and Cansdale, Lena, 'Qumran: Was it an Essene Settlement?' *BAR*, 20, 5, 1994, 25–35, 73–8.
96. The existence of such a road was inferred by Harel, M. See Crown and Cansdale, art. cit, 73 with notes 43–46.
97. Data suggesting this conjecture are set out by Crown and Cansdale on pp. 35 and 73, with notes 41 and 42.
98. Art. cit, 76.
99. Art. cit, 35.
100. Magness, Jodi writes, 'In my opinion, Qumran's location is anomalous among contemporary sites along the Dead Sea. It does not belong to the line of Hasmonean and Herodian fortresses, such as Alexandrion, Machairos, Hyrcania and Masada ... Qumran's location is not strategic, nor is it located near a source of fresh water. The main east-west road at the northern end of the Dead Sea has always followed the pass from Jericho up to Jerusalem; in fact the Roman road lay to the north of the current highway. The path up Wadi Qumran to the Buqeia is just one of many such local ascents (*ma'aloth*) on the cliffs along the Western shore of the Dead Sea.' Art. cit, 417–8. While commenting chiefly on

the fortress hypothesis, she indicates that many of the same points tell against the hostelry hypothesis (see 417, n.106).

101. Crown and Cansdale, art. cit, 73.
102. Art. cit, 73.
103. Cook, Edward M., 'Qumran: a Ritual Purification Center', *BAR*. November-December, 1996, 22, 6, pp. 39, 48–51, 73–5.
104. Humbert, J.B., 'L'Espace Sacré à Qumrân, Propositions pour l'archéologie', *RB*, 1994, 101, 161–214.
105. Art. cit, 162.
106. Art. cit, 170–4.
107. E.g. The pottery record does not support continuous community occupation from 101 BC – AD 68, pointing rather to occupation from the end of the first century BC. Again, it is difficult to establish a lacuna between de Vaux's Period Ib and Period II. Art. cit, 209f.
108. He argues that the plan of Qumran at this time (which he labels Period Ia) follows the pattern of Greco-Roman residences. Art. cit, 169f.
109. Art. cit, 178f.
110. Art. cit, 176.
111. Art. cit, 180.
112. Art. cit, 181, 211.
113. Art. 'A Villa at Khirbet Qumran?' *RQ*, 16, 1994, 414.
114. Magness, art. cit, 415.
115. Magness, art. cit, 414.
116. Schiffman, Lawrence H., *Reclaiming*, 51.
117. French, 'une implantation éclatée.'
118. De Vaux, *Archaeology and the Dead Sea Scrolls*, 5.
119. Humbert's observations, on the character of the buildings are à propos (whatever may be thought of his interpretation of them), 'Le plan de masse final de Qumrân … n'a aucune homogénéité. Il est clair qu'au noyau initial, ont été ajoutés successivement des éléments adventices, pas toujours là où la topographie commandait … Le manque de cohésion entre des unités architecturales plus ou moins juxtaposées avec des fonctions bien spécifiques, vient de ce que les raisons de modifier l'espace, étaient particulières.' Art. cit, 175.
120. De Vaux, *Archaeology and the Dead Sea Scrolls*, 11. He continues, 'Towards its western extremity a circular area stands out from the surrounding plastered floor by the fact that it

is paved. This seems to mark the place where the president of the assembly would have taken his stand.' *Ibid.*

121. De Vaux's description of the finds and a summary of various interpretations may be found in ibid., 12–16. Schiffman, L.H., has recently made the tentative suggestion that the bones may have been buried to avoid the spread of defilement in keeping with the directive of 4QMMT, 858–9, *Reclaiming*, 338.
122. See his long article, 'The Problem of Origin and Identification of the Dead Sea Scrolls', in *Proceedings of the American Philosophical Society*, 124. 1 (1980) 1–24; and his more recent treatment, *Who Wrote the Scrolls*? (New York: Scribners, 1994).
123. To date the texts have not yet been officially published. For a press report see Rabinovitch, A., 'Qumran Yields Ancient Text', *The Jerusalem Post*, Friday, February 23, 1996, 3; and Shanks, Hershel, 'So Far No Cigar', *BAR*, March-April, 1996, 22, 1, 10.
124. See the reference in Cook, Edward M., 'A Ritual Purification Center', *BAR*, November-December, 1996, 22, 6, p. 75 n. 8, together with the footnote reference to the same in Wise, Michael, Abegg, Jr. Martin, and Cook, Edward, *The Dead Sea Scrolls*, (A New Translation, San Francisco: Harper, 1996), 24, where 'gift of a house and a slave' is (presumably correctly) changed to 'a horse and a slave.'
125. *Archaeology and the Dead Sea Scrolls*, 29–31.
126. E.g. Metzger, Bruce M., 'The Furniture of the Scriptorium at Qumran', *RQ*, 1, 4, 1959, 509–15.
127. Goranson, Stephen, 'Further Qumran Archeology Publications in Progress', *BA*, 54, 1991, 110f; 'Qumran: A Hub of Scribal Activity?' *BAR*, 20, 4, September-October, 1994, 37–9.
128. Goranson, S., 'Qumran – Evidence of the Inkwells', *BAR*, 19, 6, November-December, 1993, 67.
129. De Vaux, *Archaeology and the Dead Sea Scrolls*, 49–50.
130. Magness, *Methods of Investigation*, 40–1.
131. Estimates of the population of the Khirbeh have shown considerable variation. De Vaux, admitting the difficulty of establishing the numbers because of the multiple factors involved (duration of occupation, number of graves, determination of lifespan), concluded that, 'even at the period of its greatest prosperity the group would not have

numbered many more than 200 members,' (*Archaeology and the Dead Sea Scrolls*, 86). Milik, J.T., put the total 'between 150 and 200', a result reached by dividing the number of graves by six to eight generations (*Ten Years of Discovery*, 97.) Broshi, M., reached the same conclusion as Milik by calculating the seating capacity of the assembly hall ('The Archaeology of Qumran-A Reconsideration', in Dimant, Devorah and Rappaport, Uriel, *The Dead Sea Scrolls* Forty Years of Research (henceforth *Forty Years*), (Leiden/Jerusalem, Brill, E.J./The Magnes Press, 1992), 114. Patrich, J., estimates the size of the community more probably at 50–70. (*Methods of Investigation*, 93). See below for further discussion.

132. De Vaux, *Archaeology and the Dead Sea Scrolls*, 11f.
133. De Vaux, loc. cit.
134. De Vaux divided the caves into three categories, 'those which are habitable, those which are only just so, and those which are quite uninhabitable' (*Archaeology and the Dead Sea Scrolls*, 57). Patrich concluded that the caves were not dwelling places, but stores and hiding places though he conceded that caves 4, 7, 8 and 10 – all accessible from the Khirbeh – were habitable, and could have been used as anchorite cells (*Methods of Investigation*, 93, 95).
135. See the chart of caves in the Qumran region showing traces of human occupation in de Vaux, *Archaeology and the Dead Sea Scrolls*, Plate XL. In a 1990 survey of caves in a 24 km range from 5 miles north of Khirbet Qumran to Wadi Muraba'at, 137 of sufficient size for human habitation were found, of which 85 showed signs of human use from the Chalcolithic period to the present. The number of caves per kilometre was highest adjacent to and north of Qumran. See Walker, Dennis, and Eisenman, Robert, 'The 1990 Survey of Qumran Caves', *QC*, 2, 1, December 1992, 45–9.
136. De Vaux, *Archaeology and the Dead Sea Scrolls*, 57.
137. Shanks, Hershel, 'So Far No Cigar', *BAR*, 22, 1, March-April, 1996, 10.
138. Patrich, J., '*Methods of Investigation*', 93.
139. De Vaux, *Archaeology and the Dead Sea Scrolls*, 47.
140. Hachili, R., and Killebrew, A., 'Jewish Funerary Customs during the Second Temple Period, in Light of the Excavations of the Jerusalem Necropolis', *PEQ*, 115, 1983. With

this should be compared Hachlili, R., 'Burial Practices at Qumran', *RQ*, 16, 2, 1993, 247–64.

141. A full account of the Qumran cemeteries may be found in de Vaux, *Archaeology and the Dead Sea Scrolls*, 45–8, 57f.
142. 'Burial Practices at Qumran', *RQ*, 16, 2, 1993, 263.
143. Statistics based on de Vaux's report of his own excavations as well as those of Steckoll, S.H., *Archaeology and the Dead Sea Scrolls*, 45–8, 57–8. In my reckoning, I have not included the child buried with its mother in the count of the children.
144. De Vaux, op. cit, 46–7. Other irregularities, e.g. double burial, re-inhumation are noted by de Vaux, ad loc.
145. The texts themselves offer no information on the matter. Wacholder, Ben Zion, has suggested Ezekiel's eschatological geography as the solution of some problems in the Qumran texts, including the mode of burial. Ezekiel 34 places Israel's redemption in the north, and chapters 38–9 the final destruction of Gog in the same area. Conversely, Ezekiel 47 sees the waters flowing from the new temple into the Dead Sea, sweetening it. The covenanters who have died before that event has taken place are buried looking in the direction from which victory and vindication will come. 'Ezekiel and Ezekielianism' in Dimant, D., and Rappaport, U., (eds.), *Forty Years of Research*, 194–5. If Wacholder's general suggestion is sound could a further point of contact be found in Ezekiel's prophecy to those who say, 'Our bones are dried up, and our hope is lost; we are cut off completely. Therefore prophesy, and say to them, Thus says the Lord God: I am going to open your graves, and bring you up from your graves, O my people ... and you shall know that I am the Lord, when I open your graves, and bring you up from your graves, O my people', (Ezekiel 37: 12–13; cf. 14)? A literal reading of Ezekiel's words might well explain the apparent resistance at Qumran to second burial which at that time was becoming the norm in the rest of Judaism.
146. The most apt description of the community in this regard is not that it practised celibacy, which clearly it did not, but rather that – in Cross's phrase – it practised 'apocalyptic asceticism'. 'The Essene in his daily life thus girds himself to withstand the final trial, purifies himself to join the holy armies, anticipates the coming conditions in God's in-break-

ing Kingdom. This is the situation which prompts counsels against marriage, at least for some ... at Qumran we discover counsels against marriage in *this* decisive moment when *this* world is passing away', *ALQ*[3], 83f.

147. De Vaux, *Archaeology and the Dead Sea Scrolls*, 89f.
148. For review articles see Walker, Dennis, 'Notes on Qumran Archaeology: the Geographical Contexts of the Caves and Tracks', *QC* 3, 1–3, December 1993, 93–100; and Kapera, Z.J., 'Recent Research on the Qumran Cemetery', *QC*, 5, 2 October 1995, 123–32.
149. De Vaux, *Archaeology and the Dead Sea Scrolls*, 58–87.
150. Op. cit, 64.
151. Op. cit, 66.
152. Op. cit, 69. Cf. 71.
153. Op. cit, 84.
154. The first report was published under the heading 'Chronique archéologique', *RB* 77, 1970, 398–400.
155. Bar-Adon, P., 'Another Settlement of the Judaean Desert Sect at 'En el Ghuweir on the Shores of the Dead Sea', *BASOR*, 227, 1977, 1–25. The details quoted are found on p. 1.
156. Art. cit, 5–7.
157. Art. cit, 12–16.
158. Art. cit, 20.
159. See Eshel, Hanan and Greenhut, Zwi, 'Ḥiam El-Sagha, A Cemetery of the Qumran Type, Judaean Ḍesert', *RB*, 100–2, 1993, 252–9; and Reshef, Dan and Smith, Patricia, 'Two Skeletal Remains From Ḥiam El-Sagha', op. cit, 260–9.
160. Art. cit, 258 n.16.
161. De Vaux, *Archaeology and the Dead Sea Scrolls*, 87–90.
162. Op. cit, 89.
163. Bar-Adon's hypothesis that there may have been a string of settlements throughout the area west of the Dead Sea not yet discovered has already been quoted (n.158). The only evidence that counts is evidence in hand. At the same time note should be made of D. Walker's statement that the 1990–92 survey of Qumran caves referred to in n. 135 also listed sixty non-cave sites from north of Qumran to north of Engedi ranging from walls to large structures which were of archaeological interest. See Walker, Dennis, 'Notes on Qumran Archaeology: the Geographical Context of the Caves and Tracks', *QC*, 3, 1–3, December 1993, 99.

164. De Vaux, *Archaeology and the Dead Sea Scrolls*, 22–3.
165. Op. cit, 20f.
166. Laperrousaz has written two main accounts of the excavations and his interpretation of them. The first is his book *Qoumrân, L'Éstablissement Essénien des Bords de la Mer Morte*, (Paris: A & J Picard, 1976), a very full and detailed account; the second is the sections on the archaeology and history of the sect in the article, 'Qumrân et Déscouverts au Désert de Juda' in Cazelles, H., and Feuillet, Andre, (eds.), *Dictionnaire de la Bible, Supplément*, (Paris: Tome Neuvième, 1979), cols. 749–66, 789–98.
167. Art. cit, col. 792; cf. col. 749f.
168. Art. cit, cols. 755–7.
169. Art. cit, col. 793.
170. Art. cit, cols. 765–6.
171. De Vaux, *Archaeology and the Dead Sea Scrolls*, 5.
172. Op. cit, 18f.
173. Op. cit, 5.
174. Broshi, Magen, 'The Archeology of Qumran – A Reconsideration', in Dimant-Rappaport, *Forty Years*, 105f.
175. See Barag, Dan, 'New Evidence on the Foreign Policy of John Hyrcanus I', *INJ*, 12, 1992–3, 1–12, esp. 6f, 10f.
176. Cross, *ALQ*[3], 183–4. Cross agrees with de Vaux in favouring Simon (loc. cit).
177. Broshi reviews the major trends, art. cit, 106–111.
178. Magness, Jodi, 'The Chronology of the Settlement at Qumran in the Herodian Period', *DSD*, 2, 1, 1995, 58–65.
179. De Vaux as quoted by Magness, 62.
180. Art. cit, 62–3. Dr Magness addresses the implications of her proposed reconstruction for the Herodian coins (pp. 58f, 61f) as well as for the pottery record (63–4).
181. De Vaux, *Archaeology and the Dead Sea Scrolls*, 24, 36.

Chapter Two

Approaching Qumran Theology

It is one thing to establish the existence of a community at Qumran; it is another to determine the shape of its thought. If the task is facilitated by the eight hundred manuscripts from the caves, it is also made more challenging by the need to isolate the differentiae of the thought of the sect amid such an abundance of evidence. The river is very wide; how does one locate the main channel?

Several angles of approach suggest themselves. The degree, if any, to which they are mutually supportive, would in that measure strengthen the results. First, the texts themselves must be analysed in terms of literary type, terminology and ideas. Distinctive thought forms and concepts, particularly if allied with or expressed with some consistency in language that possessed almost technical status, would have a strong claim to constituting part of the sectarian thinking. Second, confirmation for any such thinking may be sought in relevant sources outside the Qumran materials altogether, but which may, with reason, be deemed to have a bearing on them. It has already been shown not merely that the Qumran community *had* an existence but – on the basis of palaeography and archaeology – *when* it had an existence. If this can be confirmed and illuminated in any degree from sources outside of Qumran, and if, in particular, such sources give any indication of the thinking of the sect, then the case will again be stronger.

Third, it may be asked whether there are any indications within the Qumran texts themselves regarding the origin and history of the sect. Such data might have a bearing not only on when and how the sect came to exist, but the reasons which brought it into existence: in a word, its theological roots.

That there are occupational hazards in such an undertaking is self-evident. Not the least of them is the danger of circularity: accepting a document as valid evidence, and then using it to validate the reality to which it is held to bear witness. Again, in handling extra-sectarian sources there is the danger of accepting as valid testimony which accords with the Qumran sources and discounting whatever does not, with little or no attempt at justifying the decision. In many matters, therefore, probability is the most that may be attainable, and on some issues the statement of competing interpretations may be all that can be offered. With these reservations we may now turn to the point at which the investigation by any account should begin: an analysis of the texts themselves.

Analysis of the Texts

A glance at the list of contents of an English translation of the Dead Sea Scrolls will usually convey not only something of the translator's analysis of the texts but, by the same token, something of the understanding of their theological interests. Geza Vermes, for example, groups them into four major categories: the Rules; Hymns, Liturgies and Wisdom Poetry; Bible Interpretation; and Miscellenea.[1] Much fuller, and therefore more revealing, is the analysis of F. Garcia Martinez who divides them into eight groupings: Rules, Halakhic Texts, Literature with Eschatological Content, Exegetical Literature, Para-Biblical Literature, Poetic Texts, Liturgical Texts, Astronomical Texts, Calendars and Horoscopes, with the Copper Scroll in a ninth category by itself.[2] From such classifications one receives an indication of some of the topics in which the sectarians were interested and around which their literature revolves.

Far and away the most thoroughgoing analysis of the texts is that of Devorah Dimant already reviewed briefly in the Prologue, and deserving of fuller exposition here.[3] The significance of her work is that it is a self-conscious attempt to isolate from the entire corpus of texts those where the distinctive thoughtprints of the community may be found. Accordingly, she groups the texts into three main categories:

(1) Biblical manuscripts (taken to mean parts of the Hebrew Bible);
(2) Documents employing terminology connected to the Qumran community (= **CT works**); and
(3) Works which do not contain clusters of terms and ideas related to the community (= **NCT works**).

Dr Dimant's development of the second and third categories is particularly worth summarizing for our purposes.

As to the second category Dr Dimant concludes that a distinctive terminology linked with an individual set of ideas is found in four main areas. First, it is found in regard to the practices and organization of a distinct community. Examples cited include *yaḥad* ('community': IQS I 16; VI 10; IQSa I 26; CD XX 32); *serek* ('rule': IQS I 10, VI 8; IQM III 3, V 4; IQSa I 1; CD VII 6); and *mebaqqēr* ('Overseer': IQS VI 12, 20; CD IX 8, XIII 6).[4] Second, it is found in connection with the history of the community and its contemporary circumstances. Illustrations of this include the term *halāqōth* ('smooth things': CDI 18; IQH II 32); and *mōrēh hassedek* ('Teacher of Righteousness': IQp Hab. I 13; CD I 11).[5] Third, this coincidence of distinctive ideas and terminology is found in relation to the theological and metaphysical outlook of the community. Dimant cites terms related to dualism such as *rûhôth 'ôr wĕhôšek* ('spirits of light and darkness': IQS III 25; IQM XIII 11); or to predestination, such as *te'ûdah* ('appointed time': IQS I 9, III 10, 16; IQM III 4); or to divine secrets such as *rāzê 'ēl* ('mysteries of God': IQS III 23, IQM III 9).[6] And fourthly, the conjunction of distinctive terminology and ideas emerges in the form of biblical exegesis employed by the sect. Here the most characteristic (though by no means the only[7]) term is *pešer*: 'interpretation' or 'meaning', used formulaically throughout the exegetical texts or *Pesharim* to introduce the sectarian understanding of the biblical passage under consideration.

Dr Dimant is insistent that the conjunction of terms and ideas alone defines a text as belonging to the community. 'In themselves concepts and ideas are insufficient criteria for assigning a given text to the group of the CT works. Only the combination of the distinctive terminology with the respective ideas provides such criteria.'[8] Hence she sets aside ideological compatibility, identity of literary genre,[9] scribal and orthographical similarity[10] as being insufficient markers of a sectarian text. While conceding that it is not always possible to be certain that a given term is distinctive of Qumran, she concludes that this criterion provides a core group of characteristic texts which have the capacity to function as a benchmark.[11] This group, comprising Rules, Halakhic Works, Poetical and Hymnic Works, Liturgical Works, Exegetical Works, Sapiential Works, some texts in cryptic writing and other fragments amounts to 190 works, or approximately 25 per cent of the total yield of the Qumran caves.[12]

It may be useful to give particular indication of Dimant's results: of some of the main texts she attributes to the community as well as those she does not, together with some of her reasons. Chief among the former are the Rules: the *Community Rule*, the *Damascus Rule* (4Q266–273; 5Q12; 6Q15), the *War Rule* (IQM). Among the Halakhic Works are the *Halakhic Letter* (4QMMT); while the Poetical Works are represented by the *Hodayot* (IQH). Among the Liturgical Works, Dimant places the *Songs of Sabbath Sacrifice* (4Q400–407), which she describes as being 'of distinct CT character, as is evident from the various terms employed in it'.[13] The Exegetical Works include Continuous Pesharim such as the *Habakkuk Commentary* (IQpHab) and the *Nahum Commentary* (4QpNah); and Thematic Pesharim such as 4Q Florilegium (4QFlor); while Sapiential Works are represented by Sapiential Work A (4Q416–418) and Sapiential Work B (4Q413, 4Q415). On the other hand she finds various texts of the Pseudepigrapha such as the *Book of Jubilees* not to be community works; likewise Halakhic texts such as 4Q Halakhah (4Q251), and the *Temple Scroll* (11QT). Halakhic Texts indeed, provide a particular source of difficulty inasmuch as Halakhah is found in both CT and NTC texts. Here, as elsewhere, terminology must be the determining factor.[14] None of the Calendrical and Chronological Texts, and none of the Aramaic Texts is a community product.[15]

Other conclusions reached by Dr Dimant on the basis of her analysis must be set down in order to see the import of her results. She notes, for example, that the contents of most caves are similar and interlinked, showing that all housed parts of the same collection.[16] She maintains that her research shows that the two groups of texts differ in genre, with the NCT texts following mainly biblical antecedents; Rules, Pesharim belong to the CT group.[17] At the same time some genres are found in both groups, notably those modelled on biblical forms and styles: liturgical, psalmodic and wisdom compositions.[18] Even more, Halakhic texts are found in both groups, including some in which the Halakhah is identical. If however, the terminology is different, Dimant assigns them to the NCT grouping.[19] She follows the same procedure with calendrical, chronological and astrological texts.[20] Her conclusion is that such a degree of divergence indicates an origin in a circle close to the community but not identical with it.[21] It may indeed have been the parent group from which the Qumran community branched off. If so, she suggests that the NCT texts may hold the key for uncovering the origins and nature of the Qumran community.[22]

We may ask in what measure Dimant's work constitutes a secure basis for reconstructing the thought of the sect. Dimant herself concedes that the theological criterion she proposes may be problematic, inasmuch as it does not hold completely with regard to Jubilees, I Enoch and the Qumran literature.[23] Another form of the same problem is that texts occurring in the caves in multiple copies (which presumably is some index of the frequent use made of them): like 4Q *Tohorot* (as many as 9 copies) or the *New Jerusalem* texts (as many as 6 copies), fall outside the CT category. This tends to suggest that the criterion of terminology, while by no means invalid, can be applied too rigidly and must therefore be based on the widest possible induction. It may also suggest not only that the four criteria are mutually supportive, but that the presence of any one may be sufficient to validate the sectarian character of a given text.

Still further, it is important to keep in due perspective the central ideas of the texts as well as their distinctive terminology. It is easy for the terminology to assume an exaggerated role whose result can be that Qumran thought is defined in terms of its nuances rather than its undergirding concepts. For while such concepts as dualism, or predestination, or the mysteries of God, are undoubtedly parts of the sect's mental furniture, they hardly constitute the fabric of its thought, which consists of elements much more substantive. Dualism, predestination, and divine mysteries can by themselves scarcely be more than means by which the divine purposes are carried out. Apart from such purposes they are at best forms and can hardly add up to a substantive theological construct.

Accordingly, the appropriate procedure in attempting to reconstruct the thought of the sect is to start with those texts where the evidence of ideas and community terminology is clearest, the two being mutually confirmatory. This means the *Rule of the Community* (IQS), the *Hodayot* or Hymns (IQH), the *Damascus Covenant* (CD), the *War Scroll* (IQM), and the more extended Pesharim, chiefly the *Habakkuk Commentary* (IQpHab) and the *Nahum Commentary* (4QpNah) will constitute the core group. Other texts beyond this group may be drawn upon only as they are shown to exhibit coherence with these, but the coherence must be measured on a case-by-case basis, rather than by the rigid application of a single criterion.

The Contribution of the Classical Accounts

A second area in which guidance may be sought for the theology of the Qumran sect is the accounts of the sect and its thinking in sources external to it: specifically, in the writings of Pliny, Philo and Josephus. These accounts have been examined closely for assistance in establishing the identity, location and history of the sect. A near-consensus was achieved favouring the identification of the community at Qumran with the Essene sect.[24] The drift of the argument was as follows. Pliny placed a celibate, ascetic community whom he named the Essenes (*Esseni*) on the western shore of the Dead Sea.[25] He located the town of Engedi as being '*below* the Essenes', which has been taken to mean south along the shore (i.e. *below* as on a one-dimensional map) rather than west (i.e. *below* in the sense *beneath*).[26] The failure to discover any other ruins on the scale of Khirbet Qumran in that area has been seen as confirmation of the conclusion.[27]

To Pliny's evidence is added that of Philo who refers to the group as *Essaioi*. Philo, however, does not pin them down to a single site as Pliny appears to do. He does indeed depict them as living a communal (and celibate) life, but in communes in the towns and villages of Judaea.[28] But far and away the greatest source of information about the Essenes is Josephus who refers to them in the *Life*, the *Antiquities* and, most extendedly, in the *Jewish War*. Like Philo, Josephus gives no hint of a single, central site, depicting them rather as forming a colony in every town.[29] Again, like Philo, he represents them as living a communal, celibate life.[30] However, he includes some additional pieces of information that are of note. He makes reference to another order of Essenes which, while agreeing with those living in colonies in their usages and customs, nevertheless practises marriage. This evidently involved communal living in some measure since the women are said to bathe wrapped in linen, whereas the men wear a loin-cloth.[31] He makes reference to one John the Essene who was given authority in North-West Judaea during the revolt of AD 66, and was killed in battle.[32] He makes the only mention in ancient literature of an Essene Gate in Jerusalem.[33] In the *Antiquities* he records that Herod the Great excused the Essenes from taking the oath of loyalty to himself, since they refused oath-taking as a matter of conscience.[34] And finally, in his *Life* he claims that, in his youth, he received instruction as an Essene.[35]

Even as brief a summary as this indicates the problems arising from the classical accounts. Sometimes they differ among themselves. At least the impression given by Pliny that the Essenes are located above Engedi differs from that given by Philo and Josephus that they are to be found in the towns of Judaea. Again, Josephus alone mentions the existence of more than one order of Essenes. Then again, sometimes the classical writers can speak in ways that are not self-consistent. For example, Philo says both that the Essenes avoid the cities[36] and that they live in them.[37]

It is not impossible to reduce this evidence to a relative state of coherence by the making of more or less justifiable assumptions. For example, the classical authors had their own interests and tendencies which condition what they include and omit as well as their mode of presentation. Todd S. Beall, in a study designed to show how the Qumran texts illuminate Josephus[38], concludes that, while Josephus is generally trustworthy, two tendencies emerge: exaggeration, as in his claim to have taken instruction personally from Essenes, his account of Essene avoidance of oaths and of their Sabbath stringency; and second, his appeal to Greek modes of thought designed to make Essenism more intelligible to Gentile readers, as in representing the Pharisees, Sadducees and Essenes as philosphical classes.[39] Yet another factor to be taken into account is that the classical authors themselves drew upon sources of varying reliability or used their sources in widely differing ways.[40]

The inference to be drawn from this is not that, since the classical sources are not to be relied on in some places they are not to be trusted anywhere. It is rather that they are to be used critically, due account being taken of the conditioning influences at work as they can be discerned. When this is done several conclusions seem to be indicated. First, they testify to the existence of a settlement of some proportions at Qumran. This does indeed mean Pliny, and Pliny alone or Pliny's source[41], but it is not for this reason to be put down to invention. Indeed, it is difficult to provide a reason why it would be invented. Second, two of the classical writers witness to the existence of Essene settlements scattered throughout Judaea (Philo) and the whole of Palestine (Josephus). Third, Josephus testifies to a degree of divergence among them in that another order (*tagma*) of Essenes, while at one with the rest on other matters, differed from them in that they practised marriage.[42] What this amounts to is that the classical sources give evidence of a widespread Essene movement[43] which, while sharing a common mindset, was not completely monolithic. How far this elasticity extended is a point that must be taken up later.

Our chief interest in the classical accounts however, lies in the history of the sect only insofar as that history sheds light upon the theology. Here it is important to keep in mind that the authors (to our best knowledge and judgment) were outsiders and to be expected to observe practices more than beliefs, and differences rather than continuities. This is very much the case with Pliny who says little more than that the Qumran settlement was a refuge for those who sought repentance and release from the burdens of living. Philo's accounts are also predominantly ethical. In *Quod Omnis Probus Liber Sit* he commends Essene frugality, their pacific spirit, love of God, love of virtue and love of men, their community life including care of the sick and aged, and their piety, holiness and justice. The closest he comes to dealing with specifically theological issues is when he notes – almost in passing – that 'they do not offer annual sacrifice, judging it more fitting to render their minds truly holy' (75); and when he quotes their belief that 'the Deity is the cause of all good, but of no evil' (84). The prevailing tone of Philo's account is well-indicated when he virtually says that the Essenes avoid the theoretical in preference for the practical. 'As regards philosophy, they first of all leave logic to word-chasers, seeing that it is useless in the acquisition of virtue; then they leave natural philosophy to street orators, seeing it is beyond human nature, except, however, in what it teaches of the existence of God and the origin of the world. But they work at ethics with extreme care constantly utilizing the ancestral laws, laws which no human mind could have conceived without divine inspiration' (80). The Essenes, in a word, are 'athletes of virtue', and by this means they find absolute freedom (87). The tone and substance of the picture of the Essenes in the *Apologia pro Iudaeis* differs hardly at all.

Josephus is somewhat more forthcoming. It is true that in the lengthiest account in the *Jewish War* 2. 119–61 the predominantly practical, ethical perspective prevails. The main theological item of which he speaks is the Essene understanding of life after death. Souls are immortal; bodies are prisons; freed from the flesh, souls rise up to the heavenly world: the good to bliss, the evil to torment.[44] He notes the similarity to the views of the Greeks.[45]

In *Antiquities* 13.171–2 he names the three sects of the Jews 'which took different attitudes to human affairs ... The Pharisees say that some things but not everything are the work of fate, while some things either happen or do not because of the actions of individuals. The rule of the Essenes, by contrast, makes Fate mistress of all and says that nothing comes to pass for humans unless Fate has so voted.'

But by far the fullest account of Essene belief from the hand of Josephus occurs in *Antiquities* 18.18–22. Similar in some ways to *Jewish War* 2.119–66, it is much briefer, and diverges from it in important respects. While it shares some of these with Philo, and so has been thought to borrow from him[46] there is perhaps more to be said for Morton Smith's opinion that both derived it from a common source.[47] Their basic principle (*logos*) is said to be reliance on God in everything. They affirm the immortality of the soul and 'consider it necessary to struggle to obtain the reward of righteousness' (18).[48] They send offerings to the Temple, but since they use different purifications they are barred from entering the common enclosure and in consequence offer sacrifice among themselves.[49] These points are important in indicating what were apparently matters of moment in sectarian thought: reliance upon God, striving after righteousness, life after death and a view of the Temple and its worship that was both affirmative and critical, the latter dimension focusing on the correct form of purification required for the offering of sacrifice.

Finally, we may garner the contribution of the *Philosophumena* to the picture of Essene thought. The same preoccupation with the ethical found in other classical accounts is present here also: community life, abstinence from marriage and all passions, rigid sabbath-observance, and the paradoxical avoidance of oaths (22) and submission to the most fearful oaths (23). Particularly notable in this connection is the claim that the member of the sect 'will not hate a person who injures him, or is hostile to him, but pray for them' (23). But most striking is the view of the life to come credited to them: not merely the immortality of the soul, but the resurrection of the body: 'for they acknowledge both that the flesh will rise again, and that it will be immortal, in the same manner as the soul is now borne into one place, which is well ventilated and full of light, and there it rests until judgment' (27).

How far is it possible to reconstruct the theological mindset of the Essenes from these brief notices? Allowance must doubtless be made in this connection as also in the accounts of the history and general character of the sect for the perspective and purposes of the writers which themselves have been variously estimated. However, critical evaluation makes it possible at least to attempt to delineate the theological profile conveyed in the classical sources. When this is done several defining features seem to emerge.

First, and in apparent defiance of the distinction followed earlier between the predominantly practical and ethical concerns of the classical authors on the one hand,

and the strictly theological on the other, there emerges an overriding concern to depict the Essenes as being preoccupied above all with holiness. This is indeed given a heavily ethical definition in terms of selflessness which places the community before the individual, fleeing the cities because of the ungodliness of town-dwellers, frugality, simplicity, contentment, modesty – all this in Philo who indeed explains the name of the sect in such terms: 'these are called Essaeans, and I think they have merited this title because of their holiness' (*Apologeia pro Iudaeis*, 1).[50] A similar picture is painted by Josephus who not only speaks commendingly of the Essenes' community life, resistance to the passions, contempt for wealth, simplicity of life and pursuit of righteousness, but characterizes them as having 'a reputation for cultivating a particularly saintly life' (*War* 2.119).[51]

Hippolytus' general characterization in the *Philosophumena* speaks to the same conclusion, as has been indicated earlier, whatever cautions may have to be placed against some of his assertions.[52] It is clear from the classical sources, then, that the Essenes were seen to be caught up in the pursuit of holiness. The description of it given is largely phenomenological. No indication is given of the motivation behind this quest unless its value be assumed to be self-evident. Nor is any indication given of how it is to be attained, unless the various practices described are regarded as the means to the end.

Perhaps some clue to the answering of these questions is provided by a second emphasis which not only receives prominence in the classical sources, but occurs repeatedly in precisely those contexts where the Essene preoccupation with holiness is being dilated upon. The emphasis in question is that upon the law. Thus Philo, in the passage already noted in which he refers to Essene disdain for natural philosophy, contrasts with this their extreme care for their divinely inspired ancestral laws. These they instruct themselves in continually, but especially every seventh day when they avoid all other work and meet together to receive instruction (*Q.o.p.* 80).

Josephus makes the point even more forcefully in *War* 2. 145–9. The name of the Lawgiver is venerated only less than the name of God himself. Then follow what are evidently given as examples of their dedication to the law. They are forbidden 'more rigorously than any other Jew' (147) to work on the Sabbath. The *Philosophumena* likewise trace a similar sequence of thought: from their honouring of the legislator as second only to God, to their solicitous observance of the Sabbath (25).

A third feature of the Essenes which attracted the notice of the classical authors was their attitude to sacrifice. The evidence on the matter is, at the very least, ambiguous. Philo says flatly: 'They do not offer animal sacrifice, judging it more fitting to render their minds truly holy' (*Q.o.p.* 75).[53] Josephus on the other hand, as has already been indicated,[54] while stating that the Essenes were barred from offering sacrifice in the Temple, affirms nevertheless that they 'offer sacrifice among themselves' (*Ant.* 18. 19).[55] Actual practice at Qumran can only be determined on the basis of the evidence of the texts themselves. The least that can be inferred from the classical accounts is that the issue of sacrifice was one on which the Essenes adopted a distinctive stance, and that the underlying reason was a different view of the ritual purity needed for the offering of valid sacrifice.[56]

The picture of Essene theology in the classical sources also attributes to it a distinctive understanding of God and his relation to the world. The amount of data is insufficient to yield a comprehensive view, and it is not necessarily clear how the various pieces fit together. Philo avers that they hold that God is the author of all good, but of no evil (*Q.o.p.* 84). Josephus contrasts their view of fate with that of the Pharisees. 'The Pharisees say that some things but not everything are the work of fate, while some things either happen or do not happen because of the actions of individuals. The race of the Essenes, by contrast, makes Fate mistress of all and says that nothing comes to pass for humans unless Fate has so voted.'[57] Later in the *Antiquities* he writes: 'The Essenes like to teach that in all things one should rely on God.'[58] If their view of fate is as absolute as Josephus represents it to be, then it is difficult to see how it can be held together with Philo's picture. Again, then, any identification of the Essenes with the Qumran community will have to evaluate carefully the evidence of the texts from the Qumran caves.

A fifth area of thought which the classical sources raise into prominence is life after death. In both *War* and *Antiquities* Josephus represents the Essenes as teaching the immortality of the soul. 'They also declare that souls are immortal,' he writes.[59] But far and away his most detailed and emphatic treatment is found in *War* 2. 154–8. The body is corruptible serving as a prison for the soul which, freed from the bonds of the flesh as from slavery, rises up to the heavenly world (154). The concept is said specifically to be in agreement with Greek ideas and, indeed, the future life of the blessed is described in terms of the 'abode beyond the Ocean, refreshed by gentle breezes' (155). In flat contradiction to this is the account of Hippolytus in the *Philosophumena* which, as has already been noted, is very close to Josephus in *War* 2. 119–61 in many respects, and yet diverges from him startlingly in others. This is one of the divergences: 'The doctrine of the resurrection has also derived support among them, for they acknowledge both that the flesh will rise again, and that it will be immortal, in the same manner as the soul is already imperishable.'[60] The contradiction could hardly be more complete. Morton Smith's proposal that Hippolytus drew upon a Christianized version of Josephus has already been cited.[61] But while this may explain Hippolytus, it is not the only possible explanation of Josephus. Todd S. Beall, commenting on *War* 2. 154–8, and its Greek colouring, adds: 'In fact, Josephus treats the Pharisees' doctrine of resurrection in much the same way. Josephus emphasizes the Pharisees' view of the immortality of the soul (a doctrine similar to the Greeks') but does not explicitly mention their concept of bodily resurrection.'[62] This may be a fair enough comment on *War* 2. 154–8. However, in *War* 3. 374, a context in which Josephus is declaiming against the evils of suicide and extolling the glory of death for the Jewish cause, he (a Pharisee) says of such martyrs: 'Their souls ... are allotted the most holy place in heaven, whence in the resurrection of the ages, they return to find in chaste bodies a new habitation.'[63] Feldman maintains that in *Against Apion* 2. 218 and *Antiquities* 18.3 Josephus is glancing at the idea of bodily resurrection, as in the latter when he says: 'the good souls receive an easy passage to a new life', using the same Greek word for 'resurrection' (*anabaino*) as is used in other literature.[64] If this is so it constitutes presumptive evidence that Josephus was seeking to present both the Essenes and the Pharisees in a dress that would be less likely to stir the antipathy of his Roman readers;[65] and that, consequently, the Essenes, like the Pharisees believed in bodily resurrection.

A sixth dimension of the Essene mind which comes into visibility in the classical accounts is the charismatic-apocalyptic. Not least remarkable is its emergence in the context of Essene devotion to the law. Attention has already been drawn to the centrality of this.[66] Significantly, Philo not only describes the regularity with which the Law is read Sabbath by Sabbath, adding that the reading is followed by instruction by one of the more learned members; he continues: 'Most of the time, and in accordance with an ancient method of inquiry, instruction is given them by means of symbols.'[67] Taking the statement in the context beginning at *Q.o.p.* 80 where Philo refers to the Essene rejection of natural philosophy, F.M. Cross comments incisively: 'Translated into another idiom, he is saying they are interested only in biblical revelation and law.'[68] Such interpretation is presumably the basis of the doctrines of the sect (including the names of the angels) which, according to Josephus, the initiate swears to keep from outsiders and pass on to new members only as he received them (*War* 2. 141–2).

Related likewise to the study of Scripture is the exercise of prophecy which Josephus also mentions as playing an apparently large role in the life of the sect. 'There are some among them who, trained as they are in the study of the holy books and the different sorts of purifications, and the sayings of the prophets, become expert in foreseeing the future: they are rarely deceived in their predictions.'[69] In various parts of his works Josephus cites specific examples of accurate prognostication on the part of Essenes (*War* 1. 78, 2. 113 which is repeated in essence in *Ant.*17. 345–8; *War* 3. 351–4; *Ant.* 15. 371–9).

Yet another aspect of the charismatic side of the Essene mentality is their concern with healing. This again is connected with their study of Scripture, but extends beyond it to the investigation of roots and stones – these last possibly charms or amulets (*War* 2. 136).[70] And if their thought had an individual eschatology (as was seen above) it also had a global eschatology. For the passage from the *Philosophumena* cited earlier in regard to bodily resurrection concludes in a way which gathers together many of the most distinctive features of their charismatic-apocalyptic mentality. 'They affirm that there will be both a judgment and a conflagration of the universe, and that the wicked will be eternally punished. And among them is cultivated also the practice of prophecy and the prediction of future events.'[71]

Clearly, no outside text can be permitted to serve as the yardstick for Qumran theology. The texts from the caves must be heard for themselves, and be given the final say. But testimony regarding the sect from the outside, particularly contemporary testimony, can serve a confirmatory role in seeking an understanding of their thought. The classical writers are well-placed to discharge such a task.

Historical – Theological Pointers in the Texts

It was seen at the end of chapter one that the data examined there pointed to the broad parameters for the existence of a sectarian community at Qumran as being from roughly 150 BC to AD 70. The impression given by the classical sources does not greatly differ from this, even if it is less exact. This is particularly the case with Josephus.

His earliest mention of the Essenes is *Antiquities* 13. 171–2 where he injects a brief account of the three sects of the Jews into a narrative describing the struggles of Jonathan (161–143/2 BC) against the Seleucids, specifically his preparations in expectation of an attack by Demetrius II. The account, which deals with the varying attitudes of the sects to the workings of Fate, is simply introduced by the words: 'At this time there were three sects of the Jews which took different attitudes to human affairs. One sect was called the Pharisees, another the Sadducees and the third was the Essenes.'[72] The connection between the main narrative and the account of the sects is not immediately obvious, but if it is more than haphazard, then it indicates that Josephus believed the Essenes to have existed as a recognizable entity in the time of Jonathan Maccabeus.

Thereafter, further references to individual Essenes are found in his works: Judas the Essene in the time of Antigonus (105–4 BC) (*War* 1. 78–80), Manaemus in the time of Herod the Great (*Ant*. 15. 371–9), Simon the Essene in the time of Archelaus (*War* 2. 113), and John the Essene, rebel governor of north and west Judaea after the defeat of Roman forces in AD 66 (*War* 2. 567; 3. 11).

However, while such historical markers are valuable our narrower concern here is whether there are any historical indicators in the Qumran texts themselves which have theological bearings: not so much on *when* the sect came into existence (though that is not unimportant) as on *why*. If an answer to this can be found, it will go far towards defining the issue or issues which stood at the centre of the sect's theological magnetic field, as well as providing the point in relation to which any development may have taken place.

Several passages stand out in this regard.

Community Rule (IQS) VIII 1–16a.

The composite character of the *Community Rule* from Cave 1 has long been recognized.[73] The same may be said of constituent sections of the *Rule*, including columns VIII and

IX within which the passage under consideration stands. These columns consist of two types of material. On the one hand there is material which describes the character and purposes of the community as in VIII 1–10a, 12b–16a. On the other hand there is material which consists of precise regulations regarding the functioning of the community as in VIII 16b–IX 2 and IX 12–25. The two types of material are marked by distinct formulas. The legal sections are introduced by the formula, 'these are the regulations' (VIII 20; IX 12, 21). The material of more narrative character is either introduced by or contains the formula (with slight variations): 'when these things exist in Israel' (VIII 4b, 12b; IX 3a).[74] The implication appears to be that the community and its attendant functions referred to (see VIII 1–4a, 12b–16a; IX 3–12) did not yet exist at the time of writing but its establishment was envisaged. In the words of M.A. Knibb, 'at the moment when this material was first set down in writing the community was still in an embryonic state'.[75] What this amounts to is that IQS VIII 1–16a in part or in whole lays down the principles and purposes which the community would follow in its impending establishment in the desert.[76] To borrow a label which has come to be used in this connection: this passage constitutes the 'manifesto' of the community.[77]

If this is sound, the passage serves as a window on the self-understanding, as well as the aims of those who brought the desert community to birth. It is important in several specific respects. First, it marks a point of cleavage between the official religion of the Second Temple and the religious group which now brought forth the desert community.[78] 'When these exist as a community in Israel in compliance with these arrangements they are to be segregated from within the dwelling of the men of sin to walk to the desert in order to open there his path' (VIII 12b–13).[79] Second, the purpose of the establishment of the desert community was neither occasional nor ancillary, but was indispensable and central inasmuch as it was overridingly religious. This conclusion is inescapable from the twofold role which it was believed to fulfil. On the one hand it was viewed as the people of God's new covenant. Full knowledge of the covenant would be theirs (VIII 9); indeed, the purpose of their existence would be 'to establish a covenant in compliance with the everlasting decrees' (VIII 10a). Its composition of twelve men and three priests (VIII 1) speaks to the same conclusion. These are probably best understood as representatives of the true Israel: a man for each tribe and a priest for each of the three clans of the tribe of Levi (Num. 3:17). On the other hand it was also envisaged as the true temple. Temple language is used to describe it, 'a holy house for Israel and the foundation of the holy of holies for Aaron' (VIII 5b–6a. Cf. 8b–9a). Temple functions are discharged in it. Sin is atoned for: though not by the offering of sacrifice but by the practice of justice and the endurance of affliction (VIII 3–4, 6, 10). Accordingly, its functionaries are credited with executing the tasks of the Aaronic priesthood (VIII 6, 9). The initiative of establishing the desert community thus constitutes a departure of no mean order.

Thirdly, and of most importance for our purposes, IQS VIII 1–16a is laden with theological concepts which, however, carry a distinctive stamp and therefore deserve careful notice as the theological currency of the Qumran sect. These concepts are inter-related so that each carries something of the sense of all the others. For this reason it is difficult to say that any one is more important than the others. Even so, a certain logical priority belongs to the idea of covenant. The glowing description of the community in lines 4b–9 reaches its lofty conclusion in the purpose clause of line 10: 'in order to establish a covenant in compliance with the everlasting decrees.'[80] Covenant by definition rests upon divine election, and the sectarians accordingly are those who are 'chosen by the will of God' (VIII 6). In keeping with this, epithets and descriptions which are applied to Israel in the Hebrew Bible are now applied to the sect. In particular, the prophecy of Isaiah 28:16 in which Zion is spoken of as 'a tested stone, a precious cornerstone, a sure foundation' (*NRSV*) is drawn upon to describe the community 'whose foundations do not shake or tremble in their place' (VIII 8a). But election implies service, and it is this connection of thought which leads to the idea of the community's mission. The words immediately following the statement of the community's covenant function read, 'And these will be accepted in order to atone for the earth and to decide the judgment of the wicked' (line 10b).[81] These same functions are linked in lines 5–7a with the community's role as a holy Temple.

But implicit in this covenant is the idea of holiness. This is, indeed, inseparable from the role of the community as Temple. Twice it is described as a 'most holy dwelling' (*qôdeš qôdàšîm*) for Aaron (lines 5–6, 8–9) and its members as 'holy ones' (singular: *qôdeš*, perhaps in a collective or even abstract sense: 'as a holiness') (line 11). That this holiness is merely formal is disproved by the concrete qualities the sectaries are called upon to exhibit, 'truth, justice, judgment, compassionate love and unassuming behaviour of each person to his fellow to preserve faithfulness on the earth' (lines 2–3a).

A third concept which enters into this theological interplay is that of law. The opening lines of column eight state that entry into the community is for those who are 'perfect in everything that has been revealed about all the law;' while preparing in the desert the way of the Lord is defined bluntly in similar terms, 'This is the study of the law which he commanded through the hand of Moses, in order to act in compliance with all that has been revealed from age to age, and according to what the prophets have revealed through his Holy Spirit' (lines 15–16a). The law, its study and implementation thus stand at the heart of the sect's vocation. Nor is this to be taken casually; perfection in the understanding and practice of the law alone will suffice.[82] But a singular emphasis emerges at this point in association with the law: namely, revelation. This is the case in both passages just cited. It is not simply the law that is to be studied and observed, but a particular interpretation of it. Indeed, there are matters which have been hidden from Israel that have been found out by the Interpreter: evidently, a sectarian functionary since he is warned not to keep his discoveries from members of the community for fear of striking terror into them (lines 11b–12a).[83] If one inquires after the character of this revelation then, in addition to the facets of holiness already noted in lines 2–3a, it apparently includes items capable of very specific definition: walking with everyone 'in the truth and rule of the time'.[84] It is apparently an account of substantive differences on matters of 'truth' and 'time' that the sectaries will separate 'from within the dwelling of the men of sin to walk to the desert in order to open there His path' (line 13). It is on account of failings in these matters that the old Temple must be displaced by a new one.

These four theological concepts: covenant, holiness, law, revelation, and the associated ideas which they carry with them thus appear to have occupied a central place in the thought of the religious group as it stood on the brink of departing for the wilderness to assume a more specific form with a more sharply defined purpose. As such they constitute an important benchmark.[85]

Damascus Rule (CD) I 1–21 (+4Q266, 267), III 12b–IV 12a, V 15b–VI 11

A second text which sheds light on both the historical beginnings of the Qumran sect and the theological concerns which brought it into being is the *Damascus Rule*. The document first known in modern times from the Genizah text,[86] consists of two distinguishable types of material: matter of a hortatory character, in pages I–VIII, XIX–XX; and legal material in pages IX–XVI. The discovery of fragments in the Qumran caves[87] has not only established a link between the document and Qumran; it has also reinforced the likelihood that the two types of material were always united, even if in varying measure.[88] They have also placed a question mark over the suggestion that the *Damascus Rule* existed in different recensions.[89] In short, in the *Damascus Rule* we appear to be in possession of a text which has the capacity to represent the Qumran mind.[90] In what ways then, does this mind come to expression?

It comes to expression to begin with in terms of awareness of the sect's historical origins. Reference has already been made to this as a simple factual datum.[91] However, the *Damascus Rule* goes beyond this by recounting particulars of those origins, notably in column I. The details given can be summarized easily enough. Following a reference to God's abandonment of Israel to exile comes mention of a remnant which God, in fidelity to his covenant intervened to save. This took place 'at the moment of wrath, three hundred and ninety years after having delivered them up into the hands of Nebuchadnezzar, King of Babylon' when God 'visited them and caused to sprout from Israel and from Aaron a shoot of the planting in order to possess his land' (CD I5b–7). Those thus visited groped in blindness for twenty years. 'And God appraised their deeds, because they sought him with a perfect heart, and raised up for them a Teacher of Righteousness, in order to direct them in the path of his heart' (lines 10–11). Over against these stand 'the congregation of traitors' (12), and over against the Teacher of Righteousness stands 'the scoffer', who led Israel astray, causing her to transgress the covenant by propounding lax interpretations of the law and persecuting to the point of death those who stood by the covenant (18–21).

This account is clearly of the greatest importance in understanding the reasons which brought the sect into existence.[92] There has been debate as to the precise import of these data. Even though 390 years from 587 BC yields a date of 197 and a further 20 years the date of 177 BC for the beginning of the ministry of the Teacher of Righteousness: dates which place the 'age of wrath' within ready range of the convulsions under Antiochus Epiphanes which constituted the backdrop of the sect's emergence, it is questionable whether the intent of the writer is merely chronological. Rather, it is probable that all the numbers in column I together with those in XX 14–15 are also symbolical, adding up to the 490 years (seventy weeks of years) of Daniel 9: 2,24. Their intent is therefore to show that the communities of the *Damascus Rule* truly belonged to the last generation.[93] Still more important is the implicit claim that the Damascus communities are the lineal descendants and inheritors of those with whom the covenant was made 'at the very first' (*berît ri'šônîm I 4)*; they constitute the *remnant* (*šĕ'ērît*) with whom the covenant will be renewed. The import of this is that the rest of Judaism has defected and no longer constitutes the covenant people. In short, the (self-) identification of the Damascus communities as the remnant marks a decisive breach with the body of the Jewish people as a whole.

Yet while this fracture was real to the awareness of those involved, its full meaning remained opaque and inchoate for half a generation. 'They were like blind persons and like those who grope for the path' (I 9). They knew who they were not; they were less clear as to how to be what they were. This confusion was removed by the raising up for them by God of a Teacher of Righteousness (*môrēh ṣedek*) to direct them in the way of [God's] heart (I 11). The same sequence of thought is found in CD V 20–VI 8a: the breaking of the Mosaic covenant (V 20–VI 1); its renewal with men of understanding from Aaron and Israel (VI 2–3) who understood the Law (VI 4–6); and the presence of the Interpreter of the Law (*dôrēš hattôrāh*) who was the divine instrument for its exposition (VI 7b–8a). In short, the Interpreter of the Law and the Teacher of Righteousness serve the same function and so presumably refer to the same individual.[94] Accordingly, if the Teacher of Righteousness cannot be called the founder of the new movement he was certainly the guiding light.

A further factor regarding the origins of the sect which the opening column of the *Damascus Rule* makes plain is that the activities of the Teacher of Righteousness evoked a storm of opposition. Whatever may be said regarding the original form of CD I 12–II 1[95] its present form is a denunciation of the opponents of the Teacher of Righteousness. These take the shape of a party: 'the congregation of traitors' who stray from the way, and are led by a particular individual, 'the scoffer' (*hallāṣôn*). In comparison with the Teacher of Righteousness and his followers they seek lax interpretations of the law, loopholes to evade its demands, thereby violating the covenant themselves and hating those who keep it to the point of hunting them down with the sword.

It would appear therefore that, from the perspective of the *Damascus Rule* the communities whose rule it was had their origin in some kind of religious awakening which left its subjects with an awareness of their differences with Israel at large. But these did not crystallize into clear definition or distinct organization until the advent of the Teacher of Righteousness who was divinely gifted as an interpreter of the law. Even so, not all of his original disciples remained with him, a split being led by one who dismissed some of his interpretations with derision. But those who continued with him did so with the confidence with which the movement apparently began: that they were now the custodians of the covenant.

For our purposes there is no need to pursue the historical significance of the passages further.[96] What is of concern are the controlling theological themes that are to be found as close as we are able to get to the sect's historical beginnings. At least three rise to prominence, though ancillary ideas are associated with some of them. First is the idea of covenant. From one point of view this is a portmanteau idea into which all the others could be poured. For purposes of analysis, however, it is useful to treat the fact (or form) of the covenant first, turning to its content later. It is not for nothing that the document has come to be spoken of as the *Covenant of Damascus*. Its chief constituents: hortatory material or admonition (4QDb frg.1 + 4QD^{a}frg. 1:1–8 + CD I 1–VIII, XIX–XX) followed by regulations (CD IX–XVI),[97] together with specific references to entering the covenant[98] lend plausibility to Cothenet's suggestion that the *Damascus Document* may have played some part in preparation for the covenant renewal ceremony if not in the ceremony itself.[99] Of particular significance are the two points that receive recurrent stress. The first is that lying behind the long history of the breaking of the first covenant is 'stubbornness of heart' (*šerîrût lēb*): a condition that dominates the long series of breaches from the Watchers to those who fell to the Babylonian sword (II 17b–III 12a). By contrast, it is with those who remained faithful to God's ordinances that he established his covenant (III 12b–13; cf. XIX 13). The second point of significance is that the renewed covenant is for the sectarians alone. It is true that it is said to be 'for all Israel' (XV 5, cf. XVI 1) but that very context demonstrates that the community is co-extensive with Israel. Its members are enjoined to initiate their sons into the covenant (XV 6): that is to say, membership of the covenant is no longer by birth into the covenant community, but by voluntary acceptance of its obligations and privileges. In the words of S. Talmon, 'The Covenanters identify their community as the sole legitimate representative of biblical Israel'.[100] And while the *Damascus Rule* speaks of God's covenant with them as 'the new covenant' (*habbĕrît haḥădāšāh*) (VI 19, VIII 21, XIX 33), it never speaks of the community as the new Israel. It is the only Israel. If the covenant is new, it is in the sense of being renewed. Essentially it entails a return to the law of Moses (XV 8–9, XVI 1–2).

If these are the dominant notes in the covenant concept presented in these parts of the *Damascus Rule* which speak of the rise of the movement and the sect into which it evolved, there are others which, though less prominent, are nonetheless indispensable links in their connection of thought. Among these are their understanding of sin and guilt, and still more their consciousness of them without which the new movement would never have been sparked into existence. 'They realised their sin and knew that they were guilty men', (I 8b–9a). Linked with these are their understanding of repentance and acceptance by God. The former comes to expression particularly in the frequent use of the verb *šûb*: to 'turn', to 'return', to 'repent'. In the passages under review the Covenanters are characterized as 'the converts of Israel who left the land of Judah' (IV 2b–3a, cf. VI 5 which adds 'and lived in the land of Damascus'). The meaning appears to be that to 'turn' from the land of Judah, the homeland of religious traitors is to 'turn' to the observance of the covenant law; hence the expression 'to enter the new covenant in the land of Damascus', (VI 19, VIII 21, XIX 33f).[101]

Repentance, in short, as the Hebrew verb implies, is not merely an emotion, it involves action. God observed their deeds (*ma'ăśêhem*) (I 10). But it was their deeds as expressive of their inward attitude that moved God to raise up for them a Teacher of Righteousness, 'they sought him with a perfect heart' (*bĕlēb šālēm).*[102] If these ideas – sin, repentance – are only glanced at here, it does not follow that they are no more than subsidiary. It more probably means that they cannot come to fuller expression in this particular form of literature. We shall have occasion to test this.

If covenant is one controlling theme in this account of community origins, eschatology is assuredly another. The events recounted in CD I 1–12 are placed squarely in an eschatological setting, 'At the moment of wrath ... [God] visited them' (5b, 7a). Both expressions are significant. The first, 'the time of wrath' or 'the age of wrath' (*qēz ḥărôn*) is much more than a vivid description of the social turbulence of affairs in Judah during the first quarter of the second century BC. It is rather that turbulence seen through the lens of a particular view of history in which one divinely predetermined period follows another (cf. IV 9f with the references to the completing of the period (*qez*) of the years). Because that period is characterized by flagrant violation of the covenant (I 13b–16), Belial is let loose against Israel (IV 13a). Such a period can only terminate in judgment (I 17–II 1), and for this reason the present generation is the last generation (I 12),[103] and these days are 'the end days' (IV 4a). There is thus a qualified dualism in this perspective.[104]

The term 'visit' (*pāqad*) (I 7a) is likewise an eschatological term[105] as is the term 'root' (*šōreš*) associated with it. Divine visitation may be either in judgment or mercy. The visitation upon those who broke the first covenant as upon those who have broken the renewed covenant will be in judgment (VII 21b–VIII 2). But the visitation which caused the root to sprout from Aaron and

Israel in order to possess the land (I 7–8a) had a salvific intent to create a community which would remain faithful to the renewed covenant. There is also a hint of an individual dimension to this eschatology. God, having pardoned the sins of those who had been admitted to the renewed covenant, 'built for them a safe home in Israel, such as there has not been since ancient times, not even till now. Those who remained steadfast in it will acquire eternal life, and all the glory of Adam is for them', (III 19–20). The entire complex of events attending and including the emergence of the sect thus falls within the outworking of the divine purpose at the end time.

A third concept which occupied a dominant place in the sectarian mentality from its early years was that of law. This again embraces a large number of interrelated ideas which are only glanced at in the passages under review. This is scarcely surprising, since these passages stand in the hortatory prologue to the regulations, rather than in the laws themselves where one might expect fuller treatment. At the same time, the Prologue or Admonition serves to convey by implication, if not by direct exposition, something of the understanding of the formulation and functioning as well as the general content of law in the community. That observance of law stands at the centre of the community's concerns is exhibited in the opening column in the vigorous denunciation of those who have strayed from the path. Precisely what this entailed is not stated in column I, but the general meaning is not in doubt: it involved deviation from the traditional interpretation of the law: 'removing the boundary with which the very first had marked their inheritance' (I 16).[106] The only further indication given of what was involved is given in general statements about relaxation of the law and subverting it, in particular, opposing the community of the renewed covenant (I 13–21).

More specific information regarding the content and formulation of the law is found in the two later passages which also reflect on the formation of the sect. Two facets, which are related, come into view. The first is that significant stress is placed not simply on doing the right things but doing them at the right times. The earliest hint of this appears in 4QDa frg.1.4 which Garcia Martinez amends to read, '[... for there is no] before or after in his festivals.'[107] A fuller statement occurs in CD III 14b–16a where the covenant God establishes with the community is said to concern 'his holy sabbaths and his glorious feasts, his just stipulations and his truthful paths, and the wishes of his will which a man must do in order to live by them'. The sacred calendar is thus held to be of prime importance.

The second facet of the sectarian understanding of law is that its meaning is conveyed by revelation. The prologue to the foregoing statement regarding sabbaths and feast days reads, 'God established his covenant with Israel forever, revealing to them hidden matters in which all Israel had gone astray' (III 13b–14a); while the words immediately following it read, 'He disclosed (these matters) to them' (16b). The creation of the community and its continuance revolve around these two categories: things hidden (*nistārôt*) and things revealed (*niglôt*).[108] These revelations were not mediated by any kind of second sight or (apparently) by highly charged emotional experience. They were mediated rather by the study of the law on the part of 'men of knowledge (*nĕbônîm*) and men of wisdom (*ḥăkāmîm*) from Aaron and from Israel' (VI 2–3a). The text then proceeds to place their wisdom in the context of 'digging the well' (Numbers 21:18) which is taken to be the law; and more importantly, to define as their chief aid in this task a figure referred to as 'the interpreter of the law' (VI 7b).[109]

It is hardly surprising therefore that both facets should come together in VI 14–VII 6a. There the sins of the 'sons of the pit' are spelled out most specifically (even if not always clearly enough for our understanding)(VI 15b–VII 4a). Their conformity with 'the exact interpretation of the law' is repeatedly enjoined (VI 14, 18, 20 cf. VII 2a). Their walking 'according to these matters' is said to be the essence of perfect holiness (VII 4b–5a).

From these passages in the *Damascus Rule* then, which seem to be intent on tracing how the community came to be what it was, what factors shaped it, and what the shape was which it assumed, three concepts stand out clearly: covenant, eschatology and law. They are interrelated just as there are others which are implicit in them. But these assert for themselves by their pervasiveness as well as their high profile a dominant role in shaping the thought of the sect.

4Q Halakhic Letter (4QMMT)

The publication of the official edition of what may be called 4QMMT[110] to avoid begging any questions has made available another text which holds the promise of shedding light on the beginning of Qumran theology. The text consists of six manuscripts, none complete, which together yield 130 lines of material, and are reckoned to constitute about two-thirds of the original document. The surviving material comes from the middle and end of the original work.[111] The oldest manuscript dates from about 75 BC, and the youngest from about AD 50. It is unlikely that the oldest text was the archetype.[112] Both the number of surviving copies, as well as the timespan during which they were copied, suggests that the work was valued and used throughout much of the sect's history.

On the assumption that the six manuscripts witness to a single document – an assumption not universally held[113] – the official editors have woven together a composite text.[114] On this basis the text is believed to consist of three clearly definable elements. First, there is a Calendaric Section containing a list of sabbaths and feasts constructed on the plan of the 364-day calendar found in other of the Qumran texts, including the Temple Scroll. Second, there is a collection of laws, introduced by the phrase, 'These are some of our rulings' (*'ēleh miqṣat dĕbarênû*). The laws in question are largely concerned with the question of purity as this related to matters such as sacrifices and offerings, and dealings with various groups of people such as

Gentiles, women and lepers. The third section consists of an exhortation to the recipients by the senders. The most distinguishing feature of this section is its use of personal pronouns: 'we' the senders are distinguished from 'you' the recipients and both from 'they': a third group in the *dramatis personae*.

Before taking up the questions of the purpose and setting of the document which are indispensable for determining its theological bearings, it is necessary to consider further the matter of its integrity. It is of interest that one of the editors of the official edition, in a paper divulging his second thoughts before his first thoughts had been published,[115] reversed the position he had adopted in that edition, concluding that 'it is far from certain that the calendar, as found here, belonged to any other letter at all or that it formed part of the document MMT^{B+C}'.[116] Strugnell was not alone in reaching that conclusion. L.H. Schiffman, on much the same evidence as Strugnell, holds that the calendar had an independent existence, and was placed before MMT by a scribe to whom calendrical matters were important even though they are nowhere mentioned in MMT itself.[117]

Confining ourselves, then, to the legal and hortatory sections, we may inquire after their intent as a clue to their contribution to the theological understanding of the sect. If the literary genre of the document could be determined this would be a useful starting-point, but it is doubtful if this can be done with any precision. 'Letter' is the favoured designation, though Strugnell has had second thoughts about this also – or more correctly, *third* thoughts – withdrawing his suggestion that it is a treatise,[118] and viewing it now as 'a collection of laws, perhaps consciously modelled on the opening of Deuteronomy'.[119] This description (which he applies strictly to the legal section) provides him with the clue for type-casting the hortatory section. 'We would not expect formally such a conclusion (putting it broadly, a benediction) would well fit at the end of a legal code as it does in covenant formulae. Deuteronomy would thus provide a parallel for the ending of this work just as it did for the beginning.'[120]

Much as there is to be said for this, it is questionable whether covenant-form can accommodate the very specific local and personal references in Section C: '[And you know that] we have separated ourselves from the multitude of people [and from all their impurity] and from being involved with these matters and from participating with [them] in these things.'[121] 'We have (indeed) sent you some of the precepts of the Torah according to our decision, for your welfare and the welfare of your people. For we have seen (that) you have wisdom and knowledge of the Torah. Consider all these things and ask Him that He strengthen your will and that He remove from you the plans of evil and the device of Belial so that you may rejoice at the end of time, finding that some of our practices are correct.'[122] Strugnell concedes that 'treatise' is 'at least in the Hellenistic literature, a very ill-defined genre'.[123]

An address, laced with concrete personal references plus an epistolary conclusion is not unknown in Hellenistic literature, the Epistle to the Hebrews being a striking example. A covenant-form adapted to a specific historical situation, thus partaking of the forms of both covenant and letter may well be what we encounter in MMT.

What then is the setting of the document? The passages quoted above from Section C are sufficient to indicate the outline of the situation. The central issue is a dispute about Torah. The writers have separated themselves from the people at large ('them') on this account. They are sending some of their interpretations of the law to their correspondent ('you' singular), not only for his good and the good of his people, but so that he will see that some of their interpretations (*debārênû*) are correct. He himself is well-versed in the law. There is thus a two-way split: of the writers from the people at large; and of the writers and the leader being addressed. The mood is not yet of hostility; it is possible that fuller information will lead to mutual acceptance.

Is it possible to define the situation more exactly? Several features suggest that this may be so. First, the circumstance evoking the dispute is Temple praxis. Most of the laws referred to in Section B are concerned with securing the purity of the Temple: the exclusion of gentiles (lines 3–9a); the correct definition of the 'camp' so that 'outside the camp' is not merely outside the sanctuary, but outside Jerusalem (lines 27–35, 58b–62a); the avoidance of mixing clean and unclean, which is applied to marriage and the mixing of different species (lines 75–82). Second, divergent attitudes exist on these matters as between the groups referred to. The senders of the letter ('we') adopt a rigid position on the disputed issues. For example, whereas 'they' leave over parts of the sacrifices for consumption on the day after they are offered, the writers insist that all be eaten before sunset on the day they are offered, apparently interpreting Leviticus 7:15 to this effect.[124] Again, as just noted, the writers of MMT took Jerusalem in its entirety to be the 'camp' so that the purity rules must be observed throughout the city: a position which differed sharply from the developed rabbinic view which distinguished the camp of God (the Temple) from the camp of the Levites (Temple Mount) and the camp of the Israelites (the rest of Jerusalem), with most of the purity laws applying only to the first.[125]

Now the question is whether this sheds light on the theological beginnings of the sect, and if so, what light? Attempts to pin the matter down depend to some extent on finding a credible historical anchorage for the events lying behind MMT, and it can hardly be claimed that any consensus has emerged.[126] The factors most likely to give guidance would appear to be these. First, the overriding preoccupation of the document is purity, which was also a preoccupation at Qumran. Second, the halakhah propounded is stringent, another characteristic of the Qumran sect. Third, at the same time, while there are Qumran interests and Qumran features, there is no distinctive Qumran theology, even if some of the ingredients are there. It is not easy to estimate this with precision. Eisenman and Wise claim that, 'the vocabulary is rich in Qumranisisms throughout', pointing to 'violence' (*hāmās*), 'fornication' (*zenût*), 'heart' (*lēb*), and 'Belial' (*Belî'al*).[127] They also note the presence of ideas such as 'the way of the Torah' (Section C line 12) or 'seeking the Torah' (Section C line 24), thereby finding forgiveness: ideas which play a significant role in IQS and CD. Such evidence, they claim 'definitively identifies them as a group – a movement'.[128] On the other hand some things are absent from MMT that play a large role in other Qumran texts, not least any indication of organization, developed apocalyptic ideas[129] or developed dualism. While it might be argued that these were not at issue, it is surprising that the matters which are at issue are discussed in detachment from such concepts with which they are commonly associated elsewhere. Qimron's conclusion is well-judged, 'MMT is theologically less developed than the standard Qumran theology in its lack of dualistic language, typical community descriptions, apocalyptic ideas, and apocalyptic conscience. The choice of legal topics by MMT, and especially the non-choice of some topics as contrasted with the delectus of topics popular in the later Qumran literature, suggests, or is at least reconcilable with, an earlier date for MMT'.[130] If there is raw material in MMT for some of the concepts which were developed later, it seems not to have got beyond the stage of being raw material. Fourthly, the tone of the text suggests that *rapprochement* with the group to whom the letter is sent is viewed as both desirable and not yet beyond the bounds of possibility. True, the addressees will have to make the adjustments, but their position is not viewed as having hardened to the point that an appeal is wasted effort, still less that they have crossed lines that leave open as the only option their being branded as apostates.

Taken together, these considerations appear to be more consistent with an earlier rather than a later date for MMT. While the nominating of the Teacher of Righteousness as its author[131] is both speculative and improbable, it clearly comes from the hands of those who could speak with authority for the separationists. When one adds to this the very considerable probability that the theology of the sect developed quickly on the arrival of the Teacher of Righteousness in its ranks,[132] there is a strong *a priori* case for seeing in 4QMMT those concerns and conceptions which not only precipitated the creation of the movement in its earliest days before it assumed any kind of organizational form, but which laid the cornerstone in alignment with which Qumran thought would take shape.[133]

It is not going too far to say that the controlling theme of MMT is the law and its observance, especially as it relates to the Temple. Section C, while written in terms of general exhortation, by that very means exposes the underlying thrust of the entire text: namely, that wandering from the path of the Torah is the highroad to disaster (12, 23–4). What that path entails is spelled out in the regulations in Section B. Their essential content may be subsumed under two headings. First is purity. Two aspects receive particular attention. The first is ritual purity as it affects the Temple and the Temple sacrifices. The cereal offering is to be eaten on the day on which the meat has been sacrificed (9b–13); it is only at sunset that the priest engaged in the red heifer ritual becomes clean again (13–16); animal hides convey pollution, and anyone who has touched a carcase is excluded from the sacred food (21–3); all of Jerusalem is the camp and therefore holy, so the ashes of the purification offering must be buried outside the city (29–33). The other aspect of purity which receives attention is that of priestly marriage. The ruling,[134] which constitutes the last in Section B (75–82) involves, not the principle of separating clean from unclean but rather that of improper separation as the context shows. Just as there should be no mixing of species, or of clothing, or of seed sown in a single field, so there should be no marriage of priests outside the priestly family. This is simply an application of the principle that 'Israel is holy' (76).

The second heading under which the legal content of MMT may be subsumed is that of performance. Here two features are to be noted. To begin with there is the stringency of the laws of MMT to which attention has already been drawn. The document's definition of the 'camp' as incorporating the whole city of Jerusalem within which the ritual law must be adhered to (B 29–33) contrasts with more fluid and flexible definitions held by the rabbis. This stringency appears to be prompted by and rest upon a rigid and literal interpretation of Scripture. It is no accident that the hortatory section of the document gives the reason for writing as being 'so that you may study (carefully) the book of Moses and the books of the Prophets and (the writings of) David' (C 10).[135] 'It seems,' writes Qimron, 'that the sectarians strove to observe the commandments in accordance with the literal sense of Scripture, and condemned any tendency to adapt the commandments to the needs of the time.'[136] This mentality inevitably begot what must necessarily accompany the literal study of the law: namely, the exact performance of the law. God's will was not merely something to be *known*; it was something to be *done*.

Much discussion has attended the interpretation of the term *mā'āsîm* which gives the document its name.[137] The official editors take it to mean 'precepts' and so translate it in B 3 and C 27. However, they cannot translate it thus in its other occurrence in MMT C 31, where they therefore render 'This will be counted as a virtuous deed (*bā'ăśô tekā*).' Accordingly, other scholars have concluded that 'precepts' is a mistranslation, and the expression should be rendered 'deeds' or 'works of the law' in all instances.[138] This seems to fit the contexts best. The stated intent of the document is to encourage the readers 'to do what is good and righteous before Him' (C 31), a formula found elsewhere in the Qumran texts (e.g. IQS I 2–4). The critical character of such conformity to the law is enjoined through Section C in a whole variety of ways. To stray from the law is to ask for calamity (12), to unleash the curses of the law (12b–15, 18b–21a). Conversely, to contemplate the deeds of the kings of Israel shows that those who kept the law were spared trouble; more, through their righteous deeds they – David included – found forgiveness (23–6). If the readers will follow the practices of the writers 'this will be counted as a virtuous deed of yours, since you will be doing what is righteous and good in his eyes' (31).

If 4QMMT is, indeed, the window on Qumran beginnings that we have supposed then its importance is very far-reaching indeed. For even more important than its disclosure that the sect was born out of a split; even more important than its revealing that the split was occasioned by differences over Temple praxis; more important than all of these is the connection of thought which lies behind them. For what that connection of thought comes down to is that Israel's holiness depends upon her obedience to the divine will; that the divine will is known through the intense study of Scripture; that the knowledge of the divine will brings with it the obligation to live in conformity with it; and that conformity with it brings the forgiveness of sins. To the sectarian mind there was thus a direct link between observance of the ritual purity laws and the forgiveness of sins and acceptance as righteous by God.[139] For the sect there is thus a profound religious interest at the heart of their preoccupation with the minutiae of the law.[140] For this reason, whereas other groups within Judaism would still maintain association with those holding different views, the group which lay behind MMT must separate themselves in order to preserve the integrity of the law and the purity of the land.[141]

Indicators in the Pesharim

We may turn finally to the *Pesharim*[142] in quest of indications of the theological preoccupations of the Qumran sect, particularly in its beginnings. Much debate has surrounded the study of the *Pesharim*, and still does, even if the substance of the debate has somewhat changed. At an earlier stage of the debate a central focus was what constitutes a *Pesher*. Is it to be defined in terms of content or of form? If form, is there such a thing as a distinct literary genre? Given that *pesher* is some kind of biblical interpretation, is all Qumran material containing interpretation of Scripture to be classified as *pesher*, or just that which uses the specific term?[143]

It is now widely agreed that the *Pesharim* are of two main types: continuous *pesher* in which the commentary follows the text of the biblical book, explaining its meaning in order; and thematic *pesher*, in which the controlling principle is the theme chosen by the commentator who selects the biblical passages in terms of their relevance to his theme.[144] Some of the exegetical techniques employed in Qumran *Pesharim* are also found in rabbinic midrashim, which has led to the suggestion that Qumran *pesher* is but a variant form of rabbinic midrash.[145] This may be so. The important point for the understanding of the Qumran *Pesharim* lies in the recognition of the variants. Undoubtedly, the most distinctive feature of the *Pesharim* is not so much their exegetical technique as their hermeneutical assumption: namely, that the prophetic text has primary reference to the current situation of the community, and the perception of this is a matter of divine inspiration.[146] In short, their most distinctive feature is of content rather than form. That they also have a distinctive form and terminology: quotation of Scripture followed by interpretation introduced by the word *pesher* is not denied, but a definition based on form alone cannot do justice to what was clearly the quality which gave the *Pesharim* their claim to a place at the heart of the sectarian literature.

This leads to the second problem that has troubled the study of the *Pesharim*: namely their use for reconstruction of the history of the sect. The wide divergences in the identification of persons and events held to be referred to have tended to give rise to scepticism as to their usefulness for historical purposes. There can be no doubt that they were intended to convey historical information to their first readers. The occurrence of the names of historical individuals: Demetrius King of Yawan at 4QpNah I 2, and a fellow-monarch Antiochus at 4QpNah I 3 is sufficient proof of that. However, such identifications are the exception rather than the rule. Most of the *dramatis personae* appear behind theological masks: the Teacher of Righteousness

(IQpHab I 13, II 2, V 10, etc.), the Wicked Priest (IQpHab VIII 8, IX 9, etc.), the Man of Lies (IQpHab I 1–2, VII), the house of Absalom (IQpHab V 9). And this is precisely the point. The writers were not interested primarily in the chronological details of their community's history; their interest lay rather in the theological meaning conveyed through that history. Therefore, in inquiring after the theological contribution of the *Pesharim* to our understanding of the beginnings of Qumran theology we are asking a question to which there are grounds for expecting an answer. Two of the *Pesharim* hold particular promise in this regard: the *Commentary on Psalms* (4QpPs^{a}) and the *Habakkuk Commentary*.

The manuscript of 4QpPs^{a} is normally dated to the turn of the eras (approximately 30 BC – AD 20), though the work itself is older than this. What is remarkable is the role which it attributes to the Teacher of Righteousness. Thus the comment on Psalm 37:23–4, 'Its interpretation concerns the Priest, the Teacher of [Righteousness, whom] God chose to stand [in front of him, for] he installed him to found the congregation [of his chosen ones] for him, [and] straightened out his path, in truth' (4QpPs^{a}15b-17a) is noteworthy for a variety of reasons. First, the Teacher of Righteousness is identified as a priest.[147] Second, he is represented as the founder of the community: a claim which agrees essentially with the picture painted in CD I. Third, he is depicted as a teacher, divinely directed in the way of truth.[148] A similarly central role is accorded to the Teacher of Righteousness in the Habakkuk Commentary where he is mentioned no fewer than seven times. For while he is not described specifically as the founder of the community, he is represented as discharging the very work upon which the community rested: namely, interpreting the mysteries of God (II 2, VII 4). It would appear therefore, that the Teacher of Righteousness made a significant mark in the history and collective memory of the community.[149] What then is he credited with having taught?

Primarily, he is credited with being the vehicle of divine revelation. He received words 'from the mouth of God'

(IQpHab II 2b–3a), words of interpretation of the prophets regarding all that will happen to the last generation of his people (IQpHab II 6b–10a). These are 'mysteries' (*rāṣîm*, IQpHab VII 5, 8) concealed from Habakkuk himself who knew *what* would happen to the last generation, but not its full import (IQpHab III 1–2).[150] It is this mystery which God has vouchsafed to the Teacher of Righteousness: vouchsafed, it is implied, by the gift of insight into the meaning of Scripture.[151] However, the *Habakkuk Commentary* makes it clear that his teaching went beyond the question of the fulfilment of the end. His opponents are characterized as those who rejected the law (V 11–12), just as his followers are described as 'those who observe the law' (VII 11a; cf. VIII 1): a statement elaborated by reference to all of the times of God which came according to their fixed rule (VII 13).[152] By extension, law-observance is part of covenant-keeping, so that those who reject the words of the Teacher from the mouth of God are those who betray the new covenant (VIII 3).[153]

What has been attempted is an examination of texts or parts of texts from Qumran which claim directly or by implication to recount or reflect upon the beginnings of the community, and the concerns which preoccupied it from the start. Not all constituents appear in all documents, and those which do appear in all documents are emphasized unevenly. The varying purposes of the different documents may well account for such variations, at least in part. But there is a remarkable degree of consistency among the texts examined, not merely in regard to the general themes that are present, but also in regard to the way in which they are nuanced. The purity of Temple worship stands out as the primary thread which runs through the entire theological fabric. But the exactitude with and the times at which this was to be performed were themselves the subject of revelation conveyed initially through a gifted interpreter of Scripture. The failure of the Temple establishment to conform to these prescriptions meant that the nation stood in breach of covenant, but that covenant had been renewed by God with those who observed the stringent regulations which went with it. Nevertheless, judgment would fall, and it was the task of the sect to live in such holy observance that, when the end came, they would not only battle against the powers of darkness, but emerge victoriously to preserve in its purity, the purpose of God in creation. Such in outline, is the ideology cherished by the Qumran sect from close to its earliest days.

The Historical Development

The reconstruction of the history of the Qumran sect is not a primary objective of this work. However, in the conclusions reached earlier in the discussions of the archaeological evidence, the history of the occupation of the site, the interpretation of passages from the texts held to shed light on the beginnings of sectarian thought, and such like, positions have been adopted which either carry implications for, or raise questions about, the view of the sect's history which is presupposed. It seems appropriate, therefore, to indicate explicitly the stance taken. A full-scale treatment is impossible. Moreover, advantage may be taken of the earlier discussions referred to.

The history of the sect is much controverted, with reconstructions ranging from maximalist to minimalist, exhibiting moods that vary from confidence to caution, and in some cases scepticism.[154] D. Dimant, for example, argues that the origin of the sect is quite unclear. All of the accepted assumptions: that the sect began about 170 BC; in connection with the hellenization crisis; and was linked with the Zadokite origin of the Teacher of Righteousness, she finds questionable. Anti-hellenizing polemic is absent from the texts, while some pseudepigrapha antedating them reflect the sect's calendrical ideas. Accordingly, she looks for the roots of the sect, not in Hasidean times, but in a wider trend deriving from third century Palestine.[155] Again, H. Stegemann, in a wide-ranging treatment, finds the Qumran Essene hypothesis beset with difficulties, not least that it cannot do justice to the scale of the Essenes as indicated in the classical sources.[156] Accordingly, he proposes an augmented version of it which sees the *yaḥad* as the amalgamation of a number of groups: Maccabees, Hasideans, pious exiles from Judaea who migrated to Damascus during the upheavals of 170–67 BC, welded together under the leadership of the Teacher of Righteousness, a deposed High Priest, to form the new Israel.[157] Far from being a fringe group, the Essenes were the largest group in Judaism for 200 years. Qumran, founded towards the end of the second century BC, was a study centre for all members.[158] This hypothesis, immense in its scale, is essentially an attempt to answer the question: how is Qumran related to the Essenes?

In their different ways both Dimant's and Stegemann's proposals illustrate the problems inherent in tracing the history of the Qumran sect. The first is the relatively small amount of evidence; and the second is its ambivalence. In the words of F.M. Cross, 'The library found at Qumran contains no document which can be called properly a historical work. Historiography was not an interest of the sect's authors.'[159] This is not to say that history was unimportant to them: on the contrary, it was of the highest importance to them as those charged (as they believed themselves to be) with a decisive role in its climactic phase. But it was the interpretation of the persons and events who had figured significantly in their past which mattered most to them. Their names, offices and actions were well-known among them, having presumably been recounted again and again. It was the understanding of their roles and actions, particularly as concealed within and uncovered from the biblical text, which concerned them most. What to us is obfuscation: the masking of identity behind sobriquets such as 'Teacher of Righteousness', 'Wicked Priest' and so on, to them was clarification. It was the unfolding of the functions of such individuals in salvation history. Given these problems, there is room for caution. Nevertheless, the attempt must be made. The relevant data may be set forth as follows.

First, the classical sources (Philo, Josephus, Pliny), the

evidence of the site and the texts from the caves combine to link in some way the Qumran ruins, the Qumran texts and the Essenes. Second, the Essenes first appear on the stage of history in the time of Jonathan in a passage in which Josephus refers to them – along with the Pharisees and Sadducees – as one of the three main Jewish parties.[160] Josephus' reference gives no indication that these groups were of recent origin, though time of origin is not his concern in that context. His statement is entirely matter-of-fact.

Third, the Qumran texts appear to imply several critical turning-points. One is the separation of the writers 'from the multitude of the people [and from all their impurity] and from being involved with these matters and from participating with [them] in these things'.[161] It was argued above[162] that what is betokened by these words is a two-way split: of the writers from the people at large, and of the writers from the correspondent and his followers to whom the letter is addressed. The occasion of the dispute was the purity of Temple worship. A second point of crisis in the evolution of the sect is recorded in the account at the beginning of column I of the *Damascus Rule*. Like the first-noted, this also had two clearly marked aspects: the divine visitation 390 years after the exile when God caused a root to sprout from Israel and from Aaron (I 6–7); and the coming of the Teacher of Righteousness which brought to an end the twenty-and-more years of groping to find the way (I 9b–11). A third point of crisis described is the ground plan for the creation of the desert community in *Community Rule* VIII 1–15. A fourth point of crisis is the apparent split within the community of the Teacher of Righteousness by the traitors led by the 'Man of Lies' (IQpHab II 1–4, V 6–12a, cf. 4QpPs[a] I 26–7).

Now, leaving aside attempts at precise identification of these forks in the road of the sect, or whether in any given case a single event is described twice over, the question is whether it is possible convincingly to bring together the early existence of the Essenes affirmed by Josephus with the multiple data from the classical accounts, the Qumran site and the texts from the Qumran caves, including the multiple points of new departure attested in the texts. Justice can be done to all the data only within the framework of a movement which was both broadly based but sharply focused; both sufficiently widespread to become identifiable as one of the leading parties in Judaism, but sufficiently shaped to assume the sharp definition assumed in the *Community Rule*; and all of these at an early enough point to cohere with the indications of the palaeographical and archaeological evidence.[163] The data from which the history of the Qumran sect may be reconstructed presents us less with a sequence of events than with situations or sets of circumstances whose connection can only be the subject of educated inference.

We may lay it down as a beginning proposition that a major party such as Josephus depicts the Essenes to have been in the time of Jonathan Maccabaeus could hardly have emerged without prior notice. It would require the previous existence of a mentality and mood which, impacted with the right catalyst, would be likely to precipitate itself in the Essene mode and with Essene interests and values. The *Hasidim* have frequently been identified as of such a mindset on account of their devotion to the law (I Maccabees 2:42) and their backing of whatever political leadership seemed most likely to support a legitimate high priest (I Maccabees 7:12–14).[164] For such reasons, some have seen the *Hasidim* as the progenitors of the Essenes.[165] There is doubtless a degree of truth in this in the sense that some kind of transmutation overtook at least some of the *Hasidim* and within a relatively short space of time the Essenes were a recognized party within Judaism whereas the *Hasidim* had disappeared. The most likely factor to account for this would seem to be apocalyptic. Such evidence as there is would seem to suggest that the apocalyptic note was at the most very muted in Hasidic piety.[166] At Qumran, on the other hand, it was long and strong.[167] It would appear therefore, that an event or events of some magnitude not only quickened the apocalyptic consciousness in the heirs of that tradition, but drew into it those for whom it had been at best a dormant formality, but sprang to life and visibility in the new situation.

If one inquires for a setting for such a happening one need not look further than the turbulent years of 175–150. The heavy-handed incursions of Antiochus Epiphanes were all that were needed to stimulate into action the Maccabees, and after them, the *Hasidim*, 'mighty warriors of Israel, all who offered themselves willingly for the law' (I Maccabees 2:42). But the Maccabean struggles and the developments which ensued could not but trigger further misgiving. Speculation about the eschatological Temple could only stimulate agitation about the present one; and the game of musical chairs with the high priesthood culminating in a high priest from an upstart family which did not belong to the high priestly line at all could only produce bewilderment and hostility. The recognition that things had gone badly wrong was matched only by the paralysed inability to act to effect. In such circumstances withdrawal from a scene that was as offensive as it was incurable seemed to be the only option.

At exactly what point that took place we do not know. All we know – if Josephus is to be trusted – is that, by the time of Jonathan (159–2) the Essenes had become a recognized party within Judaism with an ideological base, for he defines them – along with the Pharisees and Sadducees – in terms of their respective attitudes to fate and freewill (*Ant.* xiii, 5, 9 (171). It is probable that the breach came gradually. If 4QMMT was read correctly above, it would represent an early point at which concern for Temple purity and propriety had prompted the writers to take the serious step of separating themselves from the multitude of the people. But the situation is not beyond repair. By *Damascus Rule* I 7 the separation is behind and is irreversible. The new community has come into being by divine action: '[God] visited them and caused to sprout from Israel and from Aaron a shoot of the planting in order to possess his land' (7–8a). What is clearly implied is a consciousness on the part of the members of the new community that they are the saving remnant, the inheritors of 'the covenant of the very first' (I 4). While this new departure is presented in positive terms as a gracious act of God, its obverse is that those who represented official religion had been rejected. No reasons are specified for this beyond the general consideration of unfaithfulness to the covenant. Presumably, the state of affairs indicated in the *Halakhic Letter* (4QMMT) had not been corrected as hoped for, and the breach became permanent. It would seem that in this act we are to see the founding of the Essene party.[168] The extent of its organization and ideological definition are impossible to determine with precision. But the text notes two features characteristic of that stage: first, they were a penitential movement (I 8b–9a); and second, for all the consciousness of their new role 'they were like blind persons and like those who grope for the path' (*derek*) (I 9).

That state of blindness and confusion was brought to an end by the arrival in their midst of a Teacher of Righteousness whom God 'raised up for them ... in order to direct them in the path of his heart' (I 11). Taken in the context of *Damascus Rule*, column one, the coming of the Teacher stands out clearly as the decisive moment in the sect's formation. It was his instruction which brought them to an understanding both of their enemies and of themselves and their mission (I 11b–21).

How the Teacher of Righteousness is related to the settlement at Qumran is nowhere made clear in the texts. In the *Damascus Rule* he appears as the divinely sent instructor of the 'congregation' (*'ēdah*) as a whole: a role which is confirmed in 4QPsalms Pesher[a] where he is depicted as the Priest whom God chose 'to found the congregation' (*'ēdah*) (III 16). In the *Community Rule* the word 'congregation' (*'ēdah*) appears only twice (IQS V 1, 20), the body in question being referred to rather as the 'community' (*yaḥad*). As noted earlier, the function of the wilderness community is expressed in terms of Temple and priesthood: in effect, to serve as an alternative Temple since the Jerusalem Temple had forfeited its capacity to discharge its functions (IQS VIII 4b–10a). Such a departure could not have taken place without the involvement (not to say leadership) of the Teacher of Righteousness during his lifetime, and it is difficult to imagine so radical an innovation after his death. In the words of F.M. Cross, 'It can be argued that the foundation of the community need not be coeval with the work of the founder of the sect, or with the crucial events which led to its separation from the body of Judaism. However such an argument can stand only with the greatest difficulty. All evidence points to the assumption that the Teacher led his flock into the desert.'[169] *When* it took place cannot be determined with certainty; *why* is somewhat easier, and may in turn shed light on the timing. The sacerdotal functions of the Qumran settlement could only evoke the hostility of the Temple; but then it was the failings of that establishment which almost certainly helped to evoke the creation of the Essene party in the first place. The venom of the warfare between the Priest, the Teacher of Righteousness, and the Wicked Priest, enshrined in the *Habakkuk Commentary*, is plain enough, even if the details of the battles are masked in sectarian camouflage. Likewise, the same document testifies to an internal split between the Teacher of Righteousness on the one hand, and the 'traitors', led by the 'Man of Lies' (*'îsh hakkāzāb*) on the other who came to question and eventually reject the Teacher's understanding of the renewed covenant, as well as his apocalyptic teaching (IQp Hab II 1–10a).

Of such a reconstruction of Qumran sectarian history, tentative and qualified as it necessarily is, it can be said that it coincides, broadly, with the evidence of the typological sciences.[170] As has been seen earlier[171] palaeography dates the *Community Rule* to about 100 BC, while the oldest fragment of the *Damascus Rule* is dated to 75–50 BC. Our examination of the archaeological evidence for the history of occupation of the site[172] pointed to the conclusion that the sect's arrival at Qumran took place sometime during the activity of Jonathan or Simon.[173]

If the foregoing reading of Essene history is valid, it has implications for the reconstruction of their thought. To begin with it implies that not all Essene communities were necessarily identical. Thus F.F. Bruce, who hesitated to equate the Qumran community with the Essenes, concluded, after noting that Josephus and Hippolytus recorded more than one variety of Essenes, 'the Qumran community was one Essene group, diverging in several particulars from other Essene groups'.[174] This, in turn, may explain the range of materials found in the caves, and the evident use made of them. Dimant's classification of the texts noted earlier[175] is entirely justified in seeking to establish the ideas and organization of the settlement at Qumran. But if the sect at Qumran emerged as posited here, it was the inheritor of a large body of writings with a lengthy history behind them, not all of which were equally valued but many if not most of which might be used as contributors to the tradition of which the Qumran Essenes were the custodians. That is to say, in an important sense the contents of the Qumran caves constitute an Essene library[176] and while Qumran Essene works must constitute the baseline for reconstructing Qumran thought, allowance must be made for the use of others where the evidence requires it, even if this has the effect of blurring some of our definitions and distinctions.

Notes

1. Vermes, Geza, *The Dead Sea Scrolls in English*, Harmondsworth, (Middlesex: Penguin Books, Revised and Extended Fourth Edition, 1995), v–vii.
2. Garcia Martinez, Florentino, *The Dead Sea Scrolls Translated*, The Qumran Texts in English,(trans. Wilfred G.E. Watson, Leiden: E.J. Brill, 1994) vi–xvii.
3. Dimant, Devorah, 'The Qumran Manuscripts: Contents and Significance', in Dimant, D. and Schiffman, L.H. (eds.), *Time to Prepare a Way in the Wilderness*, (Leiden: E.J. Brill, 1995), 23–58.
4. Art. cit, 27, including n.10.
5. Loc. cit, n.11 where further examples are given.
6. Loc. cit, n.12, again with further examples.

7. Dimant points to the use of sobriquets such as 'Kittim', 'Teacher of Righteousness', 'Man of Lies'. However she also goes beyond terminology to structure and application of the text to the current situation as being authentic marks of Qumran Pesharim. Art. 'Pesharim Qumran' in Freedman, D.N. *et al: Anchor Bible Dictionary*, Vol. V, (New York: Doubleday), 249.
8. Art. cit, 28.
9. Loc. cit, n.14.
10. Loc. cit, n.15.
11. Art. cit, 29.
12. See the summary table: art. cit 58. The details are set out in tabular form on pp. 37–45.
13. Art. cit, 41, n.45.
14. Art. cit, 33–4. Dimant allows that 11 QT may be a special case, emanating from a circle close to the community (loc. cit).
15. Art. cit, 34–5.
16. Art. cit, 30–2.
17. Art. cit, 32.
18. Art. cit, 33.
19. Loc. cit.
20. Art. cit, 34.
21. Loc. cit.
22. Art. cit, 36.
23. Art. cit, 27, n.12.
24. For a brief, well-documented summary see Schürer E: *The History of the Jewish People in the Age of Jesus Christ*, (Edinburgh: T&T. Clark, 1979), 583–5 (hereafter Schürer- Vermes, *HJP*. rev. ed Vermes-Millar-Black, Vol. II, 1979, 583–5.
25. For the text with translation see the handy volume edited by G. Vermes and Goodman, D. Martin, *The Essenes According to the Classical Sources*, Oxford Centre Textbooks, Volume I, (Sheffield: JSOT Press, 1989), 32–3.
26. Latin, 'infra hos Engada oppidum fuit.' For documentation that *infra* may be taken in this sense see Vermes and Goodman, op. cit, 3, n.19. The fact that Pliny's statement proceeds to speak next of Masada 'inde Masada castellum' which is a further twenty miles down the coast from Engedi tends to confirm this interpretation.
27. See Mazar, B. 'Engedi', in Thomas, D. Winton (ed.) *Archaeology and Old Testament Study*, Oxford, 1967), 223–30.

28. Philo, *Apologia pro Iudaeis*, in Vermes-Goodman, *The Essenes*, 26–31. He paints the same general picture in *Quod omnis probus liber sit*, 75–91 (Vermes-Goodman 20–25), save that he makes no mention of celibacy.
29. *War* 2.124.
30. *War* 2.120–122.
31. *War* 2.160–161.
32. *War* 2.567; 3. 11.
33. *War* 5.145.
34. *Ant.* 15. 371–9.
35. *Life*, 10–11.
36. *Quod omnis probus liber sit*, 76 (hereafter Q.o.p.).
37. *Apologia pro Iudaeis*, 1.
38. Beall, Todd S., *Josephus' Description of the Essenes Illustrated by the Dead Sea Scrolls*, (Cambridge University Press, 1988).
39. Op. cit, 130.
40. An illuminating study in this connection is Smith, Morton, 'The Description of the Essenes in Josephus and the Philosophumena', *HUCA*, 29, 1958, 273–313. The *Philosophumena*, once ascribed to Origen, are now generally credited to Hippolytus of Rome. (For the text see Vermes-Goodman, (n.25) 62–73). Smith shows that the account of the Essenes there, while closely paralleling that of Josephus in *War* 2, 119–166 nonetheless shows significant differences, tending to paint the Essenes in more Christian colours. Showing that the *Philosophumena* usually quotes without alteration; that apart from this passage it shows no knowledge of Josephus: and that the passage is a digression in the narrative of Josephus, replaced with a different, briefer account in *Antiquities*; he concludes that both authors derived it from a common source, probably Gentile.
41. There is nothing to suggest that Pliny's evidence is based on first-hand knowledge. Vermes-Goodman point out that his *Natural History*, which contains his account of the Essenes, is compiled from over 100 principal authors. The account is found in the geographical section of the work where Judaea is described after Egypt and along with other areas of Syria (*The Essenes*, 32f). At the same time it is worth noting that his description of Engedi as 'another ash-heap' (Jerusalem being the first), shows that his information was recent. (Pliny died in AD 79 in the destruction of Pompeii).
42. In the *Philosophumena* (see n.20) Hippolytus writes of the

Essenes, 'They have in the lapse of time undergone divisions, and they do not preserve their system of training after a similar manner, for they have been split up into four parties' (9.26). He then proceeds to describe these in terms used in different contexts in Josephus, though not of Essenes. One of the parties identified by Hippolytus by name is the Zealots or Sicarii. (For the text see Vermes-Goodman, *The Essenes*, 71).

43. The number is put at 'over four thousand' by Philo (*Quod omnis probus liber sit*, 75) and Josephus (*Ant.* 18.20). An elaborate argument for the hypothesis that the Essenes were the main party in Judaism of the late Second Temple has recently been propounded by Stegemann, H., 'The Qumran Essenes Local Members of the Main Jewish Union in Late Second Temple Times', in Barrera, Julio T. and Montaner, Luis V. (eds.) *The Madrid Qumran Congress* Vol. I, Leiden: Brill (1992), 83–165. Stegemann argues that at the time Menelaus became High Priest, there were at least four organized groups of Palestinian Jews: the Temple establishment, the Maccabees, the Hasidaeans and the New Covenanters in Damascus. The Teacher of Righteousness, a Zadokite who became High Priest in 159 BC, tried to unite all four groups, but failed to gain Maccabaean support and was eventually deposed by Jonathan who usurped his place. Even so the union was established throughout Israel, though against Maccabaean opposition (which gave rise to the Sadducees), and hostility from part of the Hasidaeans (who became the Pharisees). The Essenes, by far the largest party, were the followers of the Teacher of Righteousness. Qumran was a study centre for all members of the Essene movement, but not the headquarters of the movement as such. Stegemann argues that each constituent group would bring its own halakhah, officials, members and property into the union, which became the unique representative of God's covenant on earth. If Stegemann is correct the Essenes had an even higher profile in Second Temple Judaism than is indicated in the classical sources.
44. *War* 2.154–5.
45. *War* 2.156–8.
46. Vermes-Goodman: *The Essenes*, 55.
47. Art. cit, (see n.40), 278f.
48. So Goodman translates, in Vermes-Goodman, (n.25), 55. Feldman, in the Loeb edition, renders 'they believe that they

ought to strive especially to draw near to righteousness.' *Josephus*, with an English translation by Feldman, L.H. London: Heinemann, Vol. IX, (1965), 15. In a long footnote (e) he reviews various renderings, tending to favour Strugnell's 'the *approach* to righteousness' (15–16).

49. This interpretation seems to make the best sense of the text. Vermes-Goodman translate, 'They send offerings to the Temple, but perform their sacrifices using different customary purifications. For this reason, they are barred from entering into the common enclosure, but offer sacrifice among themselves.' The first sentence could mean that they offered sacrifices in the Temple in their own way, but this is impossible in view of the plain meaning of the second sentence. The textual variants noted by Vermes-Goodman (54 n.2) which negate the second half of the first sentence to read, 'they offer no sacrifices since the purifications to which they are accustomed are different', are probably best explained as an attempt to remove the ambiguity. See Feldman's note in the Loeb edition, 16–17, where he takes the text in the sense adopted here.
50. Cf. Q. o.p. 75 where he speculates that the name 'Essaeans' may be related to the word 'holiness'; *idem* 91, 'the society known as Essaeans or Saints.' While the latter might be dismissed as a pun (as by Vermes-Goodman: op.cit, 26 n1), the former suggests that Philo believed it was derived from *hosiotes*. There has been much debate over the origin of the term. See the review in Schürer-Vermes: *HJP*, II, 559f. Philo's derivation (and its semitic ancestor) has recently been reaffirmed by F.M. Cross, *ALQ*[3], 54 n.1; 183.
51. Vermes-Goodman's rendering, *The Essenes*, 37. (Greek: *dokei semnotēta askein*). See n.25.
52. Notably his claim that the Essenes will not hate any who injure them, but rather pray for them (23). Vermes-Goodman conclude that Hippolytus viewed the Essenes as deviant Jews (op. cit, 62). Morton Smith, more specifically (and more plausibly) argued that Hippolytus or his (Christian) source regarded them as prototypes of Christianity. (Art. cit, *HUCA* 29, 1958, 274).
53. Vermes-Goodman's rendering, *The Essenes*, 21.
54. See n.49.
55. Vermes-Goodman, *The Essenes*, 55.
56. It would be possible to reconcile completely the statements

of Philo and Josephus on Essene sacrificial practice if the words of the latter, 'they offer sacrifice among themselves', could be interpreted in parallel with the second half of Philo's statement, "they judge it more fit to render their minds truly holy." In that case Essene sacrifice would be purely spiritual. This has in fact been suggested by J.M. Baumgarten, 'Sacrifice and Worship among the Jewish Sectarians of the Dead Sea (Qumran) Scrolls', *HTR*, 46, 1953, 155. It might be objected to as using the term 'sacrifice' (*thusia*) with different meanings in the same context. Feldman rejects it as being unexampled. (*Antiquities* 18. 19, Loeb ed., vol. 9, p. 16 n.a.). Again then, it comes down to the evidence of the Qumran texts.

57. *Ant.* 13 172 (Vermes-Goodman's translation: *The Essenes*, 51, see n.25).
58. *Ant.* 18. 1. (Vermes-Goodman's translation, 55).
59. *Ant.* 18. 18 (Vermes-Goodman, 55).
60. *Philosophumena*, 27, as in Vermes-Goodman, *The Essenes*, 73.
61. See n.40 above.
62. Beall, Todd S., *Josephus' Description of the Essenes Illustrated by the Dead Sea Scrolls*, 150.
63. *War* 3. 374, as in *Josephus* in Loeb ed., vol. II.
64. Feldman, L.H., *Josephus* (Loeb ed. vol. IX), p. 13, n.c.
65. Andre Paul has recently sought to provide a life-setting for this in the Rome in which Josephus wrote at the end of the first century, arguing that Josephus is not only trying to commend his own people, but to distinguish them from the Christians. See his essay 'Flavius Josèphe et Les Esséniens', in Dimant-Rappaport (eds.) *The Dead Sea Scrolls: Forty Years of Research*, 126–37.
66. See item 2 above.
67. Q.o.p. 82 (as in Vermes-Goodman, 23, see note 25). F.M. Cross translates 'by means of symbols' (*dia symbolōn*) 'typologically' (*ALQ*[3], 80 n.5.)
68. Ibid.
69. *War* 2. 159 (as in Vermes-Goodman, 47).
70. Cf. *Philosophumena* 22: 'They evince the utmost curiosity concerning plants and stones, rather busying themselves as regards the operative powers of these, saying that these things were not created in vain' (as in Vermes-Goodman, 67).
71. *Philosophumena* 27 (as in Vermes-Goodman, 73).
72. *Ant.* 13. 171 (as in Vermes-Goodman, 51).

73. The view of its original and essential unity as maintained by Carmignac and P. Guilbert, (Paris: Letouzey et Ané, (1961), and in his article, 'Le Plan de la Règle de la Communauté', *RQ*, 1, 1959, 323–44, while finely nuanced, quickly gave way before a developmental view which saw the work as evolving by successive additions to a primitive core. The fundamental expression of this view is O'Connor, J. Murphy, article 'La genèse littéraire de la *Règle de la Communauté*', *RB*, 4, 1969, 528–49. Pouilly, Jean, 'La Règlè de la Communauté de Qumran, Son Évolution Littérairè' *Cahiers de la Revue Biblique*, (Paris: J. Gabalda, 1976), builds on O'Connor's foundation, elaborating it. For a review covering more recent work see Gagnon, R.A.J., 'How did the Rule of the Community obtain its final shape? A review of scholarly research', *JSPseud.* 10, 1992, 61–72; and for a more recent suggestion see Alexander, Philip S., 'The Redaction-History of Serek Ha-Yahad: a Proposal', *RQ* 17, 65–8, December 1996, 437–56.
74. VIII 12c 'When these have been established in the foundation of the Community' is fashioned on the same grammatical pattern as the three examples noted above (preposition 'b' plus the infinitive construct), and its import is the same. Interestingly, it introduces a legal passage.
75. Knibb, Michael A., *The Qumran Community, Cambridge Commentaries on Writings of the Jewish and Christian World 200 BC to AD 200*, Vol. 2 (Cambridge, 1987), 130.
76. A hermeneutical problem throughout the Qumran texts is that of determining the level of meaning to be placed on their language. A controlling term in IQS VIII 1–16a is 'desert' (13–14), quoted from Isaiah 40:3. Is it to be taken metaphorically only, or literally as well? The question has been examined closely by George J. Brooke, 'Isaiah 40:3 and the Wilderness Community', in Brooke, G.J. with Garcia Martinez, F.G. (eds.), *New Qumran Texts and Studies*, (Leiden: Brill, 1994), 117–32. Brooke concludes that IQS is best taken both literally and metaphorically (132).
77. Cf. Pouilly, J. who labels IQS VIII 1–10a, 12b–16a and IX 3 X 8a, 'Le Manifeste de Fondation' (op. cit 15). This conclusion may find support from the fact that a copy of the *Community Rule* from Cave 4 ($4QS^{e}$) lacks VIII 15–IX 11. See Metso, S., 'The Primary Results of the Reconstruction of $4QS^{e}$', *JJS* 44, 1993, 303–8.

78. The relationship between the pre-desert community and the group which established and constituted the desert community is not wholly clear. Setting aside the view that the 'council of the community' is a governing body within the sect: a use of the expression without parallel since elsewhere it refers to the sect as a whole (IQS III 2; V 7; VI 12–15), the main question is whether the community which departs for the desert is co-extensive without remainder with the group from which it evolved. A.R.C. Leaney, reading VIII 10b–12a as an integral and original part of the text, holds that they were not arguing in effect for a double separation: (a) in admission to the community following two years of perfect behaviour (VIII 10c–11a) thereby laying the foundation of the community; and (b) the departure for the desert (VIII 12b–13). He concludes, 'The community or movement therefore out of which it arose must have been represented by groups dispersed throughout the land such as we know to have existed.' Leaney, A.R.C., *The Rule of Qumran and Its Meaning* (London: SCM Press, 1966), 210–11. Leaney may well be right, though if lines 10b–12a mark a later stage in the composition of the text as many suspect (e.g. Knibb, op. cit, 133), then his case must rest on general inference plus evidence outside this passage. It is possible to read VIII 1–16a as though a single community, formed in a single action, is in mind.
79. The translation is that of Garcia Martinez, F. *The Dead Sea Scrolls Translated* (henceforth *DSST*), The Qumran Texts in English (Watson, Wilfred G.E., translator, Leiden: Brill, 1994), 12. (The slash marks denote text inserted between the lines by the copyist.)
80. The same expression occurs in the parallel passage in $4QS^d$ frag.2 line 3.
81. The words quoted are written above the line in one of the most disturbed parts of the text of IQS. See Plate VIII in Millar Burrows, *et al., The Dead Sea Scrolls of St Mark's Monastery, Vol.* II, *Fascicle 2: The Plates and Transcription of the Manual of Discipline,* New Haven: The American Schools of Oriental Research (1951). A full technical discussion can be found in James H. Charlesworth, et al. (eds.), *The Dead Sea Scrolls,* Hebrew, Aramaic and Greek Texts with English Translations, Vol. I, *Rule of the Community and Related Documents,* (Tübingen-Louisville: J.C.B. Mohr (Paul Siebeck),

Westminster John Knox Press, 1994), 34–5. Like most editors, Charlesworth places the supralinear words at the point in the text assumed above.

82. The term is used three times in VIII 1–16a: members of the community are to be 'perfect (*tēmîmîm*) in everything that has been revealed about all the law' (lines 1–2); the community will be 'a house of perfection (*bêt tāmîm*) and truth in Israel' (line 9), and they will be admitted to the community only after 'two full years in perfect behaviour' (*bitmîm derek*) (line 10).
83. It makes no difference at this point whether the Interpreter (*hadôrēš*) be regarded as a single historical individual or an official (hence spelled with a capital) or simply as a function, 'he who studies'.
84. Charlesworth renders 'time' as 'the Endtime', citing IQS IX 14, 18. In the former, Garcia Martinez renders 'period' in both occurrences.
85. It is possible both to reinforce this list and add to it if the remainder of column VIII and column IX be admitted to consideration. Pouilly, for example, includes IX 3–X 8a in his 'foundation manifesto', (*La Règle de la Communauté*, 15). If there are few grounds for including XI–8a, the case is rather different with VIII 16b–IX 2b. É. Puech, in a penetrating review of Pouilly's work (*RQ*, 10, 1979, 103–11) argues that regulations are not necessarily later than constitutional principles, and that there is therefore no reason for maintaining that the former post-date the latter. This is doubtless true. The problem is that the regulations are not always consistent. E.g. VIII 16^{b}–19 penalizes wilful sin with exclusion until repentance, while VIII 20–6 penalizes it with permanent exclusion. This lack of consonance is reinforced by the state of the manuscript in which lines 16b–19 are set apart as a separate paragraph while lines 20–26 are introduced by a new heading. It is very difficult to maintain that VIII 16^{b}–IX 26 is a unity. However, it does not necessarily follow from this that this section is therefore significantly later than VIII 1–16a. IX 12–26, for example, seems to be written from the same perspective as VIII 1–16a: namely from the midst of the 'men of sin' (16; cf. VIII 13), and at the point of departure for the desert (IX 19b–20); while the same seems to be the case with IX 3–11 (see lines 5–6). If then IX 3–26 comes from essentially the same time-frame as VIII 1–16a, not only are

some theological emphases found in the latter reinforced: e.g. holiness (6–8a), the revelation of the times (12–14a) and other mysteries (18), and conformity to God's law (22b–25); but others mentioned are filled out, and some not mentioned at all become visible. Thus the atoning function of the community as a Temple is defined specifically as being 'without the flesh of burnt offerings and without the fats of sacrifice – the offering of lips in compliance with the decree will be like the pleasant aroma of justice and the correctness of behaviour will be acceptable like a freewill offering' (4–5). Not present at all in VIII 1–16a is the note that the law practised by the sect will remain in force 'until the prophet comes, and the Messiahs of Aaron and Israel' (11). A heavy emphasis upon predestination emerges in the job-description of the Instructor (*Maskil*), specifically in regard to his responsibility to measure or weigh the sons of Zadok (14–16a). Most of these, with the possible exception of the last, are additional details which fit readily into the major themes found in VIII 1–16a. This does not mean they are unimportant.

86. See Ch. 1, n.25.
87. See Ch. 1, n.26. For a description of and introduction to the Cave 4 fragments see Baumgarten, Joseph M., with Davis, Michael T., 'Cave IV, V, VI Fragments' in Charlesworth (ed.), *DSS*, Vol. 2, 59–63.
88. Thus the oldest fragment of the Damascus Rule from Qumran (4Q267) contains material from both the hortatory and legal sections of the Genizah text. This suggests that they always belonged together, as is, indeed, the case with the covenant genre generally. Cf. Baltzer, Klaus, *The Covenant Formulary*, (Philadelphia: Fortress Press, 1971), 112–22.
89. See Ch. 1, n.30. This applies not only to the Cave 4 fragments but also to theories based on critical analysis of the Genizah text itself. See O'Connor, J. Murphy, 'La Genèse littéraire de Règle de la Communauté', *RB*, 76, 1969, 528–49; 'An Essene Missionary Document? CD II, 14–VI, 1,', *RB*, 77, 1970, 201–29; 'A Literary Analysis of Damascus Document VI 2–VIII, 3', *RB*, 78, 1971, 210–32; 'The Critique of the Princes of Judah (CD VIII, 3–19)', *RB*, 1972, 200–16; 'A Literary Analysis of Damascus Document XIX, 33–XX 34', *RB*, 1972, 544–64; 'The Original Text of CD 7:9–8:2 19:5–14' *HTR*, 64, 1971, 379–86; 'The Essenes and Their History', *RB*, 81, 1974,

215–44; *The Damascus Document* Revisited', *RB*, 92, 1985, 223–46. Sidnie Ann White, has argued powerfully that any discrepancies between CD 'A' and 'B' can be explained on the basis of scribal error and activity. 'A Comparison of "A" and "B" Manuscripts of the Damascus Document', *RQ*, 48, Read 12, 4, November 1987, 537–53.

90. The differences between CD and IQS have already been treated in Ch .1 pp. 20–6, including notes 43–50. Baumgarten and Schwartz affirm, 'CD is definitely a Qumran text. Nevertheless, it is not quite clear that CD is a document of the Qumran Community *sensu stricto*' (in Charlesworth, *DSS*, 2, 6). But having set out the divergences in organization and doctrine between the communities described in the two texts they conclude, 'Nevertheless, it seems wiser to consider CD a product of the same general movement, but to bear in mind that its laws take account of a sectarian framework which, in comparison to that of the *Rule of the Community*, was less completely separated from the outside world and its norms' (op. cit, 7). To similar effect see John J. Collins, who concludes that CD is a representative document of the New Covenant, is early, pertains to the same sect as IQS and belongs to the same period. Art. 'Was the Dead Sea Sect an Apocalyptic Movement?' in L.H. Schiffman, (ed) *Archaeology and History in the Dead Sea Scrolls*, (Sheffield: *JSOT/ASOR* Monographs, 2, 1990), 40.
91. See Chapter 1, p. 21.
92. The integrity of I 1–12 has been questioned on the ground that the numbers destroy the rhythmic structure of the lines. Knibb points out that even if this were so, the theological thrust of the argument remains unaffected (*Qumran Community*, 20).
93. For a full statement of the argument see Dupont-Sommer, A., *The Essene Writings from Qumran*, Vermes, G. (ed.), (Gloucester, Mass: Smith, Peter, 1973), 121, n.2; Knibb, M.A., *The Qumran Community*, 19f.
94. The critical and determinative influence of the interpreter of the law is underlined by the double word-play which is quite well reproduced by the English word 'staff'. CD VI 3b–4a quotes Numbers 21:18, 'A well which the princes dug, which the nobles of the people delved with the staff' (*měḥôqēq*). Line 7 goes on to say that 'the staff is the interpreter of the law'. In line 9 however the princes are said to have dug the well with 'the staves (*měḥôqqôt*) which the

sceptre (*hammĕḥôqēq*) decreed (*ḥâqāq*)', 'staff' being used as a symbol of ruling authority. Both images are applied to the interpreter of the law, showing that not only does he expound the law, but his interpretations are binding. What is conveyed by wordplay is stated unambiguously in line 10 which enjoins walking in all the interpreter's regulations throughout the whole age of wickedness.

95. Knibb, M.A., argues that I 13–II 1 is not a unity, but that the real sequel to I 12 is I 18b–II 1 which applies to Israel as a whole. I 13–18a applies to a rival group which had split from that of the Teacher, and the effect of its insertion is to make the whole of I 13–II 1 apply to the rival group. Rough as its connection may be, its positioning has the effect of branding the rivals as part of a treacherous and therefore rejected Israel. In any case, it makes the important point that the Teacher of Righteousness suffered a split among his followers, which made a deep mark in the tradition.
96. For proposed reconstructions (which favour different options) see Collins, John J., 'The Origin of the Qumran Community: a Review of the Evidence', in Horgan, Maurya P., *To Touch the Text, Biblical and Related Studies in Honour of Joseph A. Fitzmyer*, (New York: Crossroad, 1989), 159–78; and Davies, Philip R., 'The Prehistory of the Qumran Community' in Dimant and Rappaport, *Forty Years*, 117–25.
97. A text incorporating the laws from the Cave 4 manuscripts may be found in Wise Michael, Abegg Jr., Martin, and Cook, Edward, *The Dead Sea Scrolls, A New Translation*, (San Francisco: Harper, 1996), 61–74. For an examination of some of the regulations in the light of the 4Q texts see Baumgarten, J.M., 'The Cave 4 Versions of the Qumran Penal Code', *JJS*, 43, 1992, 268–76. Of their implications for CD, Baumgarten writes, 'Rather than an historical admonition to which some laws were randomly appended, CD is now seen as primarily an anthology of Torah interpretation and sectarian rulings' (273).
98. Some form of the expression 'to enter the covenant' referring either to the Mosaic covenant as the antitype of the sectarian covenant or the sectarian covenant itself occurs 15 times in CD.
99. *Les Textes de Qumran, Traduits et Annotés, II*, by Carmignac, J., Cothenet, E., and Lignée, H., (Paris: Letouzey et Ané, 1963); 'Le Document de Damas', by Cothenet, E., 137f.
100. Talmon, Shemaryahu, 'The Identity of the Community', in

Ulrich, Eugene and VanderKam, James (eds.), *The Community of the Renewed Covenant* (Notre Dame, Indiana: University of Notre Dame Press, 1994), 12.

101. The meaning of 'the land of Damascus' has been much debated. It occurs only in the *Damascus Rule* and only in the Admonition section (VI 5, 19; VII 15, 19; VIII 21; XIX 34; XX 12). Its association with escape from the sword when the Northern Kingdom fell (CD VII 9–18a) has given rise to three main interpretations. (1) It has been taken to denote a literal exodus to Damascus where the new covenant was established and whence the community returned to Judah. For a recent elaboration of this view see Stegemann, H., 'The Qumran Essenes – Local Members of the Main Jewish Union in Late Second Temple Times' in Trebolle Barrera, Vegas Montaner (eds.), *Madrid Qumran Congress*, Vol. I, 146f, 153–9. (2) It has been taken as a symbolic reference to Qumran – the sect's place of exile. See the long note in F.M. Cross, *ALQ*^{3}, 71 n.5. (3) It has been taken as a symbol for Babylonia where the Essene movement is claimed to have arisen at some point during the exile, and subsequently returned to Palestine. This position was first developed by O'Connor, J. Murphy, in a series of articles whose results are summarized in 'The Essenes and their History', *RB*, 81, 1974, 215–44, esp. 221. The first and third views are open to the objection that the earliest specific mention of the Essenes – that of Josephus – places them in Palestine in the time of the Maccabees. The problem with the second view is that it is hard to reconcile with statements which place the land of Damascus outside of Judah (CD VI 5), which Qumran assuredly was not. There seems to be a clearly symbolic element in the description of the community members as *šābê yîšrâel* (CD IV 1, VI 5): 'converts', 'penitents' of Israel; if so, there may well be a symbolic element in the following clauses, 'who left the land of Judah and lived in the land of Damascus'. In that case it will denote their separation from the religious establishment of Jerusalem as well as their fellow Jews, and their gathering of themselves into self-sustaining, separate communities, whether at Qumran or in the other settlements throughout Judaea. In short, living in the land of Damascus is a symbolic name for becoming a member of the sect of the new covenant: a kind of 'internal exile'. A useful discussion of

the relevant passages is Knibb, Michael A, 'Exile in the Damascus Document', *JSOT*, 25, 1983, 99–117.

102. The idea of 'walking in perfection' is probably to be found in 4QDa frg. 1.6, though the text is defective. It is certainly present in CD II 15f.
103. The ambiguity in I 11b–12, 'And he made known to the last generations what he had done for the last generation, the congregation of traitors', has been variously resolved. Knibb regards 'the last generation' as a gloss designed to identify 'the congregation of traitors' with the generation of the writer (*Qumran Community*, 22). Baumgarten and Schwarz take the verb, *'āśa* as a prophetic perfect, to give the meaning, 'And God informed the latter generations that which he will do in the last generation among the congregation of traitors' (Charlesworth: *DSS*, Vol. 2, p. 13 with n.8.). Either way the import of the text is the same: the present generation is the last.
104. Quoting approvingly the opinion of D. Dimant that the idea that Belial is loosed against Israel for a period overlapping the sect's existence is 'the very heart of sectarian thought,' Collins, John J., suggests that the *Damascus Rule* probably presupposes more of Qumran dualism than it shows. Art. 'Was the Dead Sea Sect an Apocalyptic Movement?' in Schiffman, *Archaeology and History*, 43. Other uses of Belial in the *Damascus Rule* are found at V 18, VIII 2, XII 2, and XIX 14.
105. It frequently stands in construct relationship with *qēz* to give 'time of visitation' as in CD VII 21b.
106. 'Those who remove the boundary' (*gĕbûl*) seems to have been a favoured description of their opponents among the sectarians. The origin of the image is biblical (Deuteronomy 19: 14). It occurs at 4QDb frg. 1.4; CD V 20; XIX 15b–16a, XX 25.
107. Wise-Abegg-Cook render: '[… for it is not permitted] to celebrate the holidays too early or too late.' *DSS, New Translation*, 51.
108. This same distinction underlies the fragmented statement 'those who examine his precepts and [walk on the perfect] path and [… exami] ne hidden things and open their ears and [hear profound things] and understand everything that happens when it comes upon them' (4QDa frg. 1. 6–8).

109. The echo of wisdom terminology is worth noting and keeping in mind.
110. *Qumran Cave 4. V*, Miqṣat Ma' aśe Ha-Tôrah (*DJD* X), by Qimron, Elisha, and Strugnell, John, (Oxford: The Clarendon Press, 1994).
111. Op. cit, 1.
112. Op. cit, 109.
113. Eisenman, R.H. and Wise, Michael, in their edition of the text, treat 4Q394–8 as the first letter, and 4Q397 (sic) – 9 as a second letter, on the basis of internal evidence, *DSSU* 180–200, especially 196, and 220 n.35.
114. *DJD* X, 44–63. So also Garcia Martinez, *DSST* 77–9.
115. Strugnell, John, 'MMT: Second Thoughts on a Forthcoming Edition', in Ulrich and VanderKam, *Community of the Renewed Covenant*, 57.
116. Op. cit, 62. The reasons Strugnell gives for his change of mind are that whereas the legal and hortatory parts are addressed by one group to another and have a polemical overtone, the calendrical section is a mere list; and that 4Q395, which gives the start of Section B, has no sign of Section A although there is enough blank manuscript to have accommodated at least some of it (op. cit, 61).
117. Schiffman, L.H., 'The Place of 4QMMT in the Corpus of Qumran Manuscripts', in Kampen, John and Bernstein, Moshe J., (eds.) *Reading 4QMMT, New Perspectives on Qumran Law and History*, SBL Symposium Series, Number 2, (Atlanta, Georgia: Scholars Press, 1996), 81–98, esp. 83–5. Wise-Abegg-Cook translate the calendar separately from 4QMMT (*DSS New Translation*, 359 with footnote). Eisenman and Wise who prefix it to 4Q394–8 (which they label, 'The First Letter on Works Reckoned as Righteousness'), concede that it is their perception only that it is an integral part of the First Letter (*DSSU*, 182–96, 220).
118. *DJD* X, 113–4. The proposal that MMT may be regarded as a treatise is withdrawn by Strugnell in Appendix 3 of the volume (204).
119. Strugnell in Ulrich-VanderKam, *CRC*, 63, as well as in *DJD*, X, 204.
120. *DJD*, X, 205 = Ulrich-VanderKam, *CRC*, 63.
121. Section C, lines 7–8 (*DJD*, X, 59).
122. Section C, lines 26b–30 (*DJD*, X, 63).
123. *DJD*, X, 204.

124. For the text see Section B, lines 9–13a. For discussion see *DJD* X, 150–2.
125. For full discussion see *DJD* X, 142–7.
126. At least four reconstructions have been proposed. (1) The word 'We' is taken to be the Qumran sectaries (at some stage of their existence) over against 'you' (sing. and plur.) regarded as the Hasmonean King and the Jerusalem establishment whom the sectaries are urging to reinstate the more rigid reading of the law, relaxation of which has caused their secession. 'They' are the Pharisees: proponents *par excellence* of laxity. So Qimron and Strugnell, *DJD*, X, 117–21, 175; Schiffman, L.H. *Reclaiming*, 83–95. (2) 'We' is the Qumran sectaries who separated over the Hellenized High Priesthood rather than Pharisaism; 'you' is Jonathan, then supported by the Pharisees; and the word 'they' is the people who followed the Hellenized priests of Jerusalem. Jonathan is being urged to use his influence against them. The letter must therefore have been written at an early point in his leadership, before he became High Priest and identified himself decisively with the Pharisaic side. So Hanan Eshel, '4QMMT and the History of the Hasmonean Period' in *Reading 4QMMT*, 59–65. (3) 'We' is the Qumran party; 'you' is the Pharisees and the early Hasmonean ruler whom they supported; 'they' is the Sadducees. MMT is thus written to the Pharisees to persuade them that, though the writers are of the priestly camp, they have separated themselves from bad priests and therefore deserve Pharisaic support in revising the laws of Temple and priesthood in alignment with the views of Qumran. So Schwartz, David R., 'MMT; Josephus and the Pharisees', in *Reading 4QMMT*, 77–80. (4) 'We' = the Qumran sect; 'you' = the Qumran congregation (reading *hā'ēdah* for *hā'ā [m]* in Section C, line 7); and 'they' = the Pharisees. The separation is thus an attempt to heal an internal split in the Qumran sect. So Abegg, Martin, 'Paul, Works of the Law and MMT' in *BAR* 20, 6, November-December, 1994, 52–5. All four interpretations depend upon historical assumptions either that Pharisees, Sadducees and Essenes were the same at the earliest time they appear as when they appear in later times; or that they differ greatly at different stages; or that they change sides for political reasons. There is some evidence supporting all of these, at least in part. The problem lies in

determining which factor or combination of factors was operative at any given stage. As if that were not confusion enough, Y. Sussmann has pointed out that it was possible to oppose Sadducean social and political pretensions, while supporting their halakhic views (against the Pharisees) at the same time. Yet to the Pharisees, support of the Sadducean halakhah made one a Sadducee (*DJD* X, 194). These factors have been fruitful of endless confusion in interpreting the import and significance of MMT.

127. *DSSU*, 197.
128. *DSSU*, 197f.
129. Eisenman and Wise affirm that the text is 'clearly eschatological' on the basis of such phrases as 'the End of Days' (Section C lines 12 and 14) and 'End Time' (lines 16 and 30) (*DSSU*, 196f.) Garcia Martinez, has examined these examples and concluded, with greater probability, that although the expression (*'aḥărîth hayāmîm*) could represent 'the first stage of an idea which in its more developed form is characteristic of the ideology of the Qumran group, much as the incipient dualism of MMT C 29 could be viewed as a predecessor to the radical dualism we know from other Qumranic writings, the concrete meaning of the expression in MMT favours a pre-Qumranic setting for this composition over the more fully-developed sectarian context' (*Reading 4QMMT*, 22f). For a study of the use of the expression in the Qumran texts as a whole see Steudel, A., *'aḥărîth hayāmîm* in the texts from Qumran', *RQ*, 16, 62, (1993), 225–46.
130. *DJD*, X, 121.
131. Qimron and Strugnell point out that if, in 4QpPs[a] IV 8 'the precepts and the law' refer to MMT then the authorship of the Teacher of Righteousness follows irresistibly (*DJD* X, 120). However, they indicate later that they hesitate to commit themselves to that view. 'Our initial description of MMT, as a letter from the Teacher of Righteousness to the Wicked Priest, pleasantly startling though it was, is probably to be modified' (op. cit, 121). Eshel, Hanan holds that 'the Law and the Torah' of the 4QpPs[a] passage do indeed refer to 4QMMT, and that the author and readers of the former assumed that MMT was written by the Teacher of Righteousness (*Reading 4QMMT*, 55).
132. As follows readily from CD I 8b–11.

133. Schiffmann, L.H., characterizes MMT as 'a document giving legal reasons for the foundation of the sect' (*Reading 4QMMT*, 84f). To the same effect Qimron and Strugnell, *DJD*, X, 121.
134. Since there is only one ruling concerned with the priesthood, it might well be questioned whether this is as significant an issue in Section B as is here implied. Qimron takes up the question, arguing that the manuscript evidence suggests that other rulings dealing with the same matter followed B 82. (*DJD*, X, 131, n.10).
135. Qimron notes that in later texts, the phrase *bîn bĕsēper*, which he translates 'study (carefully) in the book' is regularly associated with the study of the written word. (*DJD*, X, 89).
136. Op. cit, 133.
137. It is drawn from its use in C27. (*DJD*, X, 1).
138. Garcia Martinez rejects the rendering 'precepts' as being inconsistent with the meaning of the more than 130 examples found elsewhere in the Qumran Texts where its accepted meaning is 'works' or 'deeds' (*Reading 4QMMT*, 23–6). Eisenman and Wise reach the same conclusion (*DSSU*, 182), as does Martin Abegg, 'Paul, Works of the Law, and MMT', *BAR*, November-December, 1994, 52–5.
139. M. Abegg argues that MMT depends for its conclusion that *doing* the works of the law is the basis of being accounted righteous on Psalm 106:30–1, where the action of Phinehas in transfixing an Israelite and a foreign woman caught in intercourse evokes the approving comment 'Then Phinehas stood up and interposed … and it was reckoned to him as righteousness.' See the details of his argument, art. cit, 55. Eisenman and Wise likewise link 4QMMT C 31 with Psalm 106:31.
140. M. Abegg states that the phrase 'works of the law' 'appears *nowhere* in rabbinic literature of the first and second centuries AD – *only* in Paul and in MMT' (art. cit, 53).
141. See the comments of Y. Sussmann on the distinctiveness of this stance (*DJD*, X, 191).
142. *Pesharim* is the name given to the biblical commentaries found in the Qumran caves, on account of the use of the word *peser*, 'interpretation', which they commonly use to introduce an interpretation of a biblical passage.

143. A useful review of discussion up to that point, together with some fresh proposals is Brooke, George J., 'Qumran Pesher: Towards the Redefinition of a Genre', *RQ*, 10, 1981, 483–503.
144. See D. Dimant, art. 'Pesharim, Qumran', in D.N. Freedman *et al.* (edd.) *Anchor Bible Dictionary*, New York: Doubleday, (1992), V, 244–5, especially 245–8. In addition to continuous and thematic *peshar*, Dimant also distinguishes 'isolated *pesharim*' (contained *within* other works not themselves *pesharim*), and 'other forms' (use of sobriquets, word-play, etc.).
145. Cf. Brooke who concludes that *pesher* is simply a sub-genre of Jewish midrash: 'an example of early Jewish midrash because of their structure and method' (art. cit, 503). He therefore suggests that the Qumran commentaries would be more appropriately labelled 'Qumran Midrashim'. For a lucid account of midrash (including its presence at Qumran) see Bloch, Renee, art. 'Midrash' in W.S. Green (ed), *Approaches to Ancient Judaism*, BJS 1, (Missoula, Montana: Scholars Press, 1978), 29–49.
146. Cf. D. Dimant, 'Qumran Sectarian Literature', in M.E. Stone (ed), *Jewish Writings of the Second Temple Period*, (CRINT, Section Two, *The Literature of the Jewish People in the Period of the Second Temple*, Vol. II, (Assen/Philadelphia: Van Gorcum/Fortress Press, 1984), 507f. To the same effect Renee Bloch, art. cit, 45f.
147. In fact, the noun is definite. It was argued by H. Stegemann that *hakôhēn* used absolutely denoted the High Priest (*Die Enstehung der Qumrangemeinde*, Bonn, 1971, 102, n.328), but the evidence cited by Collins, John J., against this claim is decisive ('The Origin of the Qumran Community', in Horgan and Kobelski, *To Touch the Text*, 166f).
148. The text is fragmented. The options are discussed by Horgan, Maurya P., *'Pesharim': Qumran Interpretations of Biblical Books, CBQ Monograph Series, Vol. 8*, (Washington DC: Catholic Biblical Association of America, 1979), 219f. The sense is not greatly affected whichever option be followed. The translation in the *editio princeps* reads: 'Its interpretation concerns the Priest, the Teacher of [*Righteousness* whom God *(com)manded* to arise and (*whom*) he established to build for him a congregation (... and) his (wa)ys he directed towards *his* truth.'] Allegro, John M., *Qumran Cave*

4, I (4Q 158–4Q 186), *DJD*, V, (Oxford: Clarendon Press, 1968), 47.

149. It is noteworthy that IQpHab and 4QpPs[a] in which the Teacher of Righteousness is mentioned with comparative frequency there are occurrences of the root *ṣādaq* in the text which presumably could have been interpreted with reference to him without much effort, yet this does not happen. Among these are IQpHab VII 17 and 4QpPs[a] II 13, 22, III 9, all of which are referred to the community. This suggests that there were controls at work in the form of historical tradition even in a type of exegesis as open to free invention as *pesher*.

150. The expression *gĕmar haqeṣ*, 'when time would come to an end' (Verṃes); 'the fulfilment of the end-time' (Horgan) 'the fulness of that time' (Brownlee); 'the end of the age' (Garcia Martinez). That the moment when the end will come is part of the idea seems clear from VII 7, but that it comprises more than this seems equally clear from the same context, 'the final age will be extended and go beyond all that the prophets say, because the mysteries of God are wonderful' (7–8) (Garcia Matinez). For discussion see W.H. Brownlee, *The Midrash Pesher of Habakkuk* (Missoula: Scholars Press, 1979), 110.

151. If the 'interpreter of knowledge' (*mēlîs dā'at*, 4QpPs[a] I 27) is the Teacher of Righteousness as seems to be the case, then this description of him in explicit contrast with 'the Man of Lies who misled many with deceptive words' (26) would suggest that the interpretation of Scripture lay at the heart of the dispute. Knibb, M.A., comments, 'From this passage it seems clear that the dispute with "the liar" centred on doctrinal matters, particularly the proper interpretation of Scripture' (*The Qumran Community*, 249).

152. That calendrical differences were part of this seems to be implied by IQpHab XI 4–8a.

153. IQpHab II 1–10 constitutes a series of parallelisms characterizing treachery (I 16). Rejection of the inspired doctrine of the Teacher serves as a kind of inclusion (II 1–3a, 7–10) to which rejection of the new covenant (II 3–4) and rejection of the Teacher's view of the end of days (II 5–6a) are explanatory parallels. This is not to imply that only one group of individuals is envisaged in the passage. William H. Brownlee is correct in discerning three: those who had

never followed the Teacher of Righteousness; those who had followed but subsequently defected; and the contemporaries of the writer who rejected the belief that they were the last generation, op. cit., 54–6. The point is that treachery comprehends all three of the forms mentioned.

154. A good analytical review of research into the prehistory of the sect is Davies, Philip R., 'The Prehistory of the Qumran Community' in Dimant-Rappaport, *Forty Years*, 116–25. (Davies' article also illustrates the acid, not to say sceptical, character referred to: at least in some areas.)
155. Devorah Dimant, 'Qumran Sectarian Literature' in M.E. Stone (ed.), *Jewish Writings of the Second Temple Period, CRINT, Section Two, The Literature of the Jewish People in the Period of the Second Temple*, Volume II, 544–7. She concludes, 'The problem of the origins of the sectarian doctrines should be separated from the question of the historical and political circumstances which led to the actual creation of the sect' (547).
156. H. Stegemann, 'The Qumran Essenes – Local Members of the Main Jewish Union in Late Second Temple Times', in Barrera, Julio Trebolle, and Montaner, Luis Vegas (eds.), *The Madrid Congress*, Volume I, (Leiden: Brill, 1992), 89–91.
157. Art. cit, 88–91.
158. Art. cit, 138–61.
159. *ALQ*[3], 88.
160. *Antiquities*, xiii 5, 9 (171).
161. 4QMMT C 7b–8a (*DJD*, X, 59).
162. p. 97.
163. On these see Chapter 1, pp. 26–49.
164. This seems to underlie their shifting attitude towards the Maccabees whom they supported at first in their resistance to Syrian attacks on the Temple and its worship, but later distanced themselves from, supporting Alcimus (whom the Maccabees despised: I Maccabees 7:9) as high-priest – albeit to their cost (I Maccabees 7:13–18).
165. It has, indeed, been argued that the names *Hasidim* and Essene are ultimately Hebrew and Greek forms of the same original Greek word meaning 'pious or holy ones'. See Black , Matthew, *The Scrolls and Christian Origins*, Chicago: Scholars Press, (1983), 13–15. Black proceeds to say, 'The immediate ancestors of the Essenes were the Hasidim; and

it is from the period of the Hasidim the Qumran scrolls begin to date' (17).

166. M. Hengel sees the *Hasidim* as the source of the earliest apocalypses, but he makes the point very guardedly. *Judaism and Hellenism*, (London: SCM Press, 1974), Volume I, 176.
167. The presence in Qumran Cave 4 of Aramaic fragments of Astronomical Enoch (I Enoch 72–82) the earliest of which is dated by Milik to the end of the third century BC, and of fragments from the Book of Watchers (I Enoch 1–36) the earliest of which Milik places in the first half of the second century BC, testifies to both the length and strength of the tradition. Cf. J.T. Milik, *The Books of Enoch*, Aramaic Fragments of Qumran Cave 4, Oxford: Clarendon Press, (1976), 7, 22. Nor is it merely the antiquity of the fragments which is telling; it is the presence in the documents they represent of ideas which play a dominant part in later Essene thought as attested by the Qumran texts: determinism, interpretation of Scripture, communion with the world of angels and interest in the eschatological Temple. Cf. Garcia Martinez, *PDSS*, 89f.
168. It is not uncommon for the beginnings of the Essene party to be traced to this event. Cf. Schürer-Vermes, *HJP*, II, 586f. Frequently, however, this is done by equating the *Hasidim* and the Essenes. Milik, however, writes more cautiously, 'Rather than identify Asidaeans and Essenes, it seems more plausible to assume that within the vast Asidaean movement a certain group of more precise tendencies crystallized and ... the Essene group may be said to have emerged.' *Ten Years of Discovery in the Wilderness of Judaea*, (London: SCM, 1959), 81.
169. *ALQ*[3], 97.
170. F.M. Cross has consistently – and correctly – affirmed the necessity of this. Cf. 'I remain convinced that one must begin with hard evidence – that is, the evidence of the typological sciences' (*ALQ*[3], 184: see the remainder of the paragraph for the ordered methodology he spells out there). Similarly forthright is Stegemann who pronounces 'worthless' any theory incompatible with the palaeography of Birnbaum-Cross (*Madrid Congress* Vol. I, 94); likewise Garcia Martinez, who specifically includes archaeology (*PDSS*, 83).

171. Chapter One, Section A 3, pp. 26–8.
172. Chapter One, Section B 4, pp. 28–49.
173. Recent study of 4Q448, labelled commonly as the 'King Jonathan Fragment' or words to that effect, has been seen by some scholars as exploding a historical reconstruction such as that adopted here. Published originally in *DJD*, VI (*Qumran Grotte 4*, 1977) in photographic form only (Plate IV) on account of the difficulty of deciphering its semi-cursive script (see also PAM 41.371 and 43.545), it was not until 1992 that the suggestion was made by Dr Ada Yardeni that column B line 2 and column C line 8 contained the name 'King Jonathan'. (See Esther Eshel, Hanan Eshel, Ada Yardeni, 'A Qumran Composition Containing Part of Psalm 154 and a Prayer for the Welfare of King Jonathan and His Kingdom', *IEJ*, 42, 1992, 199–229. A Hebrew version appeared in *Tarbiz* 60, 1991, 295–324). Eshel, Eshel and Yardeni proceeded to argue that the 'King Jonathan' in question could only be Alexander Jannaeus (Yonathan being his Hebrew name), since the only other candidate bearing that name, Jonathan Maccabeus, did not carry the title of king. This created the historical problem of why an anti-Hasmonean group such as the Qumran Essenes should pray for the welfare of a Hasmonean King. The writers named two possibilities: one, that the Essene attitude may have changed (at least temporarily) when Jannaeus (and Jerusalem with him) were rescued from defeat as happened in 103 and 88 BC. The other was that 4Q448 gives no sign of being sectarian in origin and does not represent the mind of the sect (217–20). Other scholars, holding both that Alexander Jannaeus is in mind and that the text is a community product, have drawn much more far-reaching conclusions regarding the origins and nature of the Qumran sect: specifically that the sect was pro-Maccabaean and Sadducean in sympathy; and second, that the beginnings of the sect, and the ministry of the Teacher of Righteousness in particular, are to be sought not in the second and third quarters of the second century, BC, but late in the second or early in the first century BC. For statements of this case see Eisenman and Wise, *DSSU*, 273–80; and Wise, Abegg and Cook, *DSS, A New Translation*, 26–34, where they propound this view as a conscious alternative to what they describe as 'the Standard Model'.

It is impossible to treat the new proposal in detail here, but several facts enjoin caution. (1) The presence of the name of Jonathan in B2 is by no means certain, and is made less probable by the syntactical awkwardness created if it is present. See Philip S. Alexander, 'A Note on the Syntax of 4Q448', *JJS*, 44, 1993, 301f. Alexander notes that a thematic unity runs through all three columns, 'the deliverance of Israel from all her enemies', God dwelling in Jerusalem and establishing his Kingdom, the solidarity of the exiles with the restored Kingdom' and concludes, 'This is as far as dispassionate analysis of the grammar will take us in deciphering the meaning of the text. To what historical events (if any) the text alludes is another question' (302). (2) Even accepting the presence of 'Yohanan' in B 2, only the final *nun* in that name is in the final form, all other such letters in other words being in the initial or medial form even in the final position. But Vermes holds that, on palaeographical grounds, this would indicate an earlier date. See G. Vermes, 'The So-Called King Jonathan Fragment (4Q 448)', *JJS*, 44, 1993, 296. (3) There is evidence, as Eshel, Eshel, and Yardeni concede that Jonathan Maccabeus may have been spoken of in kingly terms (art. cit, 216, n.29). Vermes makes the same point, examining more evidence, and citing specifically I Maccabees 10:18–20 (art. cit, 297f). In the light of these data, Vermes concludes that, assuming 'King Jonathan' is referred to, it is more probably Jonathan Maccabeus before he earned the enmity of the sect. In the light of these considerations it is overly bold of Eisenman and Wise to characterize 4Q448 as a text which 'completely disproves the Essene theory of Qumran origins at least as classically conceived' (*DSSU*, 273); or Wise, Abegg and Cook in claiming that it 'undermines the idea that the Teacher and his followers were on principle opposed to the Hasmoneans' (*DSS, A New Translation*, 26). The evidence simply is not strong enough to bear such categorical and far-reaching conclusions.

174. F.F. Bruce, *Second Thoughts on the Dead Sea Scrolls*, (London: The Paternoster Press, 1966), 135. His summary statement of the chapter in question should be consulted (132–5). F.M. Cross would agree but would draw the connection between the Qumran settlement and the Essene movement more tightly, 'The Qumran settlement is probably unique,

not only in being the original "exile in the desert", the home of the founder of the sect, but also in following a celibate rule. It is possible, but not probable, I think, that more than one community could be termed the *yaḥad'*. (*ALQ*[3], 70f).

175. Chapter Two, pp. 69–71. Cf. Newsom, Carol, ' "Sectually Explicit" Literature from Qumran' in D.N. Freedman et al. (edd), *The Hebrew Bible and Its Interpreters*, (Winona Lake: Eisenbraun, 1990), 167–87.
176. See the treatment of this topic by Garcia Martinez in *PDSS*, Ch. I.

Chapter Three

Foundation: The Covenant and its Implications

The question may well be raised as to whether covenant is indeed the foundation of Qumran thought, and whether there are not ideas or postulates that are even more fundamental. The concept of God might be mentioned as an obvious example and, indeed, it has been examined, stated and analysed more than once, Ringgren making it the starting-point of his account of the Sect's doctrine.[1] Several considerations prompt caution at this point. For one thing such a procedure smacks strongly of a Greek mentality in which one doctrine follows in logical progression from its predecessor, leading back naturally in the end to the source of all, the doctrine of God. But Qumran theology was not the creation of the schools, and it is misleading to approach it in this way. A second point – not unrelated to the first – is that it would be quite impossible to deduce Qumran theology from their doctrine of God. No doubt certain aspects of their thought are more readily reconcilable with one concept of God rather than another; but that still does not mean that their theological preoccupations were inferred from their doctrine of God. The fact seems rather to be that their theological concerns were rooted in the religious pressures of their times. This does not mean that the sectaries were indifferent to theological principles; on the contrary they were perfectly capable of theological reflection as the sequence on the Two Spirits (IQS III 13–IV 26) shows. Yet their thought in large measure assumed its distinctive form in response to events, and we shall be more likely to grasp its inner meaning and characteristic emphases if we approach it from that perspective.

Another consideration which commends this approach is that the Qumran sectaries were apparently able to tolerate a high degree of unresolved tension in their thought. This does not mean that they threw consistency to the winds, but it does mean that they were ready to affirm positions which commended themselves to them as real and true, whether or not they were able to reconcile them. This is particularly the case where the life-setting of a given concept varies (and its corresponding literary genre with it): as between instruction on the one hand and worship on the other. It is important therefore to try to hold together things which they held together, even if it does not always make for tidy systematization.

Yet another caution to be kept in mind is that each of the key components of Qumran thought carries with it the flavour of all the others. The concept of covenant, for example, carries with it their understanding of revelation, purity and the end of days. Clearly, this creates problems for exposition, since it is impossible to deal with all the constituent elements simultaneously. The total picture can only be built up incrementally and one must be content with hints and indications until the element in question can be treated more fully.

With this understanding we may take up the idea of covenant. Good reasons can be given for beginning here. It was the consciousness of being the faithful remnant which brought the Essene sect into being, as we have already seen.[2] The term itself (*bĕrît*) occurs more than 150 times in the non-biblical texts.[3] Still more, the community is referred to in the texts as 'the community of the covenant' (IQS V 5) or phrases to that effect.[4]

That the covenant concept enters fundamentally into Qumran thought can hardly be surprising. It is simply part of their Jewish heritage. The covenantal tradition of the Old Testament – the covenants with Noah, Abraham,

Moses, David – was their tradition. Recent study of comparative material from the Ancient Near East[5] has illuminated the form and significance of the covenant as a political and religious instrument. As far as the Old Testament is concerned several facts seem to be clear. First, the covenant was a gift of divine grace in which God pledged himself to act in certain ways on behalf of his people whom he had chosen in his mercy, and not on the basis of any merit of theirs (Gen. 17: 1–8; Deut. 7:6–10; 2 Sam. 7:8–13). Second, the people were committed to the terms and stipulations of the covenant which, if they broke, would bring them under the penalties and curses of the covenant (Gen. 17:9–14; Deut. 7: 9–11; 2 Sam. 7:14). Third, even if the people broke the covenant on their side, *YHWH* remained faithful to his. That is to say, the breaking of the contractual aspect of the covenant did not annul the covenant itself. Chastisement would follow the breaching of the stipulations, but there was forgiveness and renewal of the covenant if the people repented, because *YHWH's* name is at stake (Lev. 26:44f). With minor variations this broad pattern persisted into the Hellenistic age as can be seen in I and II Maccabees and the Book of Jubilees.[6] G. Vermes writes, 'Since the key to any understanding of Judaism must be the notion of the covenant, it may safely be taken as an introduction to Essene religious thought … It was this same covenant theology that served as the foundation of the Qumran Community's basic beliefs.'[7] How, then, did they understand it? Their distinctive view may be said to gather around three main topics.

The Renewed Covenant

The *Damascus Rule* traces the beginnings of the Essene sect to the divine visitation of the remnant God spared 'when he remembered the covenant of the very first … and did not deliver them up to destruction' (I 4b–5a). It was this remnant which he visited 'three hundred and ninety years after having delivered them into the hands of Nebuchadnezzar, King of Babylon' (I 5b–6), and from which he caused to spring a root of planting to possess his land. It is these now entering the covenant (II 2), with whom God has entered into concert. In short, the Essenes saw the covenant, broken by their forefathers and resulting in the exile, as having been reactivated with themselves. At the core of their corporate existence stood a renewed covenant. At the same time the covenant is spoken of as 'the new covenant in the land of Damascus' (CD VI 19, VIII 21, XIX 33–4, XX 12).[8] In what sense is the covenant both renewed and new? Or must it not be one or the other?

The first thing to be noted in seeking an answer to this question is that, in contrast to the first covenant, entry into the Essene covenant was based on individual decision and choice. The terms 'those who enter (*bô'*) or pass into (*'ābar*) the covenant' or 'those who "volunteer" (*nādab*)' are very common.[9] Now this definition of the covenant implies a drastic redefinition of Israel; for its meaning is that those who have not entered the Qumran covenant do not belong to Israel at all. That this is the meaning seems clear from statements such as IQS V 10–11 in which, at the conclusion of a description of the obligations of members, the *Rule* states, 'He should swear by the covenant to be segregated from all the men of sin who walk along paths of irreverence. For they are not included in his covenant.' It is implied equally by the application to the community of terms which in the Old Testament are reserved for Israel. They are 'the elect of God' (IQpHab X:13), the 'holy people' (IQM XII 1), 'those selected by God for an everlasting covenant' (IQS IV 22), 'the chosen of Israel' (CD IV 3). No doubt it is possible to overstate the point. Jaubert points out that the idea of the remnant is akin to this,[10] and that the Qumran Psalmist saw himself not so much as entering something new as returning to something old.[11] But if anything this qualification over-qualifies, because it fails to do justice to the indubitable stress on *entering* the covenant as a matter of free decision and choice.[12]

This consideration would appear to favour the conclusion that the Essene covenant is new. However, part of the problem is that it is easy to find evidence supporting either conclusion. On the one hand it is not difficult to accumulate data favouring the view that there is only one covenant and consequently the Essene covenant is its renewal. Despite the differing perspectives of the various documents: the *Damascus Rule*, focusing on God's faithfulness to the fathers; the *Rule of the Community* stressing the present as the moment in which one must enter the covenant; the *Thanksgiving Hymns* pointing to the frailty of the fathers, but only so as to underscore human frailty in general; the *Rule of the War* affirming that the community as the Israel of the end-time will inherit the promise to the fathers; despite this variation in perspective the point is made unmistakably that the community is the legatee of the covenant with the fathers.[13] The lengthy sequence in CDII 14–IV 12a traces the spiritual history of the sect, and the line goes back to Noah and Abraham, Isaac and Jacob, Moses and Israel in the wilderness. When there has been straying it has been because they chose their own will. 'Through it', says a significant phrase, 'the very first to enter the covenant made themselves guilty and were delivered up to the sword for having deserted God's covenant ... But with those who remained steadfast in God's precepts, with those who were left from among them, God established his covenant with Israel forever, revealing to them hidden matters in which all Israel had gone astray' (III 10–14a). The language makes clear that the remnant in mind is the Qumran community. The same conclusion – that there is but a single covenant – is indicated by the epithets used to describe it. Especially is this true of the adjective 'eternal' (*'ôlām*) which is used to qualify 'covenant' six times;[14] and also the phrase 'the covenant of God' which is used absolutely at least eight times.[15] Other lines of evidence might easily be added.[16] The covenant oath in both the *Damascus Rule* and the *Community Rule* is described in virtually identical terms as an oath to return to the Law of Moses (CD XV 6–10; IQS V 7b–9).

At the same time it is just as easy to find evidence implying that the covenant is new and different. Contexts in which the adjective 'new' (*ḥādāš*) occurs qualifying 'covenant' have just been noted. Sometimes, moreover, the sectarian covenant is referred to as 'this covenant' (*habberît hazôt*: IQS II 12–13), at least suggesting that it stands in distinction from some other. This suspicion is confirmed by the appearance in descriptions of it of elements highly characteristic of the sect. Thus in IQS V 11–12 those excluded from the covenant are outside 'since they have neither sought nor examined his decrees in order to learn the hidden matters in which they err by their own fault and because they treated revealed matters with disrespect'. According to CD III 13–15 the defining content of God's covenant with those who remained steadfast was the revelation of 'hidden matters in which all Israel had gone astray: his holy sabbaths and his glorious feasts, his just stipulations and his truthful paths.' In the *Habbakkuk Commentary* treachery against the new covenant involves refusing to believe that they are the final generation, and that the Teacher of Righteousness has made clear all that is going to happen to it (IQp Hab II 1–10a). If then there is but one covenant: that made with Noah and the Patriarchs; and yet the covenant of the men of Qumran, which is entered by free decision and not by the rite of circumcision, is the only true covenant and is indeed sometimes called the 'new covenant', how are the two to be reconciled? The answer appears to depend on two factors, namely, the content of the covenant; and the nature of the covenant relationship.

As to the first, the covenant at Qumran, while repeatedly affirmed to be that made with the Patriarchs, nevertheless had a distinctive content. That content was 'knowledge' (*da'at*). According to the *Community Rule* the desert community was to be 'the most holy dwelling for Aaron with total knowledge of the covenant of justice' (IQS VIII 8b–9a). The passage from the *Damascus Rule* cited above makes clear in what this knowledge consisted: the correct times for sabbaths and festivals revealed by God to the faithful remnant (CD III 12b–16b). Jaubert observes that whereas traditionally law, knowledge and covenant were inseparable, at Qumran 'knowledge' takes a place of priority. Only those in the covenant 'know'.[17] It will have been noticed that 'knowledge' is linked with, indeed conveyed by 'revelation'. Revelation is a major factor in Qumran theology and must await fuller treatment later. Suffice it for the moment simply to observe that knowledge of some distinctive kind evidently entered into the content of the covenant, thereby compounding the problem of continuity versus originality in the Qumran understanding of the covenant.

We may be assisted in our quest for a solution to this tension by a second point of importance in the Qumran view: namely, the nature of the covenantal relationship. In a sense this is but the inside of the idea of the new covenant. The same puzzle persists here that was evident earlier. If there is but one eternal covenant, then what place can be found for a new covenant? If, on the other hand, new content can be added to the covenant in the form of 'knowledge' conveyed by 'revelation', then in what sense can the covenant be said to be eternal?

The Qumran texts speak of 'newness' in relation to the covenant in what appear to be two distinct senses. On the one hand they speak of the 'renewal' of the covenant. This seems to be the meaning of the liturgy in IQS II 19–15a, although the word 'renewal' is not used. The ceremony for the admission of new members (IQS I 19–II 18) concludes with the words, 'Thus shall they do, year by year, for as long as the dominion of Satan endures' (II 19). At first sight this might be taken as a description of the role of the Priests and the Levites, together with the novices, in the annual admission liturgy. The next lines however give a different impression. 'The Priests shall enter first, ranked one after another according to the perfection of their spirit; then the Levites; and thirdly, all the people one after another, in their thousands, hundreds, fifties, and tens, that every Israelite may know his place in the Community of God according to the everlasting design' (II 19–23). Although the word 'new' is not used in any form, it is clear that *all* the members of the Covenant 'enter' – the word *'ābar* is used – each year, in other words they renew the Covenant. But the language of renewal is explicitly used in the *Rule of the Blessings* as in III 26: 'For you may renew the covenant of [eternal] priesthood', and in V 20–21, 'And [the Instructor] will renew the covenant of the Community for him.' If, as has been suggested above,[18] the *Blessings* were not merely intended for the Messianic Age, but were used proleptically in anticipation of its arrival, then we have evidence of an eschatological renewal of the covenant in the present, as well as of the expectation of its renewal in the Messianic Age. To echo Jaubert's phrase: the renewal is past, or an actual realization (that is, in the present), or a hope for the future.[19] Indeed, Jaubert goes further still, and asks whether an affirmation such as that in IQS X 10, 'At the onset of day and night I shall enter the covenant of God, and when evening and morning depart I shall repeat his precepts', may not imply a daily renewal of the Covenant.[20]

On the other hand, we have also noted that newness is predicated of the covenant not only in the sense that it is renewed, but that it is new. Some passages which speak of the covenant as 'new' also speak of its being 'entered'. In CD VI 19 reference is made to 'those who entered the new covenant in the land of Damascus.' CD VIII 2 (which = XIX 33f) speaks likewise of 'the men who entered the new covenant in the land of Damascus' while CD XX 11f pronounces condemnation on those who 'have despised the covenant and the pact – the new covenant – which they made in the land of Damascus',[21] precisely because they did not enter the covenant, or having entered, departed from it (CD XX 10–12). As noted earlier[22] the word 'covenant' is missing from the only other example which is in the *Habakkuk Commentary*, but it is probably correct to read, '[And it concerns] the traito[rs of the]new [covenant] since they did not believe in the covenant of God' (IQp Hab II 3–4a). These examples give the impression of a distinct act by using the same language of 'entering' the covenant which we have encountered elsewhere. This in turn lends definiteness to the word 'new' as suggesting something different from that which is old. If this is so then it would appear that 'renewing' the Covenant cannot have the same meaning as 'entering the new covenant'.

Jaubert, in her thorough and incisive study, recognizes the tension but seeks to show nonetheless that both are the same. The annual liturgical renewal, she argues, is based on the recognition that the covenant ceaselessly broken, should be ceaselessly renewed.[23] The sect did not deny this. But they also believed that they were the last generation; still more that, while their sanctity did not surpass that of the Patriarchs nor their knowledge that of Moses, yet never before had the law been observed corporately with the fidelity now shown by them.[24] On such grounds the sectarians might legitimately speak of a new covenant without implying the annulment of the old or without rescinding the annual ceremony of renewal.

In principle this explanation is sound, though its detailed expression requires amendment. Thus Jaubert states that on her interpretation it would be more exact to speak of two phases of the history of the covenant.[25] Perhaps so. But the texts do not in fact speak thus; they speak rather of the new covenant. Again, she finds herself in difficulty with the history of the covenant as recounted in CD II 17–IV 3 in which the ideal of perpetual renewal sits uneasily with that of two moments of covenantal history: that of Abraham, Isaac and Jacob (III 2–4); and that of the raising of the penitent remnant, namely the community (III 12ff). The *Damascus Document* , she concludes, does not speak with one voice, and she resorts to the hypothesis of a 'binary scheme' imposed on a scheme of perpetual renewal.[26]

These attempted adjustments suggest that a factor is missing. The language of the texts is too strong to be explained in this way – even where there is no mention of the new covenant. The language is more consonant with a new beginning, even if it stands in continuity with the past. It is difficult to believe that the Qumran sectaries were not aware that their covenant differed measurably in content from its predecessors. Their belief in revelation makes it hard to think otherwise; and in their thought the covenant was linked with revelation. The *Damascus Rule* legislates that the initiate is to be enrolled 'with the covenant oath which Moses established with Israel, the covenant to rev[ert to] the law of Moses with the whole heart [and with the whole] soul to what has been discovered that has to be put into practice in all of the a[ge of wickedness] (CD XV 8–10a).

The covenant role of the sect in the end-time is spelled out almost entirely in terms of their distinctive beliefs and praxis in the lengthy description of covenant responsibilities in CD VI 11b–VII 6a. In the sense therefore in which a covenant could be called 'new' because of a change in its stipulations, the covenant of the Qumran sectaries deserved that label. But in the sense that it was the same character of covenant, made with the same God, it was still 'the covenant of the fathers' (CD VIII 18).

One further aspect of the sectarian covenant remains to be noted beyond its unique terms of entry and its character as a new covenant: namely, its community dimension. Self-evidently, this is not unique to Qumran. The idea of covenant necessarily carries that of community with it. There can be no covenant without a covenant-people. But the precisely defined structure of the Qumran sect gives the idea of community a particular flavour in their case.[27] It is no surprise therefore to find that the word 'covenant' (*berît*) slides very readily from the sense of 'covenant' to that of 'community'. In IQS II 12–18 the obverse of 'entering the covenant' (12) is being 'cut off from the midst of all the sons of light' (16). In other contexts the phrase 'covenant of the everlasting community' is used (IQS III 11–12); and conversely, the 'community of the everlasting covenant' (IQS V 5–6).[28] In what then did this community consist, and what were its marks?

First, it was a priestly community. The sense in which this was so must be carefully defined. It is everywhere insisted that the sect operates under priestly authority. This is as true of the 'congregation' of the *Damascus Rule* (CD XII 22–XIII 6; XIV 6b–8a) as of the 'community' of the

Community Rule (IQS V 2, 8–9). This last passage referred to could hardly be more explicit: The new member of the community 'shall swear with a binding oath to revert to the law of Moses with all that it decrees, with whole heart and whole soul, in compliance with all that has been revealed concerning it to the sons of Zadok, the priests who keep the covenant and interpret his will.'[29] However, more is implied than that the community was headed by priests. The community in its entirety was instituted to be 'a holy house for Israel and the foundation of the holy of holies for Aaron ... to atone for the earth' (IQS VIII 5,6). This is made clear in that, again and again, the lay members of the community are linked expressly with the priests in the exercise of authority within the community. Thus, new converts to the community are to 'acquiesce to the authority of the sons of Zadok, the priests who safeguard the covenant and to the authority of the multitude of the men of the community, those who persevere steadfastly in the covenant. By its authority, decision by lot shall be made in every affair involving the law, property and judgment' (IQS V 2–3)[30]. Not least significant in this regard is a phrase which occurs three times, speaking of the priests 'and the men of *their* covenant' (*berîtām*) (IQS V 9; VI 19; IQSa I 2). Indeed, Norbert Ilg argues cogently that what lies behind this is an Old Testament tradition in which priestly functions are accorded to such as Levi and Phineas, not on the basis of descent, but on the basis of rectitude of conduct.[31] This did not mean that the distinction between priests and laity was obliterated among the Essenes; but it appears to have meant the incorporation of the laity in the discharging of priestly functions which substituted for those of the Jerusalem Temple in which the sectaries felt unable to participate because the purity of the Temple had been compromised.[32]

A second mark of the community was holiness. This, indeed, follows necessarily from the first. The sacerdotal character of the priest, and indeed the extension of that character in some measure to all members, placed the *whole* community under the obligation of sanctity. This extended over the whole face of the community's life to such a degree that it cannot be treated adequately as an inference from the covenant, even if it originated as such. It must await fuller treatment below.

A final mark of the Essene covenant is that it involved the sharing of a common life. The precise character of that common life evidently varied between communities. The *Damascus Rule* appears to recognize this and legislates accordingly. Regulations are given for those who 'reside in the camps in accordance with the rule of the land' (VII 6);[33] apparently a reference to those who lived in the towns and villages (cf. XII 19; Josephus, *War,* II.8.4. (124); and Philo, *Apologia*, quoted in Eusebius, *Praeparatio Evangelica* VIII 11.1). It was expected that such would marry and beget children (VII 6–9), own property and engage in farming and other gainful employment (XI 12; XII 10; XIV 12–13). Yet they are obliged to 'walk in accordance with the law and according to the regulations of the teachings' (VII 7b–8a); 'to keep the unclean apart from the clean, and distinguish between holy and profane' (XII 19b–20a). Consequently, trading with gentiles is forbidden (XII 8b–11a); commerce with non-members of the sect was forbidden except on cash terms (XIII 14); and the approval of the *Mebaqqēr* was required for any commercial transaction between members of the community (XIII 15–16). It was the task of the Instructor (*Maśkîl*) to instruct members in the regulations (XII 20–1), and of the Inspector (*Mebaqqēr*) to enforce them (XIII 7–13). Clearly, even for Essenes living in the cities and villages of Judaea (in Philo's phrase), life was largely closed and separatist in relation to the world beyond the walls of the communities or camps.

In the case of the *Community Rule* the exclusiveness is defined even more sharply. The picture presented is that of not merely community living, but communal living. The general rubric with which the code of regulations begins strikes the characteristic note from the start, 'They should keep apart from men of sin in order to constitute a community in law and possessions' (V 1b–2a). Thus while association with non-members is permitted on very narrow terms (V 16b–17), the prevailing impression is that of an insulated community, living together on the very closest basis. 'They shall eat in common, and pray in common and deliberate in common' (VI 2c–3). Property was to be merged with that of the community for common use, though only after a probation of two years (VI 22f). The potential of life at such close quarters for producing stress is recognized and guidance is given accordingly. 'Each should reproach his fellow in truth, in meekness and in compassionate love for the man. No-one should speak to his brother in anger or muttering, or with a hard [neck or with passionate] spiteful intent and he should not detest him [in the stubbornness] of his heart, but instead reproach him that day so as not to incur a sin for his fault' (V 24b–VI 1a). A penal code is provided detailing penalties for such sins as angry speech (VII 2–3), wilful insult (VII 4b–5a), harbouring animosity (VII 10b, defaming fellow members (VII 17b–19a).

One does not have to look far for the reasoning which led to this insistence on closed community life. In part it is the direct consequence of the principle that membership of the covenant was based on the deliberate choice of the individual, rather than the automatic inclusion of all members of national Israel in the old covenant-people. Nor was individual decision enough to guarantee admission; examination by the *Mebaqqēr* followed by a full year of probation in the case of the *Damascus Rule* (XIII 11–13, XIV 8b–12, XV 5–15a); examination by the *Maskîl*, then by the entire membership of the community, followed by two years probation in the *Community Rule* (VI 13b–23); were required before full membership was granted. The old covenant had collapsed with disastrous consequences because it had been open indiscriminately to all; the new covenant must avoid that mistake at all costs by ensuring that it was open only to the committed. In short, to the Essenes, community, defined rigidly, was the correlative of covenant as they understood it.

With this, we are brought directly to another constituent integral to covenant: namely, law.

The Covenant Law

As a matter of definition covenant carried with it obligations, observance of which was required if the covenant was to remain in force. Such obligations were written into the terms of the covenant as stipulations or covenant-law. The Essene covenant was no exception. Such law or *halakhah*[34] is frequently referred to in the texts as 'the rule' (*serek*) (IQS V 1, VI 8; CD X 4, XII 19, 22, XIV 3, etc.) 'the regulations' (*tiqqûn*) (IQS V 7, IX 21), 'the rules' (*mišpātîm*) (IQS VI 24, VIII 20; CD XII 19,21), 'the precepts' (*hûqqîm*) (IQS IX 12, CD XII 20). So much is *halakhah* a characteristic feature of the texts that it has been claimed that the differentia of the Essene movement is to be found in its *halakhah* rather than in its theology. Y. Sussman, writing of the *Halakhic Letter* (4QMMT) says, 'what distinguished (the sect) and served as the backbone of its sectarian polemic was not religious doctrines, theology, or national or political issues, but halakhah'.[35] However, this statement for all that it is carefully nuanced, still conveys an opposition between halakhah and theology which is unfounded. It is nearer the truth to say that theological views came to expression in and through halakha. As L.H. Schiffman has put it, 'issues of theology were of central importance and often lie behind other more clearly expressed disputes.'[36] In attempting to grasp the significance of Essene halakhah it is indispensable to recognize that the presupposition of covenant law is revelation. Halakhah was not of human manufacture; it was a matter of divine disclosure. What this implied may best be seen by examining three aspects of the covenant law of the Essenes.

First, the sources of covenant law. Without doubt, the primary source of this was the Mosaic law. The 'newness' of the new covenant was never understood in an absolute sense as though no prior covenant had ever existed. The expression 'new covenant' carries overtones of acknowledgment of the existence of the old covenant as much as claims of the making of the new. The Essenes did not think of God's covenant with them as *the* covenant *simpliciter*.

This is indubitably clear from the terms of the covenant oath in which the old and new elements are repeatedly conjoined. 'Whoever enters the council of the Community . . . shall swear with a binding oath to revert to the Law of Moses with all that it decrees, with whole heart and whole soul, in compliance with all that has been revealed concerning it to the sons of Zadok,' (IQS V 76, 8b, 9a).[37] Plainly, therefore, Scripture stood at the heart of the covenant law, and the sect regarded itself as returning to Scripture.[38] Its problem lay in showing how its novel halakhah could be derived from Scripture.[39] It found the solution in revelation.

In Essene thought there could be no question that the law had been divinely revealed to Moses. But besides those things that were revealed (*nīglôt*) in the Torah and therefore accessible to all its readers, were others that were hidden (*nistārôt*) and discoverable only by exegesis of the text.[40] It was the divine disclosure of the true way of interpreting this hidden dimension of the Torah that brought the Essene sect into existence in the first place. The *Halakhic Letter* (4QMMT) points in that direction as we have seen, and CD III 12b–19 confirms it. Even the faithful remnant had 'defiled themselves with human sin and unclean paths' (III 17b) till God revealed to them 'hidden matters in which all Israel had gone astray: his holy sabbaths and his glorious feasts, his just stipulations and his truthful paths' (III 14–15a).[41] It is not surprising therefore that since the study of the Torah was the source of halakhah, communal study should be an ongoing activity in the sect (IQS VI 6–8a). Since such study was ongoing it follows that revelation was likewise ongoing. Indeed IQ VIII 15 enjoins compliance with 'all that has been revealed from age to age' and the task of the Maskil is defined as the collection and application of this accumulated revelation (IQS IX 12–16a). There is thus a growing corpus of halakhah: detailed and specific regulations derived from the general commands of the Torah. Since the discovery of these was a matter of revelation, this not only imparted to them absolute authority; it meant that the process of exegesis was inspired.[42]

However, there was another medium of revelation accessible to the Essenes: the Teacher of Righteousness. He is credited with having brought to an end the community's groping for the way by directing them in God's way (CD I 8b–11a), and, moreover, by making plain the fate of the last generation, the traitors who have strayed from the way (I 11b–II 1).[43] In the *Habakkuk Pesher*, Habakkuk 2:2 is interpreted in terms of the Teacher of Righteousness, 'to whom God has disclosed all the mysteries of the words of his servants, the prophets' (IQpHab VII 4b–5). The Teacher of Righteousness, indeed, is placed at an advantage over the prophet himself, for though 'God told Habakkuk to write what was going to happen to the last generation, he did not let him know the end of the age' (VII 1–2). The Teacher has been vouchsafed this insight.

The means of revelation thus takes a quantum leap forward. To begin with, to the Teacher of Righteousness has been vouchsafed full knowledge of the divine mysteries.[44] Second, his understanding extends beyond the Torah to the Prophetic books. Yet, third, his function as a medium of revelation is still based on the interpretation of Scripture. He thereby differs from other members of the community in terms of primacy and penetration, but not in kind. He is the founder of a tradition of interpretation, but the task of interpretation can be carried on without him.[45] However, without his unique contribution in the first place, the community's understanding of its vocation and mission would have been seriously truncated. For this reason it is not surprising that in CD XX 27b–34 conformity to the regulations (*mišpāṭîm*) (27b, 30b), including those to which the first members of the sect submitted (31b–32a) are mentioned in parallel with giving heed to the voice of the Teacher of Righteousness (28b, 32b) as conditions of eventual triumph and salvation (33b–34).[46]

It is Scripture then, interpreted in the light of divine revelation, which is the source of the community law. What can be said as to the character of this law? First, it is marked by unusual stringency. Compared with the halakhah of the Mishnah and the Talmud, says Vermes,

Qumran practice is characterized by greater severity and absolute exclusiveness. 'The sectarian interpreters tended to inject an extra measure of rigidity into the accepted understanding of the Law, thereby setting for themselves a stricter standard of ritual purity and moral behaviour. Also, in contrast to Talmudic literature ... at Qumran there was one way only ... There being, they maintained, but one God and one truth, there can be but one way.'[47] The note of stringency comes through in the language of the texts themselves. Observance must be 'according to the exact interpretation of the law' (CD IV 8, VI 14). The water of life comes from the well which is the law (CD VI 3–10). To turn from it is treachery (CD XX 25–27a). Members of the community alone observe it, and they alone will find life (CD VII 4b–6a).

The note of stringency likewise is evident in the content of the halakhah. It includes such matters as avoidance of second marriages, for the animals went into the ark two by two (CD V 1); intercourse during menstruation (CD V 6b–7a), or in the city of the Temple (CD XII 1–2a); using a ladder or rope or other instrument to rescue one who has fallen into water or a hole on the sabbath (CD XI 16–17a). The point is well-illustrated by comparing a passage like CD VI 14–21 which enjoins careful conformity to the sectarian law and CD I 12–21 which denounces those who seek 'smooth things': the easy way, and in so doing violate the covenant. The same contrast is evident in the halakhah of the *Community Rule* in which the regulations for governing community life are spelled out with great precision regarding calendar and festivals, ritual purity and the sanctuary (I 13b–15; III 2–12; VIII 10b–16; IX 3–11). In opposition to these stand 'the men of sin' (IQS V 2) who have treated revealed matters with disdain (IQS V 10b–13b. Cf. II 25b–III 3b). It is not difficult to discern the source of this stringency. Vermes accounts for it in historical terms, citing the context of religious laxity and rejection of traditional principles in which the sect arose.[48] The point may be made in a somewhat more theological way by saying that the stringency of the halakhah derives directly from the distinctive character of the Essene covenant. Since covenant was entered intentionally by the free choice of the individual, the halakhah was by that token more binding since its obligations were undertaken voluntarily. The sect was thereby in a position to insist strongly on compliance.[49] This may explain at least the strength of the emphasis upon strict conformity.

However, another factor was also powerfully at work, which leads to a second distinguishing characteristic of the covenant law: namely, it was something to be *done*. Performance of the law was an absolute desideratum. This, indeed, is implicit in the stringency of the law, which has just been considered. A stringent halakhah would serve little purpose unless it was stringently observed, and that the Essenes were intent on observance is unquestionable. They were 'doers of the law' *par excellence*. The expression 'those who do the law' (*'ôśê hattôr āh*) or an equivalent phrase is found sixteen times in the *Community Rule* and the *Damascus Rule*.[50]

But it is in the *Halakhic Letter* (4QMMT) that the most significant evidence on this count appears, as well as in other texts which treat the same theme. As to 4QMMT, the question is posed by the title given to it: *Miqṣat Mā'aśē Ha-Tôrāh*, an expression which occurs once in the original.[51] Some scholars have argued that the phrase ought to be rendered 'some legal rulings pertaining to the Torah'[52] or, in the rendering of the *editio princeps*, 'some of the precepts of the Torah'.[53] Garcia Martinez, however, has argued powerfully that this meaning cannot be sustained in the Qumran texts in general[54], or in 4QMMT in particular. The word *mā'asē* rather requires the meaning 'works' or 'deeds', which in fact, the *editio princeps* uses at 4QMMT C23, is possible at B 2 and fits well at C 27.[55]

Not less important is that in the 4QMMT contexts where the 'works' or 'deeds' of the law are spoken of, the performance of them is linked with the forgiveness of sins. Thus 4QMMT C23–26a reads, 'Think of the kings of Israel and contemplate their deeds: whoever among them feared the [Tor]ah was delivered from troubles; and these were the seekers of the Torah whose transgressions were [for]given. Think of David who was a man of righteous deeds and who was (therefore) delivered from many troubles and was forgiven.'[56] Still more, the writer of the *Halakhic Letter* commends to his readers these 'works of the law' not only so that they may find that 'some of our practices are correct'; the added advantage will ensue that 'this will be counted as a virtuous deed of yours, since you will be doing what is righteous and good in His eyes, for your own welfare and for the welfare of Israel' (C 31f).[57] The emphasis on *doing* is unmistakable in both passages, as is the forgiveness of sins in consequence. Of particular interest is the linking of the verb 'reckon' (*ḥāšab*) and the noun 'righteousness' (*ṣedāqah*), inasmuch as they are found together in the same verse in the Hebrew Bible only twice: Genesis 15:6 and Psalm 106:31. It is unlikely that the former was in the writer's mind since its emphasis is on believing, 'And Abraham *believed* God and it was reckoned to him as righteousness.' The latter verse, however, refers to the episode recorded in Numbers 25:1–8 in which Phinehas the priest, encountering an Israelite in the act of adultery with a foreign woman, transfixes them with a single spear, evoking the encomium from the psalmist, 'that has been reckoned to him as righteousness from generation to generation forever' (Ps. 106:31).[58]

It may well be asked whence this emphasis on the *doing* of the law came; even more, where the idea of forgiveness of sins as consequent upon the doing of the law and dependent upon it came from. Such a notion has been pronounced a travesty of the biblical idea of covenant according to which the covenant is a gift of God's grace in which God commits himself to enter into a saving relationship with his chosen people even though they are wholly undeserving of his favour. There are, indeed, obligations by which the people are bound, the breaking of which constitutes a breach of the covenant-bond. However, the same grace which was operative in the creation of the covenant also makes possible its restoration: forgiveness is available where there is repentance.[59]

Now these features are far from being absent from the Qumran texts. One need only look at the account of the founding of the movement in the opening column of the *Damascus Rule* to find them. God delivered Israel up to the sword when they were unfaithful to him (I 3–4a). However, he remembered his covenant and spared a remnant because they realized their sin and guilt (I 4b, 8b–9a). Seeing their good works and perfect heart (I 10), he sent the Teacher of Righteousness to direct them in his way (I 11). He is patient and forgiving to those who repent, but pours his anger on those who turn from his way (II 4b–7a). Here undeserved grace, breach of the covenant obligations, forgiveness and atonement are all to be found. How, then, can the doing of the law as a means of being reckoned righteous fit into such a scheme?

Two factors at least seem to have been at work in the mind of the sect. First, even if perfect obedience was not required, and forgiveness was available when obedience was not forthcoming, the fact was that the first covenant had been broken, with disastrous consequences (CD I 1–4a, 5b–6, II 14–III 12a). But how had this happened, given the provision made in the covenant for the remission of offences? The ideal covenanter is described in CD XX 28b–34 as the one who remains faithful to the sectarian law, who confesses his sin, for whom God atones, and who, in consequence 'shall see his salvation. For they have taken refuge in his holy name' (34). Those who have brought disaster have 'walked in the stubbornness of their hearts' (*bišrîr ut lib bām*, CD II 17b–18): an expression used repeatedly to describe those who at various times had breached their covenant obligations, incurring disaster in consequence.[60] In short, insensitivity in the observance of covenant stipulations, which would carry with it implicitly insensitivity to the need for repentance and atonement, would prove fatal to the maintenance of covenant salvation. Forgiveness was not good enough. There must be fidelity to the covenant requirements. But this is just another way of saying that 'doing the works of the law' was indispensable to the survival of the covenant relationship.

The sect was well aware of this, and their answer to it was to enjoin the utmost stringency upon members in the matter of law observance.

A second factor seems to have been operative in this connection. In their understanding God's covenant with them was not only the 'new' covenant; it was also the 'last' covenant. All that is implied in this must await fuller treatment of Qumran eschatology. At this point, suffice it to say that they believed that the end of days was upon them, and to breach the covenant would not only be fatal but final in that it would prevent the coming of the new creation (IQS IV 22b–3, 25b). Failure was therefore unthinkable. The covenant obligations were meant to be kept and could be kept, and the sectaries intended to do so.[61] It is sometimes said that the *Damascus Rule* and the *Community Rule*, being legal documents, exhibit only one side of the covenant, saying nothing of grace or hope for the future.[62] The observation has a degree of validity, no doubt, though the liturgical elements in the *Community Rule* (IQS I 1–III 12, X–XI) and the historical-hortatory elements in the *Damascus Rule* (CD I–VIII) modify it, as is shown by the mention (already noted) of grace, atonement and forgiveness.[63] What seems difficult to deny is that, however much the sectaries believed in divine grace and forgiveness – and there can be no doubt that they believed in both – that is not where the accent fell in their understanding of covenant law.

The character of the covenant is therefore responsible both for the stringency of the covenant law and the fierce and relentless insistence on its observance. The salvation of the covenant people, not to mention their survival, depended upon it. Their forefathers had failed. The Essenes were determined not to follow in their footsteps.

The Covenant God

Behind the covenant and the covenant law stands the covenant God. That very expression indicates the baseline from which the sectarian understanding of God is to be approached. The God of Essene faith is not the God of abstract speculation, but the God encountered in covenant relationship. This does not mean that there is no speculative side to Essene thinking about God; on the contrary, there is a keen awareness of the problems implicit in such belief, the problem of evil being the most notable example. However, the problems engaged are those which arise from the prior understanding of God derived from the covenant. In large measure, therefore, the Essene understanding of God is shaped by their understanding of his dealings with the chosen people in history.[64] This has the further implication that the Essene view of God will bear the stamp of their pre-existing interpretation of history. That is to say, they did not come to the Hebrew Scriptures to work out their view of God as an exercise in biblical (let alone philosophical) theology. They already knew how God had worked in the history of their forefathers as well as in their own history. It was the God whom they already knew that they wrote of in their texts.

Such an approach creates certain problems of exposition. For one thing, it means that the understanding of God passes very rapidly into issues of history and the human situation. In this way the doctrine of God can become a portmanteau for the whole of Essene theology. It will be necessary therefore, to truncate the treatment in a way that may have the appearance of being arbitrary. For another thing, the ideas which emerge most clearly in their view of God are closely intertwined, so that it is difficult to speak of one without involving the others. For purposes of analysis they may be distinguished, but this should not be allowed to obscure their essential connectedness.

Overarching the whole history of Israel is the holy and majestic God. This note is no less prominent at Qumran. The conventional ways in which it came to expression, as for example, in the use of the divine name, are present at Qumran also. The archaic name *'El*, 'God', 'the Mighty One', occurs frequently (IQS I 2, 7, 8; IQpHab I 11, II 3, 4, 8, 9), sometimes in biblical quotations or allusions as a substitute for the tetragrammaton (e.g. CD III 8 which echoes Psalm 106:40). Not only so, but on occasion it is written in palaeo-Hebrew script (4Q183 I ii 3; IQ Mic (IQ 14) XII 3). The tetragrammaton itself appears (4Q 158 1–2: 15,16,18; 7–8: 1,3 etc.; 4Q Flor 1–3 I 3): on some occasions in palaeo-Hebrew characters when the rest of the text is in square characters (IQpHab VI 14, X 7, 14, XI 10; IQp Mic 1–5: 1, 2, etc.). On occasion four dots are substituted for the tetragrammaton (IQS VIII 14, quoting Isaiah 40:3). In the *Thanksgiving Hymns* the most commonly used name for the deity is *'ādônāy*, 'Lord' (IQH II 20, 31; III 19, 37 etc.) which again is used in substitution for the tetragrammaton at IQH VII 28, which echoes Exodus 15:11. These variant names not only make clear the reverence with which God was regarded, but that it was beginning to extend to the avoidance of the covenant name itself to avoid defaming it.[65] Still more notable is the fact that the surpassing greatness of God comes to expression not merely in terms of divine power contrasted with human feebleness, but divine holiness contrasted with human sinfulness. Thus IQH X (= XVIII) 1–12 contrasts the smallness, frailty and feebleness of humans with the immeasurable greatness of God, 'What, then, is man? He is nothing but earth ... See, you are the prince of gods ... Without your will nothing happens, and nothing is known without your wish. There is no-one besides you, no-one matches your strength, nothing in contrast with your glory, there is no price on your might.' Yet elsewhere the 'nothingness' of man is associated not merely with his finitude but with his sinfulness, 'I am a creature of clay, fashioned with water, foundation of shame, source of impurity, oven of iniquity, building of sin' (IQHI (= IX) 21–2). Or again, by way of comment on God's revelation of this power, 'What is flesh compared to this? What creature of clay can do wonders? He is in sin from his maternal womb, and in guilty iniquity right to old age' (IQH IV (= XII) 29–30). In a word, God stands apart from and above humanity not simply in terms of his greatness but in terms of his holy greatness.

Nevertheless, for all that the holiness of God

constitutes the fundamental datum about God, thereby in turn giving definition to the clamant need of the human situation, the power of God is in no sense underplayed. Indeed, it is probably true to say that more space is given to the divine power in Qumran thought than to any other aspect of the divine being. This is because three pervasive elements in that thought are expressive of and converge upon the idea of God's power, together showing that everything is within divine control. These three elements overlap and interact.

First, is the idea of God's power in creation. This is stated unambiguously at the beginning of the discourse on the Two Spirits, 'From the God of knowledge stems all there is and all there shall be', (IQS III 15). Likewise in the *Thanksgiving Hymns*, 'Be blessed, Lord, creator [of all things] [mighty] in acts, everything is your work' (IQH XVI = VIII, 16). What is of particular moment is the slant given to this affirmation. The primary concern is not to assert the power of God over all other gods, or reject the existence of any and every god besides *'El*. The concern is rather to assert that the world bears the stamp of the divine order and conforms to the pattern designed for it. In the words of Devorah Dimant, 'Creation is the materialization of the divine plan so establishing its total submission to God.'[66] This becomes plain in passage after passage in which the divine creation of the world is explicated in terms of the orderly rotation of the heavenly bodies, so that everything happens at its appointed time: which regularity becomes, in turn, the grid for establishing the religious calendar with its festivals and holy days. (IQS X 1–11; IQH I = IX 1–19; hence the emphasis on keeping the appointed times in IQS I 8–9,13–15, III 9–10).

It is to be noted – and this brings us to the second idea conveying the notion of God's power – that this understanding of the principles upon which God has caused his world to operate is described in terms of 'knowledge'. To repeat the line quoted earlier, 'From the God of knowledge stems all there is and all there shall be' (IQS III 15a). The frequent use in the texts of language denoting 'knowledge'[67] has led to proposals on the one hand that the Qumran sect was Gnostic (a view which attracted support during the earlier years of Qumran scholarship[68]) and on the other that the use of 'knowing' terminology did not differ from its use in the Hebrew Bible.[69] Both views are mistaken as they stand (even if the latter is closer to the truth than the former). There is clearly at Qumran a stress on knowledge which is novel in terms of its milieu.[70] When it is examined, not in terms of its meaning for members of the community, but in terms of what it conveys about God, his being and activity, then its coherence with the idea of his commanding power stands out clearly. The accent lies not on the formal admission that, by definition, a transcendent God must be omniscient. The accent lies rather on the *character* of his knowledge. Accordingly, what is stressed is the creative aspect of his knowledge, 'By his knowledge (*da'at*) everything shall come into being, and all that does exist he establishes with his calculations and nothing is done outside of him' (IQS XI 11a). This means therefore that his knowledge is no theorem, but comes to expression in the fulfilment of his will and purpose. In Reicke's words, 'for God, knowing is the same as doing.'[71] At times knowledge is spoken of paradoxically as standing over against God, waiting on his command, 'God loves knowledge (*da'at*) he has established wisdom (*ḥokmâh)* and counsel (*tûsîah)* before him; discernment (*'ārmāh*) and knowledge (*da'at*) are at his service' (CD II 3–4a). Yet again, his wisdom is the same as his will (IQH IX = I 14–15a).

Because knowledge and action are the same to God another element is injected into the meaning of God's power: namely, a strongly predestinarian note. Exactly how this is defined will be considered later. It is enough at this point to record the fact. 'From the God of knowledge stems all there is and all there shall be. Before they existed he made all their plans and when they came into being they will execute all their works in compliance with his instructions, according to his glorious design without altering anything' (IQS III 15b–16). 'He knows the result of his deeds for all times [everlas]ting and has given them as a legacy to the sons of men' (IQS IV 25b–26a). Thus God's knowledge works both to save and to condemn (IQS III 17b–26), and extends to the knowledge of the end-time (IQS IV 18b–23b). This knowledge God shares with his creatures (IQH IX 23–4), and not to inquire into 'his decrees in order to learn the hidden matters on which they err' is to invite exclusion from the covenant and everlasting annihilation (IQS V 11–13a).

A final feature which achieves high visibility in the Qumran depiction of the covenant – God is grace. The covenant takes its rise in the divine grace. It was the recollection of the first covenant which prompted the sparing of the remnant with whom the new covenant would be concluded (CD I 4–8). That covenant is therefore birthed in compassion and love. Indeed in CD VIII 14–18, Deuteronomy 9:5 is conflated with Deuteronomy 7:8 to insist that the divine love which was the foundation of the first covenant is likewise the foundation of the second. However, several emphases characteristic of (even if not unique to) Qumran emerge at this point. To begin with, the covenant love in question is, by definition, confined to the members of the sect. For them alone God is love (IQS II 1; XI 13b). For those outside their covenant there is only condemnation and eventual destruction (IQS II 4b–10, IV 9–14). Not least remarkable is the description of the community as the child of God, and God as its Father. 'For my mother did not know me, and my father abandoned me to you. Because you are father to all the sons of your truth. In them you rejoice, like one full of gentleness for her child, and like a wet-nurse, you clutch to your chest all your creatures' (IQH XV11 = IX 35–6). What is evidently happening here is that, the representation of Israel in the Old Testament as Yahweh's child (Exod. 3:22–3; Hos. 11:1–3) and Yahweh as Israel's Father (Is. 63:16, 64:8) is being claimed by the community as the continuation of the true Israel.[72] Again, the grace exhibited in the covenant is linked inseparably with divine righteousness. It is not that God is under any compulsion external to himself to behave this way rather than that. It is that, being who he is, namely a

God who does right, he will act consonantly with his nature. Thus, having covenanted with his chosen people to fulfil his purposes through them, he for his part will remain faithful to those purposes. The grace of God, as being a righteous grace, thus comes to involve pardon, cleansing and purification; and it is remarkable how this sequence of terms: grace, righteousness, pardon, cleansing, is used interchangeably.[73] In the words of column eleven of the *Community Rule*:

> As for me,
> If I stumble, the mercies of God
> shall be my eternal salvation.
> If I stagger because of the sin of flesh,
> my justification shall be
> by the righteousness of God which endures forever ...
> He will judge me in the righteousness of His truth
> and in the greatness of His goodness
> He will pardon all my sins.
> Through His righteousness he will cleanse me
> of the uncleanness of man
> and of the sins of the children of men,
> that I may confess to God His righteousness,
> and His majesty to the Most High.[74]

Precisely what is intended by the concepts referred to: how atonement is brought about and what is meant by cleansing, are questions that will receive fuller examination in more appropriate settings. Suffice it at this point to say that they are defining aspects of the character of the covenant-God.

Notes

1. Ringgren, Helmer, *The Faith of Qumran*, Theology of the Dead Sea Scrolls, Expanded Edition Edited with a New Introduction by Charlesworth, James H. New York: Crossroad, (1995), Chapter 1; Dombrowski, B.W., 'The Idea of God in IQSerek', *RQ*, 7, 4, December 1971, 515–31.

2. Chapter 2, pp. 84–92.
3. The vast majority in the distinctively sectarian texts: IQS (32), IQM (13), IQH (24), and CD (42).
4. E.g. IQS I 16 implies that to enter the community is to enter the covenant. Cf. III 11; IQSbV21. The evidence will be examined more closely below.
5. Weinfeld, M., art. *berith* in *TDOT* II Grand Rapids: Eerdmans, (1977), 253–79; Mendenhall, G.E., and Herion, G.A., art. 'Covenant', *ABD*, I, 1179–1202; Balzer, K., *The Covenant Formulary*, (Philadelphia: Fortress Press, 1971); McCarthy, D.J., *Treaty and Covenant*, (Rome: Biblical Institute Press, 1981).
6. See Jaubert, Annie, *La Notion D'Alliance Dans le Judaisme aux bords de l'ère chrétienne* Paris: Seuil, (1963), chs. 4–5.
7. Vermes, Geza, *The Dead Sea Scrolls, Qumran in Perspective* (hereafter *Perspective*), (Cleveland, Ohio: Collins, 1978), 163f, 165.
8. A fifth probable reference is IQp Hab II 3 where the word 'covenant' is missing from the text, but the word 'new' is clearly present. The addition of 'covenant' fits the sense and most editors accept it.
9. For the first see IQS I 16; II 12, 18; V 8, 20; CD II 2; VI 11; VII 21; IX 3. For the second see IQS I 18, 20, 24; II 10. For the third see IQS I 7, 11; V 1, 6, 8, 10, 21.
10. Jaubert, *Alliance*, 120.
11. Cf. 'Pour lui, ce n'était pas une rupture avec le passé, mais une conversion du coeur à une Loi mieux connue', Jaubert, op. cit, 138.
12. Kapelrud points to the fact that entry was based not on birth or mechanical rite (circumcision); that members must take the oath freely, and were answerable as individuals to the other members of the community. Kapelrud, Arvid S., 'Der Bund in den Qumran-Schriften', in Wagner, Siegfried (ed), *Bibel und Qumran, Beiträge zur Erforschung der Beziehungen zwischen Bibel-und Qumran wissenschaften* (Fs. Hans Bardtke) (Berlin: Töpelmann, 1968), 140, 142f.
13. Jaubert, *Alliance*, 128, 33.
14. The references are IQS IV 22; V 5; IQSb I 2; II 25; and IQM XVII 3. In the sixth example (CD III 4) the use is adverbial, but the meaning is the same.
15. References include IQS V 8; X 10; CD III 11; V 12; VII 5; XIII 14; XIV 2; XX 17.
16. E.g. Such phrases as 'covenant of Abraham' (CD XII 11);

'covenant of the fathers' (CD VIII 18; XIX 31); and 'covenant of the first ones' (CD I 4; III 4, 10; IV 9; VI 2; VIII 18; XV 8–9).

17. Jaubert, *Alliance*, 122.
18. Chapter I, n. 23.
19. Jaubert, *Alliance*, 211.
20. Jaubert, loc. cit.
21. Vermes' translation, *DSSE*, 105. The argument is unaffected by the debate as to what is meant by 'the land of Damascus'.
22. See note 8 above.
23. Jaubert, *Alliance*, 215f.
24. 'Mais jamais la Loi n'avait été mieux connue et mieux pratiquée par une collectivité en Israel' (op. cit, 223, cf. 224).
25. Op. cit, 222.
26. Op. cit, 219–222.
27. It is entirely in keeping with this that the term 'community' (*yaḥad*) is used vastly more often in this sense in IQS (approximately 45 of its 68 occurrences) than in any other text. The *Damascus Rule* does not use it in this sense at all, apparently preferring the term 'congregation' (*'ēdah*) for this purpose (10 out of 15 examples); likewise IQM (15 of 11 examples). Conversely, IQS uses *'ēdah* but once (IQS V 20) in reference to the community as an organized entity. IQSa and IQSb use both terms: *yāḥad* referring to an organized entity eleven times; *'ēdah* likewise with organizational reference twenty-four times. In one of these instances however, the terms stand in construct relationship, 'congregation of the community' (IQSa II 21). Moreover, in five of the seven instances of *yaḥad* in IQSa (I 26, 27, II 2, 11, 17), and one in IQSb (IV 26) the word stands in construct relationship with *'aṣāh* to mean 'council of the community'. This latter term also appears seventeen times in IQS, in thirteen of them in construct relationship with *yāḥad* to mean 'the council of the community'. R North has shown that 'congregation' (*'ēdah*) and 'council' (*'aṣāh*) are virtual equivalents. (Art. 'Qumran "Serek a" and Related Fragments', *Orientalia* 1, (1956), 90–9. It would seem that CD uses *'ēdah* to refer to Essene sect as a whole without discrimination of individual branches. IQS uses *yāḥad* to refer to the Qumran branch of the sect, with *'aṣat yāḥad* denoting its role as representative of the whole *'ēdah*. All three terms are brought together in IQSa and IQSb because of the eschatological setting of these documents in which all the branches of the sect are brought together at the end of days. This may also explain the usage of IQM.

28. This duality of sense may explain the remarkable use at IQH V 23 (= IQH XIII 23 in the reconstruction of É. Puech followed by Garcia Martinez) which reads, 'But I have been the target of sl[ander for my rivals] cause for quarrel and argument to my neighbours, for jealousy and anger to those who have joined my covenant.' This is striking inasmuch in IQH the normal mode is 'thy covenant' (18 of a total possible maximum of 23 examples). The parallel statement in IQH V (XIII) 24, 'they have mocked me with a wicked tongue all those who had joined my council', illustrates how 'covenant' can be denoted by a related term such as 'Council'. Presumably therefore, the reverse is also possible, giving rise to the (very unusual) example under discussion. (The point is not affected by the partial lacuna in IQH V 24, which some editors complete as ['akaṣā]tî (so Lohse), and others as [*berî*] *tî* (so Vermes). A comparable example is at IQH XIV (VI) 18.
29. The priests are sometimes referred to as 'the sons of Aaron': indeed, this is the case in IQS where, after twice identifying them as the 'sons of Zadok' the author proceeds to prescribe that entrants to the community shall be tested 'under the authority of the sons of Aaron' (21). Cf IQS IX 7. The point underlying this is not that there are two kinds of priests, but rather that the Zadokite priests are the true descendants of Aaron. For elaboration see M.A. Knibb, *The Qumran Community*, 105–6.
30. Cf. IQS VIII 1 where the community council is said to consist of twelve men and three priests; and CD IV 1–4 where the argument implies that the whole community are in some sense sons of Zadok. IQS V 20–2 virtually repeats IQS V 2–3.
31. Ilg, Norbert, 'Uberlegungen zum Verständnis von *Berîth* in den Qumrântexten', in M. Delcor, *Qumrân: Sa Piété, sa Théologie et son milieu* (Louvain: Leuven University, 1978), 257–63.
32. L.H. Schiffman writes, 'The sect shared the general tendency of Second Temple Judaism to move from priestly to lay leadership,' *Reclaiming*, 113.
33. The statement is conditional, 'And if they reside in the camps', implying that there were some who did not.
34. From Hebrew *hālakh*, 'to walk', used metaphorically of conduct or behaviour. It is used frequently with the noun 'way' (*derek*), a similarly common metaphor for the ethical life.
35. *DJD*, X, 191.

36. See the whole paragraph in *CRC*, 51. For a corrective to Sussman's opinion see the comment on a similar statement in J.M. Baumgarten, 'Sadducean Elements in Qumran Law', in *CRC*, 32.
37. Cf. IQS VIII 20–6; CD XV 7b–11, XVI 1–5, XIX 26b–31a.
38. Cf. L.H. Schiffman, *The Halakah at Qumran* (Studies in Judaism in Late Antiquity, Vol.XVI; (Leiden: E.J. Brill, 1975), 9–10. H. Gabrion, pointing to the sect's self-description as 'the house of the law' (CD XX 10), and what he describes as the 'massive presence' of Scripture in every scroll, continues, 'Cette dévotion extrème á la Torah, norme de vie absolue et idéal de perfection, est donc à la base du groupement des premiers sectaires'. Art. 'L' interprétation de l'Ècriture dans la littérature de Qumran', in W. Haase (ed), *Aufstieg und Niedergang der Römischen Welt, II Principät*, 19 Band, Berlin: de Gruyter, (1979), 779, 818.
39. This problem was not peculiar to the Essenes. For an account of the centrality of this problem in Second Temple Judaism and the different solutions achieved by the main parties see Schiffman, *Reclaiming*, Ch. 15.
40. See IQS V 7–12 for one of many passages in which this distinction is presupposed.
41. M. Kister points out that this implies that, 'Even before the appearance of the Teacher of Righteousness, the sect was established because its members became aware of their sins ... The members of the sect erred along with the rest of the people ... and it was the proper observance of these commandments which was (Divinely) revealed to the sect's founders.' 'Some Aspects of Qumran Halakhah' in Julio Trebolle Barrera and Luis Vegas Montaner, *The Madrid Qumran Congress*, Volume Two, (Leiden: Brill, 1972), 572. It is this that appears to be in mind in the references to 'the first', i.e. members of the sect (CD IV 6, 9) and 'the first directives (*mishpāṭîm hāriŝônîm*) which the men of the Community began to be taught' (IQS IX 10).
42. Gabrion, art. cit, 820f; Lawrence H. Schiffmann, *Sectarian Law in the Dead Sea Scrolls*, Brown, *Judaic Studies*, 33, (Chico, 1983), 12. The point must be seen against the background of the Essene belief that the community was in communion with the heavenly world, thereby acquiring access to the divine mysteries. See Christopher Rowland, *The Open Heaven: A Study of Apocalyptic in Judaism and Early Christianity*, (London: SPCK, 1982), 115–20. At the same time this does

not mean that the distinction between Scripture and halakhah was abolished, or that halakha was regarded as Scripture. The point is well put by Markus N.A. Bockmuehl, *Revelation and Mystery in Ancient Judaism and Pauline Christianity*, (Tübingen: Mohr-Siebeck, 1990), 45f. Within this framework revelation was both *direct* as being the act of divine disclosure or the impartation of insight, but also *derived* as being mediated through Scripture. *4QMMT*, 23–5.

43. This seems to be the import of the latter part of the passage. The verbs have perfect meaning and would naturally be taken to refer to the breach of the Mosaic covenant. On the other hand, the treachery decried in I 12–II 1 is in language typical of that used to describe its contemporary opponents, including the individual behind the name 'the scoffer'. Knibb suggests that an original reference to the breach of the Mosaic covenant has been changed into a reference to apostates from the sectarian covenant (*Qumran Community*, 22–5). The point of moment is that either way, the Teacher is reported as having addressed his message to the generation (s) of the end-time.
44. This is especially so if at least some of the *Hodayoth* were written by him. The case has been argued most fully and persuasively by G. Jeremias, *Der Lehrer der Gerechtigkeit*, Studien zur Umwelt des NT.2., (Gottingen: Vandenhoeck und Ruprecht, 1963). Arguing that 'Danklieder' is a distinctive category of songs among the *Hodayot*, in which the personality of the author enters largely, speaking from concrete situations, he traces these to the Teacher of Righteousness (170–7).
45. This is confirmed by the fact that *teacher* is the title applied to him not lawgiver or prophet. For a close examination of the Teacher of Righteousness as compared to Moses see Betz, Otto, *Offenbarung und Schriftforschung in der Qumransekte* (WUNT 6. Tübingen, Mohr-Siebeck, 1960), 61–8. Betz concludes that, despite parallels, the Teacher of Righteousness is decidedly less than Moses (67f).
46. Davies, P.R., entertains the possibility that the 'voice of the Teacher' supersedes the law, if only by interpreting it definitively. Art.,' Halakhah at Qumran' in Davies, Philip R., and White, Richard T., *A Tribute to Geza Vermes*, (JSOT Supplement Series 100: Sheffield Academic Press, 1990), 48. But the text seems rather to conjoin them – which, indeed, is no small matter.
47. Vermes, G., 'The Qumran Interpretation of Scripture in its

Historical Setting', in *Post-Biblical Jewish Studies* (Leiden, Brill, 1975), 43. To the same effect, Sussmann, Y., *DJD* X 187.

48. Loc.cit.
49. It might be objected that the halakhah of 4QMMT is as stringent as any, and yet, as Sussmann correctly points out (*DJD* X 186), applied to the entire Jewish people. But if 4QMMT represents the halakhah which the nation at large had forsaken, prompting the creation of a separated group that was prepared to abide by it (as maintained above), that simply becomes another way of saying that the stringent halakhah could only find compliance within a community constituted on different principles of membership.
50. IQS I 2, 5, 7, 16, V 3, 20, 22, VIII 2, 3, 15, IX 13; CD II 21, III 8, IV 8, VI 14, XV 10, XVI 8. There are additional examples in IQp HabVII 11, VIII 1, XII 4.
51. Section C line 27, *DJD*, X, 62f.
52. Schiffmann, *Reclaiming*, 83, 86.
53. *DJD* X 47, 63, together with 5.3.2.2 on p139.
54. Of the 130 or so instances listed in Charlesworth, J.H., *Graphic Concordance to the Dead Sea Scrolls* (Tübingen, Mohr-Siebeck, Louisville, Westminster John Knox, 1991) 407–8, E. Qimron adduces two (4QFlor. 1–2 i 7 and IQS VI 18) in support of the rendering 'precepts'. But Garcia Martinez shows that the former is based on a misreading of the manuscript, and the latter does not fit the context in that meaning but does so in the meaning of 'deeds' or 'works'. "4QMMT in a Qumran Context" in Kampen, John, and Bernstein, Moshe J. (eds.), *Reading 4QMMT*, New Perspectives on Qumran Law and History, Atlanta, Scholars Press (1996), 23–5.
55. Art. cit, 25f. Sussmann likewise prefers the rendering 'deeds' at B 2 and C 27. He comments, 'From the expressions "some words regarding the deeds" and "some of the deeds of the Torah" we may infer that that letter discusses specific halakhot whose details were disputed by the sect and its opponents. It is possible that the term *ma'aśeh* is already used here in the sense of 'performance of a religious precept' (*DJD* X, 185f).
56. *DJD*, X 61–3.
57. *DJD*, X 63.
58. Eisenman and Wise discern the influence of both Genesis 15:6 and Psalm 106:31 on 4QMMT C 31 (*DSSU*, 198). Martin Abegg more precisely sees Psalm 106:31 as lying behind it. See art., 'Paul, "Works of the Law" and MMT', *BAR*,

November–December 1994, 20, 6, 55, including footnote.

59. The literature on the subject is immense. See note 3 above for literature on the covenant form. On the covenant and salvation see Sanders, E.P., 'The Covenant as a Soteriological Category and the Nature of Salvation in Palestinian and Hellenistic Judaism' in Hamerton-Kelly, Robert and Scroggs, Robin, (eds), *Jews, Greeks, and Christians*, Fs. W.D. Davies, Leiden: Brill, (1976), 11–44. On the same topic at Qumran see idem, *Paul and Palestinian Judaism, a Comparison of Patterns of Religion*, London: SCM Press, (1977), Ch. II. Sanders summarizes the general view in Palestinian Judaism as being that membership in the covenant saves, even without perfect obedience; the effort and intent to obey the law and atonement for transgressions preserve one in the covenant; certain transgressions or transgressions wilfully persisted in could remove one from the covenant and from the covenant promises. This was the case regarding national or individual salvation (art. cit, 21f).
60. The expression is used frequently in such contexts. E.g. CD III 1 (antecedent in II 17), 5, 11–12; IQS II 25, III 3, V 4, etc.
61. Cf. Sanders, E.P., 'There is no indication in the entrance regulations that all these things are not within the range of human achievement', (*Paul and Palestinian Judaism*, 264). And again, 'Perfect obedience was the aim, and, within the tightly ordered community structure was not considered a totally impossible goal' (op. cit, 286).
62. So Kapelrud, art. cit, 147.
63. There is, in any case, dispute regarding the extent to which the character of a religion can be deduced from its law. Contrary to Kapelrud (see previous note) is Vermes who writing of the sectarian list of faults with their corresponding sentences says it 'tells us more about the mentality of the Dead Sea ascetics than any isolated exposition of their doctrine and principles can do' (*DSSP*, 92). Schiffman maintains that only legal texts can show us what life meant to them (*Sectarian Law in the DSS*, 9).
64. Dombrowski, B.W., 'The Idea of God in IQ Serek', (*RQ* 7, 4, December 1971, 515–31), holds that the *Community Rule* depicts God as an acting person, revealed through his actions, but also makes references to his *essentia*, the two being complementary (518).
65. A much fuller statement of evidence to this effect may be found in Fitzmyer, Joseph A., *Responses to 101 Questions on*

the Dead Sea Scrolls, (New York/Mahwah: Paulist Press, 1992) 48–52.

66. Dimant, Devorah, 'Qumran Sectarian Literature', in Stone, M.E. (ed), *Jewish Writings of the Second Temple Period, CRINT*, Volume II, (Leiden: Brill, 1984), 533.
67. For a survey see Romaniuk, C., 'Le Thème de la Sagesse dans les Documents de Qumran', *RQ*, 9, 1977–8, 429–35. An earlier attempt at the same, which had reached much the same conclusions as Romaniuk was to reach, is Davies W.D., 'Knowledge in the Dead Sea Scrolls', *HTR*, 1953, 113–39, reprinted in *Christian Origins and Judaism*, (London: Darton, Longman & Todd, 1962), 119–44. (The survey of terminology in the latter volume is found on 124–34.)
68. E.g. Schubert, K., *The Dead Sea Community, Its Origin and Teachings*, (London: A & C Black, 1959), 71–5. Schubert characterizes Qumran thought as 'Jewish Gnosticism' (74).
69. See Reicke, B., 'Da'at and Gnosis in Intertestamental Literature', in Ellis, E.E., and Wilcox, Max (eds.), *Neotestamentica et Semitica*, Fs. Black, M., (Edinburgh: T & T. Clark, 1969), 245–255.
70. Cf. Davies, W.D., *Christian Origins and Judaism*, 140. The implications of this for the nature of Qumran religion will be considered below.
71. Reicke, art. cit. 247.
72. What is especially notable in IQH IX 35–6 is the implication that, because God is Father of all the sons of truth he is therefore Father to the psalmist as an individual, whereas in the Old Testament the prevailing sense is corporate or national. For other examples of the individual sense in the Qumran texts see 4Q372 1 16, 'My Father, my God'; and 4Q460 515, 'My Father my Lord'. (Note that the photograph of the ms. is erroneously numbered PAM 42.441. The words in question are clear in PAM 44.017 and 43.365). As to the latter, the words referred to are very plain in PAM 43.542, and are so transcribed in Wacholder-Abegg, fasc.III 345. Schuller suggests that this manner of addressing God may have been more common in Palestinian Judaism than has been suspected hitherto (362).
73. The point is well expounded in Nötscher, *Zur Theologischen Terminologie der Qumran-Texte, Bonner Biblische Beitrag*, 10, (Bonn: Peter Hanstein Verlag, 1956), 183–5.
74. IQS XI 11c–12, 14–15a (Vermes' translation). To the same effect see IQH XII = IV 35f; XVII = IX 33.

Chapter Four

The Dilemma: History, the Human Predicament and the Divine Requirement

While the covenant was the dominant reality in the minds of the Qumran sectaries, it did not function in an ideological vacuum. The covenant functioned not only in terms of its own prescriptions but also in terms of an overall world-view. Specifically, it operated within the frame of reference of a particular understanding of the *modus operandi* of God, humanity and the relationship between the two. What this implied is brought into clearer resolution by exploring the sectarian understanding of history, the human situation, or more exactly, the human predicament, and how these two gave definition to the matter of purity which had far-reaching implications for the functioning of the covenant.

History

The basic premise upon which the Qumran covenantal theology rests is that God is active in history. The two ideas are, indeed, inseparable. The God who made 'the covenant of the very first' (CD I 4b) 'delivered them up to the sword' when they were unfaithful (CD I 4a, 3a). However, he also 'saved a remnant for Israel' (CD I 4–5a) whom he caused 'to possess his land and to become fat with the good things of his soil' (CD I 7b–8a). That is to say the God who acted in history in the past is active again in the present as is shown in his renewing of the covenant with the sect. Still more, the divine intervention in history in the past and the present gives grounds for expecting his activity in the future. Thus *War Scroll*, whose concern is with the ultimate eschatological battle, thrice assures the warriors that 'the battle is yours' (IQM XI 1, 2c, 4b) by pointing to the fate of Goliath (2), the Philistines (3) and the Egyptians (9f).

Such a line of argument, however, presupposes a linkage between past, present and future. That linkage might be expressed by saying that the same God who was active in the past and present would be active similarly in the future. Ultimately, that is not untrue. However, it overlooks a middle term in Qumran thought which comes to expression repeatedly: namely that God has constructed the world, including human beings, to operate in accordance with certain prescribed patterns or along certain prescribed lines. To live in accordance with this pattern is to keep faith with his plans and purposes; to live athwart his pattern is to flout his will and way.

Another way of saying this is that behind history stands creation. The emphasis in the Qumran texts is not so much on creation as the act of God (though, of course, this is not denied); the emphasis is rather that God has designed creation to function in an orderly way. This divine order encompasses the entire created universe, human beings included, and to live contrary to it is to live against the grain of life. Thus, this order is grounded in unchanging laws. Hence, in the long sequence IQH IX (= I) 8–20 the 'will (*rāṣôn*) of God' (8, 10, 15); the 'laws (*ḥûqqîm*)' of God (10c); the 'regulation of the times' (*bemô 'ēdēh lĕmemšaltām*: 17) predetermined by God are the powers which effectively control all persons (9), supernatural spirits (10–11a), the luminaries (11c–12a), the powers of nature (12b–15a), the imposition of judgment (17–18a). The sequence concludes with the blanket declaration, 'And in the wisdom of your knowledge you have determined their course before they came to exist. And with [your approval] everything happens, and without you nothing occurs' (19–20).

It is worth tracing in fuller detail the extent to which this is taken, and the practical inferences drawn from it. To say, for example, that the courses of the luminaries are determined by God is not only to say that their order is perfect; it is also to say that their order is a transcript of what the order of worship on earth should be, in terms of the timing of its seasons, festivals and worship. Hence, there is very much a right and a wrong calendar for the regulation of religious observances; getting it wrong is much more than miscalculation; it is a breach of the divine order of the universe.[1]

Another sphere in which the outworking of the comprehensive will of God is seen at Qumran is in the ongoing movement of history. The idea emerges repeatedly throughout the texts, but comes to concise expression in 4Q *Ages of Creation* (4Q180), sometimes known as the *Pesher on the Periods*.[2] Dissenting from J.T. Milik who not only coalesces 4Q180 and 4Q181 into a single text, but sees it as concerned with the intervention of angels in human affairs and a sacerdotal interest in Mount Zion,[3] D. Dimant convincingly argues that it is concerned with the divinely pre-ordained periods of history. The text affirms that, before creation, God fixed the spans of the successive eras or periods of history. Their purpose is to bring all that is and will be to completion (*lehātēm* – I 1): a term which carries both the ideas of fulfilment and termination. That is to say, the principle at work in all the periods is to come into being and to perish. However, these periods are not mechanical; they are made by God whose will they embody. Accordingly, one follows another in pre-ordained sequence: a point expressed vividly, if typically, by saying that the sequence is engraved on the heavenly tablets (I 3). These have existed from the beginning and contain the history of humanity and all its deeds, good and evil. The power humans exercise is determined by them.

The text proceeds to work this out by tracing the order of generations from Shem to Abraham (I 4–10) with special reference to the angels who sinned with the daughters of men. Likewise, fragments 2–4 treat episodes from Lot to the destruction of Sodom making the points that all is predestined, yet nonetheless sin brings judgment. A transition is thus made from the universal plane to the individual.

This concept, which constitutes the backcloth of Qumran thought regarding the human situation, emerges at numerous points in the texts. Thus, in regard to the scale of history as a whole, the preamble to the covenant renewal liturgy in the *Damascus Rule* consists of a broad overview of history as constituted by the penitent on the one hand and the rebellious on the other. 'And he knew the years of their existence, and the number and detail of their ages, of all those who exist over the centuries, and of those who will exist, until it occurs in their ages throughout all the everlasting years' (CD II 9b–10). A similar application of the same principle reads, 'And the exact interpretation of their ages about the blindness of Israel in all these matters, behold, it is defined in the book of the divisions of the periods, according to their jubilees and their weeks' (CD XVI 2b–4a). A striking concrete illustration of the principle is its use in the *Habakkuk Commentary* to explain the delay of the eschaton. The passage of Habakkuk in question deals with the 'appointed time', which 'will have an end and not fail', even though it be delayed (Hab. 2:3). The explanation given is, 'Its interpretation concerns the men of truth, those who observe the Law, whose hands will not desert the service of truth when the final age is extended beyond them, because all the ages of God will come at the right time, as he established for them in the mysteries of his prudence' (IQp Hab VII 10–14). That is to say, the delay in the coming of the end is apparent rather than real; in truth it will arrive at the time pre-ordained by God.[4] The psalmist likewise, confesses the futility of attempting to hide his sin, because 'everything has been engraved in your presence with the stylus of remembrance for all the incessant periods in the eras of the number of everlasting years in all their predetermined times, and nothing will be hidden, nothing will remain away from your presence' (IQH IX = I 24).

It is difficult to overstate the importance of this feature of the sectarian thought. In many respects, it is the bedrock on which the entire construct rests, the covenant included. This has been reinforced by the publication (albeit in preliminary form) of two groups of texts: one, known as the *Sapiential Texts*[5], the other, as the *Book of Mysteries*[6]. The existence of such material among the Qumran texts had long been known, going back to the earliest official publications[7]; while elements of wisdom and mystery language and thought were clearly present in the leading published texts. What had been less clear was the scale of such material in the Qumran corpus, and consequently, its implications for the overall characterization of Qumran thought. In particular, it was striking that such elements were to be found not only in liturgical or quasi-liturgical texts, or in 'biblical' texts such as the *Pesharim*, but in texts whose entire character is meditative and reflective.

The longest of the *Sapiential Texts* is derived chiefly from 4Q 416–418.[8] The title given to it by Eisenman and Wise, 'The Mystery of Existence'[9], and still more 'The Secret of the Way Things Are'[10] by Wise, Abegg, and Cook indicate both its content and its angle of approach. There are features which it shares with the *Pesher on the Periods* (4Q *Ages of Creation* or 4Q180) and with the wisdom elements already noted in the Qumran corpus. For example, the term 'periods' (*qezîm*) occurs five times[11] while the related idea of the engraving of the divine decrees is also found.[12] Equally significant is the presence of other terms found readily in the sectarian texts: 'inclination' (*yēṣer*)[13], 'flesh' (*bāśar*) in a pejorative sense,[14] 'eternal planting' (*matt'at' 'ôlam*).[15]

More important, however, than the links between 4Q416–418 and the sectarian texts are the distinguishing features which are juxtaposed alongside them. Chief among these is the 'mystery of existence' (*raznihyāh*) mentioned again and again.[16] Two items are of particular note. One is the means by which the mystery is to be penetrated.

The reader is repeatedly exhorted to 'investigate' (4Q417 2 II 13, 4Q Frag.81 7), 'consider' (4Q418 Frag.9 1b, Frag.123 II 5), 'understand' (4Q418 Frag.81 15). In this way he will attain the knowledge of truth and wickedness (4Q417 Frag.2 I f), good and evil (18) and the glory of God on the one hand and the poverty of his own deeds on the other (11–13). By the examination of life in the context of the sovereign power of God, the sage will come to understanding (4Q416 Frag.2 III 14–19a; 4Q417 Frag.1 I 10b–11).[17] The second notable feature is that, coupled with this is a distinctly eschatological thrust.[18] The writer looks forward to a day when God will put an end to evil: 'every evil act will perish, and the era of truth will be complete' (4Q416 Frag. 1 13).[19] What appears to be taking place here is what L.H. Schiffman happily calls 'a wedding of wisdom and prophecy.'[20] There are references to 'divine visitations' and the 'eternal visitation' (4Q417 Frag. 2 I 6–8, 14) which appear to refer to divine judgments in all the periods, and the final judgment at the end of the last period. If this is so, then it constitutes a ready bridge between eschatology in general and apocalyptic in particular on the one hand, and wisdom on the other. This in turn has the effect of modifying the apocalyptic hue which is sometimes given to Qumran thought: not, indeed, by eliminating the apocalyptic note but by demonstrating that it co-existed peacefully with the wisdom mode of theologizing. Revelation through the Teacher of Righteousness and the inspired exegesis of Scripture were not the only ways in which the divine purposes were made plain.

The foregoing reading of the *Pesher on the Periods* appears to be confirmed by the *Book of Mysteries* (IQ27, 4Q299–301),[21] a work of related type. Several points are made which are relevant to our interest. First, it is insisted that nature and history embody the mysteries of creation, which are simply another term for the wisdom of God. Second, these mysteries have been made accessible to all, yet they have failed to penetrate them. In particular, they have failed to understand what will happen in the future, because they have failed to understand what happened in the past (IQH27: 3–4; 4Q300, Frag.3, 3–4). If it be asked why, the answer is that wisdom is morally conditioned: necessarily so, since wisdom is the ability to distinguish between good and evil. It is to the righteous that God reveals his secrets, not to '[the wiz]ards, learned in iniquity' (4Q 300 frg. 1 col. II 1). But third, at this point wisdom impinges upon apocalyptic for, as we have seen, the wisdom to understand the past contains the wisdom to understand the future. And the sign that wisdom was about to find her fulfilment was that evil would be extirpated (4Q300 frg.3 4b–6).[22] But, fourthly, if one asks why some understand and others do not, the answer is that all is in the hands of God.

> He causes every thing [which comes into being] H[e is from be]fore eternity, the Lord is his name, and for e[ternity ... the p]lan of the time of birth He opened be[fore them [...] for he tested our heart, and He caused us to inherit [...] every mystery and the tribulations [that would come] upon every creature.[23]

Again, then, we are back at an understanding of history in which all is contained within the mysteries of God and is open to discovery by the righteous. Here the predestinarian note again comes into view. But yoked with it is the emphasis that not only is history in God's hands, but one day it will come to an end with the destruction of evil. In a word, wisdom and apocalyptic are again seen to be functioning in harness.[24]

However, more needs to be said than that God is active in history, and his purposes are being worked out in it. Clearly, history is not a flawless transcript of the divine will, and while the predestinarian statements taken alone have a mechanistic ring, they are not the only mode of description of the operation of history. History is more than a mechanical process in which the divine purpose steamrollers forward on its irresistible way; it is also depicted as a war which implies opposing wills and powers. In many respects, it is the latter which is more visible.

The Qumran thought-world was peopled not only by God and his human creatures. It was populated also by spirit-beings, good and bad. While they retain a certain elusiveness inasmuch as no account is given of their origin, and most of them remain un-named, there is no doubt that they play a large role in Qumran thought. In an important measure they impart reality to history by injecting movement into what would otherwise be the relentless unfolding of the plan and will of God, human beings serving merely as tokens to be moved about the chessboard of the divine purpose. However, behind what would otherwise be a tableau if the events of history and the acts of humans were simply the moves predetermined by God, there is a conflict of supernatural proportions in progress. On the one side stands the Prince of Lights and on the other the Angel of Darkness (IQS III 20–1), each with his supporting minions (line 24a). These are apparently identical with the angel of truth (line 24b) and the spirit of deceit (IV 9a), who also travel under other descriptions (line 23b). The extent to which this was systematized is questionable.[25] The point of importance is that God's will and working in history do not go unopposed, even if his will ultimately prevails. And of particular moment is the fact that these supernatural beings, angelic and demonic, effect their purposes through direct influence upon human creatures.

On the one hand the members of the community are depicted as living in the presence of the angels of light. This accounts for a whole range of practices spelled out in the texts; from the exclusion of the defiled and deformed (CD XV 15–17; IQSa II 5b–9a) to the affirmation that in its worship the community is united with the sons of heaven (IQS XI 7–8). On the other hand, they are also exposed to the pressures of the angels of darkness. This is especially the case in the *War Rule* in which the 'people of God' and the 'men of his lot' do battle against 'all the lot of Belial' (IQM I 5). In such a setting, there is necessarily a taking of sides with the good ranged against the evil. However, individual personal experience is less clean-cut, and in describing it the notion of 'angels' who 'help' the opposing sides (IQS III 24b–25a) is supplemented with that of 'spirits': specifically the spirits of truth and deceit, of light and darkness. But this brings us to another dimension of the dilemma with which Qumran theology wrestles: namely the human predicament.

The Human Predicament

If the human predicament were merely that human beings are prisoners of the angels of darkness then presumably their plight could be resolved fairly readily by the mounting of a rescue operation by the angels of light. But that overlooks two vitally important aspects of the human situation as Qumran theology discerned it. First, it overlooks the fundamental premise that God as sovereign is the source of 'all there is and all there shall be' (IQS III 15b). In terms of the predestinarian views of the sect already noted, this means that God pre-ordains those who shall do good and those who shall do evil. Accordingly, no theological construct is admissible which makes possible the total elimination of evil. The existence of demons and their deadly work may indeed be intended to exculpate God from direct responsibility for evil,[26] but there is no denial of the existence of evil, nor promise of its extirpation without a struggle.

But, second, to construe the human situation exclusively in terms of a war between good angels and bad angels misrepresents the real state of affairs in two important respects. To begin with it depicts evil as being a phenomenon external to humanity rather than one in which human persons are themselves involved; and, deriving from that, it fails to do justice to the depth to which the human person has been penetrated by evil. In a word, the doctrine of the 'Two Spirits in Persons' is the doctrine of the Angels of Light and Darkness in the cosmos transposed into an individual, personal key.[27] According to the doctrine, God 'created man to rule the world and placed within him two spirits so that he would walk with them until the moment of his visitation: they are the spirits of truth and of deceit. In the hand of the Prince of Lights is dominion over all the sons of justice; they walk on paths of light. And in the hand of the Angel of Darkness is total dominion over the sons of deceit; they walk on paths of darkness. Due to the Angel of Darkness all the sons of justice stray ... However, the God of Israel and the angel of his truth assist all the sons of light' (IQS III 17b–22a; 24b–25a). 'Until now the spirits of truth and of injustice feud in the heart of man, and they walk in wisdom or in folly. In agreement with man's birthright in justice and in truth, so he abhors injustice; and according to his share in the lot of injustice he acts irreverently in it and so abhors the truth. For God has sorted them into equal parts until the appointed end and the new creation' (IQS IV 23b–25a).

It has been questioned whether the doctrine so expressed is wholly consistent. For example, IQS III 20–21b seems to imply that individuals are either sons of justice ruled by the Prince of Lights or sons of deceit ruled by the Angel of Darkness, whereas lines 18f and 21b–22 imply that the sons of light are exposed to the attentions of the Angel of Darkness. The latter appears to be the correct interpretation as III 18 and IV 23c seem clearly to state.[28] Moreover, the transposition of the idea from the terminology of opposing angels battling for the control of the soul to that of spirits struggling within the soul of the individual has important implications for the understanding of the human predicament. For one thing, it adds a dimension of depth to the human plight. The human person is no longer simply an external object over whom the powers of good and evil contend; rather he is possessed in some measure by both, so that the struggle takes place within him rather than around him.

It is true that predestination is not the sole factor conditioning the human situation. Much is said which implies the reality of free choice in an important measure. Membership of the community is open to volunteers:[29] there is no suggestion of converts being dragooned into the covenant. On the contrary there is an elaborate initiation course to be submitted to before full admission is finally granted. Indeed, it is fair to say that the assumption upon which the whole system rests – of conforming to the rules, repenting and doing penance for infractions, and holding firm to the prescriptions of the sect – makes sense only on the premise that the responsible commitment of the individual is meaningful. 'Those in harmony with you', prays the psalmist, 'will persist in your presence always; those who walk on the path of your heart will be established permanently' (IQH XII = IV 21–22). Nevertheless, it remains the case that the predestinarian insistence is not qualified or weakened.[30] This is illustrated strikingly in *4Q Horoscope* (4Q 186) in which the physiological features are treated as an index of the relative proportions of light and darkness present in the individual's spirit.[31] Presumably this is simply an extension to humans of the principle that the world functions in keeping with the lines along which it was made. It may be that this is what is meant by the 'weighing of the spirits' of new recruits by the Maskil in IQS IX 14. At all events, it underscores the extent to which determinism entered into the fabric of the thought of the sect.[32]

The human predicament is indicated not only by the concept of the two spirits in the individual but also by the idea of the inward inclination (*yēṣer*). The term does not always carry this sense, sometimes denoting individual creatureliness as in IQH I 21, 'I am a creature of clay' (*yēṣer haḥēmār*). Even when denoting inclination or disposition its meaning is sometimes neutral (IQH VII 13). In most instances however, it is clearly associated with evil, denoting the evil designs of the psalmist's desire (XIII = V 6) or the evil intention of his enemies towards him (XIII = V 32).[33] It is usages like the former which give definition to the 'evil inclination' as a measure of the human plight. The passage reads: '[Thou hast not] judged me according to my guilt, nor hast Thou abandoned me because of the designs of my inclination; but Thou hast saved my life from the Pit' (Vermes). The connotation here is clearly the human bent towards evil.[34] Mowinckel comments, 'Which definite *sins* he had committed he does not tell, but at all events they seem to have been sins of thoughts and desires rather than wrong deeds and ritual trespasses. His religious and moral conscience is more concerned with the status of his heart than with external things.'[35] There is no impression that the plight of the psalmist results from his failure to manipulate his good and evil inclinations into perfect equipoise. Indeed, at this point the use of *yēṣer* to denote creaturely weakness effectively crosses the moral frontier, so that he is weak because he is warped, 'I am a creature of clay, fashioned with water, foundation of shame, source of impurity, oven of iniquity, building of sin, spirit of mistake, astray, without knowledge' (IQH IX = I 21b–22. Cf. IV = XVII 19).

Remarkably, in IQS V 4–5 the term 'inclination' appears to be substituted for the word 'heart'. The passage, which evidently echoes biblical texts such as Deuteronomy 10:16, Psalms 93:10, and Jeremiah 3:17, reads thus, 'No one should walk in the stubbornness of his heart in order to go astray following his heart and his eyes and the musings of his inclination (*yēṣer*). Instead he should circumcise in the community the foreskin of his tendency (*yēṣer*) and of his stiff neck in order to lay a foundation of truth for Israel, for the community of the eternal covenant.' O.J.F. Seitz wrote, 'It would appear that the compilers of the *Manual* were already well on the way to a kind of exegesis which discovered in Deuteronomy 10:16 "uncircumcised" as one of the seven biblical names for the *yēṣer harā'*.'[36] If anything, this probably understates the case. D.R. Seely (working with texts not available to Seitz), points out how closely the language of the 'heart' is related to that of the 'covenant',[37] drawing attention to the statement in 4Q434 regarding the members of the community, 'He has circumcized their hearts and has saved them by his grace and has set their feet firm on the path.'[38]

To this may be added the concept of 'stubbornness of heart' (*šerîrût lēb*) which occurs eight times in the

Community Rule, six times in the *Damascus Document* and once in the *Thanksgiving Hymns*. The examples in the *Damascus Rule*[39] are of particular interest since it has been alleged that the view of sin in the *Damascus Document* is much more formal and shallow than that in other texts.[40] All six instances clearly show that it denotes the inward state which gives rise to individual acts of sin: a conclusion which is wholly consistent with the use of 'heart' (*lēb*) in IQS and other parts of CD. Even more notable: three of the six instances occur in the historical recital in II 14 – III 18, the example in II 17 being used in parallel with *yēṣer* in II 15,20. There is then, in CD an awareness of a deeper dimension to sin than the level of action: the human predicament lies in what the human person *is* even more than in what he *does*.[41]

The aforementioned individual elements are but components of the overall understanding of sin at Qumran with which they cohere, and which they illustrate with great vividness. They also serve as pointers to the differentia of the Qumran understanding of sin which is simply another way of saying the Qumran understanding of the human predicament. Of course, the Qumran view of sin rests ultimately on the teaching of the Old Testament which supplies both its terminology and fundamental content. Wheeler Robinson observed that 'the principal terms employed in the Old Testament with reference to sin may be grouped in four classes, according as they denote:

(1) deviation from the right way;
(2) the changed status (guilt) of the agent;
(3) rebellion against a superior or unfaithfulness to an agreement;
(4) some characterization of the quality of the act itself.'[42]

The first class would include terms like *haṭṭā, 'awĕlâ', 'åwôn*; the second words like *'ašmā' and 'reša'*; the third *peša'* which, according to Wheeler Robinson, is the most important class 'because it yields a positive idea of sin, that of *rebellion*, and because this idea conducts us along the line of the religious history of Israel to the specific sense of sin in relation to God'.[43] All of these terms are readily found in the senses indicated.[44]

However, it is none of these alone nor all of them together which bring into focus the dominant emphasis which sin receives in the Qumran texts, and in turn transmits to its perception of the human predicament. It is rather a series of usages which, without repudiating or diminishing any of the features just noted, combine to denote the gravamen of the human situation as understood at Qumran. The first, to which attention is drawn by Jürgen Becker, is that in the *Thanksgiving Hymns*, with the single exception of IQH XII = IV 10, all references to sin are in the singular: a phenomenon which he takes to mean that the chief interest lies not in individual acts of sin but in sin viewed as a unity.[45] This might be explained in that the *Hodayot*, as expressions of religious devotion, might well seek blanket absolution through blanket confession. But this hardly meets the point, since the phenomenon is found elsewhere and in a variety of forms.

Conspicuous among these forms is the account given of the human creature, *'ādam*. That the Qumran mind wrestled with the problem of the constitution of human nature is evident from the treatise of the Two Spirits in Persons (IQS III 13–IV 26) considered already. The introductory formula makes this plain, 'For the wise man, that he may inform and teach all the sons of light about the history of all the sons of man' (III 13). The word rendered 'history' (*tôldôt*) carries the meaning 'nature':[46] indeed, it is significant that the accounts of the works of the spirits of light and darkness (respectively in IV 2–6a and IV 9–11) consist almost entirely of qualities of character.

However, the picture conveyed by the usage of the term *'ādam* is even more penetrating in its depiction of the degradation of the human situation. Besides a handful of examples in Wisdom texts and apocryphal psalms examples of the term with theological connotation are concentrated chiefly in the *Community Rule* and the *Thanksgiving Hymns*. Six of the seven occurrences in IQS occur in column XI:[47] and the intensity of feeling characteristic of the *Thanksgiving Hymns* comes readily to mind. Ringgren cautions, 'There is an overwhelming impression of man's nothingness and depravity. This probably has its explanation at least partially in a radical, personal experience on the part of the author of the *Thanksgiving Psalms*. One must carefully avoid regarding these personal and subjective outpourings as dogmatic statements designed to be universally applicable.'[48] The point is well taken and its possible relevance to the closing hymn of IQS is evident. On the other hand, the hymn of IQS differs from the *Thanksgiving Hymns* in that it is incorporated in what appears to be a handbook of the faith and practice of the sect.

When the examples of *'ādam* other than those found in the *Thanksgiving Hymns* are examined, they seem to resolve themselves into three categories. Some denote humankind in its frailty. This is the case with *4Q Songs of the Sage*[b] (4Q511 [4Q*Shir*[b]]) where, after recounting the doings of God in terms reminiscent of Isaiah 40:12–15, the writer concludes, 'Man does not do these things. How, then, can man measure the spirit [of God]?'(6). 4Q *Sapiential Work* (4Q185) I 10–13 is of the same cut, describing human fragility in images like those of Isaiah 40:6–8. The other example which falls into this category, 'What, indeed, is man among all your marvelous deeds'? (IQS XI 20) stands in a comparable thought context (lines 17–19). This writer, however, is not content to leave the question a rhetorical one, but proceeds to spell out the lowliness of man's origin as a creature of dust in a series of phrases which leave no doubt of humanity's humble state, 'shaped from dust', 'maggots' food', 'spat saliva', 'moulded clay' (21–2). As against the other creations of God man is not merely the epitome of feebleness but of baseness.

Two instances seem to fall into a second category in which unprivileged mankind is distinguished from the members of the sect. 'My eyes', writes the author, 'have observed what always is, wisdom that has been hidden from mankind, knowledge and understanding (hidden) from the sons of men' (IQS XI 5b–6a). The same distinction recurs at line 16 with the reference to God's care for 'the selected ones of humankind'. Thus within column XI the line is crossed between humanity as feeble and those humans who, though feeble, are nonetheless chosen by God.

The third category of examples goes one step further and describes mankind as being not merely feeble and unfavoured, but as being sinful. This is suggested in a fragment of an apocryphal psalm (*4Q Non-Canonical Psalm B* (4Q381) where the sons of man are described as 'following the inclination (*yēṣer*) of the thou[ghts of their heart]' and (apparently) earning destruction in consequence (frg. 76 2–4). The three instances of *'ādam* in IQS XI are utterly direct. 'I belong to evil humankind', says the writer, and proceeds to deplore 'my failings, my transgressions, my sins ... with the depravities of my heart' (9). 'To man (does not belong) his path, nor to a human being the steadying of his step' (10), he continues, underlining his powerlessness to save himself from 'the sin of the sons of man' (15).

But a further usage which gives potent expression to the Qumran understanding of the human predicament is its use of the term 'flesh' (*bāśār*). Without entering into an analysis of the range of meanings which the term carries in the texts,[49] the point of relevance for our purposes is its use to denote humanity in its sinfulness. Striking in this regard is the double use in IQS XI 9,12 where the psalmist describes himself as belonging 'to evil humankind to the assembly of wicked flesh' (9) and characterizes sin (apparently generally) as 'sin of the flesh' (12). This association of 'flesh' with 'evil' in the construct state suggests that, if not necessarily so, flesh very easily becomes the locus of sin. This comes to poignant expression in several of the *Thanksgiving Hymns* in which the writer gives voice to his frustration at being in effect the unwilling prisoner of sin. 'What is flesh compared to this? What creature of clay can do wonders? He is in sin from his maternal womb, and in guilty iniquity right to old age' (IQH IV 29–30a). 'What is the spirit of flesh to fathom all these matters and to appreciate your great and wondrous secret? What is someone born of woman among all your awesome works? He is a structure of dust shaped with water, his base is the guilt of sin, vile unseemliness, source of impurity, over which a spirit of degeneracy rules' (IQH V = XIII 19b–21). K.G. Kuhn captures the point finely, saying, 'Thus "flesh" becomes a contrast to the "spirit" which rules the pious man and determines his good actions, and dwells within him; consequently, "flesh" becomes the area of weakness through the natural inclinations of man; it becomes almost synonymous with evil'.[50] But Ringgren's rider is important: 'Man is a whole and as such he is of flesh, and is weak, incomplete, impure, sinful; but the impurity is more strongly emphasized here than ever in the Old Testament.'[51]

If one puts all of this together then the human predicament as the sectaries saw it is dire indeed. Pursued by the Angel of Darkness, a battleground of an inward attack by the spirit of deceit with an inclination in his direction, even if he also experiences a counter-inclination, and by his very constitution not only weak but wicked, the human creature presents a picture as might well give rise to the despair and hopelessness which find voice in passages of the kind just quoted.

The Divine Requirement

If the religious dilemma confronted by the Qumran sectaries was defined in part by the activity of God in history and the sinful predicament of humanity, including themselves, a third element which gave it definition was God's requirement of his covenant people. As was noted earlier, the God of the covenant was a holy God, who, in consequence, could be content with nothing less than a holy people. This was true of the first covenant (Exodus 19:5f, 24:3, 5–8) as of the renewed covenant (Ezekiel 36:25–7). As the chosen remnant with whom that covenant had been renewed, it followed that God required the same of them; and it is a merely mechanical exercise in the obvious to accumulate proof-passages in support, inasmuch as it was sinful failure to keep the first covenant which had led to its rescinding.[52]

Much more important is taking account of those features of the Qumran community which bear witness to their understanding of the purity which they believed was expected of them. That purity was a central preoccupation of the community is evinced in a number of matters which, though distinguishable, share a common foundation. First, and fundamental, is their perceived relationship to the Temple. IQS VIII, which has already been noted as probably the oldest part of the *Community Rule*[53] uses Temple language several times in respect of the community. First, it attributes to it Temple functions, specifically the presentation of offerings (*rêaḥ*)[54] which effect atonement (3, 6, 10). Second, it describes it in Temple terms, 'the Community council shall be founded on truth, like an everlasting plantation, a holy house for Israel and the foundation of the holy of holies for Aaron' (5–6a): language used to describe the inner shrine of the tabernacle (Exodus 26:33–4) and the temple (1 Kings 6:16; cf. Leviticus 16:11–17). Third, it requires the presence of priests to discharge the priestly functions specified (1–3a). This is not to say that the Qumran sect regarded itself as a replacement, temporary or permanent, for the Jerusalem Temple, though this has been maintained.[55] It means rather that it saw itself as discharging functions – sometimes necessarily in alternative forms[56] – which the Jerusalem Temple had forfeited the right to discharge validly because of its failure to preserve the requisite ritual purity.[57]

All of this could have only one meaning for the community: that the purity which the Jerusalem Temple had infringed so brazenly must be scrupulously maintained if they were to discharge the functions which they believed had devolved upon them. J. Neusner has pointed out that, in truth, not many purity laws are preserved[58] in the Qumran texts, but examples are found in the *Damascus Document* particularly. Two important examples which Neusner cites are X 11–13 which specifies the amount of water required to purify a person, prescribing that to use less simply renders the water unclean; and XII 15–18 on corpse uncleanness, which rules that a corpse communicates uncleanness to the house (and certain of its contents) in which it lies.[59] But more directly relevant to the purity of the Temple is the sequence at CD IV 12b–V 15a which, though part of the Admonition, refers to specific actions involving Temple defilement. This state of affairs obtains because the present managers of the Temple have been snared in the 'three nets of Belial' (IV 15a). 'The first is fornication; the second, wealth; the third defilement of the Temple' (IV 17). The midrashic development does not follow these topics exactly, either in substance or in number,[60] but their overriding concern is with matters of ritual pollution. First, is fornication, defined as 'taking two wives in their lives', (IV 20b–21), in defiance of Genesis 1:27; 7:9 and Deuteronomy 17:17. Since the possessive adjective 'their' is masculine (*behayyêhem*) referring accordingly to husbands, the thought apparently is that marrying more than one is forbidden. The thought, however, extends beyond that to include polygamy, care being taken to provide David with an excuse and Zadok with the credit for rediscovering the divine will in the matter (V 1b–6a). The second offence consisted of having intercourse with a wife during menstruation, thereby defiling the Temple (V 6b–7a). The third offence consisted of niece-marriage (V 7b–11a); and the fourth of defiling their holy spirit, 'for with blasphemous tongue they have opened their mouth against the statutes of God's covenant, saying, "they are unfounded" ' (V 12). The offence in mind is apparently that of disparaging the halakhah of the sect, resulting in the defilement of their own 'holy spirit' which, in the eyes of the sectaries, would be their capacity to discern between right and wrong. In contrast with all of this the community must maintain a state of perfect purity.

But there is another distinguishing aspect of Qumran thought which imposed on the sectaries the obligation to maintain ritual purity, namely, the belief that in their worship they shared communion with the angels. The underlying theology was that only the angels could know God, and the Temple cult itself was part of heaven's cult by the participation of the angels in the former.[61] IQH XIV = VI 12b–13 reads, 'For you have brought [your truth and your] glory to all the men of your council and in the lot, together with the angels of the face, without there being any mediator between the intelligent and your holy ones.' That is to say, the members of the community have direct fellowship with the angels who behold the face of God, without the need of a mediator or go-between.[62] The inference is explicitly drawn that, because of their presence, the ritually impure must be excluded (CD XV 13–17; IQM VII 4b–6b). Indeed, this idea completes the circle, because the blemishes listed in the former passage are derived from Leviticus 13 and 21 which lay down the disqualifications of priests from service in the Temple. As Schiffman puts it, 'Since the sect saw itself as constituting a sanctuary through its dedication to a life of holiness and purity, it accordingly extended the Torah's legislation for the priesthood to its own eschatological assembly.'[63]

Unsurprisingly, the sectaries' view of their relationship to the Temple conditioned every aspect of their community life. For example, it conditioned their initiation rules. Non-members of the community are, by definition, unclean, inasmuch as they reject 'the statutes of God' (IQS VI 5b), that is, the halakhah of the community. IQS V–VII, which are a collection of practices in force at Qumran[64] define two stages in the process of admission to the sect. The first is entry into the covenant which took place following examination by the Instructor (apparently on his own authority) who proceeded to instruct candidates in all the rites of the community (VI 13–15a). The second stage of membership was more complex and extended. After an unspecified period the probationer was examined by the Many who, if convinced 'about his spirit and about his deeds' would advance him to a first year of probation (VI 17) which, if completed satisfactorily would be followed by a second. He would then be admitted to full membership subject to the approval of the Many and a favourable result from the lot (VI 21–2).

Now, the purpose of this elaborate system of filters and defences is simple: to preserve the purity of the sect. Joining the community meant separation from the 'men of sin in order to constitute a Community in law and possessions' (V 1b–2a). But such was the potency of impurity, that the admission of new members could take place only in carefully graduated stages. Initial admission to the covenant, while obviously bringing some degree of inclusion, nevertheless did not bring participation in the common meal nor in sharing community property (VI 16b–17). Successful completion of the first year of probation brought incorporation of his possessions and the sharing of solid food, but not sharing the common drink[65] (VI 18–20). That privilege became available only after the completion of a second year of probation and a further test by the Many and by the sacred lot (VI 20b–22). The sanctity of the common meal was such that, whereas the Pharisees washed their hands ceremonially before eating, the Qumran sectaries took ceremonial baths. Of the 'men of sin' it is said, 'He should not go into the waters to share in the pure food of the men of holiness' (IQS V 13b).

J. Neusner has said of Qumran that 'the focus for cleanness is the table'.[66] To the question 'Why?' various answers have been given. Jaubert suggested that the Qumran meals taken in sacerdotal purity, replaced the meals taken before God by the priests in the Sanctuary.[67] K.G. *Kuhn* presses this line of argument still further, contending that, since the sectaries were separated from the Temple, the meals became substitutes for Temple sacrifices and therefore, together with the baths, media of salvation.[68] L.H. Schiffman links the Pure Meal with the Messianic Banquet described in IQSa II 11–22, the two having so many common features that the Pure Meal became 'a sample of the world to come'.[69] Schiffman continues, 'The communal meals establish a link between the sectarian observance in this world, and those observances in the age to come through the crucial element of ritual purity. Total ritual purity may be seen as a catalyst which turns the ordinary communal meal into a foretaste of the great Messianic banquet at the end of the days.'[70] Perhaps it is unnecessary to choose among these options since each contains an element readily documented in Qumran thought, and all share a common principle: that purity is the bridge into the presence of God.

The foregoing may indicate the large place held by purity in Qumran thought, at least in broad terms. But it hardly explicates it: particularly why ritual purity should be of such critical significance in the Qumran religious system. Accordingly, just as it has been necessary to identify the areas in which purity was insisted upon at Qumran, so it is equally necessary to examine the differentiae of the meaning of purity at Qumran. At least three features give it distinctive definition. First, it is derived from Scripture and carries scriptural authority accordingly. This claim stands in a certain tension with the view of J. Neusner quoted above[71] that not many purity laws are preserved in the Qumran texts. Neusner recognized the incongruity, but believes the explanation lies to hand. 'When we turn from the numerous references to cleanness and uncleanness to actual rules on the subject, we find the skeleton of a system, but no rules to give substance to an autonomous and balanced, whole system. The legislation, to be sure, does tell us a bit about sources of uncleanness, loci of uncleanness, and modes of purification. *What it tells us is so meagre as to require the thesis of a sizeable corpus of law taken for granted, which obviously is Scripture's.*'[72] Since Qumran finds scriptural warrant for the purity laws which are preserved, it is a fair inference that the purity laws presupposed possess the same warrant.[73] This means that purity requirements were taken with the utmost seriousness. Hannah K. Harrington concludes her study of purity at Qumran and in the Rabbis by saying, 'the interpretation is based squarely on Scripture. The Qumran community and the Rabbis of the Mishna and Talmud were diligent students of the Torah. Their careful interpretation of each word in the Torah grows out of their sacred regard for Scripture as divine revelation. To violate its laws is to cross the will of the Almighty who will not be slack in punishing offenders.'[74]

A second distinguishing feature of the Qumran approach to matters of purity is its stringency. Stringency has long been noted as characteristic of the Qumran mindset as a whole. M. Black has observed, 'The sectaries are to be obedient in *all* that is revealed to them (cf. IQS I 8–9, V 9; VIII 1,15; IX 13,19), in "*everything* which he has commanded" (I 17;V 1,8; IX 24), to keep "*all* the words of God" (I 14; III 11), to "depart from *all* evil" (14,7; II 3; V 1), "every perversity" (VI 15; VIII 18; IX 21).'[75] This same stringency is evident in the Qumran interpretation of the purity laws. J. Milgrom affirms that there are two traditions in scripture regarding purity which left their mark on Judaism from the Second Temple onwards.[76] One is the minimalist approach which limited the laws of impurity to the area of the Temple and the priest; the other is the maximalist approach which extended the laws of purity to all Israel irrespective of its connection to the sacred. Milgrom maintains that the Qumran writers exploited both traditions in the service of their ideology, 'the imposition of maximalist conditions, i.e., holiness demands, upon a minimalist Israel, i.e., the sectaries of Qumran, within a minimalist space, the Temple-city of Jerusalem.'[77] That is to say, the most demanding interpretation of the law was brought to bear upon the smallest and most select number of people: the members of the sect.[78]

That the principle of stringency was at work in the laws of purity is evident from specific rulings. For example, the purification rules for those who have skin infections (*mĕṣōrāim*) are interpreted more sharply at Qumran. Not only must the impure live outside the city to avoid defiling persons and objects which are pure (particularly the Pure Meal: 4Q *Purification Rules* / 4Q 274 / 4Q *Tohorot* A. frg. 1, col. I 1–2), but other impure persons must avoid touching them, otherwise the degree of their impurity will be increased, and in order to eat ordinary food they must bathe and wash their clothes to reduce the degree of their impurity to what it was previously, (4Q 274 frg. 1, col 13; 4Q Ordinances/ 4Q 514 frg. 1 col. I 1–9).[79] This is an extension of the levitical law which refers to the transfer of pollution from the impure to the pure to include the transfer of pollution from the impure to the impure.[80]

Again, nocturnal emission renders impure, and the subject must leave the camp until evening when, after washing, he may return (Deuteronomy 23: 10–11). The same basic law is found in Leviticus 15:16–18 with the additional datum that it is direct contact with semen which defiles. In 4Q *Tohorot* A (4Q 274) frg. 1 col. I 86–9 however, the purification period is seven days, and any who touch them during that time must bathe and wash their clothes before eating.

Examples could be multiplied, but the general intent is hard to deny. In Harrington's words, 'the exegesis of Scripture found in the Scrolls seems overly cautious at times, but the sectarians want to be sure no transgression of the law was made. Where the Torah is ambiguous, the sectarians interpret on the side of severity. Thus, since the text requires bathing after some impurities and bathing and laundering after others, one should bathe and launder after all impurities just in case laundering was intended even when not explicitly stated.'[81]

A third feature of the Qumran understanding of purity is that it incorporates a spiritual dimension. In this regard it is unusual, not to say unique in the Judaism of its time where ritual uncleanness is an ontological rather than a moral category.[82] Jacob Neusner affirms that uncleanness is a metaphor for sin at Qumran, but not in the Mishnah.[83] At Qumran, indeed, 'moral uncleanness generates material uncleanness, and moral purification is the precondition of material cleanness.'[84] The point is not uncommon in the texts, but nowhere is it made more expressly than in IQS III 4–12, where stubbornness of heart is declared to neutralize the efficacy of ritual performance. 'By the spirit of holiness which links him with his truth he is cleansed of all his sins. And by the spirit of uprightness and of humility his sin is atoned. And by the compliance of his soul with all the laws of God his flesh is cleansed by being sprinkled with cleansing waters and being made holy with the waters of repentance' (7b–9a).[85] Within the community cultic purification alone does not avail. J.M. Baumgarten has drawn attention to the purification texts from Cave 4 as exhibiting the same point. In particular he cites 4Q *Ritual of Purification* (4Q 512)[86] pointing out that the references to rituals (usually lustration) are interspersed with either prayers for purification on the part of those being purified, or thanksgivings to God from those who have been purified. Fragments 29–32 column VII appear to constitute a *Berakhah* by one who has been cleansed, blessing God '[who forgave me all] my faults and purified me from impure immodesty and atoned so that I can enter ... the purification.' The presence of the penitential note as well as the note of thanksgiving suggests awareness of the spiritual overtones of lustration, whereas rabbinic tradition tended to treat ritual impurity as morally neutral.[87]

We may now seek to draw together the data reviewed which bear upon the understanding of the religious situation of humanity held at Qumran. The backdrop of Qumran thought is the created order, made by God to his pattern and intended to function according to the design he had laid down: his times, his ways, his will. That demand is heightened by the role which the sectarians have been called upon to play in the divine purpose: to serve as a holy temple and priesthood, by their own obedience atoning for the sin of the land. For them purity was stringent: every possible infringement of every law and regulation must be guarded against. Failure had led to disaster before: it must not happen again. Hence the elaborate system of accountability and penalties for infractions. But the stringency was made more demanding by the incorporation of inward sin into the purity system so that a wrong attitude or reaction could run through it like a virus. But given the human make-up, how were such failings avoidable? Yet perfect observance of the covenant was what was called for. That forgiveness was available they did not doubt. But the law was there to be kept. This was their dilemma.

Notes

1. For a fuller statement see M. Hengel, *Judaism and Hellenism*, 234–6.
2. That 4Q180 is a sectarian text is shown by its pesher form, as well as by its terminology. That it is neither a continuous nor a thematic pesher, but one which treats a subject rather than a biblical text or texts, does not make it less sectarian. If anything – in Dimant's words – it 'suggests that the significance of the Pesher as a literary genre as well as a technical term may be wider than hitherto suspected.' Art. 'The "Pesher on the Periods" (4Q180) and 4Q181', *IOS IX*, 1979, 96.
3. Milik, J.T., 'Milkì'-ṣedeq et Milkì' reša' dans les anciens écrits juifs et chrétiens', *JJS*, 23, 1972, 95–144.
4. The thrust of IQpHab VII is that the timing of the delayed arrival of the end is precisely what has been revealed to the Teacher of Righteousness (1–5). The problem recurred with the failure of the end to come within forty years of the death of the Teacher; once again, the resolution was sought by appeal to the same principle (CD XIX 35–XX 1, 13–15). See Armin Lange, 'Wisdom and Predestination in the Dead Sea Scrolls,' *DSD*, 2, 3. November 1995, 353 n.33.
5. The most extensive of the Sapiential Works are 4Q413, and 415–9, all transcribed in Wacholder-Abegg, Fascicle Two. In addition 4Q416 (4Q *Sapiential Work* A[b]) and 4Q418 (4Q *Sapiential Work* A[a]) are transcribed, translated and discussed in Eisenman and Wise, *DSSU*, 241–54. 4Q413 and 4Q416–9 are translated in Garcia Martinez, 382–93.
6. The Book of Mysteries (4Q299–301) is transcribed in Wacholder-Abegg, Fascicle Two. 4Q300, under the title '4Q *Mysteries*[b]: A Preliminary Edition' by L.H. Schiffman appeared in *RQ*, 16, 62, 1993, 203–23. All are translated in Garcia Martinez, *DSSE*, 400–1.
7. See IQ 26 (Wisdom Apocryphon) in J.T. Milik, DJD I, 101–2; and IQ 27 (IQ Mysteries), op. cit, 102–7.
8. For a report on the official reconstruction by D.J. Harrington and John Strugnell see Daniel J. Harrington, 'Wisdom at Qumran' in Ulrich-VanderKam, *CRC*, 139–52. Other reconstructions have been published as noted above in n.5. There is uncertainty in regard to overlaps with other texts (e.g. IQ26, 4Q415), as well as in regard to the ordering of fragments in 4Q416, and especially 4Q418 of which the number

of fragments is approximately 300. Garcia Martinez refers to this work as 4Q *Sapiential Work* A.

9. *DSSU*, 241.
10. Wise-Abegg-Cook, *DSS New Translation*, 378.
11. 4Q417 2 I 7; 4Q418 Frg. 26 (= 4Q416 Frg. 1 14), frg. 103 II 5; frg. 123 II 2,4.
12. 4Q417 2 I 14f = 4Q418 frag. 43 11.
13. 4Q416 Frag. 1 16; 4Q417 2 I 8, 11; 2 II 12.
14. 4Q416 Frag. 1 16; 4Q417 Frag. 2 I 17; 2 II 14.
15. 4Q418 Frag. 81 13. A wider induction of terminology common to 4Q416–418 and the sectarian texts is examined in Eisenman and Wise, *DSSU*, 241–4. Whether this demonstrates that the text was sectarian in origin is questioned. Harrington rejects the conclusion on the grounds that a non-Qumran setting is presupposed inasmuch as business and family life are assumed. He concludes that it is pre-Qumranic in origin (*CRC*, 144). Wise, Abegg and Cook find that, while its original setting is unknown it may have served as 'an introductory course of study for new or probationary initiates into the *Yaḥad' (DSS New Translation*, 379). The number of copies of Sapiential Work A implied by the various texts would suggest that it enjoyed significant use in the community.
16. 4Q416 Frag. 2 I 5; III 9,14,18,21; 4Q417 Frag. 2 I 2,6,18,21; 4Q418 Frag. 123 II 4, etc.
17. Wise-Abegg-Cook have arranged the fragments they have translated according to a thematic plan which underscores the 'wisdom' themes of the texts (*DSS A New Translation*, 379–91).
18. Harrington notes that he translates the phrase *raz nihyāh* as 'the mystery of what is to be (or come) since in some contexts it appears to refer to the eschatological plan of God' (*CRC*, 145).
19. Wise-Abegg-Cook, op. cit, 386. See the whole context in lines 10–15. The same idea comes to expression at 4Q418 Frag. 2 5.
20. *Reclaiming*, 210.
21. The Preliminary Edition of 4Q *Mysteries*[b] by L.H. Schiffman (see note 6 above) is a composite of IQ27, 4Q299 (= 4Q *Mysteries*[a]) and 4Q300 (= 4Q *Mysteries*[b]). (The suggestion that 4Q301 (= 4Q Mysteries[c]) was a fourth copy of the same text is one on which Schiffman now reserves his judgment, since

there is no textual overlap in this case as there is in the others. Art. cit, 203). Its Essene origin is debated, Lange maintaining that it lacks the central features of Essene theology and vocabulary, at the same time using other terms (e.g. (*ḥākam*) which are rare in other Essene texts (*DSD*, 2, November 1995, 342). Schiffman takes the contrary view, holding that it not only shares features with the Sapiential texts, but employs even more sectarian terminology. 'When read together with the *Thanksgiving Hymns*, the *Mysteries* seem more integral to the Qumran sectarian corpus than the other sapiential texts' (*Reclaiming*, 206). The presence of multiple copies of the text would suggest that it was widely used at Qumran.

22. Cf. Schiffman, *RQ*, 16, 1993, 216.
23. 4Q299 frg. 2 col. II 11–15 (Schiffman's translation).
24. It is not to be supposed that 'mystery' in the Qumran texts refers only to the meaning of history, and, in particular, to its eschatological climax. R.E. Brown finds four categories of mysteries: divine providence (including eschatology); sectarian interpretation of the law; cosmic mysteries (including creation); and mysteries of evil. Art. 'The Semitic Background of the Term "Mystery" in the New Testament', *CBQ*, 1958, 4, 417–44, esp. 436–43. For discussion see M.N.A. Bockmuehl: *Revelation and Mystery*, 53–6.
25. While some angels are named: notably Belial, who is apparently leader of the evil spirits (IQS I 18, 23f; CD V 17–19; IQM XIII 4, 11–12), and Michael who stands opposed to him (IQM IX 15f; XVII 5–8) on the side of good, most other references consist of general descriptions such as 'the sons of heaven' (IQS IV 22; IQH III 22) or the 'angels of the dominion of Belial' (IQM I 15) or 'the spirits of his lot' (IQS III 24; IQM XIII 11f) or 'of error' (IQM XV 14). The lack of specificity or delineation, and the easy movement from the idea of 'angel' to that of 'spirit' suggests that their activity rather than their personality is where the accent falls.
26. It is widely conceded that the view of predestination noted above is not typical of Judaism. Cf. Hengel, 'The conception of the *predestination of the course of history and the fate of the individual* is new in its pregnant form' (*Judaism and Hellenism*, 219). This clearly creates problems for theology the resolution of which is found in the qualified dualism which locates the active power of evil in the Prince of Darkness, and in the

declaration that in God's good time the Prince of Darkness and evil with him will be destroyed. Cf. Hengel, op. cit, 221. D. Dimant sees this as the solution only from the divine side, arguing that the solution from the human side, involving repentance and grace, can be found only in those texts which approach the question from the side of religious experience (e.g. IQH). *Jewish Writings of the Second Temple Period*, CRINT Section Two, Volume II, (1984), 536–8.

27. This does not imply acceptance of a tradition-historical account of the issue such as is propounded by von der Osten-Sacken, Peter, *Gott und Belial, Traditionsgeschichtliche Untersuchungen zum Dualismus im den Texten aus Qumran*, SUNT 6; (Göttingen: Vandenhoeck und Ruprecht, 1969), where a linear development is traced from the more personalized angels (good or bad) of IQM and IQS III 13–IV 14 to the less hypostatized powers and temptations at work within the individual in IQS IV 23b–26. As was noted in the text, the angels are always masked and muted, and the difference in usage seems to be dictated by the character of the subject (the War in IQM, and personal experience in IQS III 13–IV 26, save where a cosmic perspective is assumed) rather than by theological development.
28. M.A. Knibb argues that both are present. 'Side by side with the idea that men are assigned to one spirit or the other there is found the belief that men are influenced by both spirits, and in this way an attempt is made to take account of the fact that men are a mixture of both good and evil' (*The Qumran Community*, 95). A.R.C. Leaney concludes that the relationship between the two spirits viewed cosmically and metaphysically and the two spirits viewed anthropologically and psychologically is not clearly worked out. See his comments on IQS III 17,19, *The Rule of Qumran and Its Meaning*, 37.
29. The verb *nādab* 'volunteer' is used nine times in IQS to describe members: six of them in column 5 which introduces the regulations prescribed for members.
30. It has been argued by H. Stegemann on the basis of the 4QS mss. that the Discourse on the Two Spirits (IQS III 13–IV 2b) was not only an independent text, but even a non-Essene text in origin. E.g. the absence of the Two Spirits Discourse from 4QSb is held to support the former; while the absence of *yahad* terminology and ideas is held to support the latter.

Art. 'Zu Textbestand und Grundgedanken von IQS III 13–IV 26', *RQ*, 13, 1988, 96–100. However, these are not the only ways of accounting for the phenomena in question. Stegemann concedes that the sect was strongly influenced by this text, a conclusion that would be widely agreed; indeed III 13: 'For the Maskil, that he may inform and teach all the sons of light about the history of all the sons of man,' is virtually an official *Imprimatur*. In any case the predestinarian emphasis does not rest on the Two Spirits idea alone.

31. The official edition of the text is found in *DJD*, V, 88–91. Reference should also be made to the article by the official editor, Allegro, J.M., 'An Astrological Cryptic Document from Qumran', *JSS*, 9, 1964, 291–4; and the comments of Schiffman, *Reclaiming*, 362f.
32. An obvious question is how the sect reconciled the two sides of the predestination-human freedom autonomy. Suggestions fall into two categories. First, are those who aver that the sect made no attempt to resolve it, not being of philosophical bent, but being concerned to do justice to the facts of religious experience. Cf. Sanders, E.P., *Paul and Palestinian Judaism*, 265–8. Second, are those who believe an implicit solution is present. E.H. Merrill finds the solution in divine foreknowledge by which God, knowing who will react positively causes them to be influenced by his Holy Spirit, so bringing them into the covenant. The wicked are rejected from the womb because their tendency is always to do evil. *Qumran and Predestination*, A Theological Study of the Thanksgiving Hymns, Leiden: Brill, (1975), 51. D. Dimant distinguishes sharply between the divine and human sides of the problem, holding that, while salvation depends on God, it demands a response of repentance to indicate the capacity to receive grace. The task for humans is thus to discover, to which lot they belong: i.e. the point is shifted from freedom of action to the mystery of knowledge. *Jewish Writings of the Second Temple Period*, (1984), 536–8.
33. A standard early treatment of the theme is Murphy, R.E., '*Yēṣer* in the Qumran Literature', *CBQ*, 39, 1958, 334–44. A similar spectrum of meaning is found in Cave 4 documents such as 4Q 416, 4Q 417.
34. So Holm-Nielsen, S., *Hodayot, Psalms from Qumran*, Aarhus: Universitets-for-laget, (1960), 92 n.5 (henceforth Holm-

Nielsen, *Hodayot*); Mansoor., *The Thanksgiving Hymns*, *STDJ*, III, (Grand Rapids: Eerdmans, 1961), 148 n.11 (henceforth Mansoor, *Hymns*.)

35. Mowinckel, S., 'Some Remarks on Hodayot 39: 5–20', *JBL*, 75, 1956, 270.
36. Seitz, O.J.F., 'The Two Spirits in Man: an Essay in Biblical Exegesis,' *NTS*, 6, 1959–60, 94.
37. Referring to passages such as Deuteronomy 6:5; 10:12; 30:2; Jeremiah 31:33; Ezekiel 36: 26.
38. 4Q Bar'ki Napshi' (4Q434) frg. 1 I. 4. A similar idea may be present in line 10, but the text is uncertain. The same ideas are present in 4Q436, specifically the strengthening of the heart (frg. 1 lines 4,6), and (in all probability) the replacement of the heart of stone and the evil inclination by a pure heart. Eisenman and Wise, who treat 4Q434 and 436 as a single text, but in reverse order, translate 4Q436 line 10 thus: '(a heart of stone?). You [re]moved from me and put a pure heart in its place, remov[ing] evil inclination?' (*DSSU*, 239). Seely is certainly correct in concluding, 'The context associated with circumcision of the heart in 4Q434 is consistent with the sectarian texts from Qumran'. Art. 'The Circumcized Heart' in 4Q434 *Barki' Nafshi'*, *RQ*, 65–8, 17, 4, December 1996, 535.
39. CD II 17, III 5,11, VIII 8 (= XIX 20), 19 (= XIX 33), XX 9.
40. H. Braun contends that there is less stress on sin in CD than in IQS because it is mentioned less frequently. *Späijudisch-Häretischer und Frühchristlicher Radikalismus*, Tübingen: J.C.B. Mohr, (1957), I, 134, including n.2. He also maintains that the weakening of *Toraverschärfung* which he finds in CD, with its concomitant weakening of dualism, has the same effect, by making individuals captains of their own salvation. J. Becker carries this still further by holding that sin is depersonalized, becoming an independent existent detached from the sinner. Becker, Jürgen, *Das Heil Gottes: Heils-und Sündenbegriffe in den Qumrantexten und im Neuen Testament*, *SUNT 3*, (Göttingen: Vandenhoeck und Ruprecht, 1964), esp. 182f. He also holds that there is no sense of human fallenness in CD, as indicated by the total absence of 'flesh' (*bāśār*) in a theological sense (184f). However, he feels bound by the evidence to make admissions which, in my view, seriously qualify his case. See the continuing discussion in the text.

41. For a fuller exposition and evaluation of the positions of Braun and Becker see Deasley, A.R.G., *The Idea of Perfection in the Qumran Texts*, (unpublished Ph.D dissertation, University of Manchester, 1972), 182–6 (henceforth Deasley, *Perfection*).
42. Wheeler Robinson , H., *The Christian Doctrine of Man*, (Edinburgh: T & T. Clark, 3rd edition 1947), 43.
43. Op. cit, 44.
44. To give the statistics for IQS alone: the terms in class one occur thirty times; those in class two thirteen times; that in class three nine times. (Only substantival forms are included in the count.) It should be added that, while the terms cited bear the senses indicated, it is not difficult to find instances where one term can bear a shade of meaning chiefly associated with another. To quote Wheeler Robinson again, 'The value of such a classification is chiefly that it affords an introduction to the subject in its salient features' (op. cit, 43).
45. Op. cit, 184.
46. Cf. the different renderings of Dupont-Sommer, 'the nature of all the sons of men' (he adds in a footnote: 'it deals with the primordial and fundamental problem of the nature of man and the human condition', *Essene Writings*, 77 n.4); Vermes, 'the nature of all the children of men' (*DSSE*, 73); Knibb, 'an account of men's character, a description of their nature' (*Qumran Community*, 96).
47. The seventh is its use as a proper noun at IV 23.
48. Ringgren, *Faith*, 95.
49. The term 'flesh' (*bāśar*) exhibits a wide range of meaning in the Qumran texts.

    Sometimes it denotes the material substance as in reference to 'the flesh of burnt offerings' (IQS IX 4; 11 QT LII 18,19; LIII 2, 3), or 'human flesh' as in IQM VII 5; XV 13. Sometimes it simply means 'human being' as in CD I 2, II 20, though even there it is difficult to evade the overtone of weakness which is characteristic both of the material substance as well as of man as constituted of it: by definition it is that which decays. There is a useful brief survey in Ringgren, *Faith*, 97–100.
50. Kuhn, K.G., art., 'New Light on Temptation, Sin and Flesh in the New Testament' in Krister Stendahl (ed.), *The Scrolls and the New Testament*, (New York: Harper, 1957), 101.

51. Ringgren, *Faith*, 100.
52. IQS I 24–6; CD I 1–4a; III 10b–12a; IQSb I 1–3a, etc.
53. See above p. 83f.
54. VIII 9. The term is often used in the Old Testament in texts dealing with sacrifice. E.g. Exodus 29:18.
55. The crucial issues for this view are (1) whether, in regarding the Jerusalem Temple as defiled, the Qumran Essenes concluded that it ceased to be the Temple in any sense; and (2) whether animal sacrifice was practiced at Qumran. No altar or evidence of such has been found in the ruins, but F.M. Cross sees the deposits of animal bones as evidence of sacrifice (*ALQ*[3], 86). F.F. Bruce, referring to the same evidence, comments cannily, 'perhaps their special meals could be described as "quasi-sacrificial" (whatever meaning we may put upon the term)' (*Second Thoughts on the Dead Sea Scrolls*, 119), though this follows his statement that 'our evidence is quite inadequate for a definite answer' to the question of whether sacrifice was offered at Qumran' (loc. cit). F.M. Cross, while giving a positive answer to that question, says rather tentatively in reply to both issues under consideration, 'Though it is somewhat difficult to visualize at Qumran the maintenance of an independent sacrificial cultus by a hyperorthodox sect, I am inclined to think that our evidence now suggests that this was the case' (op. cit, 86).
56. The language of IQS VIII–IX is explicit and forceful in its insistence that atonement was effected by non-sacrificial means. VIII 3–4 attributes it to 'the practice of justice and the endurance of affliction'; line 9 to 'total knowledge of the covenant of justice', which probably means conformity to the praxis of the sect. IX 3–6 is most explicit. Negatively, it rules out sacrifice, 'to atone for the fault of the transgression ... without the flesh of burnt offerings and without the fats of sacrifice' (4 – taking the *min* in *mibbĕśar* privatively. See the listing of possibilities in H. Lichtenberger, 'Atonement and Sacrifice in the Qumran Community' in William Scott Green (ed), *Approaches to Ancient Judaism, Volume II, Brown Judaic Studies 9*, (Chico: Scholars Press, 1982), 161f). Positively, it is said that, 'The offering of the lips in compliance with the decree will be like the pleasant aroma of justice and the correctness of behaviour will be acceptable like a freewill offering' (4b–5a). It has been argued that this amounts to the concept

of a 'spiritual Temple'. Cf. Gärtner, B., *The Temple and the Community in Qumran and the New Testament*, (Cambridge, 1965). But if by this is meant the permanent repudiation of the Jerusalem Temple and its cult in favour of non-cultic worship it is very unlikely on two counts. First, it would represent a breach of the centralization of worship in the place where God had chosen to place his name. Second, it is inconsistent with the expectation of the restoration of the Temple and its cult after the eschatological war. See 4Q 174 frags. 1–3, col. I 2b–6a).

57. This might well prompt the question: When is a Temple not a Temple? Qumran is not unlike a government-in-exile. Its land is enemy-occupied, and during such time the foreign territory it occupies becomes the mother-country, and the exiled authorities execute the functions of government insofar as this is possible. In one sense the foreign territory becomes the mother-country as the seat of the legal government; in another sense the mother-country remains the real homeland. Judith Wendland expresses it well in saying that they saw themselves as acceptable even without the temple and cult because the Spirit dwelt with them as the keepers of God's covenant. They were therefore a temporary dwelling for his Spirit until God would come and build his future temple. Art. 'Unraveling the Relationship between 11QT, the eschatological Temple, and the Qumran Community', *RQ*, 14, 1, June 1989, 72.
58. Neusner J., *A History of the Mishnaic Law of Purities*, Part Twenty-Two, (Leiden: Brill, 1977), 46.
59. For discussion of an alternative translation and interpretation of CD XII 15–18 (which does not, however, affect the substance of the point being made here), see Neusner, op. cit, 47f.
60. For a discussion of the passage incorporating comments on its possible tradition-history, see Knibb, *The Qumran Community*, 39–42.
61. See Barthélemy D., 'La sainteté selon la communauté de Qumran et selon l'Évangile', in J. van der Ploeg (ed.), *La Secte de Qumran et les Origines du Christianisme, Recherches Bibliques* IV, Bruges: Desclée de Btouwer, (1959), 204–6. Ringgren thinks it may have been stimulated by the conviction that they were living in the last times (*Faith of Qumran*, 86).
62. Other passages voicing the idea of fellowship between the

community and the angels include IQS XI 7–9; IQM X 9–11, XII 1–3.

63. *Reclaiming*, 331f. The overall perspective on the Temple aspect of the community has been finely summarized by Lichtenberger, 'The Qumran community, in the time of Belial's rule, theologically dealt with two complex problems – the existence of an illegitimate place of atonement and the non-existence of the legitimate place of atonement in which God would dwell – and solved them. It did this by claiming to represent both temples and simultaneously anticipating the eschatological temple. On the one hand, it atoned by perfect life and praise to God in place of the present but desecrated Temple in Jerusalem and the non-present or not-yet-present true temple of the Temple Scroll. On the other hand, it participated here and now, through perfect life and praise to God, in that community and service with the angels which is promised for the Day of Blessing' (art. cit, 167).
64. IQS V 1–VI 8a is a statement of general principle of what community membership involves and how life within the community operated, though specific guidelines are not lacking. VI 13b–23 spells out the specific procedures for the admission of new members from probation to full membership.
65. Food was regarded as being particularly susceptible to contamination, liquids even more so.
66. Neusner, J., *Mishnaic Law of Purities*, Part 22, 38. Again, 'the rite at the heart of the system is the meal' (42).
67. Jaubert, Annie, *Alliance*, 205. She quotes Jubilees 2:30f, 50:10, in support.
68. Kuhn, K.G., 'The Lord's Supper and the Communal Meal at Qumran' in K. Stendahl (ed.), *The Scrolls and the New Testament*, 68.
69. Schiffman, Lawrence H., *Sectarian Law in the Dead Sea Scrolls*, (Chico: Scholars Press, 1983), 198.
70. Op. cit, 200. See his elaboration on 200–2.
71. See note 58.
72. Neusner, *Mishnaic Law of Purities*, Part 22, 40, my italics. Cf. his summary statement, op. cit, 41.
73. For an example of the tracing of this progress see Milgrom, Jacob, '4Q Tohora[a]: an Unpublished Qumran text on Purities' in Dimant and Schiffman (eds.), *Time to Prepare the*

Way in the Wilderness, 59–68. Note his repeated emphasis on the evident desire for scriptural support (64,65). For a more wide-ranging treatment see Harrington, Hannah K., *The Impurity Systems of Qumran and the Rabbis, Biblical Foundations*, SBL Dissertation Series 143, (Atlanta: Scholars Press, 1993). Harrington states her thesis up-front, 'It is my conclusion that much of what appears to be innovation in contrast to biblical principles is actually a valid, astute reading of Scripture itself' (1).

74. Harrington, op. cit, 261.
75. Black, Matthew, *The Scrolls and Christian Origins, Studies in the Jewish Background of the New Testament*, Chico: Scholars Press, (1983), 122. H. Braun has counted 192 instances of *kôl* in IQS alone, 64 of which refer to 'die Totalität des Geforderten oder die Ausnahmslosigkeit der Forderung Angesprochenen', *Spätjüdisch-häretischer und frühchristlicher Radikalismus*, (Tübingen: Mohr/Siebeck, 1957), I 28 n.2. He comments, 'Der Gehorsam soll nun auf der *ganzen* Linie erfolgen. Der Mensch gilt als verloren bereits dann, wenn er nicht *alles* tut' (op. cit, 29).
76. Milgrom, Jacob, 'The Scriptural Foundations and Deviations in the Laws of Purity of the *Temple Scroll*,' in Lawrence H. Schiffman (ed.), *Archaeology and History in the Dead Sea Scrolls*, Journal for the Study of the Pseudepigrapha Supplement Series 8, (Sheffield: JSOT Press, 1990), 84–9.
77. Op. cit, 89.
78. It must not be forgotten, however, that the sect constituted the true Israel so that, in principle, the maximalist demands were laid upon the whole nation. The arithmetical number of persons involved was strictly incidental.
79. Harrington, op. cit, 80f; Milgrom in Charlesworth, *DSS*, Vol. I, 177.
80. Milgrom suggests that the biblical basis is most probably Leviticus 22:6b–7. The passage is quite unspecific, 'the person who touches'. The Qumran author, through what Milgrom calls a 'hermeneutic of homogenization' gives it an application to all cases. See Charlesworth, *DSS*, Vol. I, 177.
81. Harrington, op. cit, 109. In making the case that purity at Qumran is defined more sharply than in the Bible or the rabbinic literature, Milgrom and Harrington draw heavily upon the *Temple Scroll*. Harrington regards as the most important sources 4Q *Tohorot* A, 4QMMT, 4Q *Ord*^{c} and 4Q *Flor*.

She finds that these show striking affinities with CD and 11QT and concludes, 'I think it is safe to assume for the purposes at hand that, regardless of origin, all of the Scrolls were accepted in some way by the Qumran community. The purity data of all Scrolls are compatible in most regards' (op. cit, 50). This may be true. Indeed, it was 'the draconic nature of all the laws in the scroll pertaining to matters of purity and to the holiness of the Temple' which Yadin found to be 'the determining factor of the identification' of the *Temple Scroll* as an Essene text (Yadin, Yigael, *The Temple Scroll*, Jerusalem: Israel Exploration Society, 1983), I, 399. However, the same can be said of a non-sectarian text like the *Book of Jubilees*. What the *Temple Scroll* lacks: community structure, the new covenant, cosmic dualism, is as important as features it shares with sectarian texts. Its primary intent is to depict an ideal (but not eschatological or messianic) temple: that is, the temple as it ought to be. If this is sound, then there is much to be said for the conclusion of John J. Collins, 'It is then a reformist proposal which lays claim to divine authority, but it may be representative of circles from which the sect emerged rather than of the sect itself' (art. 'Dead Sea Scrolls,' *ABD*, II, 93f.). For this reason 11QT has been left out of account in making the point about the tightening of purity laws.

82. Cf. Thiering, B.E., 'The sect is the first group within Judaism of whom we know who believed that moral failure ... incurred ritual defilement.' Art. 'Inner and Outer Cleansing at Qumran as a Background to New Testament Baptism,' *NTS*, 26, 1980, 269.
83. Neusner Jacob and Chilton Bruce D., 'Uncleanness: a Moral or an Ontological Category in the Early Centuries AD?' *Bulletin for Biblical Research* 1, 1991, 65.
84. Neusner, *Mishnaic Law of Purities*, Part 22, 45 (with parenthetical reference giving credit to Leaney, A.R.C., *The Rule of Qumran and Its Meaning*, 204).
85. IQS V 13b–14a speaks to the same point.
86. Baumgarten, J.M., 'The Purification Rituals in *DJD 7*,' in Dimant-Rappaport, *Forty Years*, 199–209.
87. Art. cit, 209.

Chapter Five

The Way: Perfection as a Means and End

It has been seen that, as the Qumran sectarians perceived it, the human situation was defined by the character, activity and claims of God on the one hand, and the powers of evil ranged against God and working in and through humanity on the other: a conjunction made the easier by the human proclivity towards sin. Most, if not all, of these factors come together in the pervasive and sensitive powers of purity and impurity. All of these factors together create and constitute the human predicament.

If one asks how the purity so deeply cherished at Qumran is to be attained the answer appears to be: by perfection. If 'a man is only able to "walk perfectly" (IQS 3.9) ... after purification, and he who fails to turn towards God is considered to be "unclean" (IQS 3.5) and cannot "be reckoned among the perfect" (IQS 3.3),' it is equally the case that, if a man becomes unclean and is excluded from the pure activities of the community, 'when "his way becomes perfect" (IQS 8.25) he is readmitted and is considered clean (cf. IQS 9.2).'[1] In a word, perfection is as contingent upon purity as is purity upon perfection. However, the connection between purity and perfection does not hang by a single thread. In the texts the notion is both common and comprehensive, constituting the hub of a network of ideas which convey the concept of salvation. Indeed, it is not too much to say that at Qumran perfection is a synonym for soteriology when that term is taken in its widest sense to denote why salvation is necessary, who are its objects, how it is effected and what is its scope.

The root word denoting perfection (*tam*) occurs almost 100 times in the non-biblical sectarian texts. However, not all of these examples, are of theological significance. Some carry the sense of 'complete' as of a measure of time (IQS VI 17; CD XV 15); others the sense of 'bring to completion or an end by destroying' (IQS IV 20; CD II 9; IQH XVII 21); and these account for approximately half the total. The theological examples are concentrated chiefly in the *Community Rule* and its appendices, and in the *Damascus Rule*, with a handful of instances being found in each of the *Rule of the War* and the *Thanksgiving Hymns*.[2] This is significant inasmuch as the *Community Rule* and the *Damascus Rule* are the two fundamental texts which give us knowledge of the organization and theological interests of the sect. If perfection is found to play a major role in such basic documents, then we shall have good reason for concluding that it occupied a sizeable role in sectarian thought.

Important as the term 'perfection' evidently is, it does not stand alone as the defining factor of the sectaries' thought. Frequently it is found in close association with other terms which assist in explicating its meaning. Chief among these is the word 'holy' (*qādaš*) and its cognates. Both in turn are yoked in harness with the terms 'way' (*derek*) and 'walk' (*hālak*), so that expressions such as 'men of perfect holiness' or 'to walk in perfection of way' are not uncommon.[3]

Without at this point trying to uncover the full soteriological import of the term 'perfect' in its various forms, it may be worth observing that the language of perfection appears to be applied on a variety of levels. Some instances imply that all members of the sect were perfect. For example, it is said of one who is inwardly resistant to the teaching of the sect ... 'in the source of the perfect he shall not be counted' (III 3b–4a).[4] Again, in the oldest part of the *Community Rule* the sect is described as a 'house of perfection' (VIII 9), and its members as 'those walking along the path of perfection' (VIII 21). Mention is made of 'the goods of the men of holiness who walk in perfection' that it shall not be merged with that of the men of falsehood (IQS IX 8); and we know from IQS VI 23 that the merging of personal property with that of the community after the second year of probation constituted 'joining the community' (IQS VI 22). What this amounts to is that the word 'perfect' had a corporate sense, and was thus applied to all members of the sect.

Besides this corporate usage however, the term is also used with an active or dynamic connotation. This is the case in several settings. For instance, initiates who had entered the covenant and were seeking admission to the community were subject to annual examination. 'And their spirit and their deeds must be tested, year after year, in order to upgrade each one to the extent of his insight and the perfection of his path, or to demote him according to his failings' (IQS V 24). This same idea of perfecting is applied also to full members who had inadvertently transgressed. 'However, if he acted through oversight he should be excluded from pure food and from the council, and the regulation applied to him: "He cannot judge anyone and no-one should ask his advice for two whole years." If his conduct is perfect in them he may return to the interpretation and to the council' (IQS VIII 24–26a). Interestingly, this same dynamic aspect is applied to full members also. The admission ceremony for new members seems to have been followed by the annual covenant renewal ceremony for existing members, and after a description of the former the text continues: 'They shall act in this way year after year, all the days of Belial's dominion. The priests shall enter the Rule foremost, one behind the other, according to their spirits' (IQS II 19b–20a).[5] Perfection was thus understood to be measurable as well as something in which progress was possible. If the *Rule of the Congregation* (IQSa) describes not only the ordering of events in the days to come but also how they were anticipated proleptically in the present, then this will provide further confirmation. The text reads that, on attaining his thirtieth birthday, one appointed to a position of leadership 'in accordance with his intelligence and the perfection of his behaviour, shall gird his loins to remain steadfast, doing the allotted duty among his brothers. Depending on whether (he has) much or little, one will be more or less honoured than his fellow' (I 17b–18). This again implies that perfection was variable among the perfect: that while all were perfect some were more perfect than others.[6] If so, then it provides a significant qualification of the point made first, that all members of the community were perfect, by injecting an ideal element into it.

Thirdly, perfection language is also used in an eschatological sense. It must suffice at this point to quote a single but highly suggestive example from the Discourse on the Two Spirits (IQS III 13–IV 26). Lines 18–23 of column IV are anthropological and individual in their reference, dealing with the struggle in the human heart of the spirits of truth and falsehood during the present time (IV 23). At the time of the visitation, however, God will destroy falsehood. 'God will refine, with his truth, all man's deeds, and will purify for himself the configuration of man, ripping out all spirit of injustice from the innermost part of his flesh, and cleansing him with the spirit of holiness from every irreverent deed. He will sprinkle over him the spirit of truth like lustral water (in order to cleanse him) from all the abhorrences of deceit and from the defilement of the unclean spirit. In this way the upright will understand knowledge of the Most High, and the wisdom of the sons of heaven will teach those of perfect behaviour. For these are those selected by God for an everlasting covenant and to them shall belong all the glory of Adam' (IV 20b–23a). What is envisaged here is the rooting out of the spirit of falsehood from the hearts of the perfect themselves at 'the appointed end and the new creation' (25a). The word rendered above as 'ripping out' (*lehātēm*) is itself a derivative of *tam*, though used here in the non-theological sense of 'make a perfect end of'. Since the subjects of this exercise are 'the perfect of way' (inconsistently rendered 'those of perfect behaviour' by Garcia Martinez, it would appear that a further perfecting lies in the future: that is perfection has an eschatological dimension.[7]

If we put these three levels of meaning of the term

together the conclusion indicated seems to be that at Qumran perfection was seen as both means and end. There was a perfection which was attainable in the present, and the process of perfecting was the means of attainment; nonetheless, a fullness of perfection lay ahead which would be the work of God at the end of days.

We may now attempt to unpack this concept more fully. Several ideas are brought into relation with perfection either by direct verbal linkage or else by ideological connection, and together they fill out what the sectaries understood by the concept.

Perfection and Law

The first idea which contributes to the definition of perfection is that of law. The terms noted earlier as being connected with perfection: namely, 'walk' (*hālak*) and 'way' (*derek*) are themselves suggestive of this, particularly when taken against their background in the Old Testament and Early Judaism. The opening lines of Psalm 119, which are typical of many others, read, 'Happy are those whose way is blameless, who walk in the law of the Lord ... who also do no wrong, but walk in his ways' (Psalm 119:1,3, NRSV Anglicized Version).[8] The same collocation of ideas is found repeatedly in the Qumran texts. Attention has already been drawn to the way in which joining the sect is construed in terms of submission to the law of Moses as interpreted by the sect (IQS I 3; V 8–11; CD XV 7b–10; XVI 4b–5). What may now be added is that observance of this law is expressed in some variation of the idea of walking in the way of perfection. In IQS I 7–8 one of the tasks of the Instructor is 'to welcome into the covenant of kindness all those who freely volunteer to carry out God's decrees, so as to be united in the counsel of God and walk in perfection in his sight.' The candidate for admission must 'steady his steps in order to walk with perfection on all the paths of God' (IQS III 9b–10a. Cf. VIII 20–6). Sometimes the word 'perfect' is used with the term 'way' (e.g. IQS IV 22, IX 2,5); sometimes with the word 'walk' (IQS I 8, VIII I, IX 6,19); and sometimes with both (e.g. IQS II 2, III 9, VIII 18, IX 8, etc.).

As to the thought lying behind all this, the meaning of several of the phrases is sufficiently concrete to give reasonably clear guidance. Thus the way of perfection is such that one can expect either promotion or demotion on the results of the annual examination (IQS V 24); two years' satisfactory probation in the way of perfection are the precondition of admission to the council of the community (VIII 10); whereas wilful infraction of the rules of the community leads to permanent expulsion, unintentional sin brings another opportunity to be tried in the way of perfection (IX 2); and while perfection of way is an impossibility without divine help (XI 2, 11, 17), yet achieved by God's aid a perfect way becomes a means of atonement for guilt and faithlessness (IX 5). From these cursory glances it is sufficiently clear that perfection of way refers to a pattern of behaviour, a mode of living, a clearly defined rule of conduct. But perhaps even more important is how this dominant feature of Qumran thought and practice contributed to the shape and character of Qumran religion. In considering this question at least three features of the view of the law at Qumran require to be taken into account.

First is the stringency of the law. This has already been observed in connection with the laws of purity, but it is typical of Qumran law as a whole. The community surrounded itself with a network of regulations which lacked nothing in breadth or depth. Conduct in the community council is carefully legislated, with penalties prescribed for offences such as speaking out of turn (IQS VII 11), falling asleep during a session (IQS VII 12–13) and laughing inanely (IQS VII 14). The sabbath law was enforced with great rigour.[9] Whereas the Rabbinic law permitted a walk of 2000 cubits on the Sabbath, the *Damascus Rule* cuts this in half (CD X 20). The same code specifically forbids going to the aid of an animal in need on the Sabbath, 'no-one should help an animal give birth on the sabbath day. And if he makes it fall into a well or a pit, he should not take it out on the sabbath' (XI 12b–14a).

The stringency of the law at Qumran is further exhibited in its inclusion of attitudes as well as actions. Speaking to a fellow-member with brusqueness (IQS VI 26) or about one of the priests with anger (IQS VII 2b–3a); feeling animosity toward a fellow-member without cause (IQS VII 10b); and above all inner resistance to the revealed laws of the sect (IQS I 6, II 14): all are placed under the ban. And as if to leave nothing out it is laid down that 'every law' (IQS I 17, V 1, 8 etc.), according to its 'exact interpretation' (CD IV 8) should be observed 'with the whole heart [and with the whole] soul' (CD XV 9–10, 12). 'The repeated admonitions to be legally perfect', writes E.P. Sanders, 'even granted the provisions for correcting transgressions – far surpass in strictness anything to be found in the Tannaitic literature.'[10]

A second feature of their view of perfection and law is that they believed the law to be capable of perfect fulfilment, even in the heightened form which they gave to it. This is the assumption on which the entire system is based, not least the *penal system* with its precise lists of demands and penalties for failure to meet them. The distinction in the *Community Rule* between entering the covenant and entering the community where the member will not be a threat to the purity of the community by contaminating their ritual food and drink is based on the assumption that the laws of purity have been perfectly observed. If these laws are not strictly observed then the penalties are at once imposed: one year's exclusion from the Pure Meal and rations reduced by one quarter for lying in regard to property (IQS VI 24–25); thirty days' penance for falling asleep during an Assembly of the Congregation (IQS VII 10); excommunication for using the name of God frivolously (VII 1); and so on. Goran Forkman says correctly that preserving the sect's order, purity and authority was the primary concern.[11]

That they believed the law could be perfectly kept is not rebutted by the provision of the penitential system. That is simply the recognition that perfect obedience is not mechanical and therefore failure is possible. But it is difficult to read the penal code (IQS V 25–VII 25) without gaining the impression that the rules were within the power of the covenanters to keep. Indeed, it is difficult to see how the community could function on any other assumption, given the basis on which it operated. E.P.Sanders again makes the point, 'Commandments were given which a man was to obey. Perfect obedience was the aim, and, within the tightly ordered community structure, was not considered a totally impossible goal.'[12]

A third feature to be taken into account in evaluating the place of the law in Qumran thought and life is that their law was the covenant law. Something has already been said of this[13] in the light of the fact that covenant is the controlling category of their system. Within such a system they do not gain admission to the covenant because they keep the law; rather, they keep the law because they have been admitted to the covenant. However, at Qumran this thoroughly biblical principle was seriously modified by other distinctive facets of the sectarian thought. The first was that entry into the covenant in the sense of becoming a full member of the community was a matter of individual choice allied with community approval (IQS VI 13b–23); indeed each member was subjected to annual testing of 'their spirit and their deeds' and promoted or demoted accordingly (IQS V 24). This necessarily introduced the element of qualifications or fitness both for admission to and continuance in the covenant. Again, failure to keep the law was a breach of the covenant commitment. In particular, it was a breach of the purity requirements by observance of which alone the community could discharge its function as 'a holy house for Israel and the foundation of the holy of holies for Aaron' (IQS VIII 5b–6a). The penitential code (IQS VI–VII) bears eloquent witness to the possibility of remission and so to the seriousness with which infraction was taken. For the fact was that the covenant law was intended to be observed. The failure to observe it had had disastrous consequences for the nation in the past (CD I 1–4a), and threatened to do so again since the larger part of the nation had once more deserted the covenant, as the sectaries saw it (IQS I 24–6). For this reason failure at the point of law observance could not be countenanced.

Under one aspect, then, perfection at Qumran consisted in total conformity to the law (which at Qumran always meant the law as the sect understood it). A.R.C. Leaney expresses the point well when he says, 'For Qumran the ideal was essentially to restore the old Israel in its purity, to bring to end or fulfilment the era of the Law in keeping the Law to the utmost. It could almost be said that the Qumran Halakah was a law to end Law; but only if you emphasize the first occurrence of the word in that gnomic phrase – you could end the period when the Law was paramount only by obeying it.'[14] Leaney's statement also alludes to another reason why legal perfection was taken with such seriousness at Qumran: the belief that a decisive turning-point in the history of salvation was impending, and that God had chosen them as the instrument of the fulfilment of his saving purposes.

Any religion which expresses itself in external performance, as most religions do, is clearly exposed to an occupational hazard at this point: the hazard of siphoning the meaning from the performance. The example which lies closest to hand in the case of Qumran is the religion of Israel of which she felt herself to be the custodian. Yet the greatest of the Hebrew prophets – Isaiah, Amos, Micah – are on record as castigating their hearers, not for failure in religious practice, but for plying punctiliously religious performance which had been emptied of all meaning (Is. 1:10–17; Amos 5:21–4; Mic. 6:6–8). It is hard to believe that the same danger was not present at Qumran where perfect observance of the law was impressed so strongly. Indeed, the heavy insistence upon the right spirit as alone guaranteeing the validity of ritual acts may be evidence of the awareness of danger. Schürer-Vermes, referring to the Pharisaic and rabbinic focusing of the laws of purity on the table in an attempt to eat their meals in the same state of purity as the priests in the Temple, say, 'this undoubtedly carried with it the risk that instead of achieving the ideal of "a kingdom of priests and a holy people" the ordinary Jew would confuse the means with the end, and the learned scholar overlook the larger spiritual issues because of his preoccupation with legal minutiae.'[15] And later, 'the religious life of Palestinian Judaism ... aimed at the sanctification of the individual and the nation. In practice however, the great accumulation of commandments and obligations could lead also to pettiness, formalism, and an emphasis on outward observance rather than true integrity.'[16] How far the theology and religious practice at Qumran fell into this snare is a question that must be kept in mind as we proceed.

Perfection and Atonement

The language and idea of perfection are brought into connection not only with the law but also with the idea of atonement. In IQS VIII – the oldest part of the *Community Rule* – the founding members are required to be 'perfect in everything that has been revealed about all the law ... to preserve faithfulness on the earth with firm purpose and repentant spirit in order to atone for sin' (1b, 3a). In lines 9b and 10b the 'house of perfection and truth in Israel' has as its stated purpose 'to atone for the earth and to decide the judgment of the wicked.' A similar statement of purpose is made in IQS IX 3–6. Perfection thus appears to be in some way the prerequisite of an atoning function carried out by the community. This would seem to bring us to the heart of the community's *raison d'être*. We may approach the subject by attempting to survey the ways in which the sect saw itself as charged with an atoning task, and, on that basis, analyse the meaning of atonement which is presupposed.

First, the sect saw itself as entrusted with an atoning

mission on behalf of the land. In IQS VIII 6 they are said to be 'chosen by the will of God to atone for the earth' (*lekappēr be'ad hā 'āreṣ*). The identical expression is used in VIII 10b. An expanded form of the phrase is found in VIII 3, 'to preserve faithfulness on the earth with firm purpose and repentant spirit in order to atone for sin'; and again in IX 4, 'in order to atone for the fault of the transgression and for the guilt of sin and for approval for the earth.' 'The verb in question (*kippēr*) is here being used with a human subject: the community; the purpose of the atonement is thrice said to be for (the forgiveness of) sin; and the means by which this is effected is by the community's doing justice and undergoing trials in order to walk with everyone in the measure of truth and the regulation of time' (VIII 3b–4a). In short, it is not by sacrificial rites but rather by living its life in community according to the law that the sect exercises its atoning ministry: a point spelled out specifically in IX 3–6. Another aspect present in these passages is that of the judgment of the wicked, which is apparently seen as part of the atoning process. 'To render the wicked their retribution' (VIII 6b–7a); 'to atone for the earth and to decide the judgment of the wicked' (VIII 10b) are perhaps the crucial clue in piecing together the meaning. The community evidently saw its atoning mission as saving the land of Israel from utter destruction by their own perfect obedience to the law and by their readiness (in the eschatological war?) to exterminate the wicked. The basic components of atonement are present: judgment upon sin; its removal by the intervention of an intermediary who offers to God the obedience he requires; and the consequent sparing of the land from destruction because the causes of offence have themselves been removed. 'Perfection of way' has thus become 'acceptable like a freewill offering' (IQS IX 5).[17]

Second, the sect saw its atoning function as extending beyond the sins of the land to its own sins. There are two distinguishable sides to this. On the one hand, there is the atonement offered for those who are in process of admission to full membership of the community. 'They should make atonement for all (*lekappēr lekôl*) who freely volunteer for holiness in Aaron and for the house of truth in Israel and for those being entered together for the community' (IQS V 6). The immediately following words: 'They should proclaim as guilty all those who sabotage the decree' (7a) suggest that the atonement is intended to cover those undergoing initiation insincerely, who consequently would not be cleansed by the purificatory rites (III 4) and might therefore pose a threat to the purity of the community (cf. IQS VIII 16b–19). However, the community was also faced with the fact of its own sins. IQS VIII 20–IX 2 deals with these in terms of the distinction between wilful and unintentional sin on the part of full members of the community ('the men of perfect holiness'). The language of atonement is not used, but that clearly is the topic. For those guilty of wilful or careless sin there is no atonement: the penalty is expulsion without possibility of return (VIII 21–24a; cf. IX 1a). As in the Old Testament, wilful sin is irremediable (Numbers 15:30f). Unintentional sin results in demotion to the rank of probationer, requiring two years' perfect conduct before he may be restored to participation in community council and in the Pure Meal. The implication of this is that, as with atonement for the land, obedience to the community's praxis has atoning value.

However, there is another dimension to the matter. The *Rule of the Community* concludes with a sample 'offering of the lips' (IX 26) prepared for the *Maskīl* as indicated by the introductory formula at IX 26. Column X is largely an affirmation of his commitment to offer praise to God spelled out in the terms such as times and seasons that were part of the sect's distinctive vocabulary; likewise his declaration not to deviate from the true way. With column XI however, his eye turns inward upon himself as a member of 'evil humankind', to his failings, transgressions, sins and the depravities of his heart. He sees that the perfection of his way belongs to God alone. 'As for me, if I stumble, the mercies of God shall be my salvation always; and if I fall in the sin of the flesh, in the justice of God, which endures eternally, shall my judgment be ... he will judge me in the justice of his truth, and in his plentiful goodness always atone for all my sins; in his justice he will cleanse me from the uncleanness of the human being and from the sin of the sons of man' (XI 11b–12, 14–15a). Here a new emphasis emerges. It is God who always atones for all his sins (*yekappēr be'ad kôl 'owônôtay*). Not only so, but a new vocabulary emerges and an old one takes on new colour from association with the fresh coinages: the 'mercies (*hesed*) of God' (12, 13); the 'goodness' (*tôb*) of God (14); the 'righteousness/righteous judgment' (*ṣedāqa'*) of God (12, 14) becomes the saving 'judgment' (*mishpāt*) (12, 13) of the *Maskīl*; while God, in atoning for his sins, will 'cleanse' (*tāhar*) him (14). The immediate point, however, is that, in this passage, another permutation emerges in comparison with those examined earlier: here, it is not the community which atones, but God. But since atonement is offered to God by definition, it follows that when God is the subject of the verb *kippēr*, the verb more probably denotes the effect of atonement: God will *forgive* all my sins. This indeed is the standard meaning in the *Damascus Rule* with the single exception of XIV 19.[18]

With data as diverse as these it is hardly surprising that widely different conclusions have been drawn as to the sect's understanding of atonement. It has been claimed that no single view was held at Qumran, and that divergent answers are found in the different documents.[19] In particular, it has been maintained that in the *Damascus Document* the view is ritualistic, the emphasis falling on ritual purity and keeping the rules of the sect, with salvation being viewed as domination of the rest of mankind by members of the redeemed community.[20] E.P. Sanders claims that there is no real soteriology in the sect's teaching at all: that the central soteriological category in Qumran thought is the covenant, and that therefore salvation simply means joining the sect,[21] with no clear distinction being made between atonement and forgiveness.[22] Paul Garnet finds an evolution in Qumran understanding of atonement, beginning with the

Founder and Community Hymns in which the accent falls on God's free forgiveness[23]; continuing through what he calls the 'Serek usage' noted above in which the community discharges an atoning function,[24] and culminating in the usage of the *Damascus Rule* where the two earlier usages are present.[25]

It is possible that the alleged divergent views and even the alleged evolutionary development are no more than the application in different contexts of varying aspects of a single reservoir of ideas. Garnet himself distinguishes the denotation of the verb 'atone' (*kippēr*) from its connotation. The denotation differs widely according to the subject or direct object of the verb, so that if man is the subject and man's wrath the object it can mean to appease; if man is the subject and sin the object it means to expiate; if God is the subject and man or sin the direct object it means to forgive. But underlying this range of denotation is a common connotation. 'The term always implies a change from wrath to favour'.[26]

In the light of the foregoing we may now attempt to piece together the sect's view of atonement. It may be laid down at once that the basic principle of their understanding was that atonement is a divine gift. Atonement language apart, it is made totally clear that the forgiveness of sins is the fruit of the grace of God. The liturgy for renewal of covenant with which the *Community Rule* begins (I 16 – II 18) is constructed around the motif of the two antithetical 'lots': the lot of God, and the lot of Belial. Each follows the same pattern: confession of sin followed by statement of consequences. The 'blameworthy transgressions' of the members of the lot of God (I 22b–26) match the 'wicked, blameworthy transgressions' of the members of Belial (II 4b–9). But the consequences are distinctly unequal. The members of the lot of God conclude their confession of sin with the words: 'but he has showered on us his merciful favour (*raḥămêy ḥăsādāw*) for ever and ever' (II 1a), and this is followed by the priestly blessing (II 1b–4a). Forthwith, the levites proceed to invoke curses on the men of the lot of Belial, which reach their climax in the invocation:

'May God not be merciful when you entreat him, nor pardon you when you do penance for your faults' (*welô' yislaḥ lekappēr 'awônêykā*) (8b).[27] In short, pardon, either granted or withheld, belongs to God alone.

The same point is made in the *Thanksgiving Hymns*. Thus column IX (= I) begins by celebrating God's power in creation (7–20), then proceeds to contrast with creation's glory the feeble and defiled state of the creature (21–26n). Yet even the creature can rise to the praise of God, because 'you, in your compassion, and in the vastness of your mercy have strengthened the spirit of man before his miseries ... you have purified him from abundant evil so that he can tell all your wonders before all your works' (31b–33a). IQH XII (= IV) 37 reads: 'For you have supported me by your kindnesses and by your abundant compassion. Because you atone for sin and cle[anse man] of his fault through your justice.' The same note recurs in III (= XVII) 11b–12: '[You have purified] your servant from all his sins [by the abundance of your co]mpassion, [forgiving rebellion], iniquity, sin, atoning for [failings] and disloyalty.' Indeed, throughout the *Thanksgiving Hymns*, the creature in his feebleness and depravity is placed in contrast with the glory and grace of the creator and one example that is repeatedly cited is God's grace in forgiving, cleansing and restoring the sinner (V = XIII 4–5, 19b–25; VI = XIV 24f; VII = XV 17b–20 etc.). It is not different in the *Damascus Rule*. In six of the seven examples of *kippēr* in the document, God is subject, with the verb followed by the preposition *be 'ad* denoting the person forgiven (II 5, III 18, IV 6, 10, XX 34) or by the preposition *'al* (IV 9) denoting the sins to be forgiven.[28]

Given, then, that atonement is a divine gift, how is it effected? It would appear that that question was answered at Qumran in terms of three distinguishable means of causation. In terms of ultimate causation atonement was effected by God. But, as has been seen, a wide range of specific motives is implied in this: mercy, compassion, goodness, righteousness. What Paul Garnet says of the *Damascus Rule* may, with only slight qualification, be said of Qumran soteriology as a whole: 'If there is any objective basis for forgiveness, it is the covenant (4:9f), but this is constantly being broken and the only real basis is God's own forgiving nature (2:5) and his free grace.'[29] And even this must be clearly understood. For one thing salvation is not on general offer; it is for the men of God's lot, not for the men of Belial's lot. As Jürgen Becker has put it: 'there is no thoroughgoing *sola gratia*, since salvation is confined to the sect'.[30] For another, God's grace is always represented as holy grace which, if it comes in forgiveness, also comes in judgment. Hence the *Maskīl* can say: 'If I stumble, the mercies of God shall be my salvation always,' and follow with the parallel statement: 'If I fall in the sin of the flesh, in the justice (*ṣedeq*) of God shall my judgment (*mišpāt*) be' (IQS XI 11c–12). And again: 'He will draw me near in his mercies and by kindnesses set in motion my judgment (*mišpāt*); he will judge me in the justice (*beṣidqat*) of his truth, and in his plentiful goodness always atone for all my sins' (IQS XI 13c–14c). The receiving of forgiveness is one side of salvation whose obverse is the acknowledgment and acceptance of God's righteous condemnation of sin.

But if God is the ultimate cause of atonement it was apparently held at Qumran that this did not exclude the use of instrumental means. It is in this sense that the community's role as an agent of atonement is best understood. As was noted above[31] the community saw this as being predicated upon two things: first, its withdrawal from participation in the Temple sacrifices; and second, its perfect observance of the law which it offered in their place (IQS IX 3–6). In this way they would be able 'to preserve faithfulness on the earth with firm purpose and repentant spirit in order to atone for sin' (IQS VIII 3). Evidently, this was regarded as an emergency measure since they saw themselves as 'chosen by the will (of God) to atone for the earth and to render the wicked their retribution' (6b–7a). There is also a stress on the visible aspect of the community's ministry: they would exhibit the positive qualities of love and justice to each other (IQS VIII 1–2); they would accept suffering and tribulation (IQS VIII 4); they would serve as true witnesses for the judgment (IQS VIII 6a). Garnet takes this to mean that 'the Community atones for sin by the spirit of holiness fostered in its midst through its discipline which forms a foundation upon which other penitents may be built like the stones of the Temple.'[32] Hence the atoning function attributed to the community is essentially metaphorical. 'The reality which is described under this metaphor of an expiatory oblation, however, is the provision of opportunity for repentance by the existence of a faithful remnant.'[33]

E.P. Sanders reads the evidence somewhat differently. Deeds and piety replace the sacrificial system. Yet these substitute 'sacrifices' are not effective in and of themselves: for the men of wickedness they avail nothing. Acts of atonement (*kippûrîm*) are powerless apart from inward conversion (IQS III 3–7). Hence the existence of the community is not effective in and of itself. 'The community, with the good deeds and pious prayers of its members, and especially those of the most pious and righteous men, constituted a substitute for the Temple sacrifices (IQS XIII 3f). As such, the community itself atoned for the sins of its members (IQS V 6; perhaps also IX.4), but more particularly for the defilement of the land, to preserve it for future occupation and use (IQS VIII 6, 10; IX 4; IQSa I 3).'[34]

Sanders' interpretation takes the language naturally, making this – in the words of F.F. Bruce – 'The most striking of all their beliefs ... the conception of their duty as the making of expiation ... for the sins of the nation which had gone so far astray from the path of His will.'[35] The thought is akin to that of the *Halakhic Letter* (4QMMT) which is much concerned with the 'deeds of the law' (*ma 'aśe hā – tôrâh*) and, in its concluding lines (Section C, 23–32)[36] exhorts the recipients to contemplate the 'deeds' of the Kings of Israel, noting that 'whoever among them feared [the To]rah was delivered from troubles; and these were the seekers of the Torah whose transgressions were [for]given.' (Lines 23–5). The letter concludes by enjoining the readers (who are also leaders of the people) to follow the practices being recommended. 'And this will be counted as a virtuous deed of yours, since you will be doing what is righteous and good in His eyes, for your own welfare and for the welfare of Israel' (lines 31–2).

If God is the ultimate cause of atonement and the community the instrumental cause, the holy spirit is the efficient cause. Whether the subject of the verb 'to atone' is the community or the individual for whom atonement is being made, 'spirit' is repeatedly involved as the instrumental preposition indicates. 'For, by the spirit of the true counsel concerning the paths of man all his sins are atoned so that he can look at the light of life. And by the spirit of holiness which links him with his truth he is cleansed of all his sins. And by the spirit of uprightness and of humility his sin is atoned' (IQS III 6b–8a). The men of the community are to set themselves apart (like) a holy house for Aaron 'when these exist in Israel in accordance with these rules in order to establish the spirit of holiness in truth eternal, in order to atone for the fault of transgression' (IQS IX 3–4a). 'I have appeased your face by the spirit which you have given me', says the psalmist (IQH VIII = XVI 19b). Only when God is the subject of the verb is the spirit generally unmentioned.[37]

But the place of the spirit in atonement is too confined a setting for a topic which plays such a large part in Qumran thought, and calls for fuller treatment below.

Before leaving the theme of perfection and atonement it will be useful, having looked at the means of atonement as seen at Qumran, to survey its effects. Some of them are already evident – necessarily, as being implied in the meaning of atonement. Forgiveness of sins is an obvious example. But in the texts several other consequences are traced to atonement: indeed, an impressively long list can be compiled: 'cleansing' (*zākāh*), 'purification' (*tāhar*), 'holiness' (*qādaš*), 'righteousness' (*ṣedāqā*), 'justice' (*mišpat*), 'salvation' (*yaša*). It is not uncommon to find these strung together (e.g. IQS III 6–8, XI 11b–15a; IQH XV = VII 30, XI = XIX 30–2, etc.): so much so that Ringgren has suggested that 'all these terms, which are well known from the Old Testament, are used apparently without differentiation.'[38] This is a tempting conclusion, particularly since some of the passages in question are quasi-poetic and emotionally intense religious utterances. However, the possibility should not be overlooked that they describe different aspects of the same reality, and rather than being resolved into a single homogenized unity, should be seen as indicating how atoning grace can cure the sinful situation in its multiple forms. Sin defiles, but atonement purifies, cleanses and sanctifies (IQS III 4,5), and a washing image denotes this.[39] Sin places the sinner in the wrong before God and in need of being put right. Atonement offers 'justice' (*mišpat*): but not the justice which would entail doom but the justice meted out by a righteous and merciful God (*beṣidqat ēl*: IQS XI 12c). Is the sinner corrupted 'in the sin of the flesh' (IQS XI 12b)? God 'will judge me in the justice of his truth, and in his plentiful goodness always atone for all my sins; in his justice he will cleanse me from the uncleanness of the human being and from the sin of the sons of man' (IQS XI 14–15a). The righteousness of God is a positive, saving righteousness which turns the heart of the penitent away from evil and falsehood towards goodness and truth.[40]

If one reviews Qumran teaching about atonement as a whole there emerges a double emphasis. On the one hand it is insisted that atonement can be wrought only by God through the working of the holy spirit. On the other hand it is written into the title deeds of the community that its chief purpose is to make atonement, particularly for the land. The tension is akin to that noted in the previous section on perfection and law: the law is covenant law; provision is made for breaches of it, and yet the insistent emphasis is that it must be kept unfailingly. So with atonement. Only God can provide atonement, yet the sect believes itself to be entrusted with an atoning function because the Temple has rendered its own sacrificial offerings null and void.

Perfection and the Holy Spirit

The place of the holy spirit in Qumran thought is by no means confined to the idea of atonement, nor even to the idea of perfection. Indeed, its significance in either can only be grasped clearly in the light of its place in Qumran thought as a whole. For its fundamentals it is indebted to the Old Testament. Accordingly, sometimes the term (*rûah*) is used in its literal sense of 'wind' or 'breath'; sometimes it denotes the 'inner nature' or 'self'; on occasion it denotes the *kind* of self as in expressions such as 'the erring spirit' or 'the haughty spirit' (IQS XI 1); while it can also be used to denote supernatural beings such as 'the spirit of light and darkness' (IQS III 24).[41]

However, the Qumran texts exhibit usages which differ either in frequency or character from Old Testament practice. For example, the expression 'Holy Spirit', found only twice in the Old Testament and in both cases in reference to God (Psalms 51:11; Isaiah 63: 10–12) occurs five times in the *Thanksgiving Hymns* alone as in the psalmist's prayer to God 'to purify me with your Holy Spirit' (IQH VIII 20 = XVI 11–12). Not only so, sometimes the expression is applied to human beings also. In CD V 11 and VI 4 members are enjoined against breaking the laws of the community because this would 'defile their holy spirit'. In some instances the human spirit is spoken of in association with God's Holy Spirit in such a way as to imply that the purity of the latter is transferred to the former.[42] It is also notable that the use of spirit-terminology in reference to supernatural beings is cultivated to greater degree at Qumran than in the Old Testament.

The classic treatment of the holy spirit in the Qumran literature is the sequence CE already referred to,[43] and variously known as the Treatise or Discourse on the Two Spirits (IQS III 13 – IV 26). This section has literary-critical problems of its own. For one thing, it is readily isolable from the rest of the *Community Rule*, and many scholars have concluded that it may have had an independent existence.[44] However that may be, there can be little doubt that it had come to occupy a central place in Qumran thought as the opening lines indicate: 'For the *Maskīl*: he shall inform and instruct all the sons of light concerning the nature (*tôldôt*) of all the sons of man according to the kind of spirit which they possess' (III 13–14a. Vermes, slightly amended). Still more problematic is its internal consistency: in particular how the psychological use of the term 'spirit' in IV 2–10, 23b–26 where it denotes the inner moods and attitudes of human beings, is to be reconciled with the metaphysical usage of III 18–26 where it refers to the Prince of Light and the Angel of Darkness. Leaney thinks the issue was never clearly resolved in the mind of the author.[45] Osten-Sacken holds that the psychological-anthropological elements represent a chronologically later development, after the metaphysical-dualistic view, which he links with IQM and the earliest thought of the sect had been de-eschatologized.[46] A.A. Anderson observes that it is not divulged how the influences of the spirits are exercised, adding that 'it is possible that the author of IQS III–IV may have thought of something *approximating* to the rabbinic doctrine of good and evil inclinations.'[47] There is no doubt that the overriding import of the section is anthropological rather than cosmological, and M. Hengel's conclusion strikes the right balance when he says, 'an exclusively psychological and anthropological interpretation of the two spirits is unjustified, though it is unmistakable that the struggle of the two "powers" finds its climax and its decision over and in man: the apocalyptic drama concentrates on anthropology, without the cosmic aspect being lost.'[48]

How then does the Qumran understanding of the spirit engage with their view of perfection? More precisely, since members of the community are repeatedly described as 'perfect in way' or those who 'walk in perfection' or constitute a 'house of perfection'[49] in what way is the spirit involved in the achieving of this perfection? There can be no doubt that the sect's emphasis on the spirit was a distinctive feature of its teaching; indeed, it is widely conceded that the Qumran community stands out as an exception in an era which confessed that, in general, the spirit was no longer at work.[50] Not only did they believe that the spirit was actively at work in their community; they believed that through their community alone the spirit could be received. In a crucially important section of the *Community Rule* which describes the meaning of membership (IQS III 6–9) the 'holy spirit' is spoken of as 'the holy spirit of the community' (III 7).[51] In short, 'the spirit' is received through joining the community. If then, members of the community are 'perfect in way' and the spirit is at work in the community presumably these two factors are connected. Is it possible to determine how?

It is well known that admission to the community involved several probationary stages, extending over at least two years. The stages are spelled out in IQS VI 13b–23a. Following admission to the covenant by the Overseer for conversion to the truth and separation from sin as well as instruction in the rules of the community (VI 14b–15a), two more stages followed. At the end of one full year, during which his participation in community affairs – especially those involving purity – was restricted, he was examined by the Council of the Community 'about his spirit and about his deeds' (17): an expression which apparently refers to his acceptance of the law and his performance of it. At the end of a second year, during which his participation in sectarian affairs involving purity was still restricted, though less so than in the first, he was again examined and, if approved, was admitted to full membership, involving full participation in all the rites and responsibilities of the community (21–3).

In the description of the stages of admission in IQS VI 14–23 the spirit is not mentioned, save for the tell-tale reference to the testing of the spirit of the candidate in IQS VI 17. This is hardly surprising in a section of legal regulations. However, since the successive stages mark progress in purity, it would be surprising if no role were found for it during the period of initiation. It is no coincidence therefore, that in the liturgy of admission to full membership (IQS I 16 – II 25) the chief disaster to befall those who turn back at the critical moment is that they will not receive the spirit (IQS II 25 – III 12). Exclusion from the Community is exclusion from the spirit and exclusion from the spirit is exclusion from cleansing.

It would seem therefore that the sectarian theology distinguished sharply not only between those outside the sect and those inside, but also between provisional and full members. The basis of this latter divide was the spirit. Moreover, it is notable that admission to full membership and reception of the spirit are associated emphatically with the inward acceptance of the sectarian teaching without which all ritual ablutions were ineffectual. 'By the spirit of holiness which links him with his truth he is cleansed of all his sins. And by the spirit of uprightness and humility his sin is atoned. And by the compliance of his soul with all the laws of God his flesh is cleansed by being sprinkled with cleansing waters and being made holy with the waters of repentance. May he, then, steady his steps in order to walk with perfection on all the paths of God' (IQS III 7b–10a). That is to say, since spirit is an element common to God and humanity, spirit becomes the medium through which the holy spirit of God takes possession of the human spirit. Whether B.E. Thiering is correct in positing a separate initiation rite for each stage, her conclusion appears to be sound that 'at the final stage the Spirit of holiness was given, as the decisive purification of the soul and the privilege of membership of the community in which the Spirit of holiness dwelt.'[52] It is by the spirit alone that it is possible to walk in perfection of way: 'The path of man is not secure except by the spirit which God creates for him to perfect the path of the sons of man so that all his creatures come to know the strength of his power' (IQH XII = IV 31b–32a).

However, Qumran pneumatology had a horizon beyond the present; they looked also for a decisive saving work of the spirit at the Visitation at the end of days. 'God, in the mysteries of his knowledge and in the wisdom of his glory, has determined an end to the existence of injustice and on the occasion of his visitation he will obliterate it for ever ... God will refine, with his truth, all man's deeds, and will purify for himself the configuration of man, ripping out all spirit of injustice from the innermost part of his flesh, and cleansing him with the spirit of holiness from every irreverent deed. He will sprinkle over him the spirit of truth like lustral water (in order to cleanse him) from all the abhorrences of deceit and from the defilement of the unclean spirit. In this way the upright will understand knowledge of the Most High, and the wisdom of the sons of heaven will teach those of perfect behaviour. For these are those selected by God for an everlasting covenant and to them shall belong all the glory of Adam' (IQS IV 20b–23b). The sect not only distinguished inward from outward sin, even though they saw the two as connected, inasmuch as inward sin incurred outward defilement. They also made a distinction between sin in the form of specific acts and sin as the source of sins; that is, they appear to have entertained a concept of innate sin which is resistant to any purification available in the present. This has, indeed, been contested[53], but it seems clear that the sectarian understanding of man as 'flesh' (*bāśār*) and man as *'ādam* sees transgression as arising from a sinful state or condition. 'What is flesh compared to this? What creature of clay can do wonders? He is in sin from his maternal womb, and in guilty iniquity right to old age' (IQH XII = IV 29b–30a). 'I belong to evil humankind, to the assembly of wicked flesh; my failings, my transgression, my sins, ... with the depravities of my heart, belong to the assembly of worms and of those who walk in darkness' (IQS XI 9–10a). By the same token it envisages an end to this condition in the conflagration at the end of days. 'Even though you burn the foundations of mountains and fire sears the base of Sheol, those who [keep] your regulations [are saved]. [You protect] the ones who serve you loyally, so that their posterity is before you all the days. You raise an [eternal] name for them, [forgiving them all] sin, eliminating from them all their depravities, giving them as a legacy all the glory of Adam and plentiful days' (IQH IV = XVIII 13–15).[54] The Qumran expectation for the end-time was the abolition of innate sin and the recovery of the creation glory of Adam. This also was the work of the spirit.

Perfection as Means and End

Why perfection is the controlling category in Qumran theology can be understood only if it is viewed against the background situation which evoked it. The texts make reasonably clear what that was: the failure of Israel to keep the covenant (CD I 1–12), and the failure of the religious leaders to preserve the worship of the Temple in its purity (IQS VIII 1–16a). It is in connection with these events that the language of perfection is found (e.g. CD I 10, II 15; IQS VIII 9,10): that is to say, in connection with the *raison d'être* of the Essene movement as a whole, and the Qumran community in particular. As they interpreted things, perfection was demanded of them if they were to fulfil their vocation.

To suggest that perfection was seen by the Qumran sectaries as both means and end is an attempt to do justice to the seriousness with which they viewed it. Without doubt it was seen by them as a means to an end: the only means to the high end of saving Israel by accepting and fulfilling her covenant responsibilities. But it was also an end in itself: the rendering to God by perfect worshippers of the perfect worship he rightly demanded. In the words of Deuteronomy 18:13 quoted in the *Temple Scroll* which describes the Temple as it ought to be, 'You are to be perfect before YHWH your God' (11QT LX 21).

In discussing the meaning of perfection at Qumran there will necessarily be a degree of overlap with the individual aspects related to it which have already been considered. But it may be useful to see the overall background against which the individual aspects find their identity and, beyond that, their unity.

The preceding treatment of perfection and the holy spirit disclosed a clear distinction between the perfecting work of the spirit in the present and the perfecting work of the spirit in the days to come. That same distinction unsurprisingly carries over into – indeed, is implied in – the idea of perfection in the texts, and we may make use of it in our treatment of the theme.

Perfection as Means and End in the Present

The idea of perfection in this sense seems to gather around three distinguishable (though not separate) themes. First is perfection as a way of life: specifically, the life of the community; that is to say, living in consonance with the sectarian law. The collocation of the terms 'walk', 'way' and 'perfect' in varying combinations is easily documented, and demonstrates the dominant role which the idea exercised in Qumran thought. One joined the sect 'so as to be united in the counsel of God and walk in perfection in his sight' (ISQ I 8)[55], one entered the covenant to 'walk perfectly on all [God's] paths' (CD II 15). In *4Q Songs of the Sage*[a] (4Q 510) 1 9 and *4Q Songs of the Sage*[b] (4Q 511) 10 1 8 there occurs the hortatory exclamation: 'May all those of perfect path praise you!' while in *4Q Songs of the Sabbath Sacrifice*[d] (4Q 403) I 1.22 and *4Q Songs of the Sabbath Sacrifice*[e] (4Q 404) 213 are found the words of assurance: 'he will bless all whose path is perfect.'[56]

To 'walk in perfection of way' then, meant to live in complete conformity with the sectarian interpretation of the law, in all its stringency. But this is not to be construed as mere external compliance with formal regulations and rituals. It had, indeed, its own forms and rites, but, as we have seen already, the ethical and the ritual were interlocked so that to defy the former was to breach the latter. The penitential code of the community (IQS VI 24–VII 25) is a remarkable fusion of the two. Interrupting another's speech (VII 9); falling asleep in council (VII 10); leaving council without permission (VII 11) are all violations of the perfect way, and are duly penalized. But intermingled with these are other offences such as angry speech (VII 2); the bearing of grudges (VII 8); slander (VII 16–18). The centrality of motive in moral action is recognized inasmuch as intentional wrongdoing is distinguished from unintentional and penalties graded accordingly. The giving of false information was punished only if done knowingly (VI 25), and likewise with harmful speech (VII 3); and in general the penalties increased in proportion to the moral turpitude of the offence.

Sin and purity, says Lichtenberger, are more than simply cultic rites. At Qumran cult-piety was not eliminated but radicalized under the aspect of obedience to the law.[57] It is therefore instructive, as Lichtenberger points out, to note that a passage such as IQS III 6–11 speaks of present salvation,[58] and, one may add, speaks of its accomplishment by both ethical and ritual means. The parallelism of the statements is significant. 'For by the spirit of the true counsel concerning the paths of man all his sins are atoned so that he can look at the light of life. And by the spirit of holiness which links him with his truth he is cleansed of all his sins. And by the spirit of uprightness and humility his sin is atoned. And by the compliance of his soul with all the laws of God his flesh is cleansed by being sprinkled with cleansing waters and being made holy with the waters of repentance. May he, then, steady his steps in order to walk with perfection on all the paths of God, conforming to all he has decreed concerning the regular times of his commands and not turn aside, either left or right, nor infringe even one of his words.' In short, cleansing, itself conditional upon submission, followed by perfect obedience is the meaning of walking in the way of perfection.

However, perfection is more than a way of life; it is also a quality of character. No doubt this is implicit in some degree in the former, especially as this was understood at Qumran. But it receives positive expression in a number of ways, some of which have already been noted. For example, it was seen that the righteousness of God is an active, saving righteousness which not only brings forgiveness, but turns the heart of the penitent away from evil towards goodness.[59] In harmony with this is the imagery of 'stubbornness of heart' considered earlier,[60] to which the cure offered is the inward work of the spirit of holiness which begets uprightness, humility and inward acceptance of the laws of God (IQS III 7b–9a).[61] To be added to these is the image of circumcision (*mûl*), which occurs once each in the *Community Rule*, the *Damascus Rule* and the *Habakkuk Commentary*. In IQpHab XI 13 the refusal of the Wicked Priest to 'circumcize the foreskin of his heart' is offered as the explanation of his impending doom. No elaboration is given. Rather more significant is CD XVI 6. The context is concerned with making binding the commitment to the sectarian covenant (1–2). The text reads: 'And on the day on which the man has pledged himself to return to the law of Moses, the angel Mastema will turn aside from following him should he keep his word. This is why Abraham circumcized himself on the day of his knowledge' (4b–6). The meaning appears to be that entry into the sect breaks the power of evil angels, and just as circumcision broke that power for Abraham when he entered the covenant,[62] so will wholehearted entry into the covenant do for the genuine convert. IQS V 4b–6a is of interest in advancing inward circumcision as the cure for stubbornness of heart. 'No-one should walk in the stubbornness of his heart in order to go astray following his heart and his eyes and the musings of his inclination. Instead he should circumcize in the community the foreskin of his tendency and of his stiff neck in order to lay a foundation of truth for Israel, for the community of the eternal covenant.'

The metaphor of inward circumcision and its effect comes to most striking expression in the texts 4Q *Bless, O my Soul*[a] (4Q 434 [4Q *Bar*[e] *ki Napshi*[a]]) and 4Q *Bless, Oh my Soul*[c] (4Q 436 [*Bar*[e] *ki Napshi* [c]]).[63] In the former the writer (and worshipper) says, 'He has circumcized their hearts and has saved them by his grace and has set their feet firm on the path' (Frg.1 col. I line 4); while the surviving text of the latter concludes ... 'you have removed from me, and in its place you will put a pure heart' (Frg.1 line 10). Again, then, there is the suggestion that perfection is more than just a matter of punctilious performance: it is a matter of inward change.

This would appear to be further confirmed in that, more than once, the expression 'perfect way' takes the form 'perfect holiness'. The 'men of perfect holiness' (IQS VIII 20) or the 'men of holiness' (17, 23) are evidently the founders of the desert community who constitute the 'council of holiness of those walking along the path of perfection' (21). The same expression is used thrice to denote the congregation of the *Damascus Rule* (CD XX 2,5,7); and to 'walk in perfect holiness' is evidently parallel to 'walking in perfection of way' (CD VII 4–5). And while the term 'holy' (*qādôš*) is used of places, things and persons by virtue of their belonging to God, it also has a moral component. The 'men of holiness' are already separated from evil (IQS V 13; VIII 17,21); already they walk in the ways of God, and are cleansed from all their sins by the spirit of holiness (IQS III 7b–8a).[64]

Yet another way in which perfection as a present condition entered the Qumran scene was in their worship. Much remains unknown about the forms and frequency of worship at Qumran, though recent research has made great progress.[65] While there are some texts whose liturgical function is unclear (e.g. 11QPs[a], IQH, IQS X–XI), there are other texts which were clearly intended for use in worship (e.g. IQS I–II, IQSb, 4Q 504f, 4Q 512, 4Q *Shir Shabb*). Not only have liturgical tables been found indicating which festivals are to be observed,[66] but others contain indications in their headings and rubrics of the occasions on which they were to be used.[67]

This is not surprising given the Temple functions which the sect believed itself to be called upon to discharge (IQS VIII 1–16). What is of particular relevance to our present concern is one distinctive aspect of their worship which the sectaries took with great seriousness: namely, the belief that in worship they were in communion with the angels. Thus in IQS XI the writer, speaking of the community of the elect, says: '[God] unites their assembly to the sons of the heavens in order (to form) the counsel of the community and a foundation of the building of holiness to be an everlasting plantation throughout all future ages'

(8). In 4Q *Songs of the Sabbath Sacrifice*[d] (4Q 403) the Maskil calls upon the sectaries to join their earthly liturgy with that of the angels who worship with them. 'This is no angelic liturgy', writes John Strugnell, 'no visionary work where a seer hears the prayers of angels, but a maskil's composition for an earthly liturgy in which the presence of angels is in a sense invoked and in which ... the Heavenly Temple is portrayed on the model of the earthly one and in some way its service is considered the pattern of what is being done below.'[68] But it is in the *Thanksgiving Hymns* that the belief comes to its most intense expression. 'The corrupt spirit you have purified from the great sin as that he can take his place with the host of the holy ones, and can enter in communion with the congregation of the sons of heaven' (IQH XI = III 21b–22a). 'For your glory, you have purified man from sin ... so that he can take his place in your presence with the perpetual host and the [everlasting] spirits, to renew him with everything that will exist' (IQH XIX = XI 10b,13). 'For you have brought [your truth and your] glory to all the men of your council and in the lot, together with the angels of the face, without their being any mediator between the intelligent and your holy ones' (IQH XIV = VI 12b–13). In all three passages the object of the psalmist is fellowship with God, which is mentioned specifically in the second passage. In the first and third passages this is expressed as fellowship with the 'holy ones' (*qedôšîm*) and in XI 13 standing before God 'with the perpetual host' (*ṣebā''ad*). In the first and second passages purification from sin is named as the precondition of such access to the presence of God; while in the last the 'men of the council' are implied to stand on the same footing as the angels of the Presence.[69]

Now it is precisely such factors as these which have led to the conclusion that the Qumran sect believed that eschatological salvation had already entered the present age in the history and experience of the community. H-W. Kuhn has explored this subject with special reference to the *Thanksgiving Hymns*, including two of the passages considered above.[70] It is not relevant to our purpose to review the full range of the evidence on which he bases his conclusion. Suffice it to say that two of his major points are communion with the angels as spoken of in IQH III 21–3[71], XI 13f,[72] and proleptic eschatological transference to heaven which he finds in III 20.[73] In this sense also, then, perfection was understood to have a present reference. The words of Otto Betz summarize it well, 'In the YHD of the realized eschaton this community will be made perfect for all those when God will cleanse with the Holy Spirit (IQSerek IV, 22), and the Qumran priests will then serve the temple of God's kingdom like the angels of the presence (IQ *Blessings* IV 25–6)'.[74] Or to echo the words of H. Lichtenberger, 'Qumran is a historical anticipation of the eschaton.'[75]

Thus, in the sectarian writings there is a very clearly defined vein of teaching according to which perfection is an achievable state in the present in respect of compliance with sectarian law, a change of heart in regard to sin and God, and an anticipation of heaven itself by the assimilation of the worship of the earthly community into the worship of the holy ones who serve God face to face. This perfection is not merely desirable and attainable: it is indispensable if the sectarian community is to discharge its appointed function of atoning for the land. But it is also indispensable as the due fulfilment of the covenant obligations which the sectaries had freely undertaken: that is, of the response of life and service which God requires. Thereby, perfection is both means and end – now.

Perfection as Means and End in the Age to Come

As remarkable as the insistence on the attainability of perfection in the present is the insistence alongside it that perfection will be achieved only in the age to come. The latter, seemingly at odds with the former, is nonetheless found throughout the literature. In the Discourse on the Two Spirits in the *Community Rule* (IQS III 13–IV 26) the picture is clear. God created man 'and placed within him two spirits so that he would walk with them until the moment of his visitation' (III 18). It is only at the last day (17) that God will purify him within, cleansing him with the spirit of holiness (20–1). But this discourse is immediately preceded by III 6–12 which affirms cleansing of flesh and spirit in the present.[76]

A similar picture, albeit with some qualifications emerges from the *Damascus Rule*. There are the familiar uses of 'walking perfectly in the way' (I 20f, II 15f, VII 4–5, XX 5,7) which clearly refer to present perfection in one of the first two senses defined above. At the same time an unfulfilled dimension remains. In CD III 20 the reward of those who remained faithful to God's precepts is said to be 'eternal life, and all the glory of Adam is for them': while VII 4b–6a reads, 'For all those who walk according to these matters in perfect holiness, in accordance with his teaching, God's covenant is a guarantee for them that they shall live a thousand generations.' To discuss the import of Qumran eschatology at this time would be to anticipate what will receive fuller consideration later. Let it suffice at this point to note that a perfection beyond that presently attainable is apparently seen as lying before the community in the future.

But the difference between perfection that is present and perfection that is to come is nowhere more intensely or more poignantly expressed than in the *Thanksgiving Hymns*. The point is not simply that there are passages in which the psalmist confesses his sin in ways that seem to allow no room for pardon or deliverance now or in the future as, for instance, 'How will a man count his sin? How will he defend his infringements? How will he answer every just judgment? To you, God of knowledge, belong all the works of justice and the foundation of truth; to the sons of man, the service of sin and the deeds of deception' (IX = I 25–7). The point is that both confession of sin and affirmation of deliverance from sin are juxtaposed with no indication of how the passage is made from the one to the other. Thus the triumphant affirmation of exaltation to praise God alongside the host of heaven in XIX = XI 10b, 13 (quoted above) is followed by the despairing confession, 'A source of sorrow has opened for me, bitterness [without end distresses me] grief has not been hidden from my eyes, when I knew man's instincts, the return of mankind [to dust], [his inclination] towards sin and the anguish of guilt. These things have entered my heart, they have penetrated my bones, [...] to plunge me into the meditation of anguish ... until iniquity is destroyed, and [fraud comes to] an end, and there are no more ravaging diseases. Then will I sing with the harp of salvation' (XIX = XI 19–21,22b). This is more than simply the stark contrast between humans as sinners and humans as graced by God with salvation such as one finds in XII = IV 29b–37. In this passage the two are intermingled throughout so as to place in explicit contradistinction the depravity and helplessness of the sinner on the one hand and the undeserved, redeeming grace of God on the other. But in the earlier passage (XIX = XI 10–22) the two appear to stand in irreconcilable conflict. Likewise, in XI = III 19–36, which is commonly regarded as a self-contained psalm,[77] the psalmist begins praising God for exaltation from the pit to communion with the holy ones (19–23b), only to relapse into querulous questioning about his fate (23–24), 'for I find myself at the boundary of wickedness and with those doomed by lot' (24d–25a). The psalm then launches into a torrential description of the destruction of the world by a river of fire which will devour the earth and the wicked, reaching even to the deep (25–34), culminating in an eschatological war which sweeps across the world unrestrained until destruction is complete, evil included (36).

This gives rise to two questions: first, what is the nature of the perfection looked for in the age to come? And second, how is it related to the perfection affirmed by the sectaries to be theirs in the present? As to the first: on the negative side it is spoken of in terms of the destruction of sin in all its forms and manifestations. This includes the annihilation of the powers of evil (IQS IV 18b–19a) and all those who have been bound by them (11b–14). It includes the purging of the spirit of darkness from the inmost part of man's flesh, and cleansing him with the spirit of holiness (20b–22a). It includes the extirpation of the human proclivity towards sin and of iniquity itself (IQH XIV

= XI 19–23). On the positive side it is spoken of in terms of eternal life (CD III 20; IQH IV 15), new creation (IQS IV 25), and – no doubt deriving from the latter – the recovery of the lost glory of Adam (IQS IV 23; CD III 20; IQH XIV = IV 13–15; 4Q 171 III 1–2). In late Jewish apocalyptic Eden was regarded as the proper setting for humanity just as unfallen Adam was regarded as the appropriate pattern of what man could and would again become.[78]

As to the second question: how is the perfection of the age to come related to the perfection claimed by sectaries in the present: the answer is complex. This is the case not only because of the sectaries' belief that their worship became one with that of the angels, but also because they believed that their life anticipated that of the age to come. Every one of the features on the positive side of the life expected in the eschaton is attributed to sectarian life here and now: length of life (CD VII 4–6; IQS IV 6–8); new creation (IQH XI = III 20–1) including the recovery of Eden (IQH XIV = VI 14–19a); access to the immediate presence of God in the company of the holy angels (IQH XIX = XI 10–14). On the negative side the picture is similar: cleansing from sin by the spirit of holiness (IQS III 7b–9b); rejecting stubbornness of heart and one's evil inclination (IQS V 4b–6a) which apparently means much the same as 'not retaining Belial within my heart' (IQS V 21); and purification from 'the great sin' (IQ III 21b–22a).[79] The question is: how can these two views, between which there is an evident tension, be held together?

Various suggestions have been advanced in the history of Qumran scholarship. Dupont-Sommer suggested that the 'confession passages' refer to and describe man before his entry into the covenant.[80] But while this might explain IQH III 19–36 where there is a marked shift in reference at line 23 from what the psalmist is, thanks to God's grace, and what he is apart from it, this hardly holds in other cases. Holm-Nielsen finds that 'the explanation is to be sought in the dual outlook of the Qumran community toward life,'[81] apparently suggesting that the dualism of the Qumran mentality naturally expressed itself in antitheses.

K.G. Kuhn offers, in effect, a variant of this view, relating the two types of passages in dialectical terms. The sectary belongs *both* to the 'company of evil flesh' *and* to the 'elect of God.'[82] But this is hardly persuasive. The confession passages are accompanied (usually followed) by passages affirming God's power to cleanse from sin as a matter of divine grace.

If a solution is to be found to the problem, or even a partial solution, it is more likely to be found in the central concerns of the Qumran sectarians than in dualistic or dialectical theologizing. Their driving preoccupation was the covenant with the God of Israel which, five centuries after it had been broken by their ancestors, was renewed with themselves as the kernel of the new Israel. The first covenant had been breached because Israel and Judah had failed to maintain their covenant obligations. The covenant was, indeed, a gift of God's grace, but grace was not to be traded on. The covenant law was to be kept – perfectly, the availability of forgiveness for failure notwithstanding. The availability of forgiveness had not spared the nation from the exile for forgiveness has no meaning to those who have become spiritually calloused. Accordingly, a companion emphasis to that on observing the law was the emphasis on the need for inward obedience and submissiveness. Rote-performance would not suffice. So much was this the case that ritual observance was valueless unless accompanied by the spirit of penitence. But equally, since the law must be kept, they must not only be punctilious 'doers of the law', but to guarantee this, the law must be tightened up to ensure that no demand was overlooked. Only by their doing the 'works of the law' would Israel be saved. A crucial aspect of this was the preservation of the purity of worship: a matter treated casually and even contemptuously as they saw it, by the Jerusalem priesthood. It was for this reason that they felt compelled to withdraw to their desert 'temple', and offer there a pure worship which could no longer be offered in Jerusalem.

Now if that is a fair summary of the main theological

and religious concerns of the Qumran it goes far to explaining why their faith assumed the form it did. It explains the central role of perfection in their thought and life. It explains the emphasis on the observance of the law just as it explains the intensified form of the law to be observed, the availability of forgiveness notwithstanding. In particular it helps to explain some of the more remarkable and distinctive features of Qumran thinking.

First, it helps to account for their profound understanding of sin. Given their calling to be the Israel with whom God had renewed the covenant, the last thing they would do would be to take sin lightly. The evidence that they avoided any such temptation there might be is twofold. To begin with they incorporated the moral within the ritual sphere so that moral offences incurred ritual defilement and so became visibly accountable. Then again, their perception of the depth of sin as being more than wrong actions but as involving a bent or inclination towards sin which lay behind and expressed itself in wrong actions underlines the seriousness with which sin was taken. The 'I' hymns in the *Hodayot* are pervaded by the sense that the confessor's primary concern is not what he has done but what he is.[83]

A second distinctive feature of the sectarian soteriology is its insistence on grace and works. E.P. Sanders has written, 'God's grace and the requirement of performance on the part of man are both stressed so strongly in the Scrolls that it is difficult to state the precise relationship between grace and works.'[84] The emphasis upon both cannot be doubted. The consciousness of grace in, for example, CD I or the *Thanksgiving Hymns* is so powerful that only the tone-deaf could miss it. But by the same token the description of the community as the 'doers of the law'; the annual examination of members' 'spirit and deeds'[85] (IQS V24. cf. 19, 21, 23; VI 13f, 17, 18); the underlining of the 'works of the law in 4QMMT, and the claim that ancient worthies received forgiveness because of their deeds[85] are equally unmistakable. It has been suggested above that this emphasis, particularly in conjunction with a greatly sharpened code of regulations, may have been prompted by the earlier disasters which befell Israel because she failed to keep the law, and did not receive forgiveness until she had first received punishment.[86] However that may be there can be no doubt of their insistence upon the need for perfection in the present. That they believed this to be attainable is shown by their self-description as 'the community of the perfect' even if the term could carry different levels of meaning. But its complete attainment in the present seems to have taken place in worship where heaven and earth, present and future were fused in a unity as they discharged their most solemn obligation: offering atonement for sin.

Nevertheless, they recognized the eschatological future as the time of full redemption from sin without and within. In that moment the world would be restored to its pristine perfection in Eden, and they themselves would be renewed in the likeness of Adam in the beginning.

To characterize such an understanding of perfection as both 'means and end' does justice both to the dynamic side of their definition of the concept as well as to the attainment of the end at successive stages along the way but also fully and finally at the eschaton.

Notes

1. Newton, Michael, *The Concept of Purity at Qumran and in the Letters of Paul, SNTS Monograph Series*, 53, (Cambridge, 1985), 39.
2. The only other texts that might have claim to consideration are *4Q Songs of the Sabbath Sacrifice*, (4Q 403–5) and the *Songs of the Maskil* (4Q 510–1), in all of which the expression 'perfect of way' is found. C. Newsom sees literary dependence of the latter on the former, while the frequent use in them of 'Elohim' distinguishes them from other Qumran texts. Her conclusion is that *4Q ShirShabb* is non-Qumranic in origin, but was taken over by and became influential at Qumran. Carol A. Newsom, 'Sectually Explicit Literature from

Qumran' in Propp-Halpern-Freedman (eds.), *The Hebrew Bible and Its Interpreters*, 180–5.

3. These will be examined later. For purposes of present documentation let it suffice to cite IQS VIII 20, CD XX 2,5,7 as examples of the former; and IQS II 2, III 9, VIII 18 as examples of the latter.
4. The context is fixed by II 25b which refers to those who 'decline to enter the covenant of God'. This would then agree with IQS VI 13–16 in which the initiate, having been admitted to the covenant as a probationer, is taught by the Instructor in all the rules of the community, and, depending on its vote, is either admitted or rejected. The reference is apparently to one who refuses this further stage of admission. 'Source' (*'ayin*) is presumably a symbolic name for the community on the analogy of 'the spring of Jacob' (Deuteronomy 33:28) in reference to Israel. Hence 'not being counted in the source of the perfect' means not joining the sect.
5. Vermes renders 'according to the perfection of their spirit'; Knibb, 'according to their spiritual status'. 'Perfection' is not in the original, but it is a true interpretation as the context shows (III 3–4).
6. Some scholars have argued for precisely this position on the basis of IQS VIII 20, 'These are the regulations by which the men of perfect holiness shall conduct themselves, each with his fellow'. E.P. Sanders says, 'It is clear that these are not the bulk of the members of the community' (*Paul and Palestinian Judaism*, 301f). He adds an appendix (op. cit, 323–5) in which, after reviewing various suggestions, he concludes that the 'men of perfect holiness' of VIII 20 were the 'twelve men and three priests' of VIII 1, i.e. there was a circle of specially holy men within the community. Theories that this group, mentioned only at VIII 20, is to be explained as belonging only to the earliest stage of the sect's history, he rejects on the grounds that they 'fail to explain how IQS, in its present form, could ever have been an effective legislative document' (325). However, even in modern societies outdated laws which still retain legal validity are conveniently ignored, and there would seem to be no reason why that could not be the case at Qumran. If the 'men of perfect holiness' were a distinct group they would constitute a further category of perfection in the ranks of the sect; a historical explanation is to be preferred, since when they are mentioned

elsewhere (as in CD XX 2–8) they are equated with the 'congregation' and exercise the disciplinary and judicial functions attributed to the entire community in the *Community Rule* (cf. IQS V 20–24; VI 13–23).

7. This seems to be the parallel or complement on the anthropological plane of the divine intervention on the cosmological plane envisaged in lines 18b–19a, 'God, in the mysteries of his knowledge and in the wisdom of his glory, has determined an end to the existence of injustice and on the occasion of his visitation he will obliterate it for ever'.
8. Further examples are Genesis 6:9; 17:1; 2 Samuel 22:33; Psalms 18:33; 101:2,6; Proverbs 11:20. For an exhaustive examination of the Old Testament usage see Nötscher, F., *Gotteswege und Menschenwege in der Bibel und in Qumran*, BBB 16; (Bonn: Peter Hanstein, 1958), 9–71. For a comparison with Qumran usage see *idem*: art. 'Voies divines et humaines selon la Bible et Qumran' in J. van der Ploeg (ed.), *La Secte de Qumran et les Origines du Christianisme*, (Bruges: Desclée de Brouwer, 1959), 135–148.
9. Josephus notes regarding the Essenes, 'They are also forbidden, more rigorously than any Jew to attend to their work on the seventh day' (*JW*, II, 127).
10. Sanders, E.P., *Paul and Palestinian Judaism*, 297.
11. Forkman, Goran, *The Limits of the Religious Community*, CBNT Series 5, (Lund: CWK Gleerup, 1972), 46f.
12. Sanders, op. cit, 286. Cf. his earlier comment on the requirements for admission to membership, 'There is no indication in the entrance regulations that all these things are not within the range of human achievement' (op. cit, 264).
13. See Chapter 3, pp. 55–8.
14. Leaney, A.R.C., 'The Experience of God in Qumran and in Paul', *BJRL*, 51, 1969, 449.
15. Schürer, E., *The History of the Jewish People in the Age of Jesus Christ*, revised Vermes, Miller, Black, Vol. II, (Edinburgh: T. & T. Clark, 1979), 457, n.63.
16. *Idem*, 486.
17. Newton appropriately points out that the connection between *tamim* ('perfect') and sacrifice in the Old Testament and at Qumran establishes in turn a link between perfection and purity, 'Purity is a prerequisite of perfection'. 'Perfection of way' presupposes purity as did the 'perfect' sacrifices of the Temple. It is in this way that the sacrifices

were replaced at Qumran. The same prerequisite for temple sacrifices was required by the community, namely, purity, and from this purity stemmed perfection of way as 'a delectable free will offering.' *The Concept of Purity*, 39.

18. *Kippēr* occurs a total of seven times in CD.
19. For a recent statement of this position see Lichtenberger, H. 'Atonement and Sacrifice in the Qumran Community' in W.S. Green (ed.), *Approaches to Ancient Judaism*, II, (Chico: Scholars Press, 1980), 159–72.
20. So Braun, H. *Spätjudisch* I, 104–6; Becker, J. *Das Heil Gottes*, 107–9.
21. Sanders, E. P., 'The Covenant as a Soteriological Category and the Nature of Salvation in Palestinian and Hellenistic Judaism' in Robert Hamerton-Kelly and Robin Scroggs (edd), *Jews, Greeks and Christians*, (Leiden: Brill, 1976), 40. Cf. idem, *Paul and Palestinian Judaism*, 282ff.
22. *PPJ*, 298.
23. Garnet, Paul, 'Atonement Constructions in the Old Testament and the Qumran Scrolls', *EQ*, 46, 1974, 152–4.
24. Art. cit, 154–5.
25. Art. cit, 155–7.
26. Art. cit, 162–3.
27. Vermes renders, 'May God not heed when you call on Him, nor pardon you by blotting out your sin.' Cf. Knibb, 'May God not show mercy to you when you call, or forgive you by making expiation for your iniquities.' Wise, Abegg and Cook translate, 'May God have no mercy upon you when you cry out, nor forgive so as to atone for your sins.' These renderings take God as the subject of *kippēr* in contrast to the translation of Garcia Martinez quoted in the text. It is not clear whether atonement is the means or result of forgiveness. Either way, it remains clear that the power to confer pardon rests with God.
28. The exception is XIV 19 where the reference is to the atoning action, not of God, but of the Messiah.
29. Garnet, Paul, *Salvation and Atonement in the Qumran Scrolls*, WUNT 2 Reihe, 3, (Tübingen: Mohr/Siebeck, 1977), 99.
30. Becker, Jürgen, *Das Heil Gottes*, Heils-und Sünden begriffe in den Qumrantexten und im Neuen Testament, SUNT, Band 3, (Göttingen: Vandenhoeck und Ruprecht, 1964), my paraphrase.

31. Pp. 82–7.
32. Garnet, *Salvation and Atonement*, 97.
33. Op. cit. 98. Cf. 'Human beings can be the subject of a verb expressing the divine forgiveness. The meaning then seems to be that their actions are a vehicle or a sign of God's forgiveness.' Op. cit, 116.
34. Sanders, E.P., *PPJ*, 303.
35. Bruce, F.F., *Second Thoughts on the Dead Sea Scrolls*, (London: The Paternoster Press, 1966), 113.
36. *DJD*, X, 61–3.
37. Garnet says correctly that 'in CD there is no stress on the spirit as a means of salvation' (*Salvation and Atonement*, 99). As has already been noted in all but one of the seven instances of *kippēr* in CD, God is the subject of the verb. See n.28 above.
38. Ringgren, *Faith of Qumran*, 122.
39. Newton points out that the use of *kippēr* to describe the ritual of the purification offering is not unknown in the biblical tradition, quoting Milgrom's view that in such contexts it means 'purge'. *The Concept of Purity at Qumran*, 47.
40. Nötscher underlies the point that, through grace, the penitent becomes a sharer in truth and righteousness and now walks in God's way, loving him with the whole heart (IQH VII 14 = XV 10, VI 23–27 = XIV 23–7), *Zur Theologischen Terminologie der Qumran-Texte*, 186–7. He points out that, within the sinner there is an inner reversal from evil to truth, quoting in support IQS V 1,14, VI 15. God does not accept sin because he is truth; man must therefore walk in the right way (IQS III 5f, 9–11): op. cit, 190. Becker, interpreting IQS XI 14, argues that there is a concreteness (*Dinghaftigheit*) to sin so that forgiveness cannot be merely spiritual or forensic; God must expel it. *Das Heil Gottes*, 113f.
41. For fuller elaboration and documentation of the issue as a whole see Deasley, Alex R.G.,'The Holy Spirit in the Dead Sea Scrolls', *Wesleyan Theological Journal* 21, 1–2, Spring-Fall, 1986, 45–73. For the point under immediate consideration see pages 48–50.
42. This phenomenon may well account for the difficulty in some contexts in knowing whether the spirit the sectary has received from God is God's or his own.
43. Pp. 181–2.

44. Cf. Leaney, A.R.C., *The Rule of Qumran and Its Meaning*, (London: SCM Press, 1966), 53–5.
45. Loc. cit.
46. von der Osten-Sacken, P., *Gott und Belial*, 116–20.
47. Anderson, A.A., art. 'The Use of "Ruaḥ" in IQS, IQH and IQM', *JSS*, 7, 1962, 299.
48. Hengel, M., *Judaism and Hellenism*, 220. Hengel writes further, 'Essene teaching was concentrated on two apparently divergent focal points, which are, however, in reality closely associated and indeed condition each other: 1. An apocalyptic dualistic interpretation of history which has now – immediately before the end – entered upon its decisive crisis, and 2, an anthropology and ecclesiology directed at the redemption of the individual, according to which God gives man knowledge of his true situation and introduces him into the *vita communis* of the Essene "Community", where alone the Torah is fulfilled: *extra exlesiam nulla salus*'. Op. cit, 224.
49. See above pp. 211–4 for references.
50. For a balanced statement of the view which prevailed in Second Temple Judaism see Jeremias, J., *New Testament Theology*, Volume I, (London: SCM Press, 1975), 80–2.
51. There is a variant reading here: 'his spirit of holiness' which, if accurate would imply that the spirit was given to the community by God. So Knibb, *The Qumran Community*, 93. For a discussion of the textual problem see Thiering, B.E., 'Inner and Outer Cleansing at Qumran', *NTS*, 27, 5, 1980, 267 n5. The point is unaffected whichever reading be adopted.
52. Thiering, B.E., 'Qumran Initiation and New Testament Baptism', *NTS*, 27, 1981, 620.
53. E.g. E.P. Sanders who argues that at Qumran sin is never more than transgression of commandments (*PPJ*, 273); that while man is such that sin is unavoidable, that condition is not itself equated with sin (284); that there is 'a kind of sinfulness which does not damn and which continues to characterize the elect, the sinfulness involved in man's inadequacy before God' (284); but that since this will not be overcome and eradicated until the end it does not become 'a basic element to be overcome in the path of salvation, since nothing can be done about it until God destroys wickedness itself at the end. For practical purposes of the sect's life, sin remains *avoidable* transgression' (284). 'In other words, *these*

profound views of human sinfulness do not touch soteriology' (282). But if this kind of 'sinfulness' begets sins (which appears to be the meaning of a statement like IQH XII = IV 29b–30), and sins entail impurity, then it becomes very much a matter of concern for the community, their inability to find a soteriological solution for it notwithstanding.

54. For a fuller examination of IQH XII = IV 29–32, IV = XVII 13–15 and the kindred passage XI = III 19–36 see Deasley, *Perfection*, 244–53.
55. The usage in IQS is especially dense. In thirteen instances the word 'perfect' is used in conjunction with the noun 'way', and in four cases with the word 'walk'; while in a further seven instances 'perfect' occurs with both. For further analysis see Deasley, *Perfection*, 15–20.
56. Whether 4Q 510–511 (*Songs of the Sage*) and 4Q 403–405 (*Songs of the Sabbath Sacrifice*) originated at Qumran has been debated. See n.2 above. Carol Newsom thinks the former are dependent literarily on the latter as well as on IQH, though there is nothing distinctively sectarian about them. Yet there is no doubt of their use and influence at Qumran. She concludes tentatively that 4Q 403–405 originated outside and prior to the founding of the Qumran settlement, but was taken over by it. Art. 'Sectually Explicit Literature from Qumran' in Propp, Halpern and Freedman, *The Hebrew Bible and Its Interpreters*, 180–5.
57. Janowski-Lichtenberger, art. 'Enderwartung und Reinheitsidee', *JJS*, 34, 1983, 49, 53.
58. *Idem*, 50.
59. See above pp. 227f, 232–4.
60. See Chapter 4, pp. 184f.
61. See Chapter 4, pp. 181–4.
62. Dupont-Sommer sees an allusion to the story of Abraham's circumcision in *Jubilees* XV, part of which reads, 'For there exist many nations and many peoples, and all are His; and over them all He has set spirits with authority to lead them astray from Him. But over Israel he has set neither angel nor spirit, for He is their sole master, and He will preserve them and will deliver them from the hand of His angels and spirits.' *Essene Writings*, 162, n.2.
63. For an earlier treatment see Chapter 4, pp. 184f with note 38.
64. For a fuller development of this point see Nötscher, F., 'Heilgkeit in den Qumranschriften' in *Vom Alten zum Neuen*

Testament, BBB 17, (Bonn: Peter Hanstein Verlag, 1962), 160f.

65. See especially Nitzan, Bilhah, *Qumran Prayer and Religious Poetry*, STDJ Volume XII, (Leiden: Brill, 1994).
66. Nitzan cites 4Q 409 (op. cit, 9), originally published by Qimron, E., 'Time for Praising God: a Fragment of a Scroll from Qumran (4Q 409)', *JQR*, 80 (1990), 341–7.
67. 4Q *Shir. Shabb* clearly belongs here. For a fuller list see Nitzan, op. cit, 9–10.
68. Strugnell, John, 'The Angelic Liturgy at Qumran', supplements to *Vetus Testamentum*, Volume VII, *Congress Volume Oxford 1959*, (Leiden: Brill, 1960), 320.
69. This point is clear however 13b is reconstructed and interpreted. Attempts to take the language of purification from sin in a strictly formal sense as implying only membership of the community (so Carmignac, J., *Les Textes de Qumran* I, ad loc.) hardly do justice to the language. Holm-Nielsen comments, '*ṭāhar* of cleansing from sin obviously comes from the cult language ... But from there the sense has passed over into a more common usage of the cleansing God gives by declaring the sinner pure'. Holm-Nielsen S., 68 n.9. Cf. The similar remarks of Nötscher on the meaning of holiness, 'Der Titel "Leilige Männer" für die Mitglieder ist deutlich dem Alten Testament entnommen (Ex. 22:30), aber nun entschieden mit ethischen Gehalt erfüllt. Diese" Männer der Heiligkeit" sind zwar auch noch exklusiv in ihren Reinigungsriten, aber die Bedingung für die Teilnahme an ihrer "Reinheit" ist jeltzt, das man sich bekehrt von einer Bosheit (IQS V 13). Es sind Leute, die in Vollkommenheit wandeln' *Vom Alten Zum Neuen Testament*, 160. The point is discussed at greater length in Deasley, *Perfection*, 224–31.
70. Kuhn, Heinz-Wolfgang, *Enderwartung und Gegenwärtiges Heil*, SUNT Band 4, (Göttingen: Vandenhoeck und Ruprecht, 1966).
71. Op. cit, 61, 114.
72. Op. cit, 113f.
73. Op. cit, 114.
74. Betz, Otto, 'The Eschatological Interpretation of the Sinai Tradition in Qumran and in the New Testament', *RQ*, 6, 1967, 91.
75. Janowski-Lichtenberger, 'Enderwartung und Reinheitsidee', *JJS*, 34, 1983, 59.

76. Cf. Janowski-Lichtenberger, art. cit, 50.
77. So Dupont-Sommer, Holm-Nielsen, and Vermes. Morawe regards it as one of the four complete 'Danklieder' in IQH: Morawe, G., *Aufbau und Abgrenzung der Loblieder von Qumran*, (Berlin: Evangelische Verlagsanstalt, 1960), 110f. H-W. Kuhn, *Enderwartung und Gegenwärtiges Heil* devotes a chapter to it (44–66), discussing the form on 61–4.
78. For a discussion of the Paradise Motif and Realized Eschatology see Aune, David E., *The Cultic Setting of Realized Eschatologyin Early Christianity*, Supplements to *Novum Testamentum* XXVIII, (Leiden: Brill, 1972), 38–42.
79. H-W. Kuhn's list is longer still, including resurrection (IQH XIX = XI 10b–14); new creation (III 21, XI 13); communion with angels (III 21–3, XI 13f); deliverance from the final power of the realm of death (III 19); and proleptic eschatological transference to heaven (III 19b–20a). *Enderwartung und Gegenwärtiges Heil*, 113.
80. Dupont-Sommer, A., *The Dead Sea Scrolls: A Preliminary Survey*, (Oxford: Basil Blackwell, 1952), 73.
81. Holm-Nielsen, *Hodayot*, 39.
82. Kuhn, K.G., in Stendahl, *The Scrolls and the New Testament*, 102–3.
83. This finding of the reason for man's transgression in the region of human frailty and beyond man's will E.P. Sanders describes as 'a more profound ... view of human sinfulness than one finds elsewhere in Palestinian Judaism. To this degree, the Scrolls do break with the definition of sin as avoidable transgression. On the other hand, this is a view which is not worked out. For one thing, there is no solution to the unavoidable transgressions ... *In other words, these profound views of human sinfulness do not touch soteriology*' (*PPJ*, 283).
84. Sanders, E. P., *PPJ*, 295.
85. *DJD*, X, Section C, lines 23–32 (pp. 59–63).
86. This could conceivably be the meaning of 4QMMT C 12, 'And it is written that [you will stray] from the path (of the Torah) and that calamity will meet [you]).' Cf. 'Think of the kings of Israel and contemplate their deeds: whoever among them feared [the To]rah was delivered from troubles; and these were the seekers of the Torah whose transgressions were [for]given' (23–5).

Chapter Six

The Goal: The End of the Days and Beyond

Qumran Eschatology

That there is a marked eschatological element in Qumran thought has become evident in the areas already examined. One need recall only such ideas as the community's worship, involving, as they believed, transference into the divine Presence in company with the angels so experiencing in this age a foretaste of the age to come;[1] or the doctrine of the two spirits in man which, while describing chiefly the way in which the two spirits struggle in the heart of man, nevertheless looks forward to the 'visitation' when the spirit of wickedness will be destroyed;[2] or the basic structure of their understanding of perfection which accords it a role in the present as well as in the age to come.[3]

The ideas just referred to belong mainly to the sphere of soteriology. Soteriology, however, is but one area of Qumran thought in which the influence of eschatology can be discerned. It is not untrue to say that the faith of Qumran as a whole is an eschatological faith, at least in the sense that its focal point is what will take place 'at the end of the days' (*'aḥărît hayyāmîm*). The expression is a biblical one, occurring thirty-three times in the Qumran texts; always in texts original to Qumran and spread over the entire Qumran timespan; always in the context of Scripture interpretation (save for IQSa I 1); and in texts of all types.[4] J. Carmignac has analysed the use of the phrase in the Old Testament (Hebrew and LXX) and concluded that, in keeping with the fundamental meaning of '*ăḥarôn* as 'that which comes after' or 'that which follows',[5] the phrase never denotes the end of the world but rather 'in the next time', referring to an ideal or messianic era[6]. This usage Carmignac finds perpetuated in the Qumran texts. He translates 4Q Flor 19–II 1 to read: 'In the next days, that is to say the time of purification which is coming,'[7] interpreting 'purification' in the light of 4QpPs 37 II 18 where it denotes the last assault of Belial before the definitive establishment of the rule of Israel. In short, it is not the end of the world but the abolition of the dominion of Belial which is in view. This meaning he finds conveyed in the remaining instances in the texts.[8]

On the basis of this understanding Carmignac concluded that Qumran eschatology presupposed two clearly defined periods. The first – the present – was that of the dominion of Belial which would be put to an end in a grand conflict between the forces of light and darkness. This would be followed by the second period: one of Paradise-like peace which would extend over the whole earth.[9] If it be asked: how long will this last, and what will happen finally, no answer is given.[10] But the implication is that Qumran eschatology is concerned with what will happen 'in the next days', not with the end of the world.[11]

Whether this is all that is conveyed by the expression 'the end of the days' is open to question. For example, in 4QMMT C 2 1 the reference of the phrase appears to be to the ongoing fulfilment of the 'blessings and curses (which) have (already) been fulfilled as it is written in the bo[ok of Mo]ses' and so to 'a presently continuing period of time'.[12] Indeed, Steudel maintains that in 4Q MidrEschat,[13] 'the end of the days' finds a parallel in 'the time of refining that has come' ('*ēt ham-maṣrēp hab-bā'āh*): a reference to the distress suffered by the pious during the last time before the final judgment and the time of salvation. That is to say, it includes the author's own time.[14] However, this does not preclude a future reference.

If 'the end of the days' reaches back to include the inauguration of the last time and its continuation in the present, it also looks forward to embrace such events as the coming of the messiahs which clearly lie in the future (e.g. IQSa II 11–22; 4Q Isaiah p[a], frgs. 8–10, col. III 11–25).[15] Indeed, there are examples of the expression with historical reference which seem best understood on the assumption that it carries such a comprehensive sense.[16]

From all of this several conclusions are indicated which help to give definition to Qumran eschatology. First, the expression 'the end of the days' which serves as the fundamental building-block of Qumran eschatology has both precision and elasticity. The former consists in regard to the definitive period which leads to, precipitates and culminates in the establishment of the rule of Israel. The latter is exhibited in the way in which eschatological import is seen throughout this critical and definitive period: past, present and future.[17] Second, notwithstanding the fact that eschatological character inheres in the 'last period' as a whole, it remains that the accent falls upon the future: upon the critical climax, the 'end of the end'. Of the various ways in which the expression *'ahărît hay-yāmîm* may be and has been rendered, the best are those which point to the happenings which will mark the conclusion of the definitive period while avoiding the suggestion that such happenings constitute the end of the world. 'The end of days' in its generality has a terminal overtone that suggests the end of history. George J. Brooke proposes 'the latter days' as allowing for the 'sense of futurity whilst embracing something of the eschatological and historical self-understanding of the community.'[18] 'The end of the days' is as good as any in accenting the future while at the same time, by its use of the definite article (denoting 'these particular days') avoiding the suggestion that the days in question are the last that will ever be.

Third, and following from what has just been said, a fundamental point to be grasped is that Qumran eschatology has a significant temporal dimension. This is not to say it has no transcendental aspect, and the degree to which it has will be taken up in due course. But its primary focus is the historical rather than the eternal future. Jacob Licht long since argued that while 'the basic notion of the Two Worlds (*This World* and *The World to Come*) can be detected underlying Qumran eschatology'; and the sect distinguished at least four periods: the past prior to its own existence, its historical present, the coming period of active struggle against the forces of evil, and the ultimate future of full eschatological peace;[19] yet their primary interest lies in showing that history – specifically their own history – makes sense. 'They accept the apocalyptic concept of "times and seasons" and base their arguments upon it, but are not deeply interested in imposing any pattern on history. *Their thought is preoccupied by the "things to be done in this time, the time of clearing the Way in the Wilderness."*'[20]

Fourth, if one inquires as to the character of the end of the days: several features are spelled out. It will be marked by notable events such as the coming of the Branch of David (4Q Flor I 11; 4QpIsa[a] frags 8–10, III 11–25) who is presumably identical with the Messiah of Israel (IQSa 11–12), and also of the eschatological Interpreter of the Law (4Q Flor I 11). Likewise, it will be marked by the building of the eschatological temple (4Q Flor I 1–10a). But the pervasive and characteristic feature of the end of the days will be turmoil, testing and conflict: but the kind of testing which effects the elimination of evildoers and the refining of the men of the community. It is the time of contempt for the law (4Qp Nah frags. 3–4 II 2; IQp Hab II 5–10; 4Q Catena[b] frag. I 1–3), and consequently of the laying waste of the land (4Qp Isa[b] I 1–2, II 1–2), with the Kittim as the instruments of judgment (Iqp Hab IX 6–7). However, the Kittim will themselves fall at the hands of the Branch of David who will rule over all the peoples (4Qp Isa[a] Frags. 8–10, III 1–22a). But this same time of testing which purifies the land also purifies the men of the community refining them by the spirit and a spiritual circumcision of the heart which will render them clean (4Q Catena[a] II 9b–10, 15b–16).

Qumran Eschatology and Apocalypticism

Apocalypticism and its Meaning

Any discussion of Qumran eschatology inevitably raises the question of its relation to apocalypticism, and the extent, if any, to which it was influenced by apocalypticism. The question is bedevilled by the difficulty scholarship has had in reaching anything approaching consensus on how apocalypticism is to be defined.[21] The methodological problem consists in whether apocalyptic is to be primarily understood from the baseline of the literary genre 'apocalypse'; or as a theological concept or construct; or as a theological or religious movement. These clearly are not necessarily exclusive of each other; the question is which is best taken as the starting-point and nerve-centre for understanding the phenomenon as a whole.

As to the third option: that apocalyptic is to be seen as a religious movement: there is little evidence to support its existence in a defined social form.[22] It is a mindset more than a movement, if 'movement' is being used as a social-historical category. The difficulty with the second suggestion: that it is to be seen primarily as a complex of theological concepts, is not that it is not such, but that some more objective basis than the variegated choices of individual scholars is needed to determine what the distinctive features of apocalyptic are.[23] This leaves the first option: that apocalyptic is best defined on the basis of the literary genre 'apocalypse'. This however is not a magician's wand inasmuch as it poses the further question: how does one define the apocalyptic genre?

The use of the term 'apocalypse' to refer to a type of literature does not occur earlier than the end of the first Christian century after which it becomes quite common. But the decisive feature is not the use of the label but whether a distinguishable group of works sharing common characteristics and showing affinities with the later works employing the label can be identified. Paul D. Hanson sees in the first two verses of the New Testament Book of Revelation the kernel of the structure of the genre:

'a *revelation* is given by God through an otherworldly *mediator* to a *human seer* disclosing *future events*. V3 contains an added feature commonly found (or implied) in apocalypses, namely, an *admonition*.'[24] This definition characterizes an apocalypse largely in terms of its form, though clearly some elements of content are implied. J.J. Collins, writing for the Society of Biblical Literature Genres Project which analysed every text from 250 BC to AD 250 with claims to being an apocalypse, and concluding that such a body of texts did in fact exist, defined the genre thus: ' "Apocalypse" is a genre of revelatory literature with a narrative framework, in which revelation is mediated by an otherworldly being to a human recipient, disclosing a transcendent reality which is both temporal, insofar as it envisages eschatological salvation, and spatial, insofar as it involves another supernatural world.'[25] Collins explicitly states that the elements that are constant in the genre 'pertain to both framework and content.'[26] Thus the narrative framework always involves an otherworldly mediator, not merely oracular utterances from heaven. The eschatological salvation which constitutes a constant element in the content is always both temporally future, yet involves present otherworldly realities. Moreover, it is always definitive in character and is marked by some kind of afterlife, involving cosmic transformation in some instances. Otherworldly beings, angelic and demonic are depicted as being at work, and celestial geography is often described in detail.

In his later work Collins distinguishes more emphatically between 'historical' apocalypses such as Daniel and 4 Ezra in which the unfolding of history is disclosed in visions; and otherworldly journeys which recount excursions through the heavenly realms in which cosmological secrets are revealed;[27] but insists, nonetheless, that both types, rather than simply the former, are to be taken into account in reconstructing the picture of apocalypticism.[28] At the same time he maintains that the content of the genre as a whole is still distinctive, with its emphasis upon the supernatural world and the activity of its supernatural inhabitants, both good and evil, which has a direct bearing upon human destiny; that knowledge of this supernatural overworld is accessible only through intermediary beings, and upon it human destiny depends; that final judgment, including the destruction of the wicked, is coming; hence warning and admonition play a large part in the texts.[29] Even so 'the literary genre apocalypse is not a self-contained isolated entity. The conceptual structure indicated by the genre ... can also be found in works that are not revelation accounts, and so are not technically apocalypses.'[30] More recently, Collins makes allowances for cases of mixed genre (e.g. *Jubilees*), or of instances where apocalypse is the dominant genre of a work without the whole work belonging to that genre (e.g. Daniel 7–12).[31]

The Influence of Apocalypticism at Qumran

Against the foregoing sketch we may now attempt to assess the extent of the influence of apocalypticism at Qumran. This may perhaps be measured best in terms of the three aspects of apocalyptic mentioned earlier: genre, thought and movement. As to the first: the data are not wholly clear and are therefore variously interpreted. The majority of texts with any claim to being regarded as apocalypses are in Aramaic, and of these only a few, if any, are regarded as having originated in the community.[32] Apocalypses in Hebrew are even fewer, leading Dimant to conclude that 'obviously, the Qumranites were not engaged in writing apocalypses.'[33] At the same time while none of the major works of the sect is an apocalypse there is at least one example of what may be called an 'embedded apocalypse' in one such text: the *Discourse on the Two Spirits* in the *Community Rule* (IQS III 13 – IV 26). Moreover, the multiple copies of Danielic and Enochic works show that apocalypses were copied and studied there.[34] Hence the – at the very most – paucity of apocalypses produced at Qumran cannot be taken safely as an index that the sect did not cherish apocalyptic interests.

If the rarity of apocalypses among the Qumran texts might be taken to imply a muted appetite for apocalypticism,[35] the same can hardly be said for engagement with and employment of apocalyptic ideas. This can be documented readily from texts which stand at the distinctive centre of the Qumran collection. Most significant in this regard is the *Discourse on the Two Spirits* already referred to. Not only are the characteristic themes of the apocalyptic world-view its very warp and woof: human life as a battleground between the spirits of light and darkness; the intervention of God in the end-time on behalf of the sons of light; the destruction of darkness and the restoration of life as God intended it to be; but this discourse is incorporated within the most authoritative text of the sect which we have: *The Rule of the Community*. If, in the *Damascus Document* apocalyptic thought does not come to the same clarity and completeness of exposition as in the *Discourse on the Two Spirits*, apocalyptic ideas are assuredly there. Periodization is present in the form of God's covenant with 'the very first', but when these years were completed (IV 7–12a) Belial was turned loose upon Israel and it is in the setting of this cosmic conflict that the sect has its existence (IV 13–18). For the penitent there is pardon, but for the impenitent destruction by fire at the hand of the angels of destruction (II 4b–10). If the language of Belial and the prince of lights is rarely used, the impression given is that it is common currency rather than freshly minted coinage for the occasion (e.g. V 17b–18).

The case is unmistakably clear with the *Rule of the War* which lays down the regulations for the conduct of the eschatological war between the sons of light and the sons of darkness, each being supported by the supernatural hosts of their respective sides, with Michael finally triumphing over Belial (IQM XIII 1–14, XVII 5–9, XVIII 1–6). The *Thanksgiving Psalms*, while less forthright in their appropriation of apocalyptic ideas, nonetheless lay them under contribution from time to time, and – like the *Damascus Rule* – in such a way as to suggest that they are accepted settlers rather than foreign intruders. The substructure of apocalyptic thought, notably the idea of periodization, appears to be taken for granted (IQH IX = I

24, XI = III 28, VII = XV 17b–21), and with it, necessarily, the figure of Belial as the lord of the hosts of evil (XI = III 28f, 32, XII = IV 12–14). The eschatological war is a detail in the vivid picture of the river of eschatological destruction in III 27–36. Also in the *Hymns* the idea of participation with the angels in worship is accepted currency (XIX = XI 10b–14, XV = VII 30f, XI = III 19–23).

On the basis of data such as has just been reviewed, it seems difficult to resist the conclusion that the Qumran sect was an apocalyptic community. Undoubtedly it was other things too, as is indicated clearly by its emphatic insistence on conformity to a particular halakah. But John J. Collins does not overstate when he writes: 'within the community at Qumran, the perspective of apocalyptic eschatology had been elevated to the status of an ideology, functioning to inform its interpretation of Scripture, to provide the basis for its understanding of Jewish and gentile adversaries, and to supply a historiographic point of view from which to develop a detailed scenario of final conflict and divine vindication of the elect.'[36] While, therefore, the Qumran sect is more than an apocalyptic community, assuredly it is not less, and stands therefore as a witness – in some respects our only concrete witness – to the organized form which such a community might take.[37]

The Nature of Apocalyptic Thinking

Before attempting to interpret the eschatology of the Qumran sect, it is necessary to consider the nature of apocalyptic thinking as being prior to and determinative of interpretation. Several features found commonly in apocalypses are particularly deserving of attention in this regard. First, language and imagery move on a supramundane level, which, in terms of the baseline of common existence, borders on the unusual and at times the bizarre. What is meant by a war in which the sons of light (i.e. the members of the community) are reinforced by the angels, and the sons of darkness by the angels of the dominion of Belial; in which each side wins three battles, but in the seventh the sons of light triumph thanks to the intervention of

God (IQM I 9b–16); and throughout which the requirements of the sacred calendar are strictly observed (II 6b–10a), as well as the demands of ceremonial purity (VII 3b–7)? What is meant by the restoration of the glory of Adam (IQS IV 23), or communion with the angels, mentioned in passages referred to above?

A further difficulty in addition to the unconventional language is that the ideas are not brought into any seemingly logical connection. For example the cosmic war of the *War Rule* does not sit comfortably with the this-worldly messianic expectations of the *Messianic Rule*, any more than these are readily reconcilable with the destruction of the world by the river of fire described in IQH XI = III 26–36. M. Philonenko therefore concludes that attempts at harmonization are futile and that the apocalyptic mind was less concerned with logical consistency than with imaginative freedom.[38] This may be so, but it gives little aid in determining what the apocalypses in general, and apocalyptic teaching at Qumran in particular was intended to convey. That it was intended to convey *something* is the minimum assumption readers must make unless they are prepared to write off apocalypses as exercises in gibberish: hardly a conclusion to be adopted save *in extremis*. The problem becomes more acute in that not only at some points does Qumran apocalyptic touch earth, but in one matter it is self-consciously corrected since an earlier interpretation was falsified by events. The *Nahum Commentary* (4QpNah), illustrates the former in that, while it is concerned with the 'time of the end' (*bĕahărîth haqqēs:* III 3; *qēs hā'ahărôn*: IV 3), yet it contains one of the few references *en clair* in the scrolls to a named historical personage: '[Deme]trius, King of Yawan' (I 3), besides others like the 'Kittim' the 'seekers after smooth things' which are plausibly taken to refer to the Romans and the Pharisees. The *Habakkuk Pesher* illustrates the latter when it appears to address explicitly the problem of the death of the Teacher of Righteousness before the expected arrival of the Messiah (CD XIX 33b – XX 1a) and to propose a new understanding. The comment on the well-known words of *Habakkuk* 2:4: 'the just shall live by his faith' is: 'Its interpretation concerns all observing the Law in the House of Judah, whom God will free from punishment on account of their deeds and of their loyalty to the Teacher of Righteousness' (IQpHab. VIII 1–3a). As F.F. Bruce observes: 'His disciples did not merely go to him for lessons in biblical exegesis, but took energetic steps to put his instruction into practice, believing that herein lay their salvation in face of the swiftly approaching day of divine visitation.'[39] Evidently the Teacher of Righteousness was seen as a messianic forerunner, the inauguration of the messianic age being expected in his lifetime. His death ended this expectation, and was re-interpreted as the launching of a more specific period which would culminate in the victorious conclusion of the eschatological war: 'And from the day of the gathering in of the unique teacher, until the destruction of all the men of war who turned back with the man of lies there shall be about forty years' (CD XX 13b–15a). This would thereby bring events to the 'end of the end of the days' and the coming of the messianic age in its fullness. (CD XX 33b – XX 1a).[40]

What is to be deduced regarding the nature of apocalyptic thinking from these confusing and conflicting phenomena and in particular, the meaning which it had for its writers and readers? Several of the features already alluded to have been advanced as mitigating in some measure the bizarre and contradictory aspects which apocalyptic thinking wears on its face. For example, development has been appealed to as accounting for at least some of the conflicting features in the apocalyptic writings. While this may account for some problems (such as the reformulation of the arrival of the messianic era just discussed) it is questionable whether it yields very much help on a wider scale, particularly at Qumran.[41] Again, the frank admission of diversity, and consequent inconsistency has been appealed to in alleviating the problem. F.F. Bruce concluded that 'a systematic eschatology cannot be constructed from the documents:'[42] a conclusion echoed more recently by John J.

Collins who writes that 'the expectations of the community should not be harmonized into a systematic body of doctrines. Rather, we must reckon with the persistence of diverse conceptions side by side in the same community.'[43]

Where then does this leave us in attempting to interpret Qumran eschatology? If, as Collins continues, 'concepts and formulations that were diverse from a tradition-historical point of view were nonetheless found to be compatible in the scrolls,'[44] what was the basis of this compatibility?[45] We seem to be pointed in at least two directions in seeking an answer to this question. First, for all the logical inconsistency of the forms of Qumran apocalyptic, there is a biblical substructure which constitutes the foundation upon which it rests and which is the source of its basic stock of images. The importance of this is that the theme conveyed by this biblical base is that the action of God in the future is shaped by his action in the past. The *Book of Mysteries* states the point clearly, 'And they do not know the future mystery or understand ancient matters' (IQ *Mysteries* I 3). Or again, 'Draw wisdom from the great power of God, remember the miracles he performed in Egypt' (4Q *Sapiential Work* I 14). The premise of the first column of the *Damascus Rule* is that the significance of the sprouting of the 'shoot of the planting' (1 7) is to be found in understanding the 'actions of God' at the exile (I 1–6). As Otto Betz has expressed it: 'there is a consistency in the history of salvation. That is why the understanding of the past and the knowledge of the future belong together: the latter is built on the former, it depends on a correct evaluation of God's mighty deeds of the past.'[46] It is because God routed Israel's enemies in the past by fire and water that the Qumran sectarians could look forward to his final victory in which their foes, including Belial himself and all his hosts, would be destroyed. To quote Betz again, 'Israel's history shows how God will act with mankind in the eschatological future.'[47] Apocalyptic expectation and expression are thus as variegated as the history of Israel.

A second direction in which we are pointed in seeking compatibility and coherence within Qumran apocalyptic thinking follows from the first. It is in the convictional affirmations underlying the variegated forms of expression that the substance of Qumran eschatology is to be sought. It is the defeat of evil and the triumph of good as embodied in the covenant people that are central. Accordingly, there is value in Collins' appropriation to Qumran eschatology of I.T. Ramsey's distinction between 'disclosure models' and 'scale or picture models.' In the latter 'a model is thought of as a replica, a copy picture … reproducing identically those properties common to the model and original which, for the particular purpose in mind, are importantly relevant'; 'whereas the former are "designed to reproduce as faithfully as possible the *structure* or web of relationship in an original" '.[48] That is to say, the picture models the events depicted would be expected to happen in exactly that way; while in 'disclosure' or 'analogue' models the important thing is the relationship implied between the elements in the model and the outcome of their interaction.[49] If this is so, then exact correspondence between the models used is not to be expected.

That there are dangers in the hermeneutical method indicated is plain: the chief being that it opens the door readily to recasting Qumran thought in terms congenial to the modern mindset. For us the line between symbol and reality tends to be drawn sharply; for them it was probably less so. What they meant by 'communion with the angels' or 'fighting against Belial' is hard for us to say in terms of the boundaries between the literal and the metaphorical. To them they were *real* and that was what mattered. It is therefore unhelpful to dispense with their preferred imagery, reducing it to prosaic statements of what we understand to have been its literal content. At the same time the impossibility of reducing the varied images to a single scheme, and the presence of diverse images not merely within the same collection of works but – as in the case of the *Community Rule* – within a single work suggests that a single, narrowly literal understanding is not what they intended. Their thinking on these matters seems to have been constituted of definable convictions describable in varied forms which they were not concerned to reduce to rigid consistency provided they gave expression to the fundamental convictions. In attempting to grasp their understanding of the last days therefore, it seems best to place it within the framework of their basic convictions but to allow the diverse forms and images to give it such definition as they may by their interaction and interplay. In that way each can shed light on the other.

Two main themes constitute the convictional core of Qumran eschatology, while a third arises from the first two, and has attracted discussion and debate.

The End of the Order

Without question a primary constituent in Qumran eschatology is the overthrow of evil. This comes to expression in a variety of forms which it will be best to describe and then seek to measure their import.

The War against the Powers of Darkness

That the sectaries envisaged an eschatological war as a distinctive and decisive factor in the achievement of God's purposes for the world is beyond dispute. The prominence of the *Rule of the War* (IQM) is sufficient testimony to this. Fragments of four further manuscripts of the *War Scroll* were found in Cave 4.[50] The oldest of these (4Q 496) is dated towards the end of the first half of the first century BC.[51] IQM itself is probably to be dated to the last half of that century.[52] Moreover, the *War Scroll* evinces much of the ideology and language in other of the sectarian texts, not least the dualism and angelology; while the organization of the community, its rules and religious forms find parallels there.[53] Likewise, the idea of conflict, including a definitive eschatological conflict, can be paralleled readily in other of the sectarian texts.[54]

The source and inspiration of the idea of the eschatological war appears ultimately to be Scripture. The most impressive evidence of this is not so much the explicit quotations of Scripture in the War Prayers (IQM X 2–8; XI 6–7, 11b–12), significant as these are; but the pervasive use of Scripture[55] in moulding the overall idea of the eschatological war[56] as well as in determining and defining special features of it.[57]

If one inquires as to the theologically significant features of the war several present themselves. First, the presupposition of the war is the active opposition of Belial which prevents the designs and purposes of God from achieving fulfilment. The present era is referred to as 'the dominion' (*memšeleth*) of Belial or the enemy (IQM XIV 10, XVII 5f, XVIII 1). This does not mean that Belial dominates the present scene but rather that his opposition prevents God's will from prevailing. The state of affairs is well reflected in the war itself in which the Sons of Light triumph during three battles but are repulsed by the army of Belial in the next three battles (I 13–14a). It is only with the direct intervention of God in the seventh lot that the stalemate is broken and Belial is vanquished (I 14b–16).[58]

A second feature of the war is that it is fought on two levels. It is a real war fought in the real world, but it is also a spiritual war fought on the spiritual plane: it is both historical and transcendental. In the sectarian mind, these are not two worlds but one. Whatever view be adopted of the compositional history of the *War Rule*[59] the important point is that the two dimensions interpenetrate throughout. Even in the description of the 'real war' in columns XV – XIX the language of the historical and the transcendental is interspersed. The battle is against the Kittim, but they are also the Sons of Darkness under the leadership of Belial (XVI 9–11). Similarly, the victorious Israelites are 'the lot redeemed by the power of the majestic angel for the dominion of Michael in everlasting light' (XVII 6).[60] As Vermes says of the *War Rule*, 'This work should not be mistaken for a manual of military warfare pure and simple. It is a theological writing, and the war of which it treats symbolizes the eternal struggle between the spirits of Light and Darkness.'[61]

A third important feature of the war is that a messianic prince plays an important role in it.[62] This is not the place to attempt an overview of the place of messianism in Qumran thought: something which will be essayed later. Here attention will be confined to the role of such a figure in the eschatological war. This has, indeed, been contested on the ground of paucity of evidence.[63] However, the objection has been overstated. To begin with, the role of the Davidic messiah in the *War Rule* must be estimated against the place of that figure in the war tradition as expressed in other texts. Important among these is *4Q Isaiah Pesher*[a] (4Q 161), a fragmentary commentary on Isaiah Chapters 10 and 11 which interprets the victory described there as the victory of the sect over the Kittim in the last days, using terms reminiscent of the *War Rule*.[64] Still more significant is the interpretation of Isaiah 10:24–7 which describes the breaking of the Assyrian yoke (frgs. 2–6, II 8–15). The text is fragmentary but enough is clear to show that, while in the biblical text the attack on Assyria is led by Yahweh, in the *pesher* the leading figure in the battle is the Prince of the Congregation (15). In frgs. 8–10, III 1–9 the felling of the forest of Lebanon by Yahweh is interpreted of the overthrow of the Kittim, and is followed by the quotation of Isaiah 11:1–5. In the *pesher* the shoot of the stump of Jesse is identified as the shoot of David who would rule over all the peoples with his sword (18–22a).[65] But this collocation of the Prince of the Congregation and the Branch of David fulfilling roles of military leadership within the same text suggests that they are one and the same.[66] The fact that a messianic figure[67] is credited with a leading role in the eschatological war is an important datum in the reconstruction of the Qumran war tradition.

Of even greater significance for our purpose is the text variously labelled *4Q Berakot Milhamah*, *4Q Serek Milhamah* or most recently *4Q War Scroll*[g] (4QM[g], numbered 4Q285).[68] The drift of the text (which is in any case fragmentary) as reconstructed by Wacholder and Abegg[69] suggests a priestly blessing in view of the imminence of the age of peace (frg. 1), followed by an account of the final war (frgs. 6 and 4) in which the evil forces are defeated and their leader captured and executed (frg. 5). The victory of Israel is celebrated and the land cleansed of the corpses of the Kittim. Several features stand out against this general background. The first is that the military leader of all Israel is identified as the Prince of the Congregation (frg. 4:2,6). The second is that the victorious leader is identified by reference to the 'shoot from the stump of Jesse' (frg. 5:2) who is further identified with the Branch of David and the Prince of the Congregation (3–4). Third, the distinctive vocabulary of 4Q285 shows links with IQM alone,[70] suggesting at the very least a close connection between the two texts, and the possibility that 4Q285 may be part of the lost concluding section of IQM: a proposal advanced by J.T. Milik as long ago as 1972.[71]

Against this background we may now turn to the evidence of the *War Rule* itself. In IQM V 1 reference is made to the shield of the Prince of the Congregation whose name, together with those of Israel, Levi and Aaron and the twelve tribes and their commanders are to be inscribed upon it. In IQS XI 6–7 Balaam's oracle of the star from Jacob and the sceptre from Israel is cited (Numbers 24:17ff). No formal interpretation is given, but several features are worth noting. First, the emphasis in the surrounding lines is upon Yahweh as the victor in the war, expressed in the words addressed to him in the refrain: 'For the battle is yours!' (XI 1,2,4). Line 5 states in the most emphatic way that it is not by the power of their own hands that they are victorious. But second, this emphasis is transmuted in the Balaam oracle in lines 6–7 to the effect that Yahweh accomplishes his victory through a human agent: the star from Jacob and the sceptre in Israel who will smash the temples of Moab and destroy the sons of Seth. This agent, moreover, is identified as star and sceptre which carry messianic overtones[72] and, further, is twice said to originate from Jacob and twice from Israel. These suggest that a central role in the battle is thus assigned to a lay messianic figure.[73] This conclusion is strengthened if the proximity of 4Q285 to IQM be admitted.

The fourth theologically significant feature of the *War Rule* is that the war results in the overthrow of evil; or as Collins puts it in more aptly measured terms, it marks a 'dramatic advance towards the extermination of evil.'[74] When one seeks fuller description of this within the text of the *War Rule* it is shown to entail the destruction of the nations (XII 11, XIV 7), of Belial and his lot (I 5b, 14f; XVIII 3), of the Kittim and their rule (I 6, 13, XVIII 3b–5), of the sons of darkness (I 10), and sometimes of several of these named within a single passage (XI 8–10). Does it receive more exact definition? In some contexts the war's outcomes are described both in theological and literal terms. Thus the permanent overthrow of the dominion of their enemies is characterized as 'eternal redemption' (*pĕdût 'ôlāmîm*) (XVIII 11). The obverse of this is Zion's dominion over the nations, depicted in terms of material wealth and the grovelling of defeated foes (XIX 4–8). At the same time there is a supra-historical dimension to the conflict inasmuch as the battle between Israel and the Kittim is also a battle between the Sons of Light and the Sons of Darkness and the day on which it is fought is the decisive day which, thanks to God's intervention, will mark the definitive extirpation of Israel's foes (I 8–14). Yet the two dimensions are aspects of a single battle fought in a single world. It should not be overlooked, however, that the eschatology of the *War Rule* is predominantly corporate, and has an unmistakably temporal reference.

The Time of Judgment and Destruction

Another feature which figures prominently in texts describing the end of the existing order is that of judgment and destruction. This is, indeed, present in the *War Rule* in which, as we have seen, the Sons of Darkness and their allies are defeated and destroyed. However, in other texts these elements emerge with more exact definition. CD XIX 5b–21a singles out for judgment on the day of visitation those who had renegaded on their commitment to the covenant (13–14, 16b–19), and it associated this judgment with the advent of the messiah.[75] The *Melchizedek Scroll* (11Q 13), an eschatological *pesher* based on Leviticus 28, with the angelic figure Melchizedek as its chief actor, sees the time following the tenth jubilee as the day when judgment will be visited on Belial and those of his lot: the day spoken of by Isaiah the prophet (II 13–16). Like the *Damascus Rule*, the *Melchizedek Scroll* links this with the arrival of one 'anointed of the spirit' (II 18).

The idea of destruction achieves a new range and scope in at least one passage in the *Thanksgiving Hymns* (IQH) in which judgment is seen as encompassing not merely the wicked but the entire created world (IQH XI, 24b–36 = III 24b–36). The lines in question are commonly regarded as part of a self-contained psalm beginning at line 19.[76] While the psalm begins with thanksgiving that the psalmist shares in communion with the angels (19–23a), it quickly changes mood as the psalmist notes that he also stands among the wicked who are doomed (24b–5), and thus is caught up in the calamities of the final struggle. This is described vividly in terms of a river of fire which devours the earth and the wicked reaching even to the deep (25–34), and culminates in an eschatological war which sweeps across the world unrestrained until destruction is complete (36).

While we are dealing here with poetic language and therefore must avoid overpressing it, several conclusions seem to be justified. First, an end has been set to the reign of Belial and his minions (28, 33). While this might be taken to refer to the destruction of wicked people, it is probable that the extirpation of evil is in mind.[77] Second, while the psalmist does not pursue his thought beyond the destruction of the world, there is no indication that he sees nothing beyond global obliteration. Exactly what order he conceived of as replacing the existing one he does not disclose here, but that he saw righteousness as superseding evil is the presupposition of his whole religious outlook. This is confirmed by IQH XIX = XI 15–34 where the sequence of thought is parallel to that of IQH XI 19–36, and culminates in a paean of praise that distress, sighing and iniquity will be no more (23–8). Indeed, in IQH IV = XVII 9–15 where the drift of thought is discernibly similar despite the fragmentary character of the text, the destruction that engulfs the world and the wicked in it is not only spared the faithful and their posterity but in its place there is given to them 'all the glory of Adam and plentiful days' (15b).

The destruction is viewed from yet another perspective in IQS III 13 – IV 26 where it is placed in the context of the conflict between the two spirits. The setting is both cosmological and anthropological, though the former is considered almost entirely as the background of the latter rather than in its own right.[78] The express purpose of the text is to give instruction regarding human nature (*tôlědôt*, III 13) and the rewards and punishments corresponding to the character and deeds of individuals (III 14f). The cosmological sequence within which the teaching is set is, as has been pointed out by M. Philonenko,[79] creation (III 15–17), the conflict between the two opposing powers in the present (IV 15–18a), and the extermination of evil at the visitation at the end (IV 18b–19a). The anthropological counterpart is the creation of man to rule the world, but this takes place in the context of the divinely appointed spirits of light and darkness (III 15–19). This means specifically the conflict of these spirits within the sons of light so that only by divine aid do they avoid falling under the control of the spirit of darkness (III 24b);[80] and the eradication from the inner being of the sons of light of the spirit of injustice, resulting in the renewal upon them of the glory of Adam at creation (IV 20–23b).

How far this eschatology coheres with that of the *War Scroll* is open to debate, depending in particular on how one interprets the third and final visitation. Philonenko views the extermination of evil in the world (IV 18f) and the cleansing of man from the spirit of perversity (IV 20–2) as taking place at 'the decisive end of the world,'[81] with the punishment of the wicked (IV 11–14) prior to this, as also the earthly blessings of the just (IV 6b–8). However, there is no specific mention of temporal death. The focal point is rather 'the appointed end and the new creation' (IV 25). This language is not inconsistent with a temporal eschatology in which case it could be simply the description in cosmological and anthropological terms of the results of the war which the *War Rule* describes in national terms.[82] This understanding appears to do justice to the language as a whole.

The Restoration of the Order of Creation

But if the existing order in its present form will be overthrown, then what will succeed it? A large body of evidence suggests that the sectarians envisaged the restoration of the existing order as it was intended to be: that is, a restoration of the order of creation. There are at least three main spheres in which this expectation was looked for.

The Restored Nation

We have already noted that the *Rule of the War* looks for the restoration of the nation of Israel, understood as Israelite hegemony over 'the nations' at large, and not least over her ancient foes.[83] This in itself is an important clue to the meaning of the restoration in mind. While on occasion the new order is described as the 'new creation' or 'renewal' (IQS IV 25) it is clear that the renewed world envisaged is not so much the world reborn in its pristine state at creation (though there are elements of that, as we shall see) but the world seen as it ought to be through Qumran lenses. The political dimension of this (so to describe it) has already been noted; but it must necessarily have had more specifically religious dimensions. A fully restored Israel requires by definition a fully restored worship which raises in turn the question of the Temple and the Temple-city.

That the Temple was seen as part of the post-war world is plain from the evidence of the *War Rule*. Indeed, the restoration of pure Temple worship as the sect understood it is one of the earliest fruits of the war, initiated in the first sabbatic year, as is evident from IQM II 1–6.[84] The calendar presupposed, requiring twenty-six courses of priests (IQM II 2), is that of the sect which counted 364 days to the year divided into twelve months of thirty days.[85] It is this which is depicted as functioning even before the war has been fought to a successful conclusion. This provides an important clue in interpreting the other texts from Qumran concerned with the Temple, which seem to speak of the Temple in several distinguishable but not unrelated ways.

Leaving aside references to Solomon's Temple (e.g. 4Q Flor I 5–6) and the Second Temple (e.g. CD VI 11), the Temple is referred to under three different aspects. First, it is viewed from a spiritual, heavenly perspective, though in such a way that participation in its worship is possible on earth, here and now. This is most strikingly illustrated in the text known as the *Songs of the Sabbath Sacrifice* (4Q ShirShabb) or the *Angelic Liturgy* as it was labelled in the preliminary edition.[86] Whether the songs were used at Qumran as part of their worship liturgy or, as Carol Newsom has suggested, 'as the praxis of something like a communal mysticism,'[87] the conclusion remains that the sectarians believed themselves to be participants in the worship of the heavenly Temple. The blessing of the sixth sovereign prince expresses the point well: 'He will bless all whose path is perfect with seven wonderful words so that they are constantly with all those who exist forever' (4Q 403 I 22b–23a).[88] The import of the *Sabbath Songs* is thus clear. In the words of Newsom: 'Both the highly descriptive content and the carefully crafted rhetoric direct the worshipper who hears the songs recited toward a particular kind of religious experience, a sense of being in the heavenly sanctuary and in the presence of the angelic priests and worshippers.'[89] And again, 'The mysteries of the angelic priesthood are recounted, a hypnotic celebration of the sabbatical number seven produces an anticipatory climax at the centre of the work, and the community is then gradually led through the spiritually animate heavenly temple until the worshippers experience the holiness of the *merkabah* and of the Sabbath sacrifice as it is conducted by the high priests of the angels.'[90] The effect of such participation in the heavenly temple is thus to make possible perfect worship in the present.[91] If this understanding is sound then the 'Temple' at Qumran was a creation for the interim when the Jerusalem Temple had forfeited its true status thanks to an illegitimate priesthood and defiled ritual.

But another view saw the Temple from a more positive and hopeful perspective: as it ought to be and would be. This was the Temple of the *Temple Scroll* (*11Q Temple*): the ideal Temple, or, in the apt phrase of Garcia Martinez the 'normative Temple'.[92] The *Temple Scroll* borrows the perspective of the book of Deuteronomy: the entry of the people into a new land and the need for exact conformity to the law. Two features are notable for our interest. First, the central and controlling fact in the scroll (and, by implication, in the situation it envisages) is the Temple. It dominates by its sheer size – not merely larger than Herod's Temple but as large as the entire city of Jerusalem itself. Still more, it dominates the scroll as being the feature around which the work is structured. The book is organized on the principle of concentric circles of holiness, beginning with the holiness of the Holy of Holies and extending progressively to include the entire land. A holy land is thus a central preoccupation of the scroll. The second noteworthy feature of the scroll is that the Temple envisaged not only has not yet been built, but it will be temporary in nature. 'I shall sanctify my temple with my glory, for I shall make my glory reside over it until the day of creation, when I shall create my temple, establishing it for myself for ever, in accordance with the covenant which I made with Jacob at Bethel' (XXIX 8–9). That is to say, the *Temple Scroll* speaks of two Temples, neither of them in existence at the time the scroll was written. The first was the Temple to be built when the true people of Israel came into effective occupation of the land: the Temple as it ought to have been from its beginning – an implied criticism of the existing Second Temple and those who controlled it. The new Temple would be constructed and operated according to the divine design; it is of this that the *Temple Scroll* largely speaks. However, even this would not be the final eschatological Temple. That would be made on the 'day of creation' (*yōm hābĕrākā*), created (*'ĕbrā'*) by God himself, and would last forever (*kōl hāyāmîm*), in keeping with the promise made to Jacob at Bethel. However, there is no indication that this Temple would differ in character from its predecessor as being a different *kind* of Temple: purely spiritual for example.[93] Rather it would be the Temple of a new order when creation would be given a new beginning. M.O. Wise has characterized these two Temples not inaptly as earthly millennialism followed by a new heaven and a new earth.[94]

A third guise under which the Temple appears in the Qumran literature is in *11Q New Jerusalem* (11Q 18) (11Q *JNar*). The text begins with a description of the city at whose centre stands a square of enormous dimensions. The description of the city is followed by a description of the Temple, including its ritual, and the number of priests involved in its execution. Garcia Martinez concludes that the Temple in mind is not the ideal, eternal Temple, beyond time, but rather the eschatological Temple which will exist at the time of the eschatological war, as noted in IQM II 1–6.[95] If that is correct, then it is also the Temple of *11Q Temple* XXIX 9 which God will create on the day of creation. This, in turn, is the same as the Temple of *4Q Florilegium* I 2–4 in which Yahweh will reign forever. If the 'temple of man' (*mîqdaš 'ādām*) of line 6 is a metaphorical reference to the Qumran community[96] then this passage makes reference to three temples: the Temple of Israel which was destroyed (I 5–6); the community functioning as an interim Temple by virtue of its participation in heavenly worship (I 6b–7a); and the eschatological Temple of the last days (I 2–5a). Thus we have, in this most sectarian of documents, references to multiple Temples, including some (but not all) of those referred to in the other texts reviewed,[97] including texts judged not to have originated with the Qumran sectaries. The point of importance to our present concern is that the Temple is viewed as a central feature in the restored nation of the days to come.

The Restored Leadership

Another aspect of restoration looked for at the end of the days was the restoration of the national leadership in what was taken to be its intended form. It is in this context that the vexed question of messiahship is to be seen; in particular its two aspects at Qumran that have attracted most debate: the number of messiahs and the nature of messiahship. It is worth keeping in mind from the start that messianism can hardly be called a dominant theme in the Qumran Scrolls. Martin Abegg has pointed out that, on a generous interpretation, no more than 23 of the 700 sectarian texts can be described as messianic.[98] In his words, 'Messianism is an eminent, but not a pre-eminent topic in the scrolls.'[99] This is largely to be explained by the fact that, in the thought of the sect, messianism comes chiefly into play in connection with the events of the end of the days: that is, it is an eschatological feature. This, in turn, suggests criteria by which – in a disputed field – passages may be considered messianic in the narrow sense. First, the word *māšiah* or a term denoting a divinely-appointed agent must be present. Second, the term must be used in an explicitly eschatological context. These criteria rule out at once examples where the term may occur but not in the sense required. Thus in CD II 12 'those anointed with his holy spirit' (*měših [e] rûah qŏdšô)*[100] seems clearly to refer to the prophets: no messianic sense is intended or indicated in the context.[101]

However, in a number of significant texts an expectation that is clearly messianic comes to expression – remarkably based on a common stock of biblical passages, even though the messianic personage is denoted by a variety of titles. Chief among the biblical passages in question are Isaiah 11:1–8; Numbers 24:17–19; 2 Samuel

7:12–16, and Genesis 49. Verses 1–5 of the first of these are cited in 4Q *Isaiah Pesher*[a] (4Q161) in fragments 8–10 column III lines 11–16, and are interpreted thus: '[The interpretation of the word concerns the shoot] of David which will sprout [in the final days, since] [with the breath of his lips he will execute] his enemies and God will support him with [the spirit of] courage ... He will rule over all the peoples' (18–19,21). The text is obviously fragmentary,[102] but enough is clear to place it beyond reasonable doubt that reference is being made to the Branch of David who will rule over the nations at the end of the days: in short, to an eschatological Davidic King. A similar reference is found in what came to be known popularly as the 'Slain Messiah' text or some such title (4Q285),[103] though it is more probably to be regarded as part of the lost ending of IQM.[104] Of particular moment to our concern is the equation here, in an eschatological context, of the Branch of David with the Prince of the Congregation (Frag. 5, line 4). But in IQSb V 27 the Prince of the Congregation is apparently further identified as the sceptre of Numbers 24:17 (cf. IQSb V 20). Furthermore, in CD VII 14–21 the 'star' of Amos 5:26[105] and Numbers 24:17 is identified with the Interpreter of the Law; while the 'sceptre' used in parallel with the 'star' in Numbers 24:17, is identified as the Prince of the whole Congregation (19–20), as in IQSb V 27. The present context is clearly eschatological, looking for the destruction of 'all the sons of Seth', who escaped at the time of the first visitation (21). Thus, both the Prince of the Congregation and the Interpreter of the Law appear to be messianic figures,[106] and it is probable that they are the Messiahs of Israel and Aaron respectively, alluded to in IQS IX 11.[107]

The image of the sceptre also appears in 4Q252, which is variously known as the '*Patriarchal Blessings*' or the *Pesher on Genesis* (4Qp Gen[a]). Column V line 1 gives an amended version of Genesis 49:10: 'A sovereign (*šallîṭ*) shall [not] be removed from the tribe (*šēbeṭ*) of Judah.' This amends the original by substituting 'sovereign' (*šallîṭ*) for 'sceptre' (*šēbet*) while retaining the latter term in its alternative sense of 'tribe', though perhaps carrying a *double entendre*. The interpretation continues: 'While Israel has the dominion, there will [not] lack someone who sits on the throne of David' (1b–2a). This ruler is then described as 'the messiah of justice' and 'the branch of David', and characterized as one to whom the covenant of royalty has been given, and to his descendants, for all generations (3b–4). 4Q252 is clearly a sectarian text since it goes on to speak of the 'men of the community', their law and their assembly (5–6), while the calendar underlying the account of the Flood in columns I and II is the solar calendar. What all of this amounts to is that in a sectarian text the Branch of David is spoken of explicitly in messianic terms, namely, as the Messiah of Righteousness or Justice.[108]

The fourth biblical context drawn upon largely for messianic purposes, namely, 2 Samuel 7:12–16, both confirms what has already been seen and advances beyond it. In *4Q Florilegium* Fragments 1–3 column I 10–11a, verses 12–14 are quoted, followed by the interpretation: 'This (refers to the) "branch of David", who will arise with the Interpreter of the law who [will rise up] in Zi[on in] the last days' (12a). This is further interpreted by reference to the fallen house of David in Amos 9:11 'who will arise to save Israel' (13b). As in 4Q285 the Branch of David and the Interpreter of the Law are again expected jointly in an eschatological setting. Of particular moment is the fact that the Branch of David is taken to be referred to in the words: 'I will be a father to him and he will be a son to me' (11a). The significance of this and other 'son of God' texts will be considered below. The point of importance for the present is that the Branch of David is yet again taken messianically on the basis of yet another biblical passage.

J.A. Fitzmyer maintains that 'there is no evidence at Qumran of a systematic uniform exegesis of the Old Testament. The same text was not always given the same interpretation'.[109] But to concede the latter is not necessarily to deny the former. Specifically, it does not exclude the existence of a common substratum of messianic understanding and expectation, grounded in the repeated use of specific biblical texts as witnessed to in multiple sectarian documents.[110]

What picture of the Messiah emerges, then, from the texts? First, and most clearly, he is a davidic figure. The emphasis that emerges most clearly in contexts where the davidic idea is mentioned or implied is upon the military prowess of the messiah, particularly in slaughtering the wicked and subduing the nations (4QpIs[a] 8–10; III 18–21; 4Q285 4,5; IQSb V 23–9). He is also depicted as an ideal ruler who will establish the kingdom of Israel and rule with justice and compassion (IQSb V 20–2, 4QpGen[a]V).

But second, the Messiah is also presented as a priestly figure. It has already been noted that the Branch of David appears in some contexts with another figure, the Interpreter of the Law (CD VII 14–21; 4QFlor 1–3, I 11f), who exhibits messianic characteristics. Still other contexts speak in priestly terms of this figure who accompanies the Branch of David or the Prince of the Congregation: notably IQSa II 17–21 where 'the priest' takes precedence over the Messiah of Israel in the feast of firstfruits of bread and new wine.[111] In the *War Rule* the 'chief priest' (*kôhēn hārō'š*) recites the prayer before the battle (XV 4), exhorts the troops (XVI 13) and pronounces the praises of God (XVIII 5), aided by his assistants. That is to say, this figure who accompanies the Prince of the Congregation is an Aaronic figure. Since he is both messianic and Aaronic, does this not explain the reference to the 'messiahs of Aaron and Israel' in *Community Rule* IX 11?[112] That is to say, the presence of the priestly dimension in messianic thought at Qumran implies that messiahship is plural: specifically, dual or dyarchic.

For long this was the dominant view on this point. IQS IX 9–11 refers unmistakably to 'the Messiahs of Aaron and Israel',[113] and the idea is implied in other documents as we have just seen. Accordingly, the evidence of the *Damascus Rule*, which might arguably read in a singular sense, since in CD XII 23–XIII 1, XIV 18–19 and XIX 10–11 the expression 'the Messiah of Aaron and Israel' is construed with a singular verb, was interpreted dually in keeping with the prevailing view.[114] More recently there have been indications of a tendency to qualify this understanding: not so much by the reassertion of a single messiahship – though this view has never lacked advocates[115] – as by the claim that the evidence of the texts points to a degree of fluidity on the subject.[116] Two things seem to be exhibited clearly in the texts. First, there is a uniform recognition of a priestly dimension in the function of the sect. Thus, in what is widely regarded as the oldest part of the *Community Rule*, and in many respects the community's constitutional charter, the community is described as 'a holy house for Israel, and the foundation of the holy of holies for Aaron' (IQS VIII 5–6a). If this was how the community was conceived, it is not merely incredible, it is impossible that this dual dimension should not be reflected in its structure and leadership. Second, this priestly dimension, while regularly present, is not regularly described in messianic terms. As has been seen, it is so described in IQS IX 9–11, but in IQSa II 17–21 'the priest' is the mode of reference used even though he takes precedence over the Messiah of Israel. Martin G. Abegg, in the article cited above,[117] has felt drawn to two conclusions. 'First, the dual messiah that we have come to accept as dogma in discussions of the *DSS* must be tempered.'[118] Second, 'There are, however, clear signs that the messianic picture was not so focused as to conclude that messianic hopes were not only or always singular.'[119]

If there was variation in messianic expectation how may it be accounted for? Attempts to reconstruct a unilinear development have not been notably successful.[120] It may be that we lack sufficient evidence to account for the degree of variation that appears to be present. The historical background may well have something to do with it. Collins points out that there is no unbroken history of messianic expectation in the post-exilic period. Rather, after a short effusion following the return from Babylon, it is largely absent, even during the Maccabaean revolt, and no davidic Messiah is in evidence until the *Psalms of Solomon* about 50 BC. The Qumran *Rules* stand between the Maccabees and Pompey which was the time of the Hasmonean monarchy: a monarchy which was Jewish but not davidic. Collins concludes, 'There is good reason to believe that the revival of hope for a messiah, or messiahs, was a reaction to the kingship of the Hasmoneans, which some Jews of the time viewed as illegitimate.'[121] At the same time the variant forms may reflect the fluctuating emphases upon the restorative as opposed to the utopian elements in eschatological expectation. Insofar as the restorative aspect was emphasised stress fell upon the davidic messiah. Where a utopian expectation of a new world following the catastrophic destruction of the old was cherished, the tendency was to invest authority in a dominant priestly leader. Such is the understanding of L.H. Schiffman.[122] How far the distinction between the restorationist and the utopian can be pressed is open to question.[123] It may be that this represents yet another dimension of the fluidity of the thought of the sect on things eschatological. However it is to be accounted for, it shows that, for the sect, the messianic age could not be envisaged without a strong priestly presence in the leadership.

Is the Messiah of the Qumran documents in any sense a suffering figure? If so, and more precisely, do his sufferings have atoning significance? In some measure this question is bound up with the presence in the texts in some form of the Isaiaic Suffering Servant. Earlier scholarship found such allusions particularly in some of the hymns. IQH X (II) 8b–9: 'I am a trap for offenders, medicine for everyone who turns away from sin' was thought to echo Isaiah 53:4–5; while the mention of the servant, his wounds and afflictions, and the light which shines upon him at the end (IQH IX 10–12,23–7) were thought to reflect the same chapter.[124] However, none of the evidence alleged attached atoning significance to suffering, or claimed messianic status for the speaker, and it was widely concluded that there was no convincing data favouring a Jewish messianic understanding of the Isaiaic Servant Songs in pre-Christian times.[125]

More recently, the question has been re-opened with the availability of newly released texts: two in particular. The first is 4Q285, the 'Pierced' or 'Slain Messiah' text already referred to.[126] Attention focuses particularly on fragment 5 lines 2–4 which Garcia Martinez translates: 'A shoot will emerge from the stump of Jesse ... the bud of David will go into battle with ... and the Prince of the Congregation will kill him.'[127] This presupposes that the final verb is to be construed as *hĕmîtô*: 'the Prince of the Congregation killed him' (i.e. the leader of the Kittim), rather than as *hēmîtû*: 'they killed the Prince of the Congregation.' Either is possible grammatically. The former is to be preferred because fragment 5 begins by quoting Isaiah 10:34–11:1 which serves as a kind of 'heading' for the sequence, and its theme is the overthrow of the mighty forest of Lebanon by the stump of Jesse.[128]

The second text which has revived the issue in question is *4Q Aaronic Text A*, edited by E. Puech as a copy of the *Aramaic Testament of Levi* (4Q541).[129] The crucial passage is as follows: 'And he will atone for all the children of his generation, and he will be sent to all the children of his people. His word is like the word of the heavens, and his teaching, according to the will of God. His eternal sun will shine. Then, darkness will vanish from the earth, and gloom from the globe. They will utter many words against him, and an abundance of lies; they will fabricate fables against him, and utter every kind of disparagement against him' (Frag. 9, I 2–6a). The personage referred to is clearly a priest, as the mention of his atoning function makes plain. There is even more reference to his teaching role, especially in earlier fragments where he is described as 'a wise man who [rises] to st[udy the instruction of wisdom] and understands the depths and utters enigmas' (frg. 2, II 6) and one who 'will open the books of wisdom' (frg. 7, 4a). He is also a suffering figure, much maligned by his opponents. He functions on a global stage, and through his action darkness will vanish from the earth.

The content of this text was reported by J. Starcky as long ago as 1963 and in it he found a suffering Messiah, cast in the mould of the Suffering Servant of the Isaianic Songs.[130] E. Puech, in his more recent edition of the text, finds it to be related to the *Testament of Levi*, dealing with Levi and his descendants.[131] While Starcky flatly identified the individual described as the High Priest of the messianic era, Puech finds three groups of characteristics: those of a sage, a priest and a maligned and rejected servant.[132] But the servant traits are adapted to the figure of the priest – the eschatological servant.[133] On this reading the Servant Messiah is the priest, not the King.[134] At the same time Puech notes important limitations in the depiction of the priest. The expiation which he offers is in his role as priest: the sufferings which he endures are not in themselves redemptive.[135] Again, his role as a messianic figure is inferred from his anointing as High Priest.[136] He is not specifically stated to be Messiah.[137]

Puech's reading of 4Q541 has commended itself to other scholars. G.J. Brooke's translation and study of the text is, as he acknowledges, 'heavily dependent on the editorial and interpretative work of E. Puech.'[138] Garcia Martinez likewise, accepts the main conclusions reached by Puech.[139] A more sceptical stance is adopted by John J. Collins who argues that the eschatological priest of 4Q541 is 'more likely to have been modelled on the career of the historical Teacher of Righteousness than on the Suffering Servant of Isaiah,'[140] concluding that 'the alleged allusions to a suffering messiah in the Scrolls disappear under examination.'[141]

It is possible both to overinterpret and underinterpret the language of 4Q541. The term 'messiah' is not used in the text. On the other hand the global scale of the function of the priest makes it difficult to see him as less than a dominant figure in the eschatological era. Again, the language of the Servant Songs is not quoted, but the ideas are so pervasive[142] that it would require more than a fair share of coincidences to account for them in any other way. The text thus stands out as singular in several respects. It is the only text in which, if the Priestly Messiah is spoken of, he is the only Messiah mentioned; and consequently it is unique in envisaging him (rather than the Messiah of Israel) as the dominant of the two Messiahs: indeed, as achieving through his priestly mission that global triumph normally credited to the Messiah of Israel by military victory. Equally it is unique in characterizing him in terms of the Servant of Yahweh. 4Q541 thus seems to bear witness to the priestly strand of messianic expectation at Qumran in more emphatic terms than any text discovered thus far: in Garcia Martinez' words: 'an independent development of the hope in the coming of the priestly Messiah as an agent of salvation at the end of times.'[143] On the basis of the available evidence it cannot be said that the eschatological Priest-Messiah-Servant is prominent, but it is there and stands as an indicator of how Qumran messianism was capable of developing.

A fourth feature of messiahship at Qumran has been proposed: the Messiah is in some sense a divine figure. The suggestion has been made on the basis of several texts which use the idea, if not the expression 'son of God'. Chief among these is *4Q Aramaic Apocalypse* (4Q246), popularly known as the 'Son of God' text.[144] The focal lines read: 'He will be called son of God, and they will call him son of the Most High. Like the sparks of a vision, so will their kingdom be; they will rule several years over the earth and crush everything; a people will crush another people, and a city another city. Until the people of God arises and makes everyone rest from the sword. His kingdom will be an eternal kingdom, and all his paths in truth and upright[tness]. The earth (will be) in truth and all will make peace. The sword will cease in the earth and all the cities will pay him homage. He is a great God among the gods(?)' (II 1–7). Even a superficial reading of the text raises questions. Why is the reference to the son of God followed by a plural verb: 'they will rule'? And what is the relation between the son of God and the people of God since the latter is said to bring an end to war? Such questions and the attendant details (which cannot be gone into here) have given rise to a wide range of interpretations, from those which see the son of God in this text as a divine figure to those which see him as diabolical.[145] At this point any judgment must be tentative, but the language and imagery, which echo the book of Daniel, seem best taken to refer to one who stands on the divine side in a special sense and identifies himself with the people of God like the Son of Man in Daniel chapter 7.[146] If this is correct then the messiah could be thought of at Qumran in quasi-divine terms.[147]

Support for this conclusion may be found in the *Prayer of Enosh* (4Q369).[148] Fragment 1 I 1–12 seems to be a description of the land of promise of which two things are said. First, it will be given 'to his seed for their generations an eternal possession' (4). The one to whose seed it will be given is later characterized as 'a prince and ruler in all your earthly land … the cr[own of the] heavens and the glory of the clouds [you] have set [on him]' (7–8). The official editors see a possible allusion to Daniel 7:13 and an eschatological ruler, while the phrase 'as a father to his son' (10) may echo 2 Samuel 7:14 as in 4Q Flor 1:11–12, where it is understood in terms of the Davidic Messiah as noted earlier. All of this serves as background for line 6: 'And you made him a first bo[rn] son to you.' C.A. Evans points out that precisely these elements: universal rule, divine fatherhood and making a firstborn son are found in Psalm 89:26–7 and that the whole sequence refers to 'my servant David; with my holy oil I have anointed him' (20).[149] The passage is thus not only messianic, but the Messiah stands in a unique relation to God: that of son to Father.

A third text which speaks to the point under consideration is *4Q Messianic Apocalypse* (4Q521).[150] Unlike the two texts just reviewed, 4Q521 does not use the expression 'Son of God'. However, it shares with these the exalted view of its protagonist: the messiah is apparently envisaged as ruler of the universe. The picture changes somewhat in that, when specific actions are spoken of: showing mercy to the poor (line 6), freeing the imprisoned and giving sight to the blind (line 8), healing the sick and raising the dead (line 12), God is said to be the actor. Most curiously, the Lord is said to be the one who 'will proclaim good news to the meek' (line 12). The echoes of Isaiah 61:1 are unmistakable. Not least significant in that context are the facts that an anointed one is speaking, and he has been sent by the Lord as the bearer of good news. Accordingly, it has been suggested that in 4Q521 the messiah is the divine agent in carrying out the tasks mentioned.[151] If this is sound then the messiah is not only a cosmic figure, but to some extent a supernatural figure. It is also notable that in this text only one messiah is spoken of, even though a wide range of activities, from ruling to raising the dead, is attributed to him.[152]

What picture of messianism at Qumran emerges from the evidence surveyed? First, no single doctrine of messiahship can be found, but rather variant forms. The variations range from the dyarchic form of IQS IX 9–11 and possibly of the *Damascus Rule* to that of the *Messianic Rule* (IQSa) where the Messiah of Israel is subordinate to the priest but the latter is not referred to in messianic language to *4Q Aaronic Text A* which not only appears to cast the Priestly Messiah in terms of the Suffering Servant, but sees him as the sole Messiah. With the texts using the idea of divine sonship (4QFlor., 4Q246, 4Q521 etc.) the range extends still more widely to depict the Messiah as in some sense a divine figure. One must therefore acknowledge a degree of fluidity arising, perhaps, from historical circumstances such as tensions between the two arms of power, and perhaps from theologizing about the character of the age to come and the consequent character of its leadership.[153] But second, while there appears to be a measure of variation in messianism at Qumran, this does not mean it was a subsidiary theme. Of course by definition it belongs largely to the sectarian eschatology even though the sect's organization and praxis reflected or anticipated that which was to come. But it is noteworthy that messianism finds a place in the chief institutional documents of the sect such as the *Community Rule* and the *Damascus Rule*. Finally, it seems safe to say that royal messianism was the fundamental form of messianism in Qumran thought as, indeed, it was in Judaism.[154] But it carried within itself the potential for enlargement because other functionaries such as priests and prophets were also anointed. Taken together with the central role of the High Priest in the history of Israel, and the importance of the Zadokite priesthood in the thought and founding of the sect, it is hardly surprising that the priest should be accorded a major and even messianic status in the new order of things at the end of the days.

C.A. Evans avers in regard to messianism at Qumran that 'we must be prepared to accept the fact that we cannot tie together all the loose ends.'[155] We have already seen that to be so of Qumran messianism as a whole. But two loose ends (which may indeed be but one) call for specific, even if brief, comment: are the Prophet and the Teacher of Righteousness messianic figures? As to the Teacher of Righteousness, one must distinguish between the figure who played a crucial role in the establishment of the sect (CD I 11; 4QpPs[a] (4 Q 171) III 15b–17a; IQp Hab VIII 1–3a) and the one who would teach righteousness at the end of the days (CD VI 11). The former is identified as both a priest (4Q171 I 27), and the 'Interpreter of the Law' (CD VI 7), but most frequently he is described as an interpreter of prophecy, understanding of which is credited to him in the most emphatic terms going beyond that of the prophets themselves (IQp Hab XII 7–10a, VII 1–5a). At the same time, he is never called a prophet. His powers lie in the interpretation of prophecy rather than in its utterance. Nor is there any clear evidence that the Teacher of Righteousness was a messianic figure.[156] If he was an eschatological figure it was in the sense that his ministry indicated that the messianic age would not be long delayed. In the apt phrase of F.F. Bruce, 'the Teacher appears to have played the part of a forerunner, "to make ready for the Lord a people prepared", rather than the part of a Messiah.'[157]

That a prophetic figure formed part of Qumran eschatological expectation is clear from IQS IX 11. But is he messianic? He might possibly be the teacher of the end of the days referred to in CD VI 11. This view has been urged on the basis that the three figures mentioned in IQS IX 11 are those referred to in 4Q *Testimonia*, the first of whom is the prophet of Deuteronomy 18: 18–19. Further, in 4Q Flor 1–3, I 11 the figure who arises with the Branch of David is the Interpreter of the Law who, in CD VII 18–21 is taken to be the 'star' of Numbers 24:13, the Prince of the Congregation being understood to be the 'sceptre'. Since an undoubtedly messianic figure is found in the last two contexts, it is inferred that the parallel figure associated with him is messianic also.[158] What this amounts to is the equation of the teacher of the end of days and the Interpreter of the Law with the eschatological prophet, understood as a messianic figure.

An alternative suggestion is that the prophet of the end is an Elijah-like figure. The basis for the suggestion is the allusion in 4Q521 2, I 2 to Malachi 4:5–6 which predicts the coming of Elijah before the day of the Lord to 'turn the hearts of fathers to their children and the hearts of children to their fathers'. While some scholars distinguish Elijah from the messiah mentioned in Fragment 2 II 1,[159] it is more probable that Elijah is the messiah or divinely anointed agent empowered to carry out the mighty works referred to.[160]

However, it has to be recognized that the available evidence is limited. Little enough is said of the historical Teacher of Righteousness, and even less of the teacher and the prophet of the end of the days. It is not improper to attempt to piece together the surviving clues, but any reconstruction must be tentative.

The Restored Humanity

A further dimension which formed a significant part of the expectation of the end of the days for Qumran thought was the restoration of fallen humanity to its original glory at creation. This may be envisioned negatively and positively. On the negative side it involved purification. This figures prominently in the concluding part of the Discourse on the Two Spirits in the *Community Rule*. At the time of the final visitation God will extinguish evil forever.

(IV 17b–19a). But this has direct effects on the individual. 'God will then purify every deed of man with his truth; He will refine for Himself the human frame by rooting out all spirit of injustice from the bounds of his flesh. He will cleanse him of all wicked deeds with the spirit of holiness; like purifying waters He will shed upon him the spirit of truth (to cleanse him) of all abomination and injustice. And he shall be plunged into the spirit of purification' (IV 20b–21b).[161] The description is far-reaching,[162] and its radicality is matched in other texts employing kindred metaphors.

The metaphor of purification is frequently defined in terms of 'purity of heart' or 'circumcision of the foreskin of the heart' (4Q *Catena*[a] (4Q177), II 9b–10, 15b–16; 4Q *Barki Nafshi* (4Q434) I 10). The image of the heart, and of the circumcision of the heart in particular, is not uncommon in the Bible to denote the inwardness of religion.[163] Nor is it unknown at Qumran. The specific image of 'circumcision of the heart' occurs, (though not frequently) in some of the central sectarian texts, (IQS V 4b; IQp Hab XI 13); while the expression that may be regarded as its opposite: 'stubbornness of heart' (*šĕrîrût lēb*) is much more common (e.g. IQS I 6, II 25, III 3, V 4 etc.). The example referred to from the so-called *Barki Nafshi Texts* (4Q434–439)[164]: 'he has circumcised the foreskins of their heart' (4Q434 1I4) stands both in the narrower context of 4Q434 in which that circumcision is spoken of in terms of the opening of the inward ears to hear God's teaching (3), as well as in the wider context of the group of texts as a whole in which the language of the 'heart' is used frequently.[165] It is worth noting that, while in 4Q434 the circumcision of the heart is spoken of as something that can happen in the present (as in IQS V 5–6 and IQp Hab. XI 13), in 4Q *Catena*[a] (4Q177) it is seen as something reserved for the last days (II 9–11,16). Something of the elasticity of the idea of the end noted at the beginning of the chapter seems to be present here also.

Akin to and associated with the idea of the purification of the heart is that of the removal of the evil inclination (*yēṣer*). The two ideas stand together in the *Community*

Rule: 'No-one should walk in the stubborness of his heart in order to go astray following his heart and his eyes and the musings of his inclination. Instead he should circumcise in the Community the foreskin of his tendency (*yēṣer*) and of his stiff neck in order to lay a foundation for truth in Israel' (V 4b–5).[166] This in turn is reminiscent of the spirit (*rûaḥ*) of wickedness in man from which he will be purged at the time appointed (IQS IV 20b–21a, 23b–25a).

If we inquire now after the positive forms which the inner purification assumes, at least two seem to be found. The first is the recovery of the lost glory of Adam. The expression occurs infrequently, but it is striking and appears in contexts of such significance that it is hard to resist the conclusion that it was a stock feature in sectarian thought. In the Discourse on the Two Spirits the climax of God's remaking of humanity is the conclusion of an everlasting covenant, 'and to them shall belong all the glory of Adam' (IQS VI 23a). Similarly, in the *Damascus Rule* the reward of those who have remained faithful to the covenant is that 'all the glory of Adam is for them' (CD III 20). In IQH IV (=XVII) 15 God forgives the sin of those who serve him loyally 'eliminating from them all their depravities, giving them as a legacy all the glory of Adam and plentiful days'; while in 4Q *Psalms Pesher*[a] (4Q171) Psalm 37:19 is taken to refer to 'those who have returned from the wilderness, who will live for a thousand generations, in safety; for them there is all the inheritance of Adam and for his descendants for ever' (III 1–2a). These passages share a common eschatological temper and their apparent expectation is a restoration of the earth to its original condition at creation, and of man upon it.

A second form which the restoration of the earth and its creatures assumes is the attainment of perfection. This has already received extended treatment[167] and a summary statement will suffice here. The point of relevance is that, while perfection in the sense of compliance with the sectarian *halakah*, a change of heart in regard to God and assimilation into the worship of the heavenly community was believed to be a present possibility, yet its full attainment was looked for only at the end of the days. These features come together strikingly in some contexts. Thus IQS IV 18b–23a describes the divine visitation which will refine and purify the human frame so that the perfect of way may gain knowledge into the wisdom of the sons of heaven and receive all the glory of Adam. A comparable collocation of these ideas is found in 4Q171 (4QpPs[a]) II 25–III 2a.

It has already been said that the achievement of this state is expected 'at the end of the days'. It is important to note the precise reference of this. It was argued at the beginning of this chapter that, while the expression had a certain elasticity, nonetheless its accent was towards the future: but not the 'end' in the sense of the termination of time but rather of the conclusion of that climactic period which is definitive in determining what will follow. If one asks, then, when the sectarians looked for the restoration of humanity as just described, the answer appears to be: at the same time at which they looked for the restoration of the nation and its leadership.

This points to a quasi-millennial conception according to which there eventuates on earth and within time a real though limited measure of the life of eternity. It is limited in time, because it does not bring freedom from death; and it is limited in scope because it is confined to the 'perfect in way'. Nevertheless, this is 'the appointed end and the new creation' (IQS IV 25). The perfect 'will live for a thousand generations in safety; for them there is all the inheritance of Adam and for his descendants for ever' (4Q171 III 1–2). 'They will inherit the high mountain of Israel [and] delight [in his] holy [mou]ntain, but those who are cursed by him will be cut off' (11–12a). The language is to be interpreted within its own frame of reference, and that seems clearly to be of the events attendant and consequent upon the arrival of the Messiah(s) and the rout of the powers of evil in the war, resulting in the restoration of Israel to her appointed pre-eminence.[168]

The evidence points strongly to the conclusion that Qumran eschatology is, in its most distinctive features, a largely temporal eschatology. Its preoccupation is with the reversal of those factors which prevented Israel from discharging her appointed role as they saw it of preserving true worship and obedience to God in the earth. That role would be restored 'at the end of the days' by the restoration of the political, but particularly the religious institutions of the nation. But besides restoration there is also – in the preferred jargon – a utopian element. For the nation betrayed her commission because of a profound inward division within the souls of her members, variously described as the 'two inclinations', the 'two spirits', a wayward heart. The coming of the new era would resolve that problem by the re–creation of man in the pattern of Adam.

The Life to Come

Was there then no transcendental eschatology at Qumran? Was their vision bounded strictly by the horizon of earth? Even the expectation of the infinite extension of life in time 'for a thousand generations' does not rule out the fact of death. What lay beyond it? There were cemeteries even at Qumran. What was the fate of the departed? And if that fate was known then how was it interpreted?

The answers to these questions are not readily come by: a fact signalized by the historic reversal of view in the article of J.Carmignac in which he repudiated his earlier position that the divine intervention in the War brought about the end of earthly history and passage to extra-terrestrial life.[169] Several factors, already noted, account, at least in part, for the problem. One is that the dominant focus of Qumran eschatology was this world. The cautionary word of A.R.C. Leaney should never be lost sight of, that 'Jewish eschatological hopes were not centred upon another sphere but on this world, transformed in a new age but still this world'.[170] Another factor arising from the preceding, and also noted earlier, is that the terminology of Qumran eschatology such as 'eternal', 'everlasting', 'end', 'judgment' is to be understood in the first instance against a temporal baseline, and not construed without remainder in transcendental terms. Where then may one begin in trying to reconstruct the sectarian understanding of life beyond death (assuming there is one)?

The fundamental datum must surely be that they believed in an extra-terrestrial sphere with which they thought themselves to be in communion. This, indeed, is one of the most striking features of their ideology just as it was one of the most prized privileges of their religious experience: '[God] unites their assembly to the sons of the heavens in order (to form) the counsel of the Community and a foundation of the building of holiness to be an everlasting plantation throughout all future ages' (IQS XI 8). Passages in the *Thanksgiving Hymns* speak to the same point (e.g. IQH XI = III 21b–22a; XIV = VI 12b–13), as do the *Songs of the Sabbath Sacrifice* (4Q Shir Shabb) which not only served as liturgies in the community, but 'also depict the world in which the sectarians hoped to share after death, in accordance with apocalyptic tradition.'[171] If this is so, how was the translation from earth to heaven conceived?

Some texts appear to envisage entry to eternal life in heaven or (alternatively) eternal extinction as taking place at judgment immediately following death. 4Q *Sapiential Work A*[a] (4Q418)[172] seems to embody such a view. The reading of history in terms of successive periods is a marked feature of the document (e.g. 4Q418 123 II 2–4), and the period of evil is seen as being brought to an end by judgment (4Q418 2 5–7). The contrasting fates of the foolish and the righteous are set out side by side in 4Q418 69 4–15. The foolish are told: '[For Sheo]l you were formed, and your return will be eternal damnation ... All the foolish of heart will be destroyed and the sons of iniquity will not be found any more, and all those who support evil will asham[ed] at your judgment' (6–8).[173] By contrast the inheritance of the righteous is 'life eternal' and 'eternal light' (13,14). 4Q *Wiles of the Wicked Woman* (4Q184) express the same view, though with greater emphasis on the fate awaiting those who succumb to the charms of Lady Folly.

'Her gates are the gates of death, and in the entrance to her house, Sheol proceeds. All those who go to her will not come back, and all those who inherit her will sink to the pit' (10b–11a). 'In the midst of eternal fire is her inheritance, and those who shine do not enter' (7b). This last clause is taken by Harrington to be akin to the thought of Daniel 12:3: 'Those who shine brightly are presumably the stars or the angels – the kind of imagery used in Daniel 12:3 to describe the immortality to be enjoyed by the righteous at the resurrection of the dead.'[174] In these and kindred texts the more vivid features of apocalyptic are notably absent: the eschatological war, the coming of the messiah(s), the restoration of Israel, and such like. For this reason it has been argued that such views represent an early stage in the eschatological thinking of the sect, or even a time prior to the sect's emergence.[175]

Interpreting the data in this way is not impossible. What seems to be clear is that the two understandings of eschatology – the temporal and the transcendental – were not thought to be incompatible. Even if an early date for 4Q *Sapiential Work A* be conceded, it is significant that no fewer than parts of six copies of the work survive: all written in the Herodian formal hand of the late first century BC, or early first century AD.[176] This shows that, however early the date of composition of the work may be, it continued to be valued and used at Qumran: a point reinforced by the presence of one of its fragments (IQ 26)[177] in Cave 1 where documents particularly cherished by the sect were stored.

Another pointer in the same direction is to be found in the Discourse on the Two Spirits (IQS III 13–IV 26), doubly significant in that it is incorporated in the Community Handbook (IQS), as well as for what it says. Its sapiential affinities have long been noted: its character as a teaching guide for the *Maskil* (III 13), and its use of wisdom ideas and terms: the 'God of Knowledge', 'all that is and shall be', 'the mysteries of God', and so on. As important as its account of the conflict between the Spirits of Truth and Error is its preoccupation with how that conflict will end.

This comes to expression in the term 'visitation' (*peqûddāh*) which is used on at least two distinguishable levels. First, it is used to refer to the recompense for good or evil of all the sons of men (III 14c–15a, IV 6b, 11b–12). The deeds in each category are listed (IV 2–6, 9–11), and the implication is that their 'visitation' takes place in return for the deeds done in their lifetime. The penalty for evil deeds is destruction (IV 11b–14), while the reward for good deeds is length of days and everlasting joy (IV 6b–8a). But second, 'visitation' is used with the third personal suffix or the definite article: 'his (God's) visitation' or 'the visitation' (III 18, IV 19,26) when the Spirit of injustice will be obliterated. At this point creation will be renewed (IV 25) and the glory of Adam restored to the perfect of way (IV 22b–23a). What this seems to amount to is that, while there was a clear recognition of eternal life beyond the grave, yet the focal point of eschatology in Qumran thought was the remaking of the earthly order; not through a redirection of the course of history but through a change in the historical order itself.

This leads directly to another question and topic. If recompense comes to the departed through the visitation of judgment at the time of death, how is this visitation related to God's visitation at the end? In particular, is the renewed world one in which the faithful departed have a share, and if so, is resurrection the gateway by which they enter it? If this is the case, then resurrection implies some sort of intermediate state between this life and the life of eternity. On the other hand, it has been argued by E.Puech, at great length and with monumental erudition,[178] that the prevailing view at Qumran was in harmony with that of Daniel 12:2–3, namely, that resurrection was the prelude to judgment which resulted in either everlasting life or everlasting condemnation.[179]

Puech's case rests to a large extent on the assumption that, since the Book of Daniel was known and used at Qumran, the sectarians must have held the Danielic understanding of resurrection.[180] But the one does not necessarily follow from the other, and many of the echoes of

Daniel alleged by Puech involve terms such as 'eternal', 'everlasting',[181] which, as we have seen, are of variable signification. One would expect to find unambiguous references, not simply to Daniel 12:2–3, but to resurrection as such, in the major *Rules*. But such evidence is not forthcoming. Puech concedes that there is none in the *Community Rule* (apart from the idea of the 'divine visitation'),[182] and that in the *War Rule* and the *Damascus Rule* it is, at best, implicit.[183] The clearest examples adduced by Puech are from the *Thanksgiving Hymns* notably IQH XIV (= VI) 34: 'Those who lie in the dust will hoist the flag, and the worms of the dead will raise the banner,' and XIX (=XI) 12 where similar imagery is used. But it is more probable that the metaphors denote the empowerment of the weak rather than the raising of the dead.

There is indeed evidence from the Qumran caves which speaks explicitly of resurrection of the dead. Most notable in this regard is 4Q *Messianic Apocalypse* (4Q 521), already considered for its contribution to Qumran messianism.[184] Whatever be concluded regarding the identity of the messiah in this text and his relationship to God, it is clear that the raising of the dead is one of the works associated with his coming. 'The Lord will perform marvelous acts such as have not existed, just as he sa[id], for he will heal the badly wounded and will make the dead live, he will proclaim good news to the meek, give lavishly [to the need]y, lead the exiled and enrich the hungry' (4Q521 2, II 11–13). But it is questionable whether the raising of dead here refers to a general resurrection of all of the departed (e.g. as the prelude to a universal judgment): rather its reference is to the raising of the dead as one of a number of mighty works such as healing the sick and providing for the needy, which were expected in the messianic age. On either assumption resurrection of the dead is in mind, but its import is rather different.[185]

Another text appealed to in the same interest is 4Q *Pseudo-Ezekiel*[a] (4Q385). The text is set in the context of eschatological judgment, namely, the reward of those who have remained faithful to the covenant with Yahweh

(2, 1–3). The prophet's question as to what this will be is replied to with the directive to prophesy over the bones on the lines of Ezekiel 37 which is then quoted. Puech argues that, whereas in Ezekiel 37 the focus is the re–creation of the nation, the setting in 4Q385 is individualized in the form of the reward of the faithful. He points out that two questions are asked: 'When will these things happen? And how will they be rewarded for their loyalty?' (2.3) The answer given is that the righteous will be raised to life: 'a large crowd of men will rise and bless *YHWH* Sebaoth who [caused them to live]' (8).[186] The question as to how this will happen is answered in the three-stage resurrection: the reassembling of the bones, their covering with flesh, and the inbreathing of spirit. The precision of this process, according to Puech, signifies 'the identity of the beings and the continuity of a form of existence beyond death.'[187] This speaks more directly to the question of resurrection at Qumran, though it is to be noted that it is the resurrection of the just only which is spoken of here. It is also to be noted that the extent to which 4Q385 is representative of Qumran thought is contested by some.[188]

The confirming piece of evidence which Puech points to in support of Qumran belief in resurrection of the dead is that of the cemeteries at Qumran and neighbouring sites.[189] This has already been reviewed[190] and their distinctiveness, in comparison with prevailing contemporary custom seems difficult to deny. John J. Collins holds that no conclusion can be drawn from it in the absence of literary evidence in the texts.[191] But the contrast with the use of family tombs and ossuaries almost universally in Jerusalem and Jericho at this period makes it difficult not to seek an explanation for so striking a difference, as does the north-south orientation of the skeletons. It is hard to believe that such features had no significance whatever. Puech finds that significance – though he is by no means the first to do so[192] – in the belief that the home of God was in the north, and likewise the New Jerusalem, the hill of Zion and the Paradise of the age of gold.[193] Qumran burial customs are an affirmation of that belief and expectation.

But the question persists as to why this comes to expression so little in the texts. The answer may be that the focus of their vision lay elsewhere. Collins has made the suggestion that the reason why death plays so little part in the Scrolls is because the attention of the sectaries rested so much on worship as communion with the angels that the life beyond was simply the continuation of the same and therefore death fell into the background.[194] In the same way, the sectarian preoccupation with the end of the days and the eschatological war may well have pushed concern with the life of the world to come into a second level of priority. But that it held a place in their thinking seems difficult to deny. And while the literary evidence for belief in the resurrection of the dead is slight it cannot be readily dismissed, especially since it offers the most intelligible explanation of Qumran's distinctive burial practices.[195]

Plainly, there are tensions within the Qumran understanding of the life to come. There is the tension between the life to come seen chiefly as the indefinite extension of life in time but in a renewed world and the life to come understood transcendentally. There is the further tension between the point of entry into the life to come as being death or resurrection. In many respects these tensions arise from another: the tension between the corporate and the individual, the re-creation of the nation and the resurrection of the individual. At Qumran the tendency seems to have been to hold all of the elements together; even if they were not formally reconciled. The tension between the temporal and the transcendental may be partly alleviated by viewing the re-creation of the nation in quasi-millennial terms without repudiating the transcendental reality of the life to come. This in turn would have implications for the corporate-individual tension, inasmuch as the nation is a temporal reality. The tension between judgment and the reward of the faithful as taking place at death or resurrection lends itself least to resolution on the basis of the available evidence. When everything is said, no single, coherent picture emerges. Schürer-Vermes point out that when expectation moves beyond that of a messianic kingdom to a blessed life in a supernatural world 'the two spheres of belief ... cannot be combined except artificially ... Accordingly, the ancient national expectation had either to be annulled or to be combined with it in appearance only. In the Apocalypses of Baruch and Ezra, and in Qumran literature, the latter course is taken.'[196] Necessarily so. To have taken any other world have meant the extinction of the sect.

Notes

1. See Chapter 5, p. 238f.
2. IQS III 18, IV 18–26.
3. See Chapter 5, p. 243f.
4. For these summary details see Steudel,A., '*Ahărît Hayuāmîm* in the Texts from Qumran', *RQ*, 16, 62, 1993, 227.
5. Carmignac, J., 'La Notion d'Eschatologie dans la Bible et à Qumran', *RQ*, 7, 1969, 18.
6. Art. cit, 18–22. He points out that when 'the end of the world is in mind', '*aḥărît* tends to be replaced by *qēs*.
7. My translation of Carmignac's original, 'Dans la suite des jours, c'est-à-dire le temps de la fournaise qui vient' (art. cit, 22).
8. Art. cit, 23–7.
9. See art. cit, 23 n.13 for documentation.
10. In reply to the first part of the question Carmignac refers to CD XIX 1, 'they shall live a thousand generations'. Of the second part he says, 'Aucun texte ne paraît envisager franchement cette question' (23). Attempts to refer IQH III 13–18, 28–36 to this period he regards as misplaced: 'cela concerne la fin de la période actuelle et non la fin du monde proprement dite' (loc. cit.)
11. 'Selon la mentalité de l'Ancien Testament et selon la mentalité de Qumran, on assigne globalement à "la suite des jours" les événements que l'on prédit pour un avenir indétermine. Mais l'on ne sous-entend pas qu'ils auront un rapport quelconque avec la fin du monde' (art. cit, 26). For a reaffirmation of this view see Carmignac's article 'La future intervention de Dieu selon la pensée de Qumrân' in M. Delcor (ed), (*Qumrân, Sa Piété, sa théologie et son milieu*, Leuven: University Press, 1978), 226–9.

12. So Steudel, A., art. cit, 228. The point is conceded by J.J. Collins who, while maintaining a future meaning for the expression, nevertheless regards 4QMMT C 22 (*sic*) as an exception. 'Teacher and Messiah? The One Who Will Teach Righteousness at the End of Days', in Eugene Ulrich and James VanderKam, *CRC*, 196.
13. '4Q Midr. Eschat' or 'Midrash on Eschatology' is the name Steudel confers on 4Q174 (4Q *Florilegium*) and 4Q177 (4Q *Catena*[a]) which she takes to be parts of a single text. An early and brief statement of her position appeared in '4Q Midr Eschat: "A Midrash on Eschatology" (4Q174 + 4Q177)' in Trebolle Barrera and Vegas Montaner (edd), *Madrid Qumran Congress*, Vol. II, 531–41. For a fuller account see idem: *Der Midrasch Zur Eschatologie aus der Qumrangemeinde* (*4Q Midr Eschat*[a-b]; Leiden: Brill, 1994).
14. *Idem*: *Madrid Qumran Congress*, Volume II, 536f.
15. *Idem*: '*Aharît Hay-yāmîm* in the Texts from Qumran', *RQ*, 16, 62, 1993, 230.
16. Perhaps most notorious of these is CD VI 8b–11a: 'And the nobles of the people are those who have arrived to dig the well with the staves that the sceptre decreed, to walk in them throughout the whole age of wickedness, and without which they will not obtain it, until there arises he who teaches justice at the end of days.' Since the *Damascus Rule* is written from the perspective that the career of the historical Teacher of Righteousness is past (CD I 11; XX 13b–15a) the implication is that a second Teacher will arise. Yet just as the historical Teacher instructed the 'last generations' (CD I 12), so the second Teacher will teach 'at the end of days'. Similarly, the 'Interpreter of the Law' in CD VI 7 seems to be understood most naturally of the historical Teacher, while in CD VII 18b–21a it seems to have an eschatological reference (note the mention of 'the star' of Numbers 24:13 which commonly has eschatological significance) as is also the case in 4Q *Flor* I 10–13. These data suggest – in the words of J.J. Collins – 'that such titles as Interpreter of the Law and Teacher of Righteousness could be variously used to refer to figures past or future, and that they are interchangeable' (*CRC*, 194). The data also imply that there is a qualitative unity to the function which these figures discharge: i.e. they stand on the same eschatological level, whatever their point on the historical continuum may be, whether they stand at

the beginning or the end or the end of the end.

17. Cf. George J. Brooke, 'This future time, this time before the end, is already being experienced. The latter days herald and anticipate, even inaugurate the end, but they are not the end except proleptically.' *Exegesis at Qumran*, 4Q Florilegium in its Jewish Context (*JSOT Supplement* Series 29, Sheffield: JSOT Press, 1985, 176).
18. Loc. cit.
19. Licht, Jacob, 'Time and Eschatology in Apocalyptic Literature and in Qumran,' *JJS*, 16, 1965, 177.
20. Art. cit, 182 (my italics). The sense in which the Qumran sect may be described as apocalyptic will be taken up later.
21. The Uppsala Colloquium of 1979 and its printed record, D. Hellholm (ed.), *Apocalypticism in the Mediterranean World and the Near East*, Tübingen: Mohr-Siebeck, (1983), is in many respects a monument to this problem. J.J. Collins comments, 'when the participants voted *contra definitionem, pro descriptione*, in a phrase often quoted since then, this did not represent a consensus on proper procedure, but was an expression of fatigue and a recognition that much more time would be needed to mediate the differing viewpoints.' John J. Collins and James H. Charlesworth, (eds.) *Mysteries and Revelations*, Apocalyptic Studies since the Uppsala Colloquium, Sheffield: Journal for the Study of the Pseudepigrapha Supplement Series 9, (1991), 12. In his contribution to this latter volume Collins concludes that, while progress has been made since 1979 there are still problems of definition (op. cit. 24–5).
22. Cf. John J. Collins: 'The main difficulty in speaking about "apocalyptic movements" in ancient Judaism does not lie in the meaning of the term, but in the lack of social documentation.' 'Genre, Ideology and Social Movements in Jewish Apocalypticism' in Collins and Charlesworth (eds.), *Mysteries and Revelations*, 23. He warns against assuming that a movement necessarily lies behind each work that may be labelled 'apocalyptic' (loc. cit).
23. Cf. J.J. Collins, art. cit, 12–13.
24. Hanson, Paul D., art, 'Apocalypses and Apocalypticism', *ABD*, I, 279a.
25. Collins, J.J., *Semeia 14, Apocalypse: The Morphology of a Genre*, SBL, (1979), 9.
26. Loc. cit.

27. Collins, J.J., *The Apocalyptic Imagination*, (New York: Crossroad, 1987), 5f.
28. Idem. *Mysteries and Revelations*, 15f.
29. Idem. *The Apocalyptic Imagination*, 7.
30. Loc. cit.
31. *Mysteries and Revelations*. 14
32. E.g. Garcia Martinez regards 4Q246, the so-called 'Son of God' text, and 5Q15 *New Jerusalem*, as such, while he views others such as the Enoch fragments as pre-Qumranic, and Danielic texts such as the *Prayer of Nabonidus* (4Q242) and the pseudo-Danielic Aramaic texts (4Q243, 4Q244, 4Q245) as being of indeterminate origin. All however were valued at Qumran. (*Qumran and Apocalyptic*, Leiden: Brill, 1992, x–xi). On the other side D. Dimant holds that none of the apocalypses found at Qumran exhibits the distinctive characteristics of Qumran literature. See *CRC*, 179, 189. John J. Collins concludes that 'it is not clear that any apocalypse was composed at Qumran' (*ABD*, I 286a).
33. *CRC*, 189.
34. For a recent survey of the Daniel material at Qumran, showing its scale and analysing its content see Flint, Peter W., 'The Daniel Tradition at Qumran,' in Craig A. Evans and Peter W. Flint (edd.), *Eschatology, Messianism and the Dead Sea Scrolls*, Studies in the Dead Sea Scrolls and Related Literature, (Grand Rapids: Eerdmans, 1997), 41–60.
35. J.J. Collins has suggested that the reason the Qumran sect produced few, if any, apocalypses was because of their belief that the Teacher of Righteousness was the medium of revelation for the community, *ABD*, I 286b.
36. *ABD*, I, 281a.
37. John J. Collins sees the Qumran community as but one representative of not merely a wider movement but a widespread mindset that may be labelled 'apocalyptist'. Cf. *Mysteries and Revelations*, 23f. See further his observations in *ABD*, I, 286b. A similar viewpoint underlies the position of Garcia-Martinez that Qumran was a repository of apocalypses originating outside the community but being valued within it (*Qumran and Apocalyptic*, xf.). This carries with it the implication that variations on other theological issues were not regarded as being incompatible with unity of apocalyptic perspective. See the discussion by John J. Collins, 'Was the Dead Sea Sect an Apocalyptic Movement?' in L.H.

Schiffman (ed.), *Archaeology and History in the Dead Sea Scrolls*, *JSOT/ASOR* Monographs 2, Sheffield, (1990), 25–46.

38. Philonenko, Marc, 'L'Apocalyptique Qoumrânienne' in D. Hellholm (ed), *Apocalypticism*, 211–217. For a fuller treatment of consistency in apocalypses see Michael E. Stone, 'On Reading an Apocalypse', in Collins and Charlesworth, *Mysteries and Revelations*, Ch. 4, esp. 70–2,77f.
39. Bruce, F.F., *The Teacher of Righteousness in the Qumran Texts*, London: Tyndale Press, (1956), 12. Bruce notes that this emphasis is also present in IQpMic. Frag. 10, 6b–7 (on Micah 1:5b) and CD XX 27b–34 (loc. cit.).
40. Extended further, this reading of the data would conclude that the title 'Teacher of Righteousness' has a double reference: to the historical Teacher of Righteousness who gave direction to the sect in its beginnings (CD, I 11–12) and is distinguished in consequence as 'the Unique Teacher' (CD, XX 1, 14, 32); and to the Teacher who would arise at 'the end of the end of days' before the eschatological war and the appearance of the Messiah(s) (CD, VI 11, XX 32–4). IQpHab II 1–10a clearly distinguishes the historical Teacher from the Priest who will give instruction as to the meaning of the teaching of the prophets in the last days. A similar multiple reference of the title 'Interpreter of the Law' as between CD, VI 7 and VII 18 together with 4Q Flor I 11f discloses the same pattern, and is best understood as another mode of reference to the Teacher of Righteousness. Cf. The comment of John J. Collins that such titles 'could be variously used to refer to figures past or future, and that they are interchangeable' (*CRC*, 194): a feature of Qumran eschatology which he characterizes as 'restorative' (op. cit. 204).
41. For cautionary comments in this regard with specific reference to Qumran eschatology see Collins, *The Apocalyptic Imagination*, 119f.
42. Bruce, F.F., *The Teacher of Righteousness in the Qumran Texts*, 14, n.1.
43. Collins, *The Apocalyptic Imagination*, 139.
44. Loc. cit.
45. The same point is made in slightly different terms by Michael E. Stone who, in reference to 4 Ezra, says, 'not strict logical consistency but coherency is a controlling category which must guide us in understanding the book. The book made sense to its author, to its readers: our task is to discover

how.' 'On Reading an Apocalypse' in Collins and Charlesworth, *Mysteries and Revelations*, 66.

46. Betz, Otto, 'Past Events and Last Events in the Qumran interpretation of History', in *Proc. World Congress of Jewish Studies*, 6, 1, 1977, 31.
47. Art. cit, 33.
48. Quoted in Collins, *The Apocalyptic Imagination*, 139f.
49. See the discussions in Collins, John J., 'Patterns of Eschatology at Qumran' in Baruch Halpern and Jon D. Levenson (eds.), *Traditions in Transformation*, Turning Points in Biblical Faith, (Winona Lake: Eisenbrauns, 1981), 352f; and *The Apocalyptic Imagination*, 140.
50. Published in Baillet, M., *Qumran Grotte 4*, III (4Q 482–4Q 520), *DJD*, 7, Oxford: Clarendon, (1982), 12–72, and denoted by the sigla 4Q 492, 494, 495 and 496. (The manuscripts designated 4Q 491, 493, and 497, while *War Scroll*-like, represent different recensions than IQM. See *DJD*, 7: 12–44, 49–53, 69–72).
51. *DJD*, 7, 56–7.
52. So Duhaime Jean, in Charlesworth, DSS, Vol. 2, 1995, 84. This implies (as Duhaime notes) that IQM is not the earliest recension of the *War Scroll*.
53. See Osten-Sacken, *Gott und Belial*, Ch. XII; and Duhaime, in Charlesworth, *DSS*, 2, 84.
54. See J. Carmignac, 'La future intervention de Dieu selon la pensée de Qumran' in M. Delcor: *Qumran* Sa Piéte, sa thèologie et sonmilieu, Leuven, (1978), 223–6, esp. 223 n1. Osten-Sacken finds the background of the dualism of IQS III 13–IV 14 in the tradition lying behind IQM (*Gott und Belial*, 116–23). To the same effect see John J. Collins, 'The Expectation of the End in the Dead Sea Scrolls' in Craig A. Evans and Peter W. Flint, *Eschatology, Messianism and the Dead Sea Scrolls*, (Grand Rapids: Eerdmans, 1997), 86.
55. Duhaime, basing on the researches of other scholars finds 'some 200 implicit quotations or allusions in the 280 lines or so preserved in IQM' (Charlesworth, *DSS*, 2, 88). He finds 'possible quotations from almost every part of the Hebrew Bible especially from the books of Numbers, Deuteronomy, Isaiah, Ezekiel, Daniel and the Psalms' (loc. cit.)
56. Yadin draws attention to 'the influence of the eschatological chapters of the Prophets in general and of Isaiah in particular', as well as to the 'enormous influence of Daniel' in the

use of apocalyptic and eschatological terminology (Y. Yadin, *The Scroll of the War of the Sons of Light Against the Sons of Darkness*, (Oxford University Press, 1962, 14). For a list of references see Duhaime, op. cit 2, 88.

57. E.g. The purity laws and the laws of exclusion (VII 3–7; cf. Deuteronomy 23:10–15); the characterization of the enemy (II 10–13; cf. Genesis 10:22–3; 25:1–4, 12–16), etc.
58. The picture is akin to that of the two spirits in man, according to which the spirits war against each other until the divine intervention at the visitation of the end-time terminates the conflict. See IQS IV 15–19a,23–4.
59. For a brief summary of research see Duhaime, op. cit. 2,83f. While noting that no consensus has been reached, and that it appears impossible to reconstruct the original *War Scroll* and its subsequent versions, Duhaime concludes that the Cave 4 fragments make it likely that 'the *War Scroll* is also a complilation of at least three different documents (cols. 2–9,10 – 14, 15–19), which may have been transmitted in various recensions and modified more than once' (84).
60. Cf. XVIII 1–5a. The same phenomenon is observable in 4Q 491 frgs. 1–3:3–5,10; frgs. 8–10:6–7,14. Since 4Q 491 'represents a different recension of the *War Scroll*' and 'both scribes were using similar sources or traditions, but worked independently and creatively on them' (Duhaime, op. cit. 2, 82) it seems clear that the fusion of the historical and the transcendental was deeply rooted in the thought of the sect.
61. Vermes, G., *The Dead Sea Scrolls in English*, (revised and extended fourth edition; Harmondsworth: Penguin, 1995), 125.
62. Collins, John J. in Evans-Flint, *Eschatology, Messianism and the Dead Sea Scrolls*, 86.
63. P.R. Davies, referring to the mention of 'the prince of the whole congregation' in IQM V 1–2, dismisses the passage as secondary on a variety of grounds: chiefly that this is the sole reference to such a figure in the entire scroll; and that there is no room for him inasmuch as the battles are directed by the priests. (*IQM, The War Scroll from Qumran*, Its Structure and History. *Biblica et Orientalia*, N 32, Rome: Biblical Institute Press, (1977), 35f). A similar objection is advanced by E.P. Sanders, who writes, 'What is most striking about the sect's "messianic expectation" is that there is no Davidic messiah in the *War Rule*, where one would expect him to

take the leading role.' (*Judaism: Practice and Belief*, 63 BCE – 66 CE, Philadelphia: Trinity Press International, 1992, 296). Sanders accounts for this in terms of the sect's priestly leanings, as well as in the need for divine aid in winning the final battle (296f). These considerations may account for the relative lack of visibility of the Davidic messiah in the *War Rule*, but it goes beyond the evidence to say that such a figure is wholly absent. See below.

64. E.g. 'On his return from the wilderness of the peoples' (4Q 161, frgs. 2–6 col. II, 14) is reminiscent of IQM I 3.
65. Again, the text is fragmentary, but the context makes virtually certain the restoration '[The Branch of] David which will sprout [at the en]d of the days' (18).
66. Cf. Garcia Martinez, F., and Trebolle Barrera, Julio, *The People of the Dead Sea Scrolls*, (Leiden: Brill, 1995), 164f.
67. Explicit identification of the Branch of David as a messianic figure is found in *4Q Genesis Pesher*[a] (4Q 252) frg. I col. 5, lines 3–4: 'For the ruler's staff is the covenant of kingship, [and the clans] of Israel are the feet, until the Messiah of Righteousness comes, the Branch of David.' (Collins' translation, *The Scepter and the Star*, 62). Collins further makes the incidental but not unimportant point that the use of 'staff (*mĕhôqēq*) in the passage just cited, where it denotes the covenant of kingship, differs from its meaning in, CD VI 7 where it denotes "the Interpreter of the Law." He comments: 'There was, then, some variation in the exegetical traditions of the sect. Nonetheless, there is also a remarkable degree of consistency in the way different messianic titles are combined and associated in different texts among the Scrolls' (63).
68. The text also acquired a good deal of attention under the popular label 'The Text of the Pierced Messiah' or 'Dying Messiah', on which see below.
69. Wacholder-Abegg Fasc. II, 223–7, and esp. PAM.43.325; and Abegg, Jr, Martin ., 'Messianic Hope' and 4Q285, A Reassessment, *JBL*, 113, 1994, 81–91.
70. See Abegg, art. cit., 82f. Abegg notes such phenomena as common occurrence of the angelic names Michael and Gabriel in 4Q285 10.3 and IQM 9:15–16 and 19:4, but not elsewhere in the Hebrew manuscripts. Again, these two manuscripts alone contain 'prince' and 'war'. Overall, 4Q285 records a unique vocabulary of only seven per cent when compared with IQM. Abegg comments, 'specialized

vocabulary of less than 15 per cent implies nearly certain relationship (83). See the further examples on 82f.

71. Milik, J.T., 'Mīlkî-sedeq et Mīlkî-reša' dans les anciens écrits juifs et chrêtiens,' *JJS*, 23, 1972, 143. Abegg concludes, 'Although no coincident text can be offered to make a certain connection with IQM, I have concluded that Milik's proposition is quite plausible' (art. cit., 82).
72. In CD VII 18–20 Numbers 24:17 is again quoted, the star being identified as the Interpreter of the Law (see note 67 above), and the sceptre as the prince of the whole congregation.
73. Collins, John J., goes as far as to say, 'In view of the messianic overtones of both the prince and Balaam's oracle, the burden of proof falls on anyone who would claim that the Davidic messiah was absent at any stage of the War Rule tradition.' *The Scepter and the Star*, 59.
74. In Evans-Flint, *Eschatology, Messianism and the Dead Sea Scrolls*, 86.
75. On the place and role of the messiah see below.
76. So Holm-Nielsen, *Hodayot*, 75; Kuhn, H-W, *Enderwartung und Gegenwärtiges Heil*, 61–4.
77. So H-W. Kuhn, op. cit., 104.
78. It is this which casts doubt on tradition-historical accounts of IQS III 13 – IV 26 such as that propounded by Osten-Sacken, *Gott und Belial*, 116–20. It is difficult to see how either the cosmological or the anthropological element could stand without the other. Hengel's comment puts the point well: 'the apocalyptic drama concentrates on anthropology, without the cosmic aspect being lost' (*Judaism and Hellenism*, I,220).
79. Philonenko, Marc, 'L'apocalyptique qoumrânienne' in David Hellholm (ed.), *Apocalypticism in the Mediterranean World and the Near East*, (Tübingen: J.C.B. Mohr – Paul Siebeck, 1983), 213–4.
80. There might be thought to be tension between the placing of the sons of righteousness under the control of the prince of lights and of the sons of deceit under the control of the angel of darkness as forces external to them on the one hand (III 20–21a); and the description of these same spirits as *possessing* them (III 18, IV 15–17). There is no doubt that the latter concept becomes the dominant idea at the end of the discourse (IV 20–25a). It may be that the two modes of speaking

are simply ways of describing the relation of the spirits to the cosmos on the one hand, and to humanity on the other.

81. 'Le "terme décisif" de l'histoire du monde,' Philonenko, art. cit., 214.
82. Philonenko points out that the rewards promised to the Sons of Light in IQM I 8–9 are the same as those of the just in IQS IV 6–8 (art. cit., 216).
83. See Section A 1 above.
84. There is an evident dislocation between IQM columns I and II. The restoration of worship in the first sabbatic year presupposes fighting during the six preceding years, though there is no direct mention of this, thanks probably to the fragmented state of the text. P.R. Davies suggests with probability that it may be that the occupation of the Temple was one of the objectives of the first stage of the war (*IQM, the War Scroll From Qumran*, 28).
85. See Yadin, *Scroll of the War*, 202–6.
86. Strugnell, J., 'The Angelic Liturgy at Qumran,' *Congress Volume: Oxford, 1959, Vestus Testamentum*, Supplements, 7, (Leiden: Brill, 1960), 318–45.
87. Newsom, Carol, *Songs of the Sabbath Sacrifice: a Critical Edition*, Harvard Semitic Studies, 27, (Atlanta: Scholars Press, 1985), 19.
88. Newsom prefers a 'radically different' rendering of the final clause (op. cit., 203), which does not, however, affect the meaning of the quotation when taken in its overall context. The rendering quoted (that of Garcia Martinez) is akin to that of Vermes, Wise, Abegg and Cook, etc.
89. Newsom, op. cit., 17.
90. Newsom, op. cit., 19.
91. The argument clearly presupposes that the *Songs of the Sabbath Sacrifice* were used at Qumran: a conclusion made probable by the number of manuscripts found there: eight in Cave 4 and one in Cave 11. Whether it is a sectarian production has been debated. Newsom is dubious, but finally concludes that it is on the grounds of points of contact with *4QBerakot* which contains specifically sectarian terminology (op. cit., 1–4). Dimant has no hesitation in concluding that it is of distinct, sectarian character, citing common terminology, *Time to Prepare the Way*, 41, n.45.
92. Garcia Martinez, Florentino, *Qumran and Apocalyptic*, STDJ Vol. IX, (Leiden: E.J. Brill, 1992), 205.

93. For a fuller statement of the interpretation of 11Q Temple XXIX 8–10 followed here, see Yadin, Yigael, *The Temple Scroll*, Volume I, (Jerusalem: The Israel Exploration Society, 1983), 182–7.
94. Wise, Michael Owen, *A Critical Study of the Temple Scroll From Qumran Cave 11*, Studies in Ancient Oriental Civilization, No. 49, Chicago, (1990), 194 n.100. Wise notes that this view was not uncommon in the late Second Temple period. Whether the *Temple Scroll* is a sectarian document continues to be widely debated, as do most other questions regarding its origin, such as date, authorship and purpose. Wise provides a survey of scholarship on these issues up to 1990, indicating wide divergences on all points (op. cit, Ch. 1). Nor has consensus emerged since then. However, certain data seem to provide parameters within which any probable solution should be sought. (1) The palaeographical evidence points to a date prior to or contemporaneous with the establishment of the sect. Whereas the scripts of *IIQ Temple*[a] are Herodian the script of *II Q Temple*[b] is about half a century earlier than that of *II Q Temple*[a]. Cf. van der Ploeg , J.P.M., 'Les Manuscrits de la Grotte XI de Qumrân', *RQ*, 12, 1985, 3–15, esp. 9); and van der Woude, A.S., 'Ein bisher unveröffentliches Fragment der Tempelrolle', *RQ*, 13, 1988, 89–92, esp. 89 n3). The further fact that the script of the last named is identical with that of IQp *Hab* implies ongoing use within the community in some degree. This is confirmed by the presence of two hands in *IIQ Temple*[a] – and in such a manner as to suggest restoration work (for details see Yadin, op. cit, I 11f, 17–20). (2) Other lines of evidence have led scholars to posit an origin prior to or contemporaneous with the origin of the sect. E.g. Garcia Martinez who, on the basis of legal similarities, including some shared with 4QMMT, dates *IIQTemple* to the early years of the sect (see refs in *Qumran and Apocalyptic*, 204 n69). Cf. M.O. Wise who on the basis of redaction critical analysis, dates the *Temple Scroll* to 150 BCE, (*A Critical Study*, 199f). D.D. Swanson thinks precision is unattainable, but considers that the absence of any sense of crisis or schism in the practice of the cultus favours a pre-Maccabaean date (*The Temple Scroll and the Bible*, Leiden: Brill, 1995, 242f). (3) *IIQTemple* does not exhibit the characteristic terminology of the sectarian documents, and cannot be regarded as a sectarian product. Cf. Dimant, *Time to Prepare the Way*, 33f. Yadin qualifies his

affirmation of its sectarian character by conceding that it may incorporate 'to a greater or lesser extent, the teachings of a wider movement,' (*The Temple Scroll* I, 398). (4) At the same time the scroll embodies interests and positions that would not be uncongenial to the sect. This is true of the Temple itself, as well as the calendar. Hence scholars increasingly concede a connection of some sort. E.g. Dimant, 'produced by a circle close to the community but not identical to it' (op. cit, 34 n26); Garcia Martinez, 'a work originating during the formative years of the community ... and ... played an important role in the process leading to the formation of the sect' (*Qumran and Apocalyptic*, 204 n.69); M.O. Wise, who finds connections with the CD community, thinks 'it is not a "sectarian" writing. But in saying this I do not mean that it has no possible sectarian connections' (*A Critical Study of the Temple Scroll*, 202). However, there are those who distance it as far as possible from Qumran in both origin and use. Cf. Stegemann, H., 'The Literary Composition of the Temple Scroll and Its Status at Qumran', in G.J. Brooke (ed.), *Temple Scroll Studies*, (Sheffield: JSOT Press, 1989), 123–48, esp. 143–5.

95. Garcia Martinez, *Qumran and Apocalyptic*, 201. To similar effect Dimant describes it as, 'the Temple of the eschatological future' (*CRC*, 183).
96. This understanding, which is expressed at least as early as the first edition of Vermes, G., *The Dead Sea Scrolls in English*, Harmondsworth, (1962), 245, and remains unchanged in all subsequent editions, has been much criticized. E.g. Schwartz, D.R., 'The Three Temples of *4Q Florilegium*,' *RQ*, 10, 1979–81, 83f. However, the publication of 4QMMT gives verisimilitude to the expression, 'to offer him in it ... the works of the law' (4QFlor I 6–7) as a description of the community.
97. There is no reference to the normative Temple of the *Temple Scroll* as this has been interpreted above.
98. For details see Abegg, Jr., Martin G., 'The Messiah at Qumran: Are We Still Seeing Double?' in *DSD*, 2.2, 1995, 143, together with n.64.
99. Loc. cit.
100. The photograph clearly reads *měšîhô rûah qŏdšô* (Broshi, *The Damascus Document Reconsidered*, 12) but the editor affirms the plural (p. 13 n.10). Likewise Charlesworth, *DSS*, 2, 15 n.18.
101. A similar example is found at CD VI 1.

102. For the official edition see *DJD* V 14 together with Plate V.
103. Leaving aside somewhat sensational accounts in the press, the argument that 4Q285 refers to a Messiah who was killed was pressed by Eisenman-Wise, *DSSU*, 24–30; and Tabor, James D., 'A Pierced or Piercing Messiah? The Verdict is Still Out', *BAR*, (November–December, 1992), 58–9. The tenuous nature of such claims has been made clear by Vermes, Geza, 'The Oxford Forum for Qumran Research Seminar on the Rule of War from Cave 4 (4Q285)', *JJS*, 43, 1992, 85–90; and Bockmuehl, M., 'A "Slain Messiah" in 4Q Serekh Milḥamah (4Q285)?' *TB*, 43, 1992, 155–69.
104. Vermes, art. cit., and Abegg M.G., 'Messianic Hope and 4Q285: A Reassessment,' *JBL*, 113, 1994, 81–91, esp. 81–3.
105. Not present in the quotation in CD VII 14–15a, but present in the original Hebrew of Amos 5:26.
106. For a specific use of the latter in a messianic sense see 4Q*Flor* 1–3, I 11.
107. Cf. Knibb, *The Qumran Community*, 63.
108. Craig A. Evans points out correctly that the messianic interpretation of Genesis 49:10 is 'little more than a digression and apparently does not represent a major concern of the document as a whole' (*Jesus and His Contemporaries, Comparative Studies*, Arbeiten zur Geschichte des Antiken Judentums und des Urchristentums, (Leiden: E.J. Brill, 1995), 103. But the fact that it can be spoken of in an unstudied way suggests that it was an accepted understanding at Qumran, particularly in the light of its appearance in other texts to be noted below.
109. Fitzmyer, Joseph A., 'The use of explicit Old Testament quotations in Qumran literature and in the New Testament,' in *Essays on the Semitic Background of the New Testament*, (London: Geoffrey Chapman, 1971), 55.
110. Collins, John J., summarizes the data in similar terms, concluding that these amount to exegetical traditions. Op. cit, 64–7.
111. For a discussion of the whole context, including the problem of textual reconstruction see Vanderkam, James, *CRC*, 221–4.
112. Brooke, George J., finds the direct link in the Interpreter of the Law and the priestly function of instruction in the Law in Deuteronomy 33:10: both referred to in 4QFlor 6–11 (*Exegesis at Qumran*, 204, cf. 94f, 126).

113. It is true that the section of IQS in which these words occur is absent from the oldest manuscript of the work (4QS[e]). But this is capable of more than one explanation. For a recent discussion see VanderKam, J., *CRC*, 212–4.
114. For a classic statement of this reading of the evidence see Schürer-Vermes, II 550–4. A more recent exposition is VanderKam, J., *CRC*, 229–31. Whether the Hebrew allows a singular understanding has been, and continues to be, hotly debated. F.M. Cross, after examining the syntax of CD XIV 19, concludes roundly, 'the putative single messiah is a phantom of bad philology.' Art. 'Notes on the Doctrine of the Two Messiahs at Qumran and the Extracanonical Daniel Apocalypse' (4Q246), in Donald W. Parry and Stephen D. Ricks (eds.), *Current Research and Technological Developments on the Dead Sea Scrolls*, STDJ XX, (Leiden: Brill, 1996) (hereafter *Current Research*), 3. Martin G. Abegg, on the other hand, examines the syntax of the CD passages, concluding that they 'would appear to argue for the existence of a singular messianic expectation' ('The Messiah at Qumran: Are We Still Seeing Double?' *DSD*, 2.2, 1995, 127–31).
115. See previous note, and also Wise, Michael O. and, Tabor, James D., 'The Messiah at Qumran,' *BAR*, 18, 6, 1992, 60–5, especially their examination of 4Q521 on 60f. See also *DSSU*, 17f, 226.
116. For a survey of relevant texts underlining the variegated forms of reference see Schiffman, L.H., 'Messianic Figures and Ideas in the Qumran Scrolls' in J.H. Charlesworth (ed.), *The Messiah*, Ch. 6. Schiffman reiterates his conclusion in his more recent work, *Reclaiming the Dead Sea Scrolls*, 323–6.
117. See note 115.
118. Art. cit, 143. The use of messianic nomenclature in reference to a priest he finds only in 4Q375 I i.9 and 4Q376 I i.1, and in both cases he thinks the term 'anointed' is being used adjectivally rather than appositionally (140).
119. Art. cit, 144.
120. Cf. Starcky, J., 'Les quatres étapes du messianisme à Qumrân', *RB*, 70, 1963, 481–505.
121. Collins, John J., 'Messianic Authority in the Dead Sea Scrolls,' *DSD*, 2.2, 1995, 149. A historical explanation, though against a wider background is advanced by

Talmon, S., 'The Concept of Māšîah and Messianism in Early Judaism' in Charlesworth (ed.), *The Messiah*, Ch. 5. Talmon sees the dyarchic pattern as a reaction against the pre-exilic period when the king wielded control over sacred institutions (106–8, 113).

122. Schiffman, L.H., 'Messianic Figures and Ideas in the Qumran Scrolls' in Charlesworth (ed.), *The Messiah*, 128f.
123. Schiffman, while insisting that the restorative-utopian dichotomy is real, nevertheless concedes that both trends are sometimes found side by side in the same text. Art. cit, 129. This he sees as the beginning of a process in which the two would be merged to yield the messianic ideal of rabbinic Judaism. (*Reclaiming the DSS*, 327).
124. See Black, Matthew, *The Scrolls and Christian Origins*, Studies in the Jewish Background of the New Testament, (Chico, California: Scholars Press, reprint, 1983), 143f.
125. Schürer-Vermes, II, 547–9.
126. See pp. 270–1 with notes 68–71 and p.280, n.103–4.
127. *DSST*, 124.
128. In addition to the literature referred to in notes 68–71 and 103–4 see now Martin G. Abegg, 'The Messiah at Qumran', in *DSD*, 2.2, 1995, 138–9, where he lists the factors favouring the first option.
129. Puech, E., 'Fragments d'un apocryphe de Lévi et le personnage eschatologique, 4Q Test-Lévi [c–d(?)] et 4QAJa' in *The Madrid Qumran Congress*, 449–501.
130. Starcky, J., 'Les quatre étapes du messianisme', *RB*, 70, 1963, 481–505, esp. 492.
131. *Madrid Qumran Congress*, 490f.
132. Op. cit, 491–9.
133. Op. cit, 496–7. For a scrutiny of these traits as found in 4Q541 see 497–9.
134. Op. cit, 500.
135. Op. cit, 498f.
136. 'Il au moins reçu l'onction comme prêtre ou grand-prêtre' (op. cit, 500 n.60).
137. Even so, Puech finds the text of the highest interest as constituting the earliest known interpretation of the Servant Songs in an individual sense. Op. cit, 500.
138. Brooke, George J., '4Q Testament of Levi[d] (?) and the Messianic Servant High Priest', in Marinus C. DeBoer (ed.), *From Jesus to John*, Essays on Jesus and New Testament Christol-

ogy in Honour of Marinus de Jonge, JSNT Supplement Series 84, (Sheffield: JSOT Press, 1993), 83 n.1.

139. Garcia Martinez-Trebolle Barrera (eds.), *PDSS*, 170–3.
140. *SS*, 125.
141. *SS*, 126.
142. See especially Brooke, art. cit, 92–6.
143. *PDSS*, 170f.
144. The text has been published in full by Puech, E., 'Fragment d'une apocalypse en araméen (4Q246=pseudo-Dan[d]) et le Royaume de Dieu,' *RB*, 99, 1992, 98–131; Fitzmyer, J.A., '4Q 246: The Son of God Document from Qumran,' *Bib*, 1993, 153–74; and *DSSU*, 68–71 (with plates).
145. For a powerful statement of the latter view see Cook, Edward M., '4Q246' in *BBR*, 5, 1995, 43–66.
146. For a reconstruction and interpretation of the text on the assumption of a Danielic background see F.M. Cross in Parry-Ricks, *Current Research*, 5–13. Garcia Martinez interprets the Son of God in the text as 'an eschatological liberator, heavenly being similar to Melchizedek ... an almost divinized messiah.' Art. 'Two Messianic Figures in the Qumran Texts', in Parry-Ricks, op. cit, 29f. John J. Collins understands the Son of God as 'one who stands in a special relationship to God', though 'no metaphysical speculation is presupposed' (*SS*, 16B).
147. This does not necessarily depend on 4Q246 having originated at Qumran – a view denied by E. Puech, *RB*, 49, 1992, 102 n.14. Garcia Martinez, on the basis of ideas parallel with these in other Qumran writings, finds the text 'compatible with the outlook of the Qumran group' (Parry-Ricks, *Current Research*, 27).
148. For the official text see J. VanderKam et al. (eds.), *Qumran Cave 4. VIII – Parabiblical Texts Part I*, DJD XIII, (Oxford: Clarendon, 1994), 353–62.
149. Evans, Craig A., 'A Note on the First-Born Son of 4Q369', *DSD*, 2.2, 1995, 185–201, esp. 198.
150. Puech, E., 'Une Apocalypse Messianique (4Q 521)', *RQ* 15, 1992, 475–519.
151. So Collins, John J., 'The Works of the Messiah', *DSD*, 1.1 , 1994, esp. 99–102.
152. Puech argues that the royal messiah is in mind (art. cit, 479). Collins on the other hand, holds that the messiah spoken of is an Elijah-like, anointed prophet (art. cit, 102–5).

153. E.g. L.H. Schiffman connects the davidic messiahship with the restorative trend, the priestly with the utopian. *Reclaiming*, 326f.
154. So Collins, *SS*, 68.
155. Evans, C.A., *Jesus and His Contemporaries*, 127.
156. For an evaluation of the case that he was so regarded see Knibb, Michael A., 'The Teacher of Righteousness – A Messianic Title?', in Philip R. Davies and Richard T. White, (edd.) *A Tribute to Geza Vermes*, Essays on Jewish and Christian Literature and History, *JSOT, Supplement Series 100*, (Sheffield: JSOT Press, 1990), 51–65.
157. Bruce, F.F., *The Teacher of Righteousness in the Qumran Texts*, (London: The Tyndale Press, 1956), 13. Bruce suggests that at one time the followers of the Teacher believed the messianic age would be inaugurated in his lifetime. His death required a revision of this view, which may be alluded to in CD XX 13b–15a (loc. cit.)
158. A recent statement of this view is Garcia Martinez , F., 'Two Messianic Figures in the Qumran Texts' in Parry-Ricks, *Current Research*, 16–40, esp. 30–6.
159. For the context see the discussion above together with note 150. The proposal is Puech's, art. cit, 497.
160. So John J. Collins as in note 150, pp. 102–6. Cf.*SS*, 116–122.
161. Vermes' translation, *DSSE*, 74f.
162. The use of collective terms for man (*geber* and *'îsh*) does not weaken the individual reference, since what is in mind is the recreation of humanity (IV 22b–23a,25a).
163. For a summary see Seely, David Rolph, 'The Circumcised Heart in *4Q434 Barki Nafshi*', *RQ*, 17, December 1996, 528f, 530f.
164. For a partial edition of these texts together with discussion see Seely, David Rolph 'The *Barki Nafshi* Texts', in Parry-Ricks, *Current Research*, 194–214.
165. Seely finds 15 examples. RQ, 17, 1996, 528 n.7. Seely makes the further important point that the vocabulary of 4Q434–439 is consistent with that of the sectarian texts in general. *Current Research*, 211–3, esp. 212.
166. There may be a similar collocation in 4Q436 I 9b–10, but the text is too fragmentary to be sure.
167. See Ch.5, Section D above (pp. 234–46).
168. Terms such as 'eternal', 'everlasting', 'endless' (*'ad, 'ōlām, nēṣaḥ*) which occur frequently in passages describing the

reward of the righteous and the fate of the wicked (as in IQS IV 7, 12–13), are not necessarily transcendental in meaning. They may denote only long duration, as is pointed out by Nötscher, F., *Zur Theologischen Terminologie der Qumran-Texte*, Bonner Biblische Beitràge 10, (Bonn: Peter Hanstein Vertag, 1956), 150–2. All of the terms cited are used in Ps. 21 of an earthly king. The context is the decisive factor though, as Nötscher observes, some contexts are not clear (152).

169. Carmignac, J., 'La future intervention de Dieu selon la pensée de Qumran,' in M. Delcor (ed), *Qumrân* Sa piété, sa théologie et son milieu, *BETL*, XLVI, (Louvain: University Press, 1978), 219–29, esp. 219, 228f.
170. Leaney, A.R.C., *The Rule of Qumran and Its Meaning*, (London: SCM Press, 1966) 152.
171. Collins, John J., *Apocalypticism in the Dead Sea Scrolls*, (New York: Routledge, 1997), 143. Collins' survey of views of the content and function of the *Songs* is valuable (op. cit, 136–43).
172. 4Q418 is apparently the longest copy of the work of which 4Q416 and 417 are shorter copies. A transcription of the text may be found in Wacholder-Abegg, Fasc. II, 77–154. For a translation and exposition see Harrington, Daniel J., *Wisdom Texts From Qumran* (New York: Routledge, 1996), 40–59.
173. Collins' rendering, 'Wisdom Reconsidered, In Light of the Scrolls', *DSD*, 4.3, 1997, 275.
174. Harrington, *Wisdom Texts From Qumran*, 33.
175. Cf. Elgvin, T., 'Early Essene Eschatology: Judgment and Salvation according to *Sapiential Work A'* in Parry-Ricks, *Current Research*, 133, 142.
176. *Ibid*, 127.
177. The official edition of IQ26 is found in *DJD*, I, 101f.
178. Puech, Emile, *La Croyance des Esséniens en la vie future: immortalité, resurrection, vie éternelle? Histoire d'une croyance dans le Judaïsme ancien*. I *La Résurrection des morts et le contexte scripturaire*. II *Les Donnés qumraniennes et classiques*, (Paris: Gabalda, 1993). Hereafter Puech: *Croyance*).
179. *Ibid*, 83f. Against a Hellenistic understanding which affirms immortality of the soul over against resurrection of the flesh, Puech finds at Qumran a 'linear eschatology' in which the life to come takes the form of resurrection of the

(transformed) body in a renewed earth in which the faithful enjoy everlasting communion with God and the angels (ibid, 498, 574, 777, 784, 792, 797f) i.e. he collapses the temporal and the transcendental into one, claiming that this represents the semitic and biblical view. Whether bodily resurrection necessarily excludes immortality is questionable. Whether it does so in Qumran thought depends on the texts examined below.

180. He applies this argument particularly to the *Hymns* in IQM and IQH which he attributes to the Teacher of Righteousness, ibid, 496. Cf. his even more generalized statements in 'Messianisme, Eschatologie et Résurrection dans les Manuscrits de la Mer Morte', *RQ*, 70, 18, 2, 1997, 289, 293.
181. Puech, *Croyance*, 435f, 437f, 452f, 474.
182. Ibid, 433f.
183. Ibid, 495, 497f; 513f.
184. See pp. 288–9.
185. This leaves aside the question of the provenance of 4Q521. E. Puech regards it as contemporary with IQH, IQS and IQM on grounds of common vocabulary, concluding that an Essene attribution 'seems to be justified or at least quite possible' (*CRC*, 253 n.42). In a later article Puech expresses himself more affirmatively (*RQ*, 18, 1997, 290, n.74), rejecting the objections of John J. Collins (*SS*, 121), who leaves the question open.
186. Puech, *Croyance*, 613.
187. Ibid, (my translation).
188. The original editors while conceding that 4Q385 was much read and even copied at Qumran, had difficulty in deciding whether it was of Qumran origin, since it shared some Qumran ideas and terminology, but exhibited a distinctive style and form. Strugnell, John, and Dimant, Devorah, '4Q Second Ezekiel', *RQ*, 13, 1988, 46–8, 58f.
189. *Croyance*, 693–702.
190. Pp. 41–5.
191. See his review of Puech, *Croyance* in *DSD*, 1, 2, August 1994, 252.
192. For references by earlier scholars see *Essene Writings*, 65 with n.1.
193. Puech, *Croyance*, 700.
194. Collins, John J., *Apocalypticism in the DSS*, 129, 143.

195. To the evidence cited may be added that of Hippolytus who credits the Essenes with holding 'both that the flesh will rise again and that it will be immortal in the same manner as the soul is already imperishable' (*Refutation of all Heresies*, 27; in Vermes and Goodman, *The Essenes According to the Classical Sources*, 73). Hippolytus' testimony has been questioned on the ground that he claims that some of the Essenes were Zealots or Sicarii; as well as on the ground that his version of the Essene view of the life to come is flatly contradicted by Josephus who affirms that they saw immortality as the deliverance of the soul from its bodily prison (*Jewish War* 2, 154–6). But it is not impossible that it is Josephus who gives the mistaken impression, in attempting to explain an alien view to his Roman readers. For a close examination see Puech, *Croyance*, Ch. XIII and pp. 785–7.
196. Schürer-Vermes, II 546.

Conclusion

The Shape of Qumran Theology

If the controlling themes of Qumran thought have been identified and expounded above with anything approaching accuracy, it remains to ask whether they congeal into any coherent form. How may one fairly characterize the sect and its thought?

Numerous attempts at epitomization of the distinctive character of Qumran thought have been made throughout the history of Qumran studies. Matthew Black labelled the sect a 'perfectionist mystery cult'.[1] 'In the form in which it confronts us in the actual documents from Qumran, it was a legalistic puritanism or perfectionism, with its secret code jealously guarded, and presented as a divine mystery or gnosis.'[2] Garcia Martinez has identified apocalyptic as 'the most defining characteristic of Essenes:'[3] a conclusion anticipated by some of the earlier generation of Qumran scholars,[4] though Garcia Martinez refines his characterization by placing the sect 'between legalism and apocalyptic.'[5] The same two motifs are found by James VanderKam, who writes: 'An intriguing, over-arching feature of Qumran thought is that it combines an intense awareness that the latter days are here with an equally intense conviction that conduct must accord with the most stringent legal precepts.'[6] S. Talmon finds the same combination, which he summarizes succinctly as 'hyper-nomism wedded with a fervent messianism.'[7]

There is a remarkable degree of commonality among these characterizations. Apocalyptic expectation, secret knowledge, rigorous law-observance are identified as leading ideas in the stock current at Qumran. Even if there are important aspects of Qumran thought which do not come to direct expression: election and covenant for instance, yet it does not require much analysis to discover such related elements within those that are mentioned. No less interesting is the note of tension expressed in several of the epitomes: 'between legalism and apocalyptic,' 'hyper-nomism wedded with a fervent messianism', suggesting a combination of the unexpected, as well as a high degree of intensity.

If we take an overview of Qumran thought as it has been surveyed in these pages, and seek for a unifying theme or undergirding principle, it does not seem wide of the mark to say that soteriology is a strong candidate for that role. The overriding concern of the Qumran literature is how Israel would be saved, not only following the decimation of the Exile, but also in face of the blindness of those who constituted the new sprout from Israel and the shoot from Aaron (CD I 3–10a). The answer to this came in the person of the Teacher of Righteousness and the instruction which he brought. (CD I 11). The sweep of his teaching comprehended entering the covenant (CD II 2), walking perfectly in its precepts (CD II 14–16a; III 12b–18) and, in the end, acquiring eternal life and all the glory of Adam (CD III 19–20). However, the work and instruction of the Teacher of Righteousness have a markedly eschatological conditioning. An important part of his work would be 'to make known to the last generations that which he would do to the last generation, the congregation of the faithless' (CD I 12):[8] a mission echoed remarkably in the *Habakkuk Commentary* where members of the covenant are said to 'hear all that is going [to happen to] the final generation, from the mouth of the Priest whom God has placed wi[thin the Community], to foretell the fulfillment of all the words of his servants, the prophets, [by] means of whom God has declared all that is going to happen to his people [Israel].'[9] A broadly concordant, even if not wholly identical, connection of themes was found above in other texts which appear to bear on the beginnings of the sect.[10]

If the foregoing may be taken as a fair statement of the aims and purposes of the sect as they took form under the guidance of the Teacher of Righteousness, then the shape of its theology becomes discernible at least in broad outline. It is fundamentally a covenantal theology, and its individual features are, for the most part, components of the covenant-form expressed or developed in terms of the theological outlook distinctive of Qumran. Something has already been said of the unique character of the covenant as understood at Qumran: the distinctive 'revelation' or 'knowledge' which informed it, making it 'new' and, as peculiar to the sect, exclusive.[11] But covenant brings with it obligation. The covenant promises are balanced by the covenant stipulations. And it is at this point that the intense stress on law observance comes into visibility, as was noted earlier.[12] It was observed there that, not only was the *halakah* unusually stringent, but heavy emphasis was laid upon conformity to it down to the last detail: an insistence possibly to be explained by the disastrous consequences of non-compliance in the past as well as by the critical eschatological events which the sect believed to lie immediately in the future.

However, another factor also plays into the equation at this point: side by side with the insistence upon perfect conformity to the covenant prescriptions as the sect understood them was a searching understanding of the direness of the human situation. 'There is no doubt,' writes E.P. Sanders, 'that in seeking reasons for man's transgression within the covenant which lie beyond man's will and in finding them in human frailty on the one hand and in the predestining grace of God on the other, the theologians of the community reached a more profound ... view of human sinfulness than one finds elsewhere in Palestinian Judaism.'[13] But this merely underlined the sharpness of their dilemma, for, as was argued above,[14] the fulfilment of the divine requirements was thwarted by the 'spirit of injustice' in 'the innermost part of man's flesh' (IQS IV

21f). Only by the spirit of holiness could he be cleansed from his wicked deeds (IQS IV 21–2) and that would take place only at the time of the visitation (IQS IV 18b–19a).

It is to this dilemma that perfection is offered as the solution. But in the form in which it is offered – as means and end[15] – it is, in the strict sense of the term, a match for the problem rather than a solution to it. For while it recognizes the necessity of perfect compliance with the requirements of the covenant and ostensibly accepts the possibility of doing so, it also concedes that the perfection demanded cannot be attained until the visitation at the end of the days. To quote E.P. Sanders again, 'these profound views of human sinfulness ... do not state a plight to which a soteriological solution within this life is offered.'[16] The sectarians were thus caught in a soteriological cul-de-sac. Fully aware of the divine pardon, they were equally aware of the demands of the covenant law and their obligation to keep them. The consequences of failure to do so, well illustrated by history, stood in the forefront of their consciousness, heightened by their conviction that they were the pivotal generation between the old creation and the new. What this amounts to is that they lived at a point of soteriological tension for which they found no theological resolution within the present.

How then is the sectarian theology best characterized? Its fundamental shape is unquestionably covenantal, but inasmuch as the covenant was for the end of the days, its functioning was heavily conditioned by the apocalyptic expectations of the sect. This gave rise to the stringency of its stipulations as well as its insistence on perfect compliance. But allied with this was a profound insight into the inward character of sin: a perception which did not sit easily with the requirement of perfect conformity to the covenantal law. The soteriological reach of the latter was too short to impinge upon the former. To describe it as an apocalyptic salvation cult is not untrue inasmuch as it acknowledges the two driving interests of Qumran thought. But no sobriquet can convey more than a generalized picture. To move beyond that one must trace out the multiple individualities of their mind. This is what has been attempted in this book

Notes

1. Black, Matthew, *SCO*, 170.
2. *Ibid*, 124.
3. *PDSS*, 50.
4. E.g. Cross, F.M., 'The Essenes prove to be the bearers, and in no small part the producers, of the apocalyptic tradition of Judaism,' *Ancient Library*, 144. Cf. M. Hengel, '[The Essenes] represent a further development of apocalyptic historical thinking, with a tendency on the one hand in the direction of a theodicy ... and on the other of a soteriologically determined anthropology,' *Judaism and Hellenism*, I 218.
5. *PDSS*, 67.
6. VanderKam, James, *The Dead Sea Scrolls Today*, 109.
7. *CRC*, 24.
8. Translation of Rabin, Chaim, *The Zadokite Documents*, (Oxford: the Clarendon Press, Second revised edition, 1958), p. 4.
9. IQ pHab II 7–10a. Cf. VII 1–5.
10. See chapter 2, Historical – Theological Pointers (pp. 82–106).
11. See chapter 3, The Renewed Covenant (pp. 140–50).
12. See chapter 3, The Covenant Law (pp. 151–8).
13. Sanders, *PPJ*, 282f.
14. Chapter 4.
15. See chapter 5.
16. *PPJ*, 283.

Author Index

Subject Index